PAIR-IT BOOKS®

Nana's Kitchen

Written by Darwin McBeth Walton
Illustrated by Pauline Rodriguez Howard

STECK-VAUGHN
ELEMENTARY · SECONDARY · ADULT · LIBRARY
A Harcourt Classroom Education Company

www.steck-vaughn.com

“Nana, I’m here!” called John Claude.

He ran into his grandmother’s kitchen.

“It smells good in here,” John Claude told Nana.

“It makes me hungry.

Can we have egg nests?” he asked.

“Mom doesn’t know how to make them.”

Nana nodded.

EGG NESTS

"I will be the cook," Nana said.
"You can be the helper," she told him.
Nana got a spatula and her special black pan.

John Claude got out eggs and bread.
Then he gathered a small glass, a cup, and a fork.
He used the glass to cut holes in the bread.

"I want to crack an egg," John Claude said.
He hit an egg on the cup.
Egg splattered all over.
"Uh-oh," he said and looked at Nana.

Nana smiled and cleaned up the mess.
"Watch me," she told John Claude.

EGG NESTS

Nana tapped an egg on the rim of the cup.
John Claude gently tapped an egg, too.
It cracked just right.
Then Nana showed him how to open his egg.
It slid into the cup.
"I did it!" John Claude said with a grin.

Nana put the bread in the pan and let it brown.
Then she turned the bread over.
"What do I do now?" John Claude asked.

"You beat the eggs," Nana said.
John Claude got the fork.
He beat the eggs until Nana said to stop.

Nana poured the eggs into the bread holes.
John Claude listened to the eggs sizzle.
"I like cooking with you," he told Nana.
"And I like egg nests a lot," he added.

"You're a good helper," Nana told John Claude.
"My special pan helps, too," she added.

Nana put the egg nests on plates.
John Claude took a bite of his egg nest.
"I wish my mom had a special pan," he said.
"Then she could make egg nests."

Nana looked out at her back yard.
John Claude could tell she was thinking.

"I want you to have my special pan," Nana said. "You can teach your mom to make egg nests."

"Will you come eat with us?" asked John Claude. "You can be the helper, and **I** will be the cook!"

ENSURING DATA BASE INTEGRITY

William E. Perry

A Ronald Press Publication

JOHN WILEY & SONS

New York · Chichester · Brisbane · Toronto · Singapore

Library of Congress Cataloging in Publication Data:

Perry, William E.
Ensuring data base integrity.

"A Ronald Press publication."
Bibliography: p.
Includes index.
1. Electronic data processing departments—Auditing.
2. Data base management. I. Title.

HF5548.35.P472 1983 657'.453 82-25922
ISBN 0-471-86526-5

Printed in the United States of America

10 9 8 7 6 5 4 3 2 1

PREFACE

Data base technology is frequently cited as the fastest-growing segment of data processing. The growth of data base technology has been inhibited by the cost-effectiveness of computer processing and the size of storage devices. Current strides in data processing technology have eliminated those restrictions through cost reductions in processing and storage hardware.

Data base technology has been in use for almost 20 years, and during that time span has been greatly ignored by auditors. This book was written to answer the question, "Do auditors need to do anything different because of data base technology?" The answer, of course, is yes, and this book is also meant to provide the methodology necessary to conduct the data base audit.

During the past five years, I have been researcher on two significant data base audit and control projects. The first was a joint data base auditing research project sponsored by the American Institute of Certified Public Accountants, the Canadian Institute of Chartered Accountants, and The Institute of Internal Auditors. The second project was for the United States National Bureau of Standards and resulted in the 1981 publication of Federal Information processing Standards Publication 88 entitled *Guideline on Integrity Assurance and Control in Data Base*.

In the preparation of this book, I am indebted to action with Walter Pugh, partner, Price Waterhouse & Co. and chairman of the joint data base task force, Allan Goldfine, National Bureau of Standards and manager of the NBS research project, and the CODASYL Systems Committee for their work on the selection and acquisition of data base management systems. I am also indebted to Ken Pollock of the U.S. General Accounting Office, Wayne Gould of Bankers Trust Company, and the workshop members who participated in numerous National Bureau of Standards data base workshops. Much of the thinking of the above individuals has been incorporated into this book and I want to express my appreciation publicly for their pioneering efforts in data base audit and control.

WILLIAM E. PERRY

Orlando
March 1983

CONTENTS

PART 4 ASSESSING THE DATA BASE

ENSURING DATA BASE INTEGRITY

part one

DEVELOPING A DATA BASE STRATEGY

Data base is too complex just to begin an on-site audit. The strategy helps one decide whether special auditing procedures are necessary and, if so, what procedures and how much labor to devote to data base.

one

DATA BASE AUDITING STRATEGY

In the beginning (of the computer era), programmers had complete control over the computer resources. Programmers had certain objectives, and the computer was a tool used to accomplish those objectives. The entire resources of the computer were available to the programmers, and anything they wanted to accomplish they had to accomplish themselves.

The first commercial programs were written in machine language. This was an exceedingly difficult language to use, and one that was almost impossible to maintain. There were many problems in computerland.

Over the years, the computer resource has been carved into ever smaller pieces of responsibility in an effort to simplify the programming task and to improve productivity. Many of the tasks performed by the computer programmer in the early days of computing are now performed by compilers, operating systems, and data base management systems. The computer programmer is no longer in control of computer operations; instead, he or she is now one member of a team. However, there are still problems in computerland, as systems are becoming more complete and integrated.

THE NEED FOR DATA BASE

The objective of data base technology is to manage data independently of the programs that use those data. It is but another step in dividing the programming task. However, unlike many of the other divisions of programming, data base has significant implications for an organization's information system strategy.

Prior to the introduction of data base technology, data were considered "owned" by the applications that used those data. The concept of ownership came about because many users justified, budgeted, and were charged for the applications associated with their area. In other words, the users paid for the data and thus felt they owned them.

Ownership of data dedicated to a specific application carries with it the ability to orient data toward the user's specific requirements. For example, in a payroll application it is unnecessary to include new employees who have not yet earned salary, or terminated employees. Thus, while the payroll view of employees may be satisfactory from their perspective, other users may want a different view of those same data.

Let's look at the classical accounting/marketing dispute over the recording of the sale. The accountants only want the sale recorded on the records of the organization when title passes between the seller and the buyer. The marketing perspective of a sale is when the "handshake" occurs and there is an intent to buy. Both perspectives are valid. If the organization does not record the event, inventory may not be sufficient to deliver the customer's merchandise promised at the time of the "handshake," while others purchasing at a later time will get the coveted merchandise. If the marketing people control the computer system they will view sales from a marketing perspective, while if the accountants control the computer system, their view of sales will be the legal view.

Data base technology permits data to be managed independently of the applications that use those data. Managing data independently of the applications that use them permits multiple "views" of data to occur concurrently. In our previous example, in a single data base the accountants could view sales data from the legal perspective, while marketing could view those same data from a sales commitment perspective.

As computer systems became more integrated, and the computer becomes an integral part of the day-to-day process, it is necessary to reconcile the different views of data so that diverse users can use the same data. The process of coordinating and reconciling different views of data when those data were maintained by two or more independent applications became unmanageable. The solution to modern business information system needs was to divide data processing responsibilities into data and processing. If the data are maintained independently of the process application, the concept is called data base.

WHAT IS A DATA BASE?

A data base is a data collection so organized for computer processing as to reduce duplicate storage and improve the independence of the stored data structure from the using program(s). This commonly accepted data base definition implies the following:

Data in a single storage location can be used by many different programs.

More than one program can access the same piece of data concurrently.

Data are managed independently of the programs that use them, thus requiring a data base management system.

Data must be organized to optimize the use of those data by the programs using them.

One of the key concepts of data base is that data are "managed" independently of the applications that use those data. This leads to a practical working definition of data base which is: "a collection of data managed by a single piece of software called a data base management system (DBMS)."

Data base as used in this book encompasses both of the above data base definitions. The first definition, which is the National Bureau of Standards definition, is the conceptual definition, while the second definition requires that the organization must have a data base management system in order to be considered to be using data base technology. This second definition is important because data base and related terminology are used in different ways by different people. However, the commonly accepted definition of data base is one involving a DBMS.

A data base management system (DBMS) is a software package designed to meet common application goals by:

Providing features and preprogrammed functions to organize and process many different types of data in an integrated structure called the data base

Providing for data base definition in generic or logical terms, independent of physical storage and machine-dependent factors

Facilitating a rapid and economical development of many applications

Providing a rather complete operational facility, with features for security, error recovery, monitoring, and so on

If data are managed independently of the programs that use those data, there is an implied organizational structure needed to manage the data. It would be illogical to establish new responsibilities and then not assign someone to be responsible for those tasks. The function that performs this management service is frequently referred to as the data base administration function.

Data base administration (DBA) is a function concerned with the technical design and maintenance of data bases used in information systems. Data base administration is a highly technical activity which requires significant technical training. Among other things, the function is responsible for assuring the integrity of the data base and the proper definition and use of data in the organization.

The individual in charge of the data base administration function is frequently referred to as the data base administrator. Sometimes both the individual and the function are referred to as the DBA. The data base administrator is normally the manager of an organization's data, responsible for the specification, acquisition, and maintenance of the data base software, and for the design, validation, and security of the files or data bases.

The complexity of the management process and organizational structure is consistent with the complexity of data base technology. This is necessary because data base administration covers a broad band of activity. The activities range from working with management in order to accomplish the organization's mission to assessing the adequacy of controls on highly sophisticated data base technology.

KEY CONCEPT

Data base means that data are managed independently of the application that uses those data.

HOW DOES DATA BASE WORK?

Conceptually, a data base is simple, but technically it is very complex. The concept involves identification of the information that will be recirculated or reused by the application systems and its storage in a single place or file called a data base. In concept, a data base is similar to a central file in an office for the storage of paper documents. Anyone having a document of interest to others stores that document centrally. Then whenever the document is needed, the individual needing it can go to the central location and obtain the document.

The data base is the central file of information for data processing applications. The data base management system is the equivalent of the organization and retrieval system used in a central file. The data base administrator would be the equivalent of the individual who administers the central file of documents.

The major difference between the central file of documents and the data base is that in the central file the documents are paper and in the data base the information is electronic. Paper documents are only available once, while electronic information can be used by multiple programs concurrently. Therefore, while the central file's concern is the location of a specific document, the data base's concern is that data may be lost or abused because of inadequate data usage controls.

From a user's perspective, data base technology separates the physical and logical perspectives of data. The physical view of data indicates where data are physically stored on a data storage device. The logical view of data explains how the data elements interrelate.

In a data base environment, the DBMS controls the physical view of data and their storage location, so that it is not necessary for the user of data to know or understand the physical view. All the data base user needs to know is the logical view of data. For example, what the data base user needs to know is:

Specific pieces of data wanted, such as the number of hours an individual worked, his or her pay rate, and payroll deduction information

Sequence in which data are wanted (for example, whether an entire grouping of data is wanted, such as all the employees, or whether a specific employee's data are wanted and, if so, in which sequence)

DBMS interface, because the user of data base technology must understand the method for interfacing with the data base management system, the equivalent of which in a central office document storage system may be the completion of a form in order to have a clerk retrieve a specific document

The physical and logical concepts of a data base are important to the understanding of how a data base works. The physical data base is established by the data base administrator and managed and used by the data base management system. The logical view of data is independent of the physical view, but is the method by which data are known, understood, and used by the application programs interfacing with the data base.

The physical and logical equivalents of data base in a business organization are the physical layout of the office and the organizational chart. The physical layout determines where people sit, how much space they are allocated, and the difficulty of accessing those individuals. It is important to the efficiency of a business organization that people be located in an efficient manner. For example, to place a guard or receptionist in an obsolete corner of an upper floor would make his or her function very ineffective. Likewise, if heavily used data in a data base are not conveniently located, the use of those data can be very ineffective. In addition, the office departments which have interfacing functions are normally physically close. If there is a lot of movement and activity between the two departments, the closer those departments are physically the more effective their operation. However, physical location, while important to effectiveness and efficiency, is relatively unimportant with regard to how actions and decisions are made. Actions occur using the logical structure which is the organizational chart for the business.

When the president of a corporation has a financial problem, the president needs to interface with the comptroller. It is unimportant to the president, except for efficiency and economy, where the comptroller is physically located. What the president wants is to interact with the comptroller so that information can be passed or action taken.

In a data base environment, the user does not need to know where the data are physically stored. All the user must ask in order to obtain data is the equivalent of, ''I would like to see the comptroller'' or ''Deliver this to the comptroller.'' The data base management system, in that example, becomes the equivalent of the organization's mail room which retrieves and delivers data according to the instruction of the user.

KEY CONCEPT

Data base technology eliminates the need for the user to know or understand how data are stored.

How Data are Obtained from the Data Base

The functioning of a data base can be explained by stepping through the process of obtaining data from the data base. Understanding how a data base functions makes the concepts more understandable. This process is illustrated in Figure 1.

The example used is that of an on-line data base system. Since most data base systems are coupled with on-line communication capabilities, the example is illustrative of the more common use of data base technology. The following three components are involved in this process:

User terminal. The method by which the user communicates with the computer is called the user terminal. The introduction, use, and acquisition of data through that terminal are an integral part of the user process.

Central processing unit. The computer and the program stored within the computer to perform the desired processing tasks are the central processing unit.

Data base. The collection of data that will be used in satisfying a user requirement is the data base.

Four functions are defined within the central processing unit. While these four functions are necessary to execute obtaining data base data, there may be other functions in the central processing unit which are also involved in this process, such as communication systems and security systems, but are not important in understanding how a DBMS functions. The four major functions are:

Application program. This is the computer program that performs the user requirements, such as payroll, accounts receivable, demand deposits, or order entry.

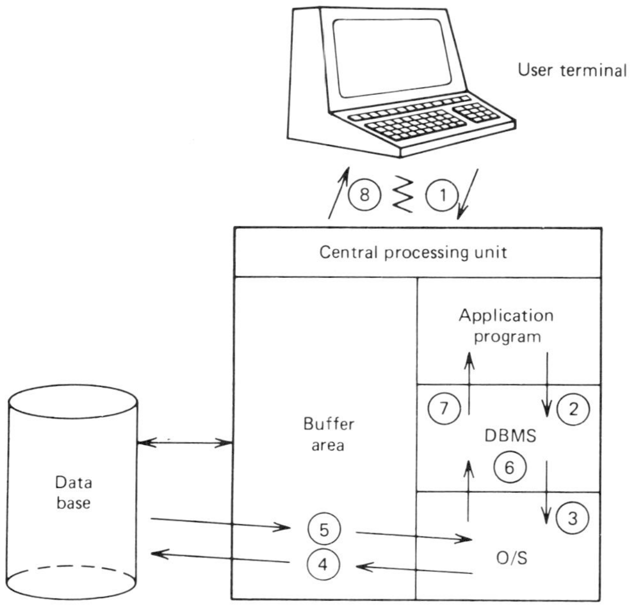

Figure 1. How Data Are Obtained in a Data Base Environment.

Data base management system. The management system is the single piece of software that manages the data base. Note that the term "management" means that the DBMS is, in fact, a manager, and not a doer.

Operating system (O/S). The operating system is the piece of software that directs the operations of the computer and physically reads and writes records to and from the output devices.

Buffer area. The portion of computer storage used to hold large blocks of data until needed by the application program, or complete and ready to place on an output device, is the buffer area.

Let us walk through, step by step, a user request for information from the data base. To make the example simple, let us assume that our user wants to know the balance due from a specific customer, such as customer number 123. The user sits at his/her terminal and from a menu (list of available preprogrammed functions) selects one to inquire and obtain customer 123's outstanding accounts receivable balance. The user types in the customer number and the customer balance seems to appear on the screen like magic. Let's look at what really happens. (Note: The steps are illustrated in Figure 1.)

Step 1: Select application program. The user selects the specific application program that will obtain the accounts receivable customer balance, and in response to that application program enters the customer number. The application program must then convert customer 123 into a message understandable by the DBMS.

Step 2: DBMS read request. The application program passes parameters to the DBMS indicating that the application program would like the account balance for customer 123. The DBMS must then search through a directory to determine the physical record in which that information is located. Note that a directory is like an index. Knowing the information is wanted, and assuming that information is in the index, the method of determining the physical location of the desired information can be determined from the index. Building the proper directory is a highly technical activity, and the directory may consume large segments of the available disk space.

Step 3: O/S read request. The information about locating the physical record as communicated to the operating system by the DBMS may not indicate the physical location of the record.

Step 4: Locate physical record. Depending on the DBMS characteristics the operating system may have to refer to another index to determine on which part of the physical storage device the record is actually located. The process involves first looking to determine if the record is in the buffer area (storage area in memory used to hold data), in which case no physical read is needed. However, should a physical read be needed, large amounts of computer time in proportion to process time will be required. Depending on the physical location of data, several reads may be required, in which case the service level from a data base may be seriously degraded.

Step 5: Move data to buffer area. Physical data requested by the DBMS must be located and moved to the buffer area. If the needed physical data are already in the buffer area, this step becomes unnecessary. If the physical data must be read from the input device, the necessary instructions must be executed in order to ensure the correct delivery of the physical record to the buffer area.

Step 6: DBMS notification. The operating system notifies the DBMS that the physical data required are located in the buffer area, and provides the exact location of physical information.

Step 7: Creation of a logical record. The information needed by the application program may be part of a single physical record, or parts of multiple physical records. The DBMS will locate the exact pieces of information wanted from the buffer area and assemble them (if necessary) for the application program and then deliver a record containing the desired information. In this instance, the record contains a single field showing the outstanding accounts receivable balance for number 123.

Step 8: Delivery of wanted information. The application program must make whatever logical and editing processing are required and then deliver the information to the user. In this instance, the application program would need to insert the monetary punctuation, and then place the amount in the screen so that the information provided is comprehensible to the user on the terminal screen.

The above events, and the sequencing of events, are typical of those that occur in a data base environment when acquiring information. However, the reader should be cautioned that the process will vary depending upon the specific DBMS used. The important concept for the reader to understand is how the DBMS acquires and translates physical records into the logical information needed by the application program. The reader should also note that in the above example there was only a single application program, while in a true DBMS environment there will be multiple application programs. Thus, the DBMS does not just service a single program, but must service multiple programs and at the same time protect the integrity of the data base.

KEY CONCEPT

The DBMS is the technique that permits data to be managed independently of the applications that use the data.

WHERE DOES DATA BASE FIT INTO THE EVOLVING DATA PROCESSING TECHNOLOGY?

Data processing from the time of the invention of the punched card in the late 1800s until the early 1960s meant the processing of sequential data files. A file is a collection of data held together by a common bond, for example, as a payroll employee file, an accounts receivable customer file, a savings account file, or an unearned premium reserve file. The common bond in an employee payroll file is the fact of employment by that same firm. This common bond is normally the basis for determining the sequence of the sequential file. For example, a payroll file would be in sequence by employee payroll number, or perhaps by social security number. Let us assume it is employee number. The first employee in the file is normally the employee with the lowest payroll number, and the last employee in the file is the one with the highest numerical payroll number.

As the file is processed, all of the information is read into computer memory. Those records needed for processing are used, and those not needed are either ignored or passed through to an updated version of the file from which the data have been read.

The sequential file has one major disadvantage. If only one record, or a few records, are wanted from the file, the file must be read. Thus, sequential files are not suited to a processing strategy when the computer is involved in the process. However, sequential files are very effective when all of the processing can be batched and processed together.

For example, payroll which is run weekly or biweekly is still an ideal candidate for a sequential file processing system. Rules of thumb state that when access at any one point in time will exceed 10% of the records in the file, sequential files are normally a preferred mode for processing.

In the early 1960s, direct access devices became available for commercial computers. These devices permitted direct access to a single record or groups of records. With this data processing innovation, it was no longer necessary to process entire files. With this innovation came on-line banking, on-line airline reservation systems, inquiry as to the status of inventory, and so on. Direct access files opened new processing concepts for business organizations.

The direct access file placed two limitations on information processing. First, the file mechanisms were normally more complex than sequential files, and thus more difficult to organize, access, and maintain. Systems designers needed to devote significantly more time and attention to file maintenance of direct access files than they did to file maintenance of sequential files. Second, except for very sophisticated direct access file structures, the files were organized in a single sequence. A payroll file would be organized employee number, and while any single employee could be accessed directly, the only way to access was by employee number. If processing was wanted by social security number, the file needed to be sorted for that purpose. In both the sequential and direct access mode, data could be shared, but only in a manner designed into the data file by the application system creating that file.

Data base was introduced to overcome these two direct access file restrictions, while at the same time providing the full benefits of direct access processing. Data base technology permits a single grouping of data to be shared concurrently by multiple users without the technical complexity associated with data base capabilities.

KEY CONCEPT

Data base permits files to be accessed in more than one sequence.

OVERVIEW OF DATA BASE TECHNOLOGY

Data base administrators and data base security officers need to understand how data base technology affects the accuracy, completeness, and security of data. The overview of data base technology presented in this section is designed to emphasize data base integrity. Data base technology will be divided into its functional components. References are provided explaining basic concepts for those needing to understand how a data base system works technically. This section is designed to provide a technological framework for building and reviewing data base controls.

Difference between Data Base and Non-Data Base Technology

Data base technology provides for a concurrent sharing of data among multiple users. This is in contrast to non-data base technology in which sharing, if it occurs, is sequential rather than concurrent. It is these differences between data base and non-data base technology that provide the systems opportunities as well as the integrity challenges. The following are the differences:

File Maintenance is a Centralized Function

A single software package administers the data used by application systems. This software package, the DBMS, is interposed between the set of application programs using the data and the operating system that reads and writes data to a physical storage area. It manages the data for each application program so that the program need only ask for specific pieces of data and they are delivered. The DBMS maintains whatever indices are needed in order to translate application program data needs into the information needed by the operating system to read or write data to the physical data base.

Data Management is Organizationally Independent of Application Development

The DBMS is managed by data administration personnel who are, in general, organizationally independent of the application users. It is frequently unnecessary for the user of an application or the application system personnel to understand how data are retrieved for use by the application. Those functions of application programs that would have been designed by programmers in non-DBMS technology to structure the data are not provided by the data administration group.

Data are Organized Into Complex Data Structures

The technical complexities of data bases should not be underestimated. Normally, sophisticated software packages are needed to aid in the design, maintenance, reorganization, and verification of the integrity of the data base. It is not uncommon for the indices to consume one-fifth to one-third of the total data base storage space. A single write command may cause the execution of thousands of computer instructions needed to update the indices, pointers, and overflow areas. This is essential to ensure the continued integrity of the data base.

Data Can be Shared Concurrently

A major advantage of data base technology is the fact that multiple users can share the same piece of data concurrently. This ensures consistency and reliability of data throughout all the applications using any particular data element. However, this concurrent sharing poses a technological problem and an integrity problem.

The technological problem of concurrent sharing is protection against the loss of data updates. For example, if two users were permitted to update the same data element, one update would overlay the other. This would cause one of the updates to be lost randomly or to be garbled.

The integrity problem relates to the sequence in which those updates occur. In some processes, the order of update is important. For example, in an invoicing operation, all of the items ordered should be accumulated before sales tax is calculated. These are normally application system concerns, but they are ones which need to be considered during the data base application design.

Understanding the Data Base Structure

The data base structure must be viewed from three perspectives. These are the physical, logical, and individual user's views of the data. The data base administrator is concerned with the physical and logical views of the data base, while the user and application system personnel are interested in the user view of data. To design or verify data base integrity requires an understanding of all three views.

The physical view of data shows where data are physically stored on a data storage device, while the logical view explains how the data elements interrelate. The structured architecture (e.g., hierarchical, network, or relational) is used to describe the logical view of data. That subset of the data base used by any individual user is considered to be the user view of data.

All three views of data must be controlled. It is important to ensure the integrity of the physical, logical, and user's views of data. Later sections of this book will describe the methods of ensuring the integrity of the different data views.

Components of a Data Base Environment

Control does not start or stop with the physical data base and is not limited to the hardware and software of data base technology. Control includes the data base personnel, and the policies, procedures, and activities supporting the data managed by the data base administration function. Only when viewed in its totality can the adequacy of control be determined. Understanding the special characteristics of a data base environment clarifies what must be controlled.

A Data Base Uses a Single Software Package Called a Data Base Management System

In a data base environment, data are organized and maintained independently of the programs that use those data. Many of the file integrity functions previously performed by application programs are now performed by the DBMS. These functions include organizing the data, verifying the completeness of data, and providing for the backup and recovery of those data.

The Data Base Architecture Affects the User's Approach to the Data Base

Data bases are currently designed using hierarchical, network, or relational structures. The architecture of the structure determines how one item of data is related to other items of data. Hierarchical data bases are composed of relationships that begin at the top and extend downward. Network structures are more flexible in that they enable downward relationships to cross hierarchical boundaries. Relational data bases permit almost unlimited flexibility in that a direct relation or access between any two pieces of data is achievable.

There is the normal tradeoff between flexibility and efficiency. A hierarchical structure is the most efficient but the least flexible, while a relational one is the most flexible but the least efficient. Some of the inflexibility of hierarchical data bases can be overcome through redundancy of data. When the same data item is needed in two parts of a hierarchical data base, it may be duplicated in both segments. This common practice leads to a concern over consistency of redundant data.

Data Dictionaries Structure and Formalize Data Documentation

Since multiple users share common data, it is important that each user understand the content, reliability, timeliness, and consistency of the data. This type of information needs to be documented in a standardized format comprehensible to all users. A data dictionary system (DDS) can fulfill that need.

A data dictionary system is a software package used to record, store, and process information about all of an organization's significant data entities and associated data processing function. Many DDSs are specifically tailored to operate in conjunction with a DBMS, requiring the DBMS facilities to perform DDS functions. Others are self-contained software packages. Either type can be used to ensure consistent data definition and usage within an organization.

A Special Data Base Administration Function Needs to be Made Responsible for the Technical Functioning of the Data Base

Data bases are technically complex. The structuring and maintenance of the data base require a matching of the technological capabilities with the organization's needs. After design, the data base must continually be fine-tuned to ensure an acceptable level of performance and to meet the changing needs of users.

The Data Administration Function Establishes Data Policy

Data policy describes the organizational philosophy of data. The data policy should be developed by management, possibly through a data administrator, to explain to users management's intent for the use of data. The data policy should cover such things as security, accessibility, retention, accountability, and documentation.

In smaller organizations, data base administration and data administration may be combined. When combined, the emphasis of the function is normally dependent upon the background of the managing individual. When the manager is an administrator by training, the emphasis is normally on policy and data usage, while a software specialist in that job emphasizes the technical performance of data base software.

KEY CONCEPT

Because the same data are used by multiple users, it is necessary to establish a central function to administer the data. This function is normally called the data base administration function.

THE IMPACT OF DATA BASE ON THE AUDIT PROCESS

Most commercial computer installations use data base technology. It is even possible to get sophisticated data base management systems for the personal computers used by business people in their homes and offices. Thus, it becomes increasingly likely that auditing in an organization with a computer will involve an assessment of the audit risk in using data base technology.

On the other hand, data base technology has been in use since the 1960s. From the introduction of data base technology until today, very few auditors even recognized the existence of the DBMS and yet from all appearances the audit community does not seem overly concerned about data base technology.

However, all is not well in auditing computerland. Data base, which in the mid-1970s appeared to be the shining star of data base technology, is becoming tarnished. The advantages claimed by the technicians have rarely materialized in organizations using data base. In addition, many of the early data base concepts, such as a single data base for an entire organization, have fallen into disfavor.

Data base can be an effective and efficient tool to improve the management and control of data maintained in a computer-based system. The effectiveness of the data base system will depend on proper planning and control. An extensive study conducted by the United States General Accounting Office in 1979 stated that federal agencies need to receive technical assistance on the proper use of data base technology. After the study, the GAO concluded that most federal agencies did not adequately plan before acquiring data base management systems; consequently, they may have spent substantial amounts for automatic data processing resources that they did not need.

A similar study by one of the large public accounting firms concluded that most of their clients felt they moved into data base technology too quickly. The data base users stated that if they had the opportunity to change their data base decisions, they would delay the installation of data base until more extensive planning could occur. The data base problems do not appear to be technological but, rather, administrative, involving integration of an information resource concept into their organization.

As organizations change from a philosophy of data dedicated to a single application to one in which data are managed as a resource of an organization, the implementation impact is significant. Many noted data processing experts state that the movement to data base technology may be more difficult and have a greater impact on the organization than that which occurred when that same organization moved from manual processing to computer processing.

KEY CONCEPT

Without extensive organization-wide planning, the use of data base technology is rarely successful.

The Multiple Uses of Data Base Technology

Data base is not a single thing, such as on-line processing, but, rather, multiple concepts incorporated into a single concept called data base. When an organization moves to on-line processing, the users of a system are provided communication capabilities and it is easy to understand what has happened. When the same user moves to data base technology, there is no clear line of demarcation, for the organization nor the auditor.

There are literally millions of ways in which to implement data base technology in an organization. In its simplest usage, a non-data base file structure concept is unplugged and the data base is plugged in. For example, an application system may use an indexed sequential access mechanism and decide they want capabilities not available in the index sequential access method. The same applications, using all the same logic and program structures, merely change the read and write interfaces and use data base instead of the previous access mechanism.

An organization would want to do this, for instance, in order to:

Access a single file by more than one sequence without sorting

Gain utilities for generalized processing against the file, such as a query language which is common with data base technology

Gain experience in the use of a DBMS

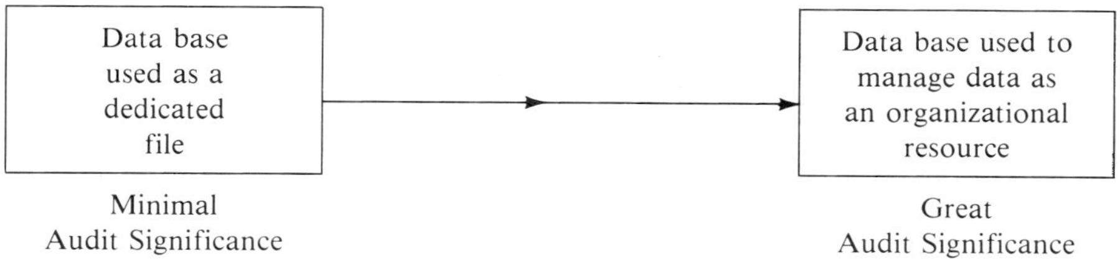

Figure 2. Data Base Technology Continuum.

At the other end of the data base technology continuum (see Figure 2), data base is used to manage data as an organizational structure. In this implementation mode, data are viewed as a resource of the organization and are managed at an organizational level as opposed to an application level. (Note: These concepts will be explained in more detail later in the book.)

The audit implication will be dependent upon the type of implementation of data base in the organization. When data base is used as a dedicated file in a single application, the audit implications are little different than for any other file structure. On the other hand, if data base is used to manage data at the organizational level, the audit implications are huge. As data base moves along the continuum from minimal audit significance to great audit significance, the determination of where on this continuum an organization resides is an important aspect of defining the audit strategy.

KEY CONCEPT

The audit implications of data base are directly related to how data base technology is utilized.

The Data Base Audit Strategy Cycle

While the use of data base varies significantly, the process of introducing data base into organizations is relatively consistent. The auditor needs to understand the cycle of introducing data base technology into an organization. Once the cycle is understood, a data base audit strategy can be developed to complement the use of data base technology.

Rarely do organizations understand the full impact of data base when the technology is introduced into the organization. The organization's commitment to data base creeps into the organization slowly. If organizations truly understood their commitment, few would use the technology.

The data base "creeping commitment" theory states that a small commitment is all that is asked for. Normally this is to acquire a DBMS, and thus the low end of the continuum (Figure 2) of data base installations is a logical starting point. Once the organization buys off on this commitment, then the next commitment, usually the hiring of a data base administrator, is approached. When this commitment is made, the next calls for the development of standards and procedures. The process continues, commitment by commitment, until the organization's information strategy is also restructured.

As data base is introduced into the organization, new data base activities exist (see Figure 3 for the data base audit strategy cycle). As discussed in the creeping commitment theory, one of the first activities is the introduction of the data base management system. Each time a new activity is introduced into an organization, it results in new risks to the organization. For example, the DBMS results in a risk of unauthorized access because the

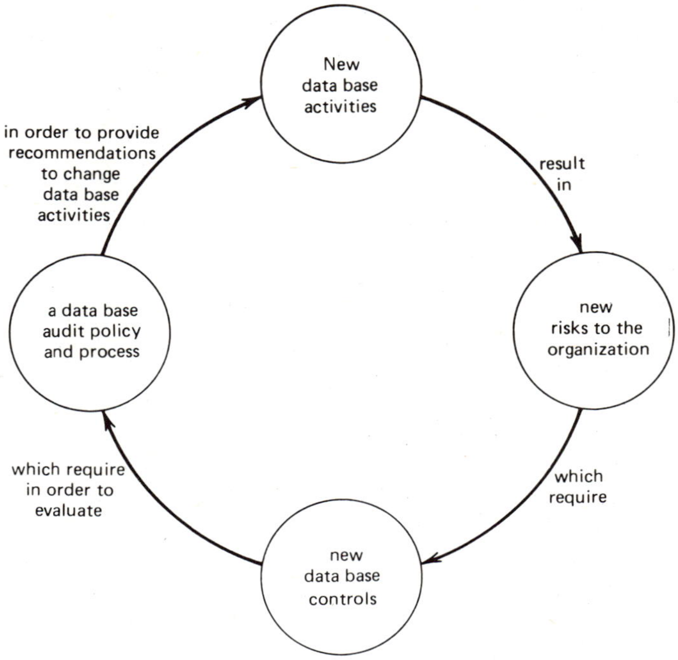

Figure 3. Data Base Audit Strategy Cycle.

DBMS is structured to permit multiple users access to the same data base. Each time a new data base activity is created, one or more new risks occur.

The risks caused by the introduction of data base require new data base controls. In our example of the DBMS access risk, the control most commonly used is password protection of the data in the data base. Each of the new risks requires one or more new controls. However, some of the controls will be a reemphasis of controls currently in use. For example, with an on-line data base it may be even more important to restrict the computer operations area to authorized individuals.

The new data base controls require an audit policy and process for the data base in order to evaluate the adequacy of the controls. For example, assessing the adequacy of access controls over data resources will require a policy decision on whether those controls are evaluated at the application or environmental level, and a process that can evaluate and test the effectiveness of the new data base controls.

The audit strategy must be built upon a data base audit policy. The audit process will be the strategy for implementing policy in the organization. The strategy must be built around the new activities, risks, and controls.

The development of an audit strategy encompasses the following considerations:

Evaluate long-range data base plan. The auditor must be familiar with how the organization is currently using data base technology, and the plans for using that technology in the future. If a data base technology plan does not exist, the audit strategy should be to perform those evaluations that would highlight the problems associated with not having a long-range plan, and encourage such a plan to be developed.

Identify new activities, controls, and risks. the auditors need to be familiar with the current situation in order to create an effective audit program to evaluate the use of that technology.

Identify audit data base resources and skills. The audit department should know the staffing and skill levels available to evaluate the use of data base technology so that the specified audit process will be achievable.

Develop data base policy. A clear audit policy on the evaluation of data base technology provides the framework for evaluation.

Match resources to risks. The final step of the strategy is to optimize the audit resources. Allocating the resources in accordance with the significance of the data base risk ensures the organization the maximum protection against the failure to diagnose inadequate controls for the minimum resources.

KEY CONCEPT

Data base is not just another audit—it requires new methods, skills, and tools.

Data Base Audit Policy

The data base audit policy of an organization should address the following three data base audit issues:

Whether to audit data base technology independently of the applications that use that technology

Whether the auditor evaluating data base needs data base skills

Whether the sequencing of the data base audit steps is important

Data base technology is used for multiple applications and thus is more an environmental control than an application control. While some may argue that it is not a general or environmental control in a true sense, it is a new type of control that is emerging in data processing. Because it is common to all of the applications that use the data base, it should be considered an environmental control.

> The control environment is shaped by several factors. Some are clearly visible, like a formal corporate conduct policy statement or an internal audit function. Some, like organizational structure and the way in which management communicates, enforces, and reinforces policy, vary so widely among companies that they can be contrasted more easily than they can be compared.
>
> Although it is difficult to measure the significance of each factor, it is generally possible to make an overall evaluation. The committee believes that an overall evaluation of a company's internal accounting control environment is a necessary prelude to the evaluation of control procedures and techniques.[1]

Data base technology involves new activities, new risks, new controls, and a new audit process. Without an understanding of data base technology, it is difficult for an auditor to assess properly the adequacy of control in this environment. The question appears to be what skills are needed, as opposed to whether or not data base skills are needed at all. The

[1]*Tentative Report of the Special Advisory Committee on Internal Accounting Control,* American Institute of Certified Public Accountants, New York, 1979.

remainder of this book is intended to identify the needed skills, and provide the necessary guidance to acquire those skills.

Good audit policy dictates that environmental controls should be assessed prior to evaluating the application controls. The AICPA Special Task Force on Internal Accounting Controls went on to state in its report: "A poor control environment would make some accounting controls inoperative for all intents and purposes because, for example, individuals would hesitate to challenge a management override of a specific control procedure. On the other hand, a strong control environment, for example, one with tight budgetary controls and an effective internal audit function, can have an important bearing on the selection and effectiveness of specific accounting control procedures and techniques."[2]

The above discussion of the three data base audit policy questions leads to the adoption by an audit department of a policy on data base audit such as:

DATA BASE AUDIT POLICY

In order to assess the adequacy of data base controls and to evaluate the integrity of processing by data base applications, an auditor skilled in data base technology should first determine the impact of data base on the organization, and second (if the impact of data base is significant) evaluate the reliance that can be placed on the data base controls prior to auditing the applications that rely on the data base management system controls.

DATA BASE AUDIT STRATEGY

The data base audit strategy is the means of implementing the audit policy. The policy must come first, and it is good practice for an audit department to document their policies formally.

The recommended data base audit strategy is a seven-step process. The process is briefly described in Figure 4 and explained below. The remainder of the book explains how to audit data base using this strategy. The chapters describing each step are noted in Figure 4.

Step 1: Acquire and understand the organization's long-range data base plan. Data base can be used both technically to improve the effectiveness of data processing, and as an organizational philosophy to manage data as a resource. The approach taken will significantly affect the amount of audit resources needed to evaluate the use of data base technology. Without a data base plan, the implementation process will "creep." This is normally the most expensive route and one in which risks may occur without proper management or audit attention.

Step 2: Identify the risks associated with the use of data base technology. Effective auditing assigns resources based upon the organizational risks. This allocation of audit resources cannot occur until the risks are identified. The data base risks are new and normally require an auditor skilled in data base to identify those risks.

Step 3: Determine the significance of each risk. The risks vary in magnitude. An auditor skilled in data base technology and knowledgeable in how data base is used in his or her organization can assess the magnitude of a risk, which in turn is used to determine the quantity of audit resources allocated to that risk.

[2]Ibid.

Step	Description	Purpose	See Chapter
1.	Acquire and understand the organization's long-range data base plan.	Determine scope of the audit.	2
2.	Identify the risks associated with the use of data base technology.	Determine auditor concerns with the implemented use of data base technology.	3
3.	Determine the significance of each risk.	Determine where to use audit resource.	3
4.	Locate the data base activities where those risks may result in a loss.	Determine which data base activities to audit.	4
5.	Develop an audit program for evaluating those data base activities.	Determine how to audit data base.	5
6.	Conduct the data base audit (where the risk is high).	Determine needed audit tools and techniques.	6–12
7.	Assess the actual or potential loss due to risk, and make recommendations accordingly.	Report audit results and recommendations.	13

Figure 4. The Data Base Audit Strategy.

Step 4: Locate the data base activities where those risks may result in a loss. Risks cannot be audited; only activities can. An activity is a function needed to operate and use data base technology. An activity is also a place where controls are placed to reduce risks. Therefore, an audit program cannot be constructed until it can be determined which activities should be audited.

Step 5: Develop an audit program for evaluating those data base activities. An audit program needs to be developed and/or customized for each data base activity under audit in order to evaluate the impact of the identified risks within those activities.

Step 6: Conduct the data base audit (where the risk is high). The audit process needs the appropriate tools and techniques for each of the risk areas under audit. The evidence produced by data base technology is unique to that technology, and normally requires new audit methods and tools for effective auditing.

Step 7: Assess the actual or potential loss due to risk, and make recommendations accordingly. The bottom line of each audit is a report which assesses the impact of risk to the organization. In a data base audit, this is performed by assessing the adequacy of data base controls, and then evaluating the potential or actual losses associated with identified control weaknesses. Recommendations should provide the data base organization solutions to data base control weaknesses.

Data base is more technically complex than non-data base. The audit of data base can be overwhelming for an auditor, even one with average data processing skills, unless that auditor has an audit methodology that leads him or her through the process in a logical manner. This book is designed to fulfill that need. Each part of the audit process is outlined in a step-by-step format similar to that of the above audit process. Following the methodology outlined in this book should provide the auditor with minimal data processing and data base skills a high probability of success in identifying major weaknesses in the use of data base technology.

KEY CONCEPT

Just as the implementation of data base technology is unsuccessful without extensive planning, so are data base audits unsuccessful without extensive planning.

part two

PLANNING THE DATA BASE AUDIT

Planning is the single most important productivity tool in a data base audit. Data base provides an easy opportunity to get lost during the audit.

two

SCOPING THE DATA BASE AUDIT

Data base technology is only a part of an organization's strategy for using information. The auditor must understand this strategy in order to scope the audit. Scoping is an important aspect of audit planning.

There are two parts to an organization's information strategy. One part is its management philosophy on the use of information. Currently this is being called information resource management. The second part is the administration of the data and the interaction with the application programs that use those data. This is called data base administration.

Any organization that maintains information for subsequent use performs an information management function, and cannot help but use some concepts of data base technology. Even if its present techniques include only sequential access of tape records, these belong to the branch of computer/information science concerned with the structure, storage, and retrieval of information. In recent years, this technology has evolved a body of new concepts and terminology aimed at synthesizing the entire discipline into a global perspective more conducive to analysis and management.

Information management and data base administration can be formal functions or informal functions. When information management is formalized, the manager of that function is normally called the data administrator. When data base administration is formalized, the manager of that function is usually called the data base administrator. If these are informal functions they must be performed by the application project leaders.

This chapter is designed to provide the auditor with the tools needed to scope the audit. The auditor should collect background information on the information management philosophy and data base administration as implemented in the organization in order to scope the audit. The chapter includes background checklists on information management and data base administration. The information gathered in the completion of these background checklists will be helpful throughout the audit in evaluating the controls over the structure, storage, and retrieval of information in the organization under review.

INFORMATION AS AN ORGANIZATION RESOURCE

Information, like people, does not appear on the balance sheet of an organization as an asset. Therefore, to most individuals in an organization, data do not have a value and thus do not require much management attention. That concept is false, and many organizations are beginning to realize that data may be their most valuable resource.

Data have always been considered a resource of an organization, and as such are owned by the corporation. What until very recently has been missing is the management attention needed to formalize and control the process of managing information. One of the reasons information resource management is growing as a discipline is the fact that the technological capabilities are now emerging as the tools necessary to implement this process.

One of the earliest efforts to manage information was a formal record retention program. These programs had two primary goals. First was to inventory ''records'' existing within the corporation; second was to establish retention dates so that the data would be available if needed and also be destroyed promptly when no longer needed. Unfortunately, the emphasis in many of these programs was on the destruction of data, as opposed to the management of data.

The logical progression for an organization moving into data base technology is first to establish the information management function, and, second, the technical data base administration function. Unfortunately, many organizations reverse the process, thereby establishing the tools to manage data before they have put into place their data management policies. It is a technology-first approach that has resulted in the inability of many data base organizations to achieve their data base objectives.

KEY CONCEPT

The plans to use data base technology should precede the acquisition of the technology.

The Decision to Go Data Base

It becomes eminently clear after reviewing many data base installations that the data processing profession has almost calculatingly given an almost impenetrable aura of complicatedness to an essentially straightforward function—the management of a data base. Out of this obfuscation seem to be arising enough common descriptors and measures to begin to qualify data base technology as a discipline. What is confusing the issue is that this discipline embodies many segments of information processing previously vested in other disciplines of the profession. There is also an overraction to implications of standardization, avoidance of cost-effectiveness analysis, inadequate education and training, and a great fear of a commitment to ''go data base'' on the part of most users. ''Going data base'' is only an evolutionary step along a path which has been followed for many years; it involves the application of new and diverse tools to make the data management function more effective, more productive, and more reliable than has been the case for the past decade.

An initial questionnaire was distributed to the members of a working group, and some of the responses to the questions (with some editorial commentary) are as follows.

A logical question is whether data base technology is necessary or desirable for an organization. Is there a break-even point in size, type, or complexity of information processing needs? If so, how is it measured? Is there a way to determine the cost/benefit?

If your organization needs three or more of the following, then data base technology is probably necessary for you:

An integrated data environment
Rapid retrieval of data from large files
A query/update language for use at terminals
Backup and recovery requirements
Privacy/security protection of your data
Complex data structures

There is a break-even point, but it is difficult to define. Items that should be considered primarily are those relating to the user:

What is the desired goal?

What is the impact on the user's environment?

Will greater data availability improve or impede increased productivity?

The larger the file, the more likely you are to need data base technology. The type of query to be run is a factor. The more unpredictable the query, or the more complex the query, the more likely you are to need data base technology. The type of data structure is also a factor.

UNDERSTANDING WHAT YOU ARE GOING TO AUDIT

One of the auditing standards addresses the auditor's skills. One of the needed skills is a knowledge of the area under review. This can be obtained by gathering information about this area. For a data audit, this involves a knowledge of (1) the organization's information resource management policy, and (2) the organization's data base administration.

Information Resource Management Background Information

Organizations approach the management of their information resource from different perspectives. The policies and strategies used by the organization under audit affect the scope and approach used in the audit process. Understanding management information philosophy, either a formal or informal philosophy, partially defines the scope of a data audit.

Without a formal information resource management function, auditing must concentrate on the technical aspects of data base. With a formal function, the audit can start at a policy level and assess compliance to that policy instead of only assessing the technological aspects of data base management. A survey checklist is the tool used by auditors to acquire the types of information needed to understand the organization's approach to managing data.

Need to Understand Data Base Management Approaches

Understanding the use of data base technology is more complex than understanding an organization's information resource management philosophy. The use of data base technology involves not only the data base management system, but also a series of tools to assist in the data documentation, organization, and use.

The background information collection process is frequently referred to as a "preliminary review." The objective of the review is to provide the auditor the opportunity to walk through the area under audit in order to become familiar with that area. In a data base environment, much of the walk-through may have to occur within the documentation because much of the activity occurs electronically within the computer.

The purposes of the auditor's obtaining background information on the data base systems, in addition to gaining a general understanding of the area, are:

To identify the types and extent of data base documentation available

To acquire an "impression" of the orderliness and control level within the data base function

To meet the key individuals in the data base administration function

To learn to whom to go for specific information and/or documents
To scope the size of the data base operation

One major intangible benefit can be derived from the preliminary walk-through: a better personal understanding of data base technology. When an auditor is provided the opportunity to "look, touch, and question" the data base processing, that individual has an opportunity to gain personal insight into the why, when, where, how, and what of that technology. If an auditor misses an opportunity to take a tour through the data base area and talk to the data base administration personnel, the auditor is missing an opportunity to improve himself or herself technically.

INFORMATION RESOURCE MANAGEMENT BACKGROUND CHECKLIST

The checklist for use in obtaining background data on an organization's information resource management program is a listing of items to be obtained for analysis. A background search is an investigation designed to provide the auditor with sufficient knowledge to conduct the audit effectively. The objective is not to uncover audit findings, but to understand the area under audit.

An investigation is not as structured as the typical audit process. Therefore, the checklist contains categories of items which if available will provide the auditor with valuable information on how the organization manages information. This information is necessary in order to understand the role, responsibility, and functioning of the data base administration. It may not be necessary to audit the management of information, but it is necessary to understand the formal or informal information management policy and procedures in order to assess the data base administration function effectively.

The background checklist provided identifies the items to be obtained (see Figure 5). The items themselves should be stored in a permanent workpaper file for use in this and subsequent audits. The checklist provides space to indicate the workpaper index where the background documents are located. In situations where there is no formal documentation, such as may occur with the lack of a formal data policy, the auditor should interview the appropriate management personnel and document on an interview sheet the informal description of the item in question (in our example it would be the data policy) and store that in the workpaper.

Data Policy

The data policy is the organization's position on managing information as a resource of the organization. The data policy items that need to be collected are:

Organization's Data Policy

a. Purpose. The organization's data policy is a statement by senior management defining the organization's approach to information management. The policy may be written for both employees and customers of the organization. Financial institutions frequently issue a public data policy describing how they handle customers' information. The type of information that is typically included in a data policy is:

Organizational responsibility for information
Protection and/or disclosure of information
Commonality of definition and use

Number	Items to Be Obtained	Workpaper Index
	Data Policy	
1.	Organization's data policy	
2.	Policies and procedures that affect information processing	
	Organization Structure	
3.	Information management organization chart	
4.	Functional description of organization's information management role and responsibility	
	Data Plans and Programs	
5.	Copies of long- and short-term information resource management planning documents	
6.	Copies of external review reports prepared by independent consultants or auditors	
7.	Copies of relevant internal audit reports	
	Justification and Costs	
8.	Copies of documents justifying new methods of information resource management	
9.	Information resource cost/benefit analysis worksheets	
10.	Information resource annual budgets and year-to-date costs	
	Data Security	
11.	Data security policy and programs	
12.	Data security officer function and job description	

Figure 5. Background Data on Information Management Checklist.

Ownership
Retention of information
Consistency and reliability of information
Protection of information

b. Typical response. Few organizations have formal data policies. When formal data policies do not exist, it is helpful to obtain the opinion of senior data processing management, especially those in a policy-making position, on their understanding of the organization's position on the above data policy items.

Policies and Procedures That Affect Information Processing

Many policies and procedures of an organization address the area of information processing. For example, a manufacturing organization may have a policy on the confidentiality and/or the intent to patent or not patent inventions which address manufacturing information.

a. Purpose. Policies and procedures explain how to use and store documents. Procedures in many areas of an organization, such as payroll, describe methods of handling and protecting employee information. If there is not a formal data policy, other related policies may comprise a de facto data policy for the organization.

b. Typical response. The policies and procedures that relate to information management are normally not consolidated. In many instances, they will not be viewed as information management policies and procedures. A suggested method to gather this information is to interview the senior auditing personnel for the purpose of gathering a list of potential policies and procedures containing information management directives. The auditor can then investigate and collect those policies and procedures that are truly applicable to information management. Note that it is not necessary to have an exhaustive list of policies and procedures; a representative sample which includes the main areas such as personnel, finance, and production will suffice.

Organization Structure

The method of organizing the information management functions has a direct bearing on the effectiveness of the implementation of information management policy and procedures. Ideally, a senior manager, one equivalent to a treasurer, would be charged with information management responsibilities for the organization. The organizational location of the people responsible for information management, including data base administration, provides insight into the senior management perspective of the importance of information. The items that should be obtained regarding organizational structure are:

Information Management Organization Chart

a. Purpose. The information management organizational structure shows the process for implementing information policy. The structure should be the equivalent of a comptroller's organization for managing financial resources. The structure may be a complete entity, or it may use a "dotted line" relationship indicating that one individual does not formally report to another, but receives direction from another individual.

b. Typical response. Few organizations have formalized an information management organizational structure. A sample structure is given in Chapter 6. If there is not a formal structure, the auditor should identify those individuals with information management responsibilities and then show the structural relationships among those individuals.

Functional Description of Organization's Information Management Role and Responsibilities

a. Purpose. Understanding the role and responsibility of the individuals and units responsible for information management serves two purposes. First, it familiarizes the auditor with the way the organizational structure works. Knowing who does what pinpoints where the real information management authority resides. Second, it provides the auditor with a list of contacts for use during the conduct of the audit.

b. Typical response. Most organizations define the role and responsibility of their units and individuals. This information is normally easy to obtain. However, the auditor should be cautioned that information management responsibilities may be imbedded as part of other more encompassing positions.

Data Plans and Programs

The information management policies and procedures are implemented through plans and programs. For example, if the policy should state that the information of the organization will be safeguarded in accordance with its importance to the organization, then plans and programs need to be established to achieve the desired level of security. The information management plans and programs are normally developed by or under the direction of the senior information management person in the organization. The items that need to be obtained about these plans and programs are:

Copies of Long- and Short-Term Information Resource Management Planning Documents

a. Purpose. The planning documents explain both the short-term and long-term goals and objectives for information management, as well as the method of achieving those goals and objectives. Short-term plans normally cover one year, while long-term plans frequently cover a span of five years. Properly established, the short-term plan is the initial step in achieving the long-term plan. The information resource management plan should be an integral part of the organization's short- and long-term planning documents.

b. Typical response. Most data processing organizations have planning documents. It is important in a function that has grown as rapidly as data processing to develop long- and short-term plans. This is particularly important when the lead time for needed equipment may be 12 to 36 months. Unfortunately, many of these plans are not integrated into the organization's planning documents. Therefore, they become data processing plans, and not information management plans. If the data processing plan is not properly integrated into the organization's plan, the auditor should obtain both in order to determine if there are inconsistencies between the planning documents.

Copies of External Review Reports Prepared by Independent Consultants or Auditors

a. Purpose. Many organizations use consultants to help them analyze information management deficiencies and to make recommendations for improvement. These consulting reports and auditors' operational audit reports may comprise the plans and programs for information management. If these recommendations have been adopted, the auditors should ensure that they have been or are in the process of being implemented.

b. Typical response. Generally, consultant reports are not available to the auditors unless they specifically request them. In other words, the organization requesting the consulting service does not typically send the auditors a copy of that report. The auditor can identify such studies by asking senior information management personnel or by reviewing the information management budget and/or cash disbursements for consulting service fees.

Copies of Relevant Internal Audit Reports

a. Purpose. During the conduct of internal audits, many information management problems may be uncovered and reported. In addition, auditors may make information management recommendations. If the audit department consolidates all findings and recommendations, a perusal can quickly identify those relating to information management. If findings and recommendations are not consolidated, the identification of the relevant audit reports can be accomplished by scanning audit reports for the past couple of years, or by interviewing the individuals who are normally assigned in-charge audit positions and having identify the appropriate information management finding and recommendations.

b. Typical response. Previous audit reports are readily available and should be reviewed.

Justification and Cost

Many organizations indicate that the implementation of data base management systems has not been a cost-effective program. The reason which has been previously cited is the lack of planning. An integral part of planning is justifying the data base management system and then quantitatively stating costs and benefits for that implementation. Earlier sections of this chapter explained why organizations move to data base, and the more common benefits to be derived from that move. The cost and benefit statements should be prepared in accordance with the financial procedures of the organization. The items that should be obtained in this area are:

Copies of Documents Justifying New Methods of Information Resource Management

a. Purpose. Understanding the purposes for installing new methods of information resource management helps put the plans and procedures into the proper perspective. This information can also be used by the auditor to measure whether or not those new methods have achieved their objectives. Unless this step has been formalized and monitored, data processing resources may be expended unnecessarily.

b. Typical response. Few organizations prepare formal information resource management justifications. Normally the data base processing tools are obtained as a productivity tool because it is easier to justify the concept without identifying all of the costs and uses that will be associated with tools such as a data base management system or data dictionary. Lacking formal documents, the auditors should interview those responsible for acquiring new methods to obtain their perspective on the acquisition objectives.

Information Resource Cost/Benefit Analysis Worksheets

a. Purpose. The development of cost/benefit analysis worksheets indicates that considerable thought, effort, and energy has gone into acquiring new methods for information management. For example, if the cost and benefits of introduction of a data base management system have been documented, this is indicative that good planning has occurred. In addition, the auditor can use this information to determine whether or not the costs are within estimate, and that the benefits have been achieved.

b. Typical response. Normally, the cost/benefits of information management methods are not clearly identified. Reasons for this may be numerous. Some organizations have cited benefits so large as to be unbelievable, while others, knowing the full cost implications, are reluctant to document those costs. If the costs and benefits are not clearly stated, the auditor should attempt to put together a cost/benefit worksheet for data base.

Information Resource Annual Budget and Year-to-Date Costs

a. Purpose. If the costs and benefits have been estimated, they should be monitored. The cost and benefit information should be available from normal organization accounting systems, assuming that costs and benefits are recorded in such a manner that they can be analyzed as part of an information management budget.

b. Typical response. If organizations have gone to the time and effort to develop justification documents and cost/benefit worksheets, they normally also collect those costs and benefits so that they can be monitored. If it becomes necessary for the auditor to reconstruct cost/benefit and justification documentation, the auditor should also evaluate whether the actual costs and benefits are in compliance with those estimates.

Data Security

The consolidation of information poses a security threat to that organization. Passage of the Privacy Act of 1977 in the United States was directly attributable to the consolidation of information by governmental agencies. Many of the privacy laws throughout the world are a direct result of the consolidation and easy retrieval of information. The auditor needs to understand the methods of protecting that information, and in that process should obtain the following items:

Data Security Policy and Programs

a. Purpose. The security policy defines the degree and type of protection required, and the programs outline the method for implementing those policies. In an automated environment, many of the programs will be automated security systems. Because the information will be stored electronically and may be accessible to many organizations over common carrier communication lines, protection must be within the computer, not external to it.

b. Typical response. Most organizations have addressed the subject of computer security. Sometimes the emphasis is on physical security, and other times it is on both physical and logical security. The auditor should be aware of a computer security paradox. Frequently the security within the computer is extremely strong, but once the valuable information leaves the computer, security lapses occur as the methods of enforcement deteriorate. The auditor should be concerned with security policies and procedures in both manual and automated environments.

Data Security Officer Function and Job Description

a. Purpose. The security officer function may be a full-time or part-time function. If security is an issue, an individual or group of individuals must assume the responsibility for security, and that becomes the data security officer function. Understanding this function through job descriptions or equivalent provides the auditor with insight into the security enforcement mechanism as well as the monitoring and improvement process.

b. Typical response. Many financial institutions have formalized the data security officer function. In these organizations, the description of that function is readily available. Other organizations have chosen to use a data security committee comprising part-time people, in which case the functions and duties may be more sketchy. Still other organizations have attempted to make each project leader responsible for the security of that project, and computer operators responsible for security in the computer room. In these instances, the security responsibilities may be included in individuals' job descriptions.

KEY CONCEPT

Organizations have an information resource management policy; however, it may not be formalized and thus may be difficult to identify and document.

BACKGROUND DATA ON DATA BASE MANAGEMENT CHECKLIST

The data base management function is normally more precisely defined than is the information resource management function. Furthermore in this area there is normally an overabundance of documentation available to the auditor. The auditor may have to conduct investigations and interviews to acquire the desired information while investigating information resource management, but in reviewing the data base management function the auditor may be overwhelmed with data. This makes it necessary to be more selective in the type of documents collected. The auditor may choose to reference an external source rather than to accumulate documents within the audit workpaper file.

Auditors with minimal understanding of data base concepts should use this background-gathering period to improve their own personal data base skills. In conducting this background investigation, many auditors question why it is necessary to gather a lot of the detailed information that is included on Figure 6. You will probably have that same question as you go through the checklist and begin to use it. One good reason is completing the background questionnaire provides a learning experience for the auditor. If he or she merely gathers the information, some of it may be questionable from an audit purpose. For example, the questionnaire asks for a lot of information about the hardware that is used to process the data base management systems and applications. However, if the auditor uses it to learn more about the hardware and how the hardware and data base software interact for efficiency and control, the exercise can be extremely valuable.

The checklist in Figure 6 is both a reference document and a documentation tool. Items that should be available from the data base administration area are listed as items to be obtained, and a column is provided in which to indicate where in the workpapers those items are filled. For items for which documentation is not normally available, space is provided on the checklist iteself to record that information. Should that information be available from the DBA area, it should be acquired and the fact noted in the workpaper index. The following sections explain how to use the data base management checklist.

KEY CONCEPT

Use the data preliminary review step for growth in your knowledge of data base technology.

Organization and Staffing

The data base administration function is normally a formal function. Most data base administration functions organizationally report within the data processing organization. The role and responsibility of that group vary significantly from organization to organization, making it necessary for the auditor to understand the role prior to commencing the audit. The following five items are identified as helpful in understanding the organization and staffing of the data base administration function:

1. Data base administration (DBA) department organization chart
2. Functional description of DBA department organization
3. List of key officials in the DBA department
4. Staffing level of the DBA department by division or office
5. Major position descriptions:

Number	Items to Be Obtained	Workpaper Index
	Organization and Staffing	
1.	Data base administration (DBA) department organization chart	
2.	Functional description of DBA department organization	
3.	List of key officials in the DBA department	
4.	Staffing level of the DBA department by division or office	

Item 3:

Section and Supervisor	Location and Telephone Number	Major Responsibilities
______	______	______
______	______	______
______	______	______
______	______	______
______	______	______
______	______	______

Item 4:

	Number		Names of Supervisors
	Authorized	Assigned	
DBA general management	______	______	______
Security personnel	______	______	______
System programmers	______	______	______
Data definition analysts	______	______	______
Data base design analyst	______	______	______
Data base systems coordination	______	______	______
Data base software support specialists	______	______	______
Data base operations assistant	______	______	______
Data coordinator	______	______	______
Data base quality assurance analyst	______	______	______
Other technical support Specify ______	______	______	______

Figure 6. Background Data on Data Base Management Checklist.

Number	Items to Be Obtained				Workpaper Index
4.	Continued				
		Number			
		Authorized	Assigned	Names of Supervisors	
	Data entry operators	______	______	______	
	Control clerks	______	______	______	
	Schedulers	______	______	______	
	Librarian(s)	______	______	______	
	Secretaries and clerks	______	______	______	
	Other Specify ______	______	______	______	
	Total	______	______		
	Anticipated staffing additions and deletions during the next two years: ______ ______ ______ ______				
5.	Major position descriptions				
	Data Base System Design, Development, and Modification				
6.	Data base system documentation standards				
7.	Data base system documentation procedures				
8.	Data base system development procedures				
9.	Data base computer program change procedures				
	Data Base Operations				
10.	Data base operations procedures manual				
11.	File library procedures manual				
12.	User billing procedures, including the billing algorithm				

Figure 6. *(Continued)*

Number	Items to Be Obtained				Workpaper Index
13.	Statistics on DBMS utilization				
				Total DBMS Processing	
	Number of scheduled eight-hour shifts per day			________	
	Number of scheduled days per week			________	
	Average number of jobs per day			________	
	Total hours scheduled for past three months			________	
	Actual hours used for past three months:				
	Production			________	
	Testing			________	
	Rerun			________	
	Maintenance			________	
	Idle			________	
	Other			________	
	Average number of crashes per month			________	
	Explain how the numbers of actual hours used were derived:				
	____				
	____				
	Multiprogramming factor (average number of programs running concurrently)			________	
14.	Budgeted, actual, and projected costs for current and next fiscal year				
		Budgeted Costs	Actual Costs	Projected Costs	
	Costs of rented data base equipment				
	Disk storage	________	________	________	
	Central processing units	________	________	________	
	Data communications	________	________	________	

Figure 6. *(Continued)*

Number	Items to Be Obtained				Workpaper Index
14.	Continued				
		Budgeted Costs	Actual Costs	Projected Costs	
	All other	______	______	______	
	Costs of purchased data base equipment				
	Disk storage	______	______	______	
	Central processing units	______	______	______	
	Data communications	______	______	______	
	All other	______	______	______	
	Hardware maintenance costs	______	______	______	
	Data base personnel costs:				
	DBA general management	______	______	______	
	Security personnel	______	______	______	
	System programmers	______	______	______	
	Data definition analysts	______	______	______	
	Data base design analyst	______	______	______	
	Data base systems coordination	______	______	______	
	Data base software support specialists	______	______	______	
	Data base operations assistant	______	______	______	
	Data coordinator	______	______	______	
	Data base quality assurance analyst	______	______	______	
	Other technical support Specify ______	______	______	______	
	Data entry operators	______	______	______	
	Control clerks	______	______	______	
	Schedulers	______	______	______	

Figure 6. *(Continued)*

Number	Items to Be Obtained				Workpaper Index
14.	Continued				
		Budgeted Costs	Actual Costs	Projected Costs	
	Librarian(s)	________	________	________	
	Secretaries and clerks	________	________	________	
	Other				
	Specify ________	________	________	________	
	Data base software	________	________	________	
	DBMS (specify)				
	________	________	________	________	
	________	________	________	________	
	________	________	________	________	
	Data dictionary	________	________	________	
	Other (specify)				
	________	________	________	________	
	________	________	________	________	
	Contracts				
	Data base consultants	________	________	________	
	Other services	________	________	________	
	Facility costs				
	Space	________	________	________	
	Utilities	________	________	________	
	Other costs (specify)				
	________	________	________	________	
	________	________	________	________	
	Total costs	________	________	________	

Figure 6. *(Continued)*

Number	Items to Be Obtained			Workpaper Index
		Number	Application Name	
15.	Applications using data base	________	________	
			________	
			________	
			________	
16.	DBMS recovery procedures			
	Data Definition and Documentation			
17.	Method of documenting data			
18.	Inventory of data elements in data base			
19.	Data base statistics			
	Number of data elements in data base		________	
	Data organizational structure		________	
	Size of physical data base		________	
	Number of data bases		________	
	Location of each			
	________			
	________			
	________			
	Data Base Security Protection			
20.	Data center security procedures			
21.	Emergency plan			
22.	Backup and recovery procedures			
23.	Security software			
	Data Base System Software			
24.	DBMS system description			
25.	DBMS utilities description			
26.	Program library system description			
27.	Data base file maintenance system description			
28.	Security software description			
29.	Data communications system description			

Figure 6. *(Continued)*

Number	Items to Be Obtained	Workpaper Index
30.	Data dictionary description	
31.	DBMS reorganization procedures	
	Data Base Hardware	
32.	Complete the inventory and description of the computer system used for data base: CPU manufacturer __________ CPU model number __________ Date CPU installed __________ CPU physical location __________ Internal storage capacity __________ Direct access storage capacity __________ Console model number __________ Peripheral devices: Number of Devices Magnetic tape drives ____track____density __________ ____track____density __________ ____track____density __________ Magnetic disk drives ____series or model number __________ ____series or model number __________ ____series or model number __________ Magnetic drum units __________ Other mass storage units (specify type) ____________________ __________ Card readers __________ Card punches __________	

Figure 6. *(Continued)*

Number	Items to Be Obtained		Workpaper Index
32.	Continued	Number of Devices	
	Card reader/punches	______	
	Line printers		
	_____lines per minute	______	
	_____lines per minute	______	
	On-line terminals	______	
	Remote batch terminals	______	
	Communication controllers	______	
	Optical scanners	______	
	MICR readers	______	
	Mark sense readers	______	
	Key-to-tape units	______	
	Key-to-disk units	______	
	Keypunch/verification units	______	
	Card sorters	______	
	Card collators	______	
	Card accounting machines	______	
	Other (specify)		
	______	______	
33.	Schematic of telecommunication network		
34.	What percent of the above hardware is used for data base technology?	______%	

Figure 6. *(Continued)*

a. *Purpose*. Staffing within the data base administration function defines the scope of activities, and the potential contacts during the audit process. The checklist provides space to indicate the key officials of the department. It is frequently beneficial during the background-gathering phase to meet these key officials.

b. *Typical response*. This information is normally easy to acquire. Note that the DBA function may be included on the data processing organizational chart, and the functional descriptions within broader data processing documents. The staffing levels may need to be acquired through interview, as the up-to-date staffing status may not be readily available in a formal document.

Data Base System Design, Development, and Modification

Data base systems are constructed differently than non-data base systems. While the data base is designed to alleviate the technical complexities of accessing data, it does place restrictions on system designs and system structures. Once the data base has been structured, the application design should attempt to optimize the interface with that structure in order to gain operational efficiencies.

a. Purpose. A highly structured system design, development, and modification process is necessary for the successful effective use of data base technology. If applications are permitted to be developed without consideration for the organizational structure of the data base and the needs and concerns of other users, a chaotic operating environment may occur. Many data base administrators review each proposed application system and major enhancements to existing systems in depth to ensure that those proposals are consistent with the data base structure and that the proposal optimizes the use of data base technology.

The method of interfacing with data base technology affects the cost/benefit from data base technology. Understanding the process in which systems are designed, developed, and modified can assist the auditor in understanding the operational effectiveness of that technology. Once the audit commences, problems detected by the auditor are often traced to a faulty design methodology.

b. Typical response. Most data base administrators establish standards and procedures for the development of data base applications. The auditor's concerns are the effectiveness of the methodology and the enforcement of the methodology.

Data Base Operations

When the data base is first installed, most of the operations are performed by the data base administrator. However, as the installation matures, more and more of the daily function is assumed by computer operations personnel. The data base administrator normally trains these data base operators and gradually turns more and more of the operations functions over to them. The last aspect to be turned over to computer operations is normally the reorganization function. This section of the checklist contains a series of items to be obtained during the background phase.

a. Purpose. Background information on the operation of the data base provides a means to assess the operational performance of the data base. This operational information can be used to determine the data base workload, how that workload is distributed, the division of data base costs, and the problems being encountered in the use of data base technology.

The operational information provides background about the data base operation, and it can also be used to begin to pinpoint data base control weaknesses. For example, if a large amount of processing time is being used for reruns, that may be indicative of inadequate operational controls. Some analysis of the raw information can help develop the data base audit work program.

The operational questions cover both the operation of the physical data base and the operation of the data base administration function. The information is divided equally between procedures and statistical information about the operation. The ease with which this information can be gathered will be dependent upon the structure of the accounting system for data base costs.

In order to gain an appreciation of the magnitude of the data base operation, it is necessary to obtain operating statistics. These statistics show whether data base is an insignificant part of the data processing function, or whether it is an important segment of data processing. While the checklist does not specifically request it, growth rates on data base operations would be extremely valuable, showing the rate of growth during the last several years, assuming data base has been installed that long, so that future growth in operations can be projected.

b. Typical response. Most organizations can provide operational information on data base. Even if the figures are not directly reportable to the accounting system, it is normally easy to identify the segment of data processing costs directly attributable to data base technology.

Data Definition and Documentation

The data base administration function administers data. Data are the major ingredient in the process. Therefore, complete and accurate documentation is essential in a well-run data base environment. The documentation of data is performed in many organizations by using a data dictionary.

This section is designed to provide information on the size of the data base, organizational structure of the data base, and an inventory of data elements. The inventory can be provided by the data dictionary, or independently compiled based upon the documentation methods used by the organization. This section lists items that should be obtained about data definition and documentation.

a. Purpose. The auditor is concerned about the adequacy of the data documentation. The auditor is also a user of that documentation. During the audit, some of the tests may be examining data within the data base. In order to do this, the auditor must become ''friendly'' with the data in the data base. This is a data processing term meaning familiar with something in an easy-to-do manner.

b. Typical response. Organizations that have made extensive use of the data dictionary can normally supply the data documentation information easily. These organizations may also have an inventory of data elements. On the other hand, those organizations without a data dictionary, or in which the data dictionary is a documentation tool and not integrated into the process, may not be able to provide the type of up-to-date information needed.

Data Base Security Protection

The data base must be protected from both intentional and unintentional destruction and disclosure. As the importance to the organization of the information contained in the data base increases, so does the need to protect that information. The security measures are the totality of the procedures and processes implemented to ensure the continual operation of the data base without any loss or disclosure.

The security measures for the data base will be both physical and logical. Physical security measures encompass restricting access to the computer room and off-site storage areas for use in the event of a computer room disaster. Logical security measures include those measures designed to restrict access to the data base and prevent unintentional destruction or modification of electronic media, and the appropriate steps to ensure continuity of processing. Three items to be obtained in this area are described.

a. Purpose. The actual protection of the data base is dependent more upon the data base procedures than the information resource security policies. The auditor needs to understand those procedures in order to assess the effectiveness of the data base security procedures. The auditor must also assess the technical complexity of the security measures in order to determine whether security consultants are needed to assess the adequacy of the security measures.

b. Typical response. Physical security procedures are frequently easier to understand than logical security procedures. This is because it is easier to identify the physical risks than it is to identify the logical risks. Security experts state that people have difficulty identifying with problems they have not personally experienced. Thus, security may be exceptionally strong in areas where the organization has previously experienced security problems and weak in those areas where problems have not previously been encountered.

Data Base System Software

The data base function is under the control of the data base management system. This piece of software performs many functions as a manager of the data base. It establishes the initial structure, manages the day-to-day operation, provides operating statistics, assists in the reorganization and recovery of the data base, and also offers numerous utilities for the maintenance and analysis of data base information.

The auditor does not want to become a data base technical expert, but he or she should understand the data base management system capabilities. It is also helpful to know the analysis and printout capabilities included as part of the data base software. These features may be an aid to the auditor during the conduct of the audit. The items to be obtained about data base software are identified in this section.

a. Purpose. The auditor should understand the data base software in order to understand data base technology. The capabilities and constraints are frequently incorporated within the software. A knowledge of the software also becomes a communication vehicle between data base administration people and the auditor, and an understanding of the software may help increase the auditor's respect for the technical problems in the data base administration area.

b. Typical response. Data base administration people are normally very willing to discuss and describe data base software. If the auditor is unfamiliar with the capabilities, that should be explained to the data base administration people so that they can keep the explanation at a conceptual level, rather than at a technical level. Frequently, introductory books to data base management systems are available, and these should be requested by the auditor.

Data Base Hardware

Computer hardware is hardware used for computing purposes. Data base is but one of many purposes for using hardware. Therefore, if the question is asked about what hardware has been acquired specifically for data base, the answer may be, "None." It is more appropriate to ask what hardware is available, what percentage is dedicated to data base usage, and what percentage is partially used for data base usage, and what percentage is partially used for data base technology. The process is twofold. First, the hardware on which data base technology is used should be identified. Note that data base may be used on several different computers, and if so the hardware from each computer should be identified. Second, the percentage of those resources consumed by data base technology should be identified.

a. Purpose. The purpose of identifying the hardware is to familiarize the auditor with hardware terminology and capabilities, as well as to identify hardware available to run auditor software on. This inventory show whether or not audit software can be operated on the hardware facility.

b. Typical response. Most organizations have an inventory of hardware and can supply that information upon request. Even when such a list is available, it may be helpful for the auditor to take a tour of the computer room in order to identify the specific pieces of hardware. If a list of hardware is not readily available, the auditor should look for a bill of sale if the hardware has been purchased, or a rental agreement if it is rented. Both should identify the hardware components.

USING BACKGROUND INFORMATION TO PREPARE FOR THE AUDIT

In developing an audit finding, the auditor must identify the following four characteristics about each identified data base audit concern:

Statement of condition. This tells what the auditor has uncovered.

Criteria. These tell what the specific condition should be.

Effect. The difference between what it is and what it should be determines the effect or significance of the finding.

Cause. This tells the reason for the deviation between what is (statement of condition) and what should be (criteria).

In gathering the background information, the auditor is establishing a base for two of the four attributes of an audit finding. Background information provides the criteria (what data processing should be) and will provide input into determining the cause of the condition. Since the auditor will not know what the findings will be during the background review, it is important to collect as much information as possible and to organize it in the best possible manner to help define and evaluate problems when they are uncovered.

The background information is also used in the data base risk analysis process. The recommended data base audit process begins by identifying the risks associated with the data base installation under audit. A careful scrutiny of the background information is helpful in identifying the specific risks that require audit investigation.

three

SELECTING DATA BASE AUDIT AREAS

Auditors use many different methods to determine the areas to be investigated during the review. Some of the more common include predetermined audit programs, auditor intuition and judgment, recommendations by senior management, and the conduct of preliminary reviews. All of these methods have a common thread which is risk.

Auditing is a risk business. The objective of auditing could be stated as providing opinions regarding the magnitude of risk faced by an organization. These opinions can be expressed in terms of the adequacy of control, the degree to which the financial records represent the condition of the business, or the effectiveness, economy, and efficiency of operations.

This chapter outlines a process for selecting the data base areas for audit. The recommended process identifies the magnitude of the risk present in the use of data base technology. The process uses the criteria that correlate to risk in data base as a basis for determining the magnitude of risk.

The purpose for performing the risk analysis process is twofold. First, it is a nontechnical assessment of the data base permitting auditors with minimal data processing skills to achieve a high degree of success in data base auditing by identifying the high probability problem areas. Second, the process optimizes the use of limited auditing resources by concentrating audit effort on the high-risk areas, while applying only minimal audit resources to the low-risk areas.

RISK DRIVES AUDITING

Risk as used in this book is defined as the probable result of the occurrence of an adverse event, such as the destruction that could be caused by fire. Risks are ever present and rarely can be completely eliminated. For example, fire is a risk which is always present. It is possible to reduce the probability of fire by the type of construction used and care exercised in preventing and detecting fire, but the risk will always be present.

Risk management is an important function in conducting business. Management deals with risk every day. There is a risk that new products will be unacceptable to the marketplace; a risk that needed supplies will not arrive on time; a risk that employees will defraud the organization; and a risk that management will make improper decisions because of being provided erroneous information by data base applications.

A control is that which prevents, detects, corrects, or reduces a risk. The stronger the system of controls, the less of a threat the risk becomes to the organization. Auditing is a function used by management to assess the adequacy of control. Once apprised of the adequacy of control, management can then determine whether the level of risk in a specific situation is acceptable, or whether action needs to be taken to reduce the risk further.

Auditors have always understood the concept of risk and used it within the audit process. Unfortunately, most of the risk analysis was performed by experienced auditors using intuition and judgment. Management paid auditors for their experience, intuition, and judgment, which was applied more as an art than as a science.

The introduction of the computer brought consistency to processing. Prior to the computer, the consistency of processing depended upon the consistency of people and the ability of supervision and the system of internal controls to detect inconsistencies. In this environment, auditing relied heavily upon sampling to measure the level of inconsistency as a basis of appraising the effectiveness of controls.

Data base technology automates not only processing but also many of the application and environmental controls. In this type of processing environment, it is possible to formalize some of the risk analysis concepts that in a manual environment were based upon auditor intuition and judgment. The risk scoring concept proposed in this chapter breaks down auditor intuition and judgment into a structured process that attempts to quantify the level of risk in a data base environment so that the process can be used by less experienced auditors.

KEY CONCEPT

Data base risk analysis is the formalization of audit judgment and experience.

DATA BASE COST-EFFECTIVENESS CURVE

An important element in understanding risk is the cost-effectiveness curve for risk in a data base environment. The curve illustrates the relationship between risk and control. The curve shows that as the adequacy of controls increases, the loss due to risk decreases.

The cost-effectiveness curve demonstrates that risk can be measured and that the effective control on risk can also be measured. This concept, if understood and practiced, not only helps auditing, but also helps data processing professionals develop cost-effective controls. The curve identifies those points where a data base risk is undercontrolled, as well as those where that risk is overcontrolled.

The cost-effectiveness curve for data base controls is illustrated in Figure 7. The curve shows that without any controls, or minimal controls, the loss due to any given risk can be extremely high. In most instances, as controls are added the loss due to risk drops rapidly until a level of loss is reached which is hard to reduce. The figure also implies that it is almost impossible to reduce the level of loss due to risk to zero. The figure assumes a relationship between the adequacy of control to the cost of control. Assuming this relationship, the figure shows that as controls are increased so does the cost, but, in turn the loss due to risk is reduced.

Let's examine an example of how this might work with an on-line data base banking credit card system. Let us start at the point where the bank designs an on-line data base credit card system to record purchases and bill customers. Without any controls, the bank would issue a credit card to anyone who wants it, and allow unlimited use of the credit card. In this situation, there are practically no controls, and the loss due to the risk of customers not paying for items charged would be extremely high. In fact, it could be so high that the bank would go out of business. Therefore, the bank must introduce controls to reduce those risks. The bank might decide that these three controls are necessary:

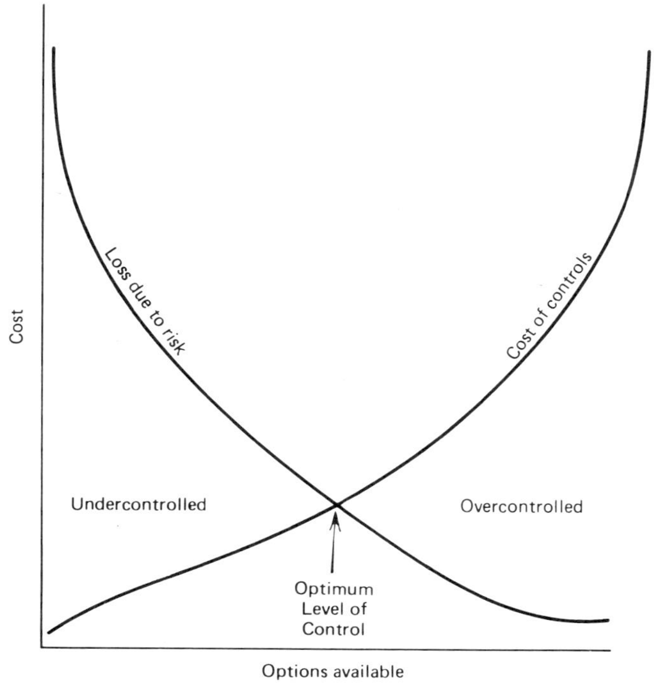

Figure 7. Cost-Effectiveness Curve for Data Base Controls.

Initial credit check

Limiting a customer's credit

Invalidating cards which are lost or those of persons with whom the bank no longer desires to continue a credit relationship

There are hundreds of variations of these three basic controls. For example, a credit check can be minor, such as filling out a simple form, or it can involve personal investigation, interaction with a credit bureau, and so on. The method by which the bank provides information to the merchants can involve establishing a battery of telephone operators, regular issuance of lists of bad cards, and so on. The controls over invalidating credit cards can include monitoring of credit risks, lists of invalid cards, and paying a bounty to recoup a bad card.

The first step in using the cost-effectiveness curve is to estimate the most probable loss with minimal controls. It is almost impossible in an organization with strong environmental controls not to have some control over any given risk. The method for quantifying the loss due to risk is the application of the following risk formula:

$$\text{ALE} = \text{frequency of occurrence} \times \text{average loss per occurrence}$$

This formula states that the annual loss expectation (ALE) from a risk equals the frequency at which the losses occur times the average loss per occurrence. In our credit card example, we might assume that we would have 100 uncollectible charges per day, at an average loss of $100 each, or an annual loss expectation of $10,000 per day. We must now analyze what comprises that frequency of 100 and the average loss of $100 so that we can begin to apply controls realistically.

The annual loss expectation formula demonstrates that effective controls must accomplish one of the following two tasks. They must (1) reduce the frequency of occurrence of loss, or (2) reduce the average loss per occurrence.

Let's look again at our bank credit card situation. We find that the bank's suggested controls are designed to:

Create an effective credit-checking process to reduce the frequency of occurrence of charges due to bad credit risks

Issue the merchant a list of invalid credit cards to reduce the frequency of occurrence of bad charges

Limit an individual to a predetermined amount of credit to reduce the average loss per occurrence

Require the merchant to call in for approval for all charges over $50 to reduce the average loss per occurrence

The proper use of the cost-effectiveness curve to determine the need for these controls is as follows:

Identify the risks that are present in the data base environment.

Estimate the magnitude of those risks.

Identify the types of controls that will be effective in reducing the identified risks.

Select that mix of controls which appears to reduce the risk to the optimum cost-effectiveness level.

Monitor the controls to ensure that they are cost-effective in an operational environment.

The controls must now be evaluated using the cost-effectiveness curve to determine which mix of controls will reduce the risks to the optimum level. The curve will show that it is not economical to reduce the level of loss too low. As the number of controls cross the optimum level of control, the system is overcontrolled, while insufficient controls permit the loss due to risk to be too high and the data base process would be undercontrolled. The optimal level of control can be estimated during design, but can only be verified if the effectiveness of controls is monitored after the data base system goes into operation.

KEY CONCEPT

Too many controls can be as costly as too few controls.

DATA BASE RISKS

Data base auditing is concerned not only with the integrity of the data base, but also with the effectiveness, economy, and efficiency of the data base operation. Experience has shown that the greatest losses attributable to data base appear to be operational, and not financial. Therefore, as we evaluate the data base risks, we will evaluate them from an operational perspective.

The data base risks stated in this book are used to illustrate a potential data base technology problem. Data base technology risks are needed to identify the concerns that must

Number	Data Base Risk	Description of Risk
1.	Inadequate assignment of responsibilities	There is inappropriate segregation of duties or failure to recognize placement of responsibility.
2.	Inaccurate or incomplete data in a data base	The integrity of data entered in the data base is lost due to inadvertent or intentional acts.
3.	Losing an update to a single data item	One or more updates to a single data item can be lost due to inadequate concurrent update procedures.
4.	Inadequate audit trail	The use of data by multiple applications may split the audit trail among those applications and the DBMS audit trail.
5.	Unauthorized access to data in a data base	The concentration of data may make sensitive data available to anyone gaining access to a data base.
6.	Inadequate service level	Multiple users contesting for the same resources may degrade the service to all due to excessive demand or inadequate resources.
7.	Placing data in the wrong calendar period	Identifying transactions with the proper calendar period is more difficult in some on-line data base environments than in others.
8.	Failure of DBMS to function as specified	Most DBMSs are provided by vendors, making the data administrator dependent upon the vendor to assure the proper functioning of the software.
9.	Fraud/embezzlement	Systems that control resources are always subject to fraud and embezzlement.
10.	Lack of independent data base reviews	Most reviewers are not skilled in data base technology and thus have not evaluated data base installations; in addition, many auditor software packages cannot access a DBMS.
11.	Inadequate documentation	Documentation of data base technology is needed to ensure consistency of understanding and use by multiple users.
12.	Continuity of processing	Many organizations rely heavily upon data base technology for the performance of their day-to-day processing.
13.	Lack of performance criteria	Without established performance criteria, an organization cannot be assured that it is achieving data base goals.
14.	Lack of management support	Without adequate resources and "clout," the advantages of data base technology may not be achieved.

Figure 8. Data Base Risks.

be addressed by data base auditors. The applicability of any risk to an organization will vary with the extent of use of data base technology by that organization and the amount of attention paid to control of the data base. The data base risks are listed and briefly described in Figure 8.

Each of the data base risks will be explained separately to assist the auditor in understanding the risk and to aid the auditor in determining the magnitude of the risk. Later in the chapter, risk analysis worksheets will be provided for each of the data base technology risks. The objective of these worksheets is to provide the auditor with a method for determining the magnitude of each of the identified risks.

The data base technology risks that need to be evaluated in each data base audit are described in the following sections.

KEY CONCEPT

Understanding the data base risks provides the basis for a data base audit.

Inadequate Assignment of Responsibilities

Data base technology creates new activities, such as administering and coordinating the use of common data. These activities may cause a shifting of responsibility. Responsibilities residing in user area when users process dedicated data shift to a centralized area when the data is centrally administered.

Two "assignment of responsibility" concerns surface when responsibilities are shifted. The first concern is the concentration of responsibility at the central location, which may reduce or eliminate some of the checks and balances that were present prior to centralization. Second, when responsibilities move, some task may not be performed. This occurs when responsibilities are not clearly defined and documented; one or more of the parties involved may assume that some other party is still fulfilling the task.

The insertion of a data base administration function into the design and operation of application systems creates a need for additional communication. Non-data base systems normally involve only EDP systems and programming personnel, and users. With the advent of data base technology, the data base administration function frequently encompasses the system development and operation process. This new arrangement requires increased, and more formal, communication.

There is a tendency in organizations using data base technologies for the users to feel that data base is not "their system." Many organizations have spent the last decade convincing users that they are responsible for the application systems, and that data processing is merely a service organization to help them use technology effectively. Now data base technology has reversed the decentralization of data processing, and has tended to centralize functions that previously were user functions into the data base administration function. This attitude about who "owns the data base" is a contributing factor to lapses in the proper assignment and acceptance of responsibilities associated with data base technology.

Inaccurate or Incomplete Data in a Data Base

The need for accurate and complete data increases as more uses are made of those data. An inaccurate data element in a dedicated system only affects that system, but in an environment where multiple users use the same data, the problem can be much more acute. The advantages of data base can only be achieved when the integrity of the data base can be ensured.

Inaccurate or incomplete data can be both an application and a data base problem. The application may fail to enter data, enter them twice, or perform events in the wrong sequence. The updating process used by the data base technology may lose data, or it may inaccurately place those data into the data base. When many users depend upon, create, and update data, the risk of inaccurate or incomplete data increases.

The data base administrator should take the steps necessary to ensure the accuracy and completeness of data entered into the data base. Because of the multiple uses of data, additional resources should be allocated to the validation of input. The validation rules should be specified along with the definition of data in the data dictionary or equivalent.

A difficult problem for many data base organizations has been assuring the consistency of data that are deliberately redundant in the data base. There are many reasons for including a single item of data more than once in the data base, or in multiple data bases, but the primary reason is operational efficiency. Unfortunately, many data base administrators feel they do not have adequate tools, techniques, or time to ensure the consistency of redundant data.

Losing an Update to a Single Data Item

Data base technology permits multiple users to access, and perhaps update, the same data element concurrently. For example, in an airline reservation system, any agent in the system can sell the last seat available on a flight. Most data base management systems have lockout procedures to prevent the second individual wishing to update a data element from doing so until the first is finished with his or her update procedure. Without such a control, airline agent A may call out a flight record on which there is a single seat available to sell that seat to a customer. At the very same moment, airline agent B may also call for that flight record in hopes of selling the very same seat. Without adequate controls, overbooking could occur due to inadequate data base controls.

Equally important is the correct sequencing of events. For example, if a sequence of events is to change pay rates and then calculate pay, the change pay rate action should occur prior to the payroll calculation step. Data base applications need to determine that appropriate controls are established to ensure the proper sequencing of events.

Inadequate Audit Trail

Data base technology has two audit trails: one for the applications using the data base and one for operations to reconstruct processing. The audit trail is needed both to substantiate prior processing should the integrity of processing be questioned and to reconstruct processing should problems occur. The audit trail includes source documents and computer logs and files as well as the procedures and documentation needed to understand and utilize the audit trail. The data base administration function should assist in the design of both audit trails, because in some instances the data from both will be needed to prove or restore processing integrity.

The application audit trail should provide the capability to trace source documents to control totals, and to identify all the source documents supporting the control totals. The data base audit trail should contain sufficient information to enable transaction processing to be reconstructed. The audit trail needed to accomplish all these objectives may be quite extensive.

In dedicated applications, the audit trail is normally easy to follow, provided sufficient data have been retained. However, in a data base environment, following the audit trail is much more complex. First, the trail is split among multiple applications and the data base itself. This makes identifying and obtaining the needed evidence more difficult technically. Second, the data base audit trail is frequently enormous in scope. It is not uncommon to produce several hundred thousand audit trail records in one day. This is particularly true when the DBMS is accessed using sophisticated data communication technology.

The data base administrator needs to determine that the audit trail has been clearly established, identified, and documented. In addition, it is important to determine the retention time for all parts of the audit trail. The voluminous DBMS log records may have a much shorter audit trail life than the application audit trail.

Unauthorized Access to Data in a Data Base

The accessibility control issue in a centralized data base environment is increased when the DBMS is accessed on-line. Management must be concerned with both unintentional and intentional unauthorized access.

The data base administration function should match user needs with data base resources. Users should then be restricted to accessing only those elements of data for which they have a need. "Users" should be defined in the broad sense here, to include data base administration, operations, and data processing systems personnel.

Current DBMSs offer many opportunities to achieve sufficient access control. Specific users can usually be restricted to specific subsets of the data base. In more sophisticated systems, access can be restricted according to the type of data usage. Some data might be read only, while other data might be accessible or not based upon the value of the data. For example, access to pay rates in a payroll application could be restricted, for clerical personnel, to those not exceeding $10 per hour.

Many organizations have established a data base security officer function to enforce access rules. The security officer normally develops a profile of user, which becomes the specification for designing access authorization systems.

Inadequate Service Level

Providing multiple users concurrent access to data may create a service level problem. One user can downgrade the service level for other users by consuming too large a portion of the data base resources. In addition, if the data base structure gets out of synchronization with user requirements, the time required to satisfy requests may become excessive.

The data base administration function should continually monitor the service level to users. As the service level begins to deteriorate, the DBA should fine-tune the data base to improve service.

Three options are available for improving service. First, the data base structure can be reorganized to make it more responsive to user needs. Second, it is sometimes possible to encourage users to spread out their service requests in order to avoid peak service periods. Third, additional hardware and software can be added to improve performance.

Placing Data in the Wrong Calendar Period

The placement of events in the proper calendar period may be a very complex process in a data base environment, and it becomes even more so with continuous on-line processing. In some systems, events are entered and stored awaiting the appropriate processing date to occur. For example, if bank customers have direct access to the bank's computer, they can indicate that banking transactions should occur at some predetermined date in the future, frequently limited to 30 days.

Some data base organizations date entries so that they can be recorded in the appropriate accounting period regardless of when they are entered into the data base. This accounting period identification avoids any ambiguity that may be caused by the time of entry, but requires some additional processing effort and storage space. Generally, recording events in the proper accounting period is more of a business problem than a data base problem.

However, it must be recognized that data base technology provides the ability to enter transactions in one accounting period that belong in another accounting period.

Failure of the DBMS to Function As Specified

Data base management systems are complex software packages. Most DBMSs are obtained from independent vendors. In addition, the vendors continually release updated versions of their DBMS.

It is the job of the data base administrator to verify the proper functioning of the data base software. Each new DBMS release should be thoroughly tested by the DBA before it is put into operation. Agencies, of course, frequently contract for the actual maintenance of the DBMS software.

The failure of the DBMS to function properly could result in substantial erroneous processing due to the heavy use of the data base. Data base administrators should be alert to DBMS problems, and establish procedures for contractor call-in should problems occur.

Fraud and Embezzlement

The state of the art of control of advanced data base technology may be encouraging fraud and embezzlement. Two of the major fraud detection methods in any system are the internal controls and routine internal audits. With any new technology, control tends to lag behind technology, and this appears to be true in data base technology. In addition, routine audits of data base technology are not common.

Most computer frauds require many transactions. For example, the AICPA computer fraud task force indicated that 20% of the computer frauds in banks involve over 100 transactions. Since data base technology makes it easy to control a large number of transactions over data, it is an ideal environment for fraud.

The primary method of fraud is manipulation of input data. The large majority of computer fraud cases occur through either the introduction of unauthorized input or the manipulation of otherwise proper input. This would indicate that the strongest controls data base could exercise over fraud are data validation and integrity controls.

No Independent Data Base Reviews

All activities need to be assessed periodically by an independent group. In most organizations, this independent review is performed by internal auditors. Their function is to verify compliance with the organization's policies and procedures and to determine that the operation is adequately controlled, that it is performed in an efficient, effective, and economical manner, and that it meets the intent of organization management.

Data base reviews can be conducted by groups other than internal auditors. Many data processing functions have established a quality assurance function, and have provided this group the authority to review data base technology. The groups do not report to the data base administrator. Other functions that review data base technology are certified public accountants, independent consultants, internal management consultants, and a special task force established by data processing management or senior management. Sometimes these task forces are part of a data base steering committee.

The initiation of a review normally occurs outside the data base administration function. However, data base administrators can request a review. The objective of making such a request would be to have the adequacy of data base controls reviewed.

Inadequate Documentation

Documentation of a data base environment includes documentation of both the individual data items and the data base structure. Many organizations use documentation aids such as a data dictionary system. Many DDSs can document the data base structure as well as the data items in the data base.

The types of documentation on the data base structure that should be kept include:

Principles of the schema
Principles of the subschemas
How security is achieved
Recovery actions
Reorganization changes required

The types of documentation that should be kept on each data element include:

A precise and unambiguous definition
Source of data
Frequency of change
The individual accountable for correctness
Relationship to other data items
Location
Program/individuals authorized access (and the type of access)
Reports in which the data item appears

Continuity of Processing

The development of data base technology has accelerated the integration of automated systems into day-to-day processing. A result of this trend is the elimination of hard-copy documentation. Individuals use computer terminals to enter information directly into processing, and receive many of the results directly from processing on a terminal screen as opposed to receiving a piece of paper. In data base technology, there are many users accessing a single data base. The focal point for ensuring continuity of processing is the data base. Information contained in an electronic format must have sufficient controls to ensure the ability to reconstruct processing should problems occur.

As organizations rely more heavily on their automated systems, their ability to continue processing without those systems is diminished. However, some organizations, such as banks, cannot stop processing when the data base is not operational. This poses two challenges to data base administration function. The first is the development and implementation of those steps necessary to assure the continuity of processing of the automated systems. The second is the development of procedures to aid individuals in the conduct of their business during those periods in which the automated systems are not operational. The completeness of the performance of these two tasks may determine the success of the data base installation.

No Performance Analysis

Many data base installations fail to define performance criteria before implementing data base technology. The implementation is made solely upon technical recommendations and arguments by data processing personnel. In those instances where performance criteria are established, there is often no follow-up made to verify that the estimated performance goals were accurate and that anticipated benefits were achieved.

The implementation of the data base management system can be costly. Only a small part of the cost is the procurement and installation of the DBMS. Organizations indicate that training and systems redesign costs exceed by many times the cost of DBMS acquisition and installation.

Performance criteria should be included in both data base objectives and cost/benefit analysis. Not only does the establishment of performance criteria, including cost/benefit analyses, provide a means to measure data base performance, but it also leads to more economical and efficient use of data base technology. However, the value from establishing such criteria will be minimal if follow-up is not made to verify whether or not the criteria have been achieved.

Lack of Management Support

The costs of acquiring data base management systems are generally small compared with the costs of using them in a "true data base environment." This requires a long-term management commitment to application software, computer hardware, communications, procedures, training, and support which will cost far more than the DBMS itself.

Senior management support for a true data base environment is essential if that environment is to be successful. Not only does data base technology centralize many of the application functions, but for most organizations it changes their information processing procedures. Without management oversight and direction, some users may dominate requirements, causing the system to be more responsive to the needs of a few rather than to the total organization.

To guarantee adequate management support, some agencies have established a data administration function. This is a senior management position responsible for data policy, direction, coordination, and arbitration of disputes. Other organizations have established a sufficiently powerful central review board which establishes implementation priorities and oversees the use and extensions of data base technology.

ASSESSING THE MAGNITUDE OF DATA BASE RISKS

The identification of a data base risk is the first part of the data base process. Determining the magnitude of that risk within the organization is the key to successful data base auditing. Risks with a potential of low losses do not warrant much audit effort or are perhaps not worth auditing. It may be advisable to bring such risks to the attention of management, but it makes little sense to spend $3,000 to audit a risk whose maximum loss to the organization is $1,000.

There are four commonly used methods to determine the magnitude of a data base audit risk. They are:

Historical cost. The auditor uses history as a basis for projecting future losses. This is particularly valuable in areas where the previous losses have been well documented, and there is a relationship between the magnitude of the volume of transactions in an area and the loss. For example, bad debts on accounts receivable is such a risk.

Formula method. The annual loss expectation can be calculated by estimating the frequency of occurrence and average loss per occurrence. This requires an in-depth knowledge of the application in order to develop reliable estimates. Without this type of knowledge, the stated magnitude of the risk may imply a much higher precision than actually exists.

Judgment. The auditor uses experience and intuition in estimating the magnitude of the risk. The auditor may use a qualitative estimate such as high, medium, or low risk; or the auditor may use a quantitative estimate, usually expressed in a range such as a potential loss in the range of $100,000 to $300,000. Highly experienced auditors are more successful than auditors with less experience at using judgment.

Risk scoring. The auditor identifies the criteria that correlate to loss and then determines the number of those criteria present in the area being evaluated. The greater the number of criteria present, the greater the risk. Auditors can assign numerical values to these criteria, and then add up those values to arrive at a score which is representative of the degree of risk.

The historical method, the formula method, and the judgment method all suffer from a lack of experience with the use of data base technology. Rarely are there any historical data relating to loss, and there is normally not enough knowledge about the use of data base technology in an organization to use either the formula or judgment method effectively. This leaves risk scoring as the most promising risk analysis method for data base technology.

The risk scoring concept uses the experiences of many organizations that have used data base technology. As organizations using data base encounter problems, many of these problems are documented together with the cause of those problems. These causes then become the criteria upon which other organizations can assess the magnitude of risk present in their use of data base technology.

Of the risk assessment methods discussed, risk scoring provides the greatest transfer of knowledge between organizations. For this reason, risk scoring is recommended in this book for the auditor to use in assessing the magnitude of data base technological risks. Risk scoring has another advantage in that it is an easy-to-use audit tool which does not require much audit time. However, while it predicts the magnitude of risk, it should not be considered a high-precision estimator. Risk socring is a planning tool and therefore many organizations use the concept to categorize risks as high, medium, and low.

A risk scoring model follows for each of the 14 identified data base audit risks. These risk models are presented as Figures 10 through 23. These worksheets permit the assessment of the magnitude of each risk individually, and then a method is presented to enable the magnitude of the 14 risks to be compared.

Using the Risk Model Worksheets

The data base risk assessment worksheets are designed to be used by either the auditor or the data base administration personnel. The worksheets can be given to the data base administration personnel to complete as self-assessment documents, or the auditor can complete the documents through interviews and investigations. Experiences in other areas of auditing indicate that the reliability is approximately the same regardless of who completes the worksheet.

The advantage to having the auditor complete the worksheet is that the interview process is a learning experience about data base technology. When the auditor must perform sufficient investigation to gather the information, the auditor's knowledge of data base increases. On the other hand, the process may be performed more effectively by using the worksheets as self-assessment questionnaires.

If the documents are to be given to data base administration personnel to complete, the DBA personnel should not be apprised of the scoring algorithm used to rate the risk. Knowing this would bias their answers to the questions. They should be presented to data base administration personnel as information-gathering documents.

There is one worksheet for each of the 14 data base risks. The worksheets contain a brief description of the risk so that they can be copied and given to data base administration personnel for completion.

The criteria are designed to be answered yes or no. It is recognized that not every criterion can be answered so exactly, so the user of the questionnaire should be instructed that if the answer is more yes than no, it should be answered yes, and vice versa. Room for comments is provided on the worksheet.

The score column on the data base risk assessment worksheet is the weight given to a no answer to any of the criteria. The weight score determines how that item contributes to the total risk score in relationship to the other risk. *The number itself has no meaning*. The numbers add to a score of 20, so each item is scored to show its contributing part of that maximum score of 20.

To determine the risk score for each of the individual risks, the score for all of the no answers should be accumulated. Note that if the self-assessment worksheet is given to data base administration personnel to answer, the score column should first be deleted.

KEY CONCEPT

Identifying a risk is of marginal value until the magnitude of that risk has been estimated.

DEVELOPING THE RISK SCORE

At the completion of the risk assessment exercise, a score should be developed for each of the individual risks. The number in the score column by each criterion is the weight given to that specific criterion if it is not present in the area under review. Note that this is based on the judgment of the author in working with numerous data base installations, and has not been developed through statistical regression analysis.

The worksheets are established so that yes answers are indicative of good control practices, and no answers indicative of poor control practices. The risk score is established so that the higher the score, the higher the risk. Therefore, the criteria receiving a yes answer are assigned zero risk points, and the criteria receiving no answers are assigned 1, 2, 3, 4, or 5 risk points, which is indicated in the score column. The number of risk points for each "no" score is accumulated to give a total risk score for a risk being evaluated.

Alternate Rating Method

Some organizations feel that the evaluation by any single individual may be biased. Therefore, they ask three individuals to rate the criteria for each of the risks. The no risk points scores are accumulated for each criterion and divided by the number of evaluates. For example, if a criterion is rated no by either two or three of the raters and it is valued at three risk points, the final criterion scoring will be 2 (i.e., 2 no answers at 3 points each = $6 \div 3 = 2$).

The same individual may not be selected to rate all of the risks. For example, the risks dealing with computer operations may be rated by computer operations personnel, and the risks relating to data documentation may be rated by the data base administrator. The successful use of this process will be dependent upon identifying the appropriate individual either to interview or to rate each of the criteria.

Establishing a Data Base Risk Profile

After all 14 risks have been scored individually, the score should be placed upon the data base risk profile chart (Figure 9). This chart is used for comparing the degree of risk among the 14 individual risks. The recommended way to present the risk scores is a risk profile or bar chart, although a simple risk score listing would suffice.

The data base risk profile chart is designed to be used as a bar chart. The developed risk score for each of the individual risks should be posted on the data base risk profile chart as a bar above the name of each risk. The vertical score column equates to the number of risk points. For example, if the first data base risk (inadequate assignment of responsibilities) received 10 risk score points, the bar for that risk should be extended to the 10 level on the vertical score column.

After all 14 risks have been posted, the profile chart quickly identifies in graphical format those risks that are the highest. This chart becomes a workpaper document, and is the basis for determining which risks will receive the most audit attention.

DEVELOPING AN AUDIT PLAN USING RISK SCORING

The recommended way to use the risk profile is to divide the profile into high, medium, and low risks. A dotted line on the profile chart can be used to illustrate high, medium, and low data base risks.

The risk profile provides an indication of the magnitude of risks in a data base environment under audit. Those using risk scoring indicate that the precision is no greater than plus or minus 10% of the risk score. In other words, if two risk scores are within 10% of one another, they should be considered a tie. A rule for this risk exercise is if the risk scores are within three risk points of one another they should be considered a tie.

The maximum risk score for any risk is 20 points. Twenty points indicate the highest risk possible, and zero points the lowest risk possible.

Interpreting the risk score into high, medium, and low can be done as follows:

High risk score: 14 to 20 points
Medium risk score: 7 through 13 points
Low risk score: 0 through 6 points

Again, note that a risk scored low with six points may be just as great a risk as a risk scored seven and put into the medium category. If the score is a borderline score, and the auditor is categorizing risk into low, medium, and high, the auditor may wish to use judgment on the final categorization. In other words, if a risk gets a score of six and normally would be scored low, because of the criteria comprising the six points the auditor may wish to reclassify that risk as a medium risk.

To optimize audit effort, all of the high risks should be audited first, followed by medium and low risks if time and resources permit. The objective for developing the data base risk profile is to identify the high-risk areas, and then allocate either:

Audit by risk score. Available audit resources are allocated first to the high risks; then, if resources remain, they are allocated to medium risks, and if resources are still available the low risks are audited.

Proportional-to-risk auditing. All of the risks are evaluated under this method, but the resources allocated are proportional to the risk. In other words, more time and effort are spent on auditing the high risks than on auditing the medium risks, and more time and effort are spent on auditing the medium risks than on auditing the low risks.

Score	Rating	1. Inadequate assignment of responsibilities	2. Inaccurate or incomplete data in a data base	3. Losing an update to a single data item	4. Inadequate audit trail	5. Unauthorized access in a data base	6. Inadequate service level	7. Placing data in the wrong calendar period	8. Failure of DBMS to function as specified	9. Fraud/embezzlement	10. Lack of independent data base reviews	11. Inadequate documentation	12. Continuity of processing	13. Lack of performance criteria	14. Lack of management support
20 19 18 17 16 15 14	High														
13 12 11 10 9 8 7	Medium														
6 5 4 3 2 1 0	Low														
Magnitude of Risk / **Data Base Risks**															

Figure 9. Data Base Risk Profile Chart.

The remainder of the book will present a data base audit process that is risk oriented. The audit process will be centered around activities, but using risk as a basis for auditing those activities. The magnitude of each of the data base risks in the area under audit should be the determinant in building the audit program. Once the magnitude of risk has been identified, an audit program can be developed using the material in the remainder of the book to audit those risks.

KEY CONCEPT

Allocate audit resources to evaluate the high data base risks.

Data Base Risk Inadequate Assignment of Responsibilities (1).

Description of Risk
There is inappropriate segregation of duties or failure to recognize placement of responsibility.

Data Base Risk Analysis—Criteria and Assessment

Number	Criterion	Response		Comments	Score
		Yes	No		
1.	Has a charter been established for the data base administration function outlining the role and responsibilities for the function?				5
2.	Have the user responsibilities regarding the integrity of the data base been defined?				4
3.	Have job descriptions been modified for all individuals interfacing with the data base to define their data base responsibilities?				1
4.	Have job descriptions been developed for full-time data base administration personnel?				2
5.	Has a formal method of resolving data base disputes been established?				2
6.	Does the organization have a data policy which outlines organizational data responsibility?				3
7.	Are the functions being performed by data base administration functions within that function's formal role and responsibility?				2
8.	Where responsibilities shift to/from users and the data base administration function, have dates for that switch been established?				1

Figure 10. Data Base Risk Assessment Worksheet 1.

Data Base Risk Inaccurate or Incomplete Data in a Data Base (2).

Description of Risk

The integrity of data entered in the data base is lost due to inadvertent or intentional acts.

Data Base Risk Analysis—Criteria and Assessment

Number	Criterion	Response		Comments	Score
		Yes	No		
1.	Has each element of data in the data base been identified?				1
2.	Have the data validation rules for each data element been documented?				3
3.	Have the data validation rules for each data element been implemented?				3
4.	Are the data validation rules adequate to ensure the accuracy of data?				3
5.	Have procedures been established to ensure the consistency of redundant data elements?				3
6.	Have procedures been established for the timely correction of data entry errors?				3
7.	Are procedures established to notify promptly all users of the data base when an inaccuracy or incomplete data condition has been identified?				2
8.	Are the data base administration tools and techniques adequate to ensure the consistency of redundant data elements?				2

Figure 11. Data Base Risk Assessment Worksheet 2.

Data Base Risk Losing an Update to a Single Data Item (3).

Description of Risk

One or more updates to a single data item can be lost due to inadequate concurrent update procedures.

Data Base Risk Analysis—Criteria and Assessment

Number	Criterion	Response		Comments	Score
		Yes	No		
1.	Does the DBMS in use have a lockout feature to prevent concurrent updates to a single data item?				5
2.	Does the DBMS have a feature to resolve deadlock in accessing data (for example, user A has item 1 and wants item 2, while user B has item 2 and wants item 1)?				3
3.	Has the sequencing of updates to the data base been defined?				4
4.	Are there controls in the DBMS to ensure that events can only be recorded in the predetermined sequence?				4
5.	Have the parties that can create, update, or delete a data element been identified?				4

Figure 12. Data Base Risk Assessment Worksheet 3.

Data Base Risk Inadequate Audit Trail (4).

Description of Risk

The use of data by multiple applications may split the audit trail among those applications and the DBMS audit trail.

Data Base Risk Analysis—Criteria and Assessment

Number	Criterion	Response: Yes	Response: No	Comments	Score
1.	Has the audit trail for data base applications been identified and documented?				3
2.	Has the retention period for each part of the data base audit trail been determined?				2
3.	Is a DBMS log maintained?				3
4.	Does management determine what information will be maintained on the DBMS log?				1
5.	Can the audit trail trace source transactions to control totals and trace control totals back to the initiating transactions?				3
6.	Can the audit trail provide the evidence needed to reconstruct transaction processing?				2
7.	Is the audit trail in operation whenever the data base is in operation?				2
8.	Are all overrides of normal DBMS procedures recorded on the DBMS log?				3
9.	Can the application audit trail records be cross-referenced to the DBMS log audit trail records?				1

Figure 13. Data Base Risk Assessment Worksheet 4.

Data Base Risk Unauthorized Access to Data in a Data Base (5).

Description of Risk

The concentration of data may make sensitive data available to anyone gaining access to a data base.

Data Base Risk Analysis—Criteria and Assessment

Number	Criterion	Response		Comments	Score
		Yes	No		
1.	Have all of the data elements requiring security procedures been identified?				3
2.	Have all of the data base users been identified?				3
3.	Has a user profile been established indicating which resources can be accessed by which users?				3
4.	Has the enforcement of the user profile been automated?				2
5.	Is the access mechanism, such as passwords, protected from unauthorized manipulation?				2
6.	Has the organization established a data base security officer function (note that this need not be a full-time function)?				2
7.	Are security violators promptly punished?				3
8.	Are formal records maintained on security violations?				1
9.	Are security violation summaries presented to management in regular reports?				1

Figure 14. Data Base Risk Assessment Worksheet 5.

Data Base Risk Inadequate Service Level (6).

Description of Risk

Multiple users contesting for the same resources may degrade the service to all due to excessive demand or inadequate resources.

Data Base Risk Analysis—Criteria and Assessment

Number	Criterion	Response		Comments	Score
		Yes	No		
1.	Has the level of service that is desired been documented?				4
2.	Are procedures established to monitor the desired level of service to users?				4
3.	Are users encouraged, by the use of such techniques as varying chargeout rates, to spread out their nonurgent processing?				1
4.	Have the identified options to improve service when it degrades been identified?				2
5.	Does the DBA continually monitor the service level and make adjustments where appropriate?				3
6.	Are steps to take established at points where service level degrades?				3
7.	Do procedures identify the cause of degradation in service, such as a single user consuming exorbitant amounts of resources, so that action can be taken to eliminate those causes where appropriate?				3

Figure 15. Data Base Risk Assessment Worksheet 6.

Data Base Risk Placing Data in the Wrong Calendar Period (7).

Description of Risk

Identifying transactions with the proper calendar period is more difficult in some on-line data base environments than in others.

Data Base Risk Analysis—Criteria and Assessment

Number	Criterion	Response		Comments	Score
		Yes	No		
1.	Do procedures identify the criteria for determining into which accounting period transactions are placed?				5
2.	Are all postdated transactions date-stamped to identify the accounting period in which they belong?				4
3.	Are procedures established to cut off processing at the end of significant accounting periods, such as at year-end?				5
4.	For applications where data must be segregated into accounting periods, are significant transactions entered both immediately before and immediately after the accounting cutoff period manually reviewed to ensure they are in the appropriate accounting period?				3
5.	Are formal procedures established to move data from one accounting period to another if appropriate?				3

Figure 16. Data Base Risk Assessment Worksheet 7.

Data Base Risk Failure of DBMS to Function as Specified (8).

Description of Risk

Most DBMSs are provided by vendors, making the data administrator dependent upon the vendor to assure the proper functioning of the software.

Data Base Risk Analysis—Criteria and Assessment

Number	Criterion	Response		Comments	Score
		Yes	No		
1.	Have the processing expectations been determined?				4
2.	Is the DBMS evaluated to determine that it performs in accordance with the predetermined requirements?				4
3.	Is each new release of DBMS software thoroughly tested?				1
4.	Has a maintenance contract for the DBMS been established?				1
5.	Are procedures established to identify DBMS problems?				2
6.	Are operations personnel trained to identify and report DBMS problems?				2
7.	Have backup procedures been developed for use in the event of a DBMS failure?				3
8.	Are DBMS failures recorded and regularly reported to the data base administrator?				1
9.	Are the vendors promptly notified in the event of a DBMS problem so that they can take appropriate action?				2

Figure 17. Data Base Risk Assessment Worksheet 8.

Data Base Risk Fraud/Embezzlement (9).

Description of Risk

Systems that control resources are always subject to fraud and embezzlement.

Data Base Risk Analysis—Criteria and Assessment

Number	Criterion	Response Yes	Response No	Comments	Score
1.	Do data base administration personnel have access to the data in the data base?				3
2.	Has a methodology been established for designing data base controls?				4
3.	Has the data base been reviewed within the last year by an independent reviewer?				3
4.	Have procedures been established to identify and report errors, omissions, and frauds to senior management?				1
5.	Are all data base resources access controlled?				2
6.	Are passwords or other access control procedures changed at least every six months?				2
7.	Are all error messages acted upon in a timely fashion?				2
8.	Are deviations from normal processing investigated?				2
9.	Do data validation routines anticipate and report on unusual processing?				1

Figure 18. Data Base Risk Assessment Worksheet 9.

Data Base Risk Lack of Independent Data Base Reviews (10).

Description of Risk

Most reviewers are not skilled in data base technology and thus have not evaluated data base installations; in addition, many auditor software packages cannot access a DBMS.

Data Base Risk Analysis—Criteria and Assessment

Number	Criterion	Response: Yes	Response: No	Comments	Score
1.	Is there an internal audit function having jurisdiction over reviewing data base technology?				3
2.	Is there an EDP quality assurance group having jurisdiction over reviewing data base technology?				3
3.	Does either of these groups have adequate skills to perform such a review?				4
4.	Has an independent review of data base technology been performed within the last 12 months?				4
5.	Was a report issued describing the findings and recommendations from that review?				2
6.	Were the findings and recommendations reasonable based upon the current use of data base technology?				2
7.	Is an independent review of data base technology planned during the next 12 months?				2

Figure 19. Data Base Risk Assessment Worksheet 10.

Data Base Risk Inadequate Documentation (11).

Description of Risk

Documentation of data base technology is needed to ensure consistency of understanding and use by multiple users.

Data Base Risk Analysis—Criteria and Assessment

Number	Criterion	Response		Comments	Score
		Yes	No		
1.	Do data documentation standards exist?				4
2.	Are data documentation standards enforced?				4
3.	Is a data dictionary used to document the attributes of data elements?				4
4.	Is the data dictionary integrated into the DBMS operation so that the only entry into DBMS-controlled data is through the data dictionary?				3
5.	Does the data base administration group provide counsel in documenting and using data?				2
6.	Does the data documentation contain the data validation rules?				3

Figure 20. Data Base Risk Assessment Worksheet 11.

Data Base Risk Continuity of Processing (12).

Description of Risk

Many organizations rely heavily upon data base technology for the performance of their day-to-day processing.

Data Base Risk Analysis—Criteria and Assessment

Number	Criterion	Response		Comments	Score
		Yes	No		
1.	Have the potential causes of data base failure been identified?				4
2.	Has the impact of each of those failures on the organization been assessed?				3
3.	Have procedures been developed to continue processing during a data base failure?				3
4.	Are procedures established to ensure that the integrity of the data base can be restored after data base failure?				3
5.	Has the sequence of actions necessary to restore applications after a data base failure been documented?				1
6.	Have computer operations personnel been trained in data base recovery procedures?				2
7.	Is sufficient backup data stored off-site to permit reconstruction of processing in the event of a disaster?				3
8.	Are records maintained on data base failures so that periodic analysis can be performed?				1

Figure 21. Data Base Risk Assessment Worksheet 12.

Data Base Risk Lack of Performance Criteria (13).

Description of Risk

Without established performance criteria, an organization cannot be assured that it is achieving data base goals.

Data Base Risk Analysis—Criteria and Assessment

Number	Criterion	Response		Comments	Score
		Yes	No		
1.	Have measurable objectives for data base technology been established?				5
2.	Are those objectives monitored to determine whether or not they are achieved?				5
3.	Can the cost associated with data base technology be identified?				2
4.	Can the benefits associated with data base technology be identified?				2
5.	Was a cost/benefit analysis prepared for the installation and operation of data base technology?				3
6.	Has the cost/benefit projection been monitored to measure whether or not those projections have been achieved?				2
7.	Is the achievement of the performance criteria evaluated by an independent group, such as EDP quality assurance?				1

Figure 22. Data Base Risk Assessment Worksheet 13.

Data Base Risk Lack of Management Support (14).

Description of Risk

Without adequate resources and "clout," the advantages of data base technology may not be achieved.

Data Base Risk Analysis—Criteria and Assessment

Number	Criterion	Response: Yes	Response: No	Comments	Score
1.	Has a member of senior management been appointed responsible for managing data for the organization?				5
2.	Was senior management involved in the selection of the organization's data base technology approach?				3
3.	Has a review board been established comprising users, EDP personnel, and senior managers to oversee the use of data base technology?				4
4.	Has data processing management attended courses on the use of data base technology?				1
5.	Has senior management requested regular briefing and/or reports on the implementation and use of data base technology?				1
6.	Has senior management been involved in the preparation of a long-range plan for use of information in the organization?				3
7.	Is senior management involved in the settlement of disputes over the attributes or use of information in the organization?				3

Figure 23. Data Base Risk Assessment Worksheet 14.

four

AUDITABLE DATA BASE ACTIVITIES

An organization normally undergoes a number of changes when its data processing system is upgraded to include a data base management system. Changes in computer system design and operation require a reallocation of responsibilities and the acquisition or development of new skills. These changes, coupled with modification to the methods of conducting business, normally result in changes to the organizational structure.

The audit concern is risk, but the audit process focuses on activities. The new activities created by the introduction of data base technology should be audited. The auditor should identify and evaluate the new data base activities in order to ensure that data base controls are adequate and that the new risks are reduced to an acceptable level.

This chapter describes the data base environment and identifies the auditable activities in that environment. An activity is defined as a task or group of tasks in which controls reside, which can be audited as a stand-alone entity. The auditable activity may or may not be a separate organizational entity.

Each of the identified data base activities is described individually. The major tasks for each activity are listed. In addition, the methods for controlling these activities are covered. A description of the more common data base controls is provided in Appendix A.

THE RELATIONSHIP OF DATA ADMINISTRATION TO MANAGEMENT

Management must be convinced that a new function is worthwhile before it can be adopted and implemented into the organization. If the new function is a data processing function, such as data base administration, the approval to implement comes directly or indirectly from data processing, user, and senior management. If these three types of management are not convinced of its value and committed to its success, the probability of success is diminished significantly.

The introduction of data base technology to an organization is normally through data processing management. The data processing manager understands data base technology, and has the responsibility to explain the concepts and operation of data base technology to senior and user management. It is important that they understand the effect upon the existing organization and functions if they are to be supportive of data base technology.

Information is the lifeblood of an organization. Without timely, accurate, complete, and secure information, organizations cannot operate effectively. The value of information increases as the presentation of that information is customized to the needs, size, and facilities of the organization. Ensuring the correctness and integrity of information is everybody's responsibility.

Senior management, user management, and data processing management interact based upon the type of information received. The data administration function is defined as the function responsible for developing and administering the policies, procedures, practices, and plans for the definition, organization, protection, and efficient utilization of data within an organization. The function exists regardless of the organizational structure of the data administration function.

The data administration role and management are illustrated in Figure 24. This shows data administration as the central core of interchange among the three types of management. The introduction of data base technology has provided the vehicle to implement a formal data administration function. Unless formalized, each of the three types of management must perform all or some part of the data administration function.

As this function is being created, new activities start to occur. In many organizations, the activities are centered around the data base management system, as opposed to a formal data administration function. Without central direction, the risks may be larger, and the controls not as well established.

The introduction of data base technology has a significant impact on information processing. In order to understand the data base environment and the resulting activities, it is helpful to understand how data base changes the methods of processing. Also, many of the controls that will be described later in the chapter are directly related to these new processing concepts.

KEY CONCEPT

Data administration always exists, but it is not always a formal function.

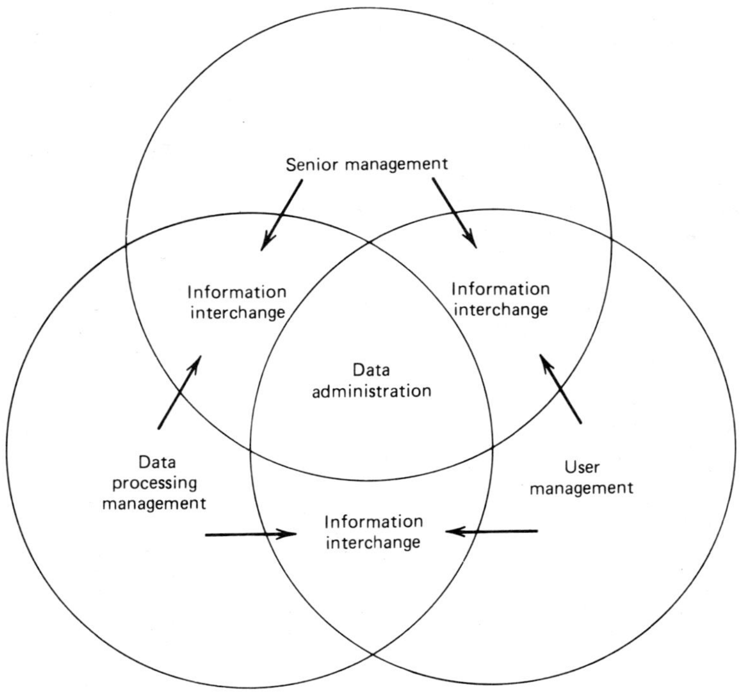

Figure 24. Data Base Administration Function Relationship to Management.

IMPACT OF DATA BASE ON THE ORGANIZATION

The implications of the selection and acquisition of a data base management system within an organization will vary depending on the organization, but in no case should the decision be taken lightly. Installation of a data base management system will have a major impact on the organization, its people, procedures, capital, and resources. The acquisition system will have a procedural, economic, and technological effect on the organization.

Procedural Implications

Prior data processing experience does not fully equip an organization for this new approach, because the data base management approach differs in a number of important ways from conventional data processing. Significant changes in perspective are required when converting to a data base management system, such as:

Change from program orientation to data orientation. The primary focus must be on data and their relationships, and not on data as by-products of programs.

Change from single-purpose files to a multipurpose data base. Data must be brought together from isolated files where they could be accessed by only a few specialized programs, into a unified data base from which they can be used by all present and future programs.

Change from single use to shared use. Data are a resource which should be available to all authorized elements of the organization, and not just to those responsible for their collection and maintenance.

Change from EDP professional orientation to user orientation. The adoption of a data base management system implies a significant step toward a more user-oriented environment, with correspondingly less emphasis on the orientation toward the data processing professional.

These changes will require corresponding changes in the personnel responsible for generating, maintaining, and using data. Various individuals in the organization must learn and apply new skills and disciplines, and integrate them into the organization's way of doing business.

New skills must be acquired or developed in such areas as data administration, system administration, information analysis, and other data base management specialties. Some of these skills can be filled only by specialists in the field (who are already in high demand and short supply).

A data base management system will affect current business procedures because a centralized data processing function will allow more automation of the peripheral support functions of the organization. Consequently, the organization will become more oriented to the computerized flow of data and dependent on this flow. This dependence should not be underestimated. Failure of the computer data processing will in a large degree disrupt the data processing system. The longer a system is used, the more acute is the attrition of the human skills it replaces. Consequently, the ability to back up the system manually degenerates over time.

Organizational changes may also take place. The development of new organizational structures to utilize the information systems approach effectively is necessary. One example is the development of an information systems department to manage the system; another example is the emergence of the role of the data base administrator. Often the development of automated systems serves to highlight organizational problems which have been evolving for a number of years. The recognition of such problems will be associated with the introduction of a data base management approach, but this should not be blamed for the already existing problems.

Economic Implications

The major costs an organization incurs in automating its data processing system include data conversion, training personnel, and the hardware and software system. For the benefits of generalized processing using a data base management system to be realized, the data must be transformed into a format the system can process. Transformations of this type currently cost industry and government millions of dollars annually, partly because there is not yet an effective methodology to accomplish this task more economically. If the data are already machine readable, then the transformation consists of writing a translation program to adapt the existing data to the new system format. If the data are not machine readable, the translation cost will be even greater.

Utilization of the capabilities of data base management systems requires trained personnel. The cost will be significant even if the vendor supplies personnel training support. Personnel training, coupled with the development and learning of new procedures, is one of the largest costs.

The organization will also face different hardware and software costs. The software costs include system acquisition and any modifications necessary to use the system. The hardware costs may include those of upgrading the present system or those of acquiring new hardware to provide sufficient power for effective utilization of a data base management system.

Technological Impacts

Inherent in the design and implementation of a data base management system are a number of technological tradeoffs which vary from system to system and from one organization to another. These tradeoffs will have to be discussed and understood by users in the organization. Some of the more important tradeoffs are:

Machine time versus people time. Probably the most obvious external tradeoff in the use of a data base management system is the substitution of the utilization of hardware resources for the use of analyst/programmer time. These systems generally require more hardware resources and take more hardware execution time. On the other hand, they produce data for a new application more quickly, using less of the analysts' time than conventional methods.

User language versus integrity. Some functions of a user language are at odds with the data base integrity objective and with the provision of an economical checkpoint-restart facility. For example, the command: "CHANGE SALARY TO SALARY* 1.05" can change every salary in the data base, providing a powerful capability for the user. However, the need for integrity of the salary data implies a system logging function in which the expense of logging all of the "before" images required by this command is very high.

Data independence versus performance. Data independence at item level is generally at odds with a requirement for high-speed, high-volume, sequential processing. Data independence demands that attention be given to each item as it is moved to or from the data base, whereas high-volume, sequential processing will normally be expedited by data movement at the group or record level.

User interface versus complexity of data structure. The need for a simple user language is in direct opposition to the need for complex data structures. The more powerful the data structure being manipulated, the greater the complexities of the user language need to be.

Complexity of data structure versus storage overhead. The more complex the data structure, the greater the cost for the increase in data storage. Hence, the desire for minimum storage use is in direct opposition to a desire for complex data relationships.

Gathering of statistics versus optimum performance. The need for accumulation of statistics concerning the use of data will add significant overhead to all the data manipulation processes. The extent of an improvement in performance must be related to the cost of providing the required information.

The decision to upgrade the data processing system by installing a data base management system will have major impact on the whole organization. The difficulty of the transition from the current way to the new approach should not be underestimated. Economically, acquiring and installing the system will require an allocation of more resources, hardware, and perhaps people to operate the data processing system. The procedural impact includes developing new organizational structures and employing people with new and varied qualifications to work in this organization. A large amount of training will be necessary at all levels of the organization to assure a smooth and effective operation, so that the organization will be able to invest the resources necessary to realize the benefits of using a data base management system.

As we examine the data base environment, keep in mind these procedural, economic, and technological impacts on the organization. An understanding of how the environment works, its advantages and disadvantages, and the benefits derived from the use of data base will help provide the necessary background to evaluate the impact on your organization. A look at the data base environment will also provide the basis for identifying the auditable data base activities.

KEY CONCEPT

The impact of data base technology will be greater than the impact of data processing.

THE DATA BASE ENVIRONMENT

An organization which has decided that the data base approach is the best method for satisfying its data processing requirements can choose from a wide variety of data base management system software packages. Each package has a unique set of features and methods for describing the data base and manipulating the data. Because each package provides a general, yet different, set of data management functions, a particular DBMS cannot operate equally effectively in all data processing environments.

The data in the data base are in two parts—a logical data structure and a physical storage structure. A DBMS provides the bridge between these two structures. The logical data structure describes the way that the data are viewed by the user and is often called the data model because it "models" an organization's data in terms of their logical relationships. The physical storage structure determines how the data are actually accessed and maintained on computer storage devices such as magnetic disk or drum. Different physical storage structures can be used to implement the same data model.

The two most prominent data models are the hierarchical and network models. The major commercially available DBMS packages primarily support one or the other. An-

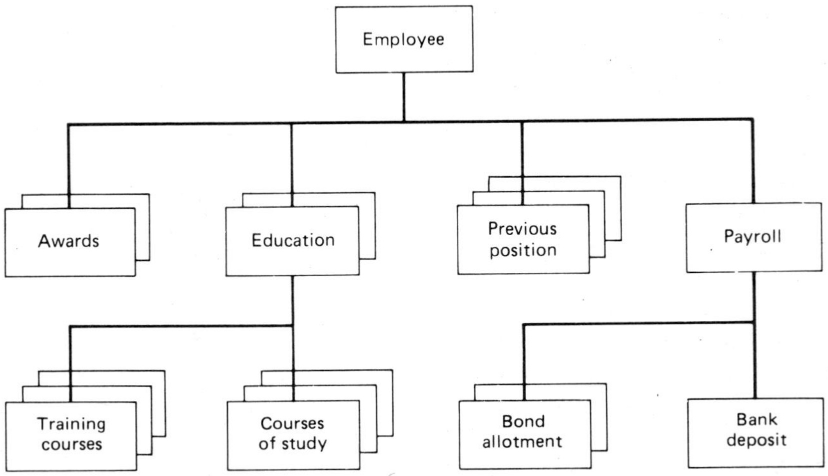

Figure 25. Hierarchical Data Model.

other data model, called the relational model, is under development. The relational model has few implementations, but some industry advocates believe that it will be the primary model used in the future.

The hierarchical data model supports a logical data relationship commonly referred to as a ''tree structure'' and allows the development of a hierarchy. The diagram in Figure 25 illustrates the hierarchical data model.

Each record (a record may consist of only a single data element) may be related to any number of data records at any level below it, but only one record above it in the hierarchy. The data records are called nodes, and the node at the top is called the root. Every node except the root has a ''parent,'' which is the node immediately above it. Thus, in the diagram in Figure 25, EMPLOYEE is the root node and parent node of AWARDS, EDUCATION, PREVIOUS POSITION and PAYROLL. The hierarchical data model differs from other data models in that each record has only one parent and therefore has only one logical access path.

The network data model supports a logical data relationship—also referred to as a ''plex structure''—and can represent complex data structures more readily than can the hierarchical data model. The network data model is illustrated in Figure 26.

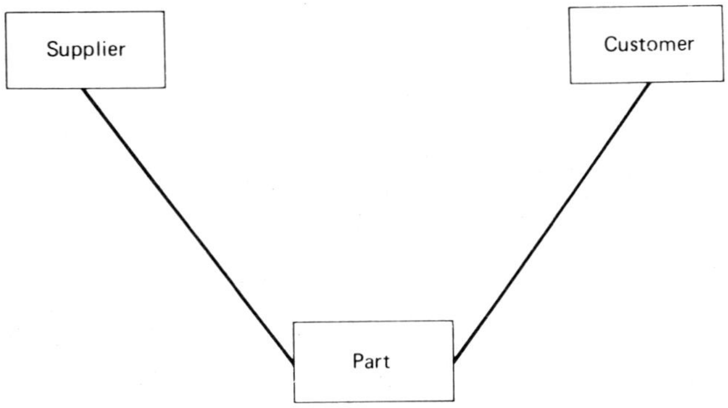

Figure 26. Network Model.

In a network model, any given record can be logically related to any other. The network mode differs from the hierarchical model in that every node can have more than one parent, thus allowing multiple access paths through the data base. In Figure 26, PART has two parent nodes. More than one CUSTOMER can order from the same PART and the same PART can be obtained from more than one SUPPLIER.

Physical Storage Structures

The data in the data base are organized into a physical storage structure which determines the method of placement of and access to the data on the computer storage device. The types of storage structure include: sequential, random, index sequential, chain, and inverted. Some DBMS packages can support more than one physical storage structure. User information processing requirements are the most important and overriding consideration when choosing which storage structure to use. If user requirements as known, the potential mismatch of requirements and improper storage structure can be eliminated.

In the sequential structure, records are stored according to some specified sequence. To order the records in a sequence, one common attribute—called a ''Key''—is chosen. The key is a data element or set of data elements which have unique values for each record within the data base. For example, records in an employee file could be stored in numerical order by social security number. In this instance, the employee's social security number would be the key. Sequential access implies data storage where access to the next record is by association to a previous record in sequence. The next logical record is also the next physical record. The sequential structure is simple to understand and can provide for fast retrieval for the next record in the file. However, it is not possible to add records, and generally not possible to delete or modify records, without rewriting the file.

The index sequential storage structure is simply a sequential storage structure with an index. Records can be accessed either by using indexes or in a sequential fashion. Each index contains the address of a record in the data base. If a record is to be retrieved by its index, the indexes are searched until the desired key is found, and the pointer (a pointer is a method of referencing another part of the data base) from that index to the record is used as a direct address to retrieve the desired record. Record retrieval in an index sequential storage structure is much faster than in a sequential storage structure because the index is much smaller and therefore can be searched more quickly. However, additions, deletions, and modification (called maintenance) of records is more time-consuming for the whole file than in the sequential structure because both the sequential order and the index must be maintained.

In the random storage structure, records are stored and retrieved based on a predictable relationship between the key of a record and the record's physical location on the storage device (called the address). The address is usually determined by an arithmetic operation on the value of the record's key. For example, records in an employee file could be randomly accessed based on the conversion of the last four digits of an employee's social security number to an address on the storage device. Random access means that access to a given record in the data base is not related to the access of other data base records. The random storage structure can provide very fast retrieval on a single key value; it is good if every key value yields a unique physical location because then only one physical access is required for the desired record. However, different record key values can generate the same address on the computer storage device, which results in a ''collision.'' The techniques for resolving the collision increase both retrieval and maintenance processing times. Random accessing does not readily allow for complex query processing. This storage structure is best suited for applications requiring fast retrieval on a single key value and is often used in conjunction with other storage structures.

A chain storage structure is one in which the records are linked together by pointers which are physically a part of the record. Several techniques can be used to link records in a data base, but the principle of having the pointer physically part of the record does not change. The basic concept of the chain structure is that pointers are used to separate the logical structure from the physical structure. To link records together, one of the records must be accessed by a key which is relevant to all of the linked records, and then the pointers are used to access all subsequent records in the chain. The records in a chain are logically related.

For example, it may be desirable to link the records contained in a personnel file of all employees who work in the organization's finance and accounting department. By accessing the personnel file in the data base by department, it would be possible to retrieve the personnel record of the first employee in the department which would contain a pointer to other employees in the same department. Since any data element in a record may be treated as a key, it is possible to have many chains passing through a single record. For example, in addition to linking all employees within a particular department, it may also be desirable to link employees who have special job skills, such as a foreign language proficiency. Record retrieval is normally slower in this structure because the search is sequential through the chain. However, file maintenance can be efficient because record additions and deletions are made simply by changing the pointers. A disadvantage of the chain storage structure is that it requires additional storage space for the pointers. This structure is often used in conjunction with other storage structures.

The inverted storage structure can make every data element in a record available as a key. With this approach, a key value is stored in a directory which contains the addresses of all like-valued records. The directory is physically separated from the data and can be as large as or larger than the data themselves. (This approach is in contrast to the chain storage structure in which the pointer to the next logical record is physically a part of the record.) If every data element in a data base record is used as a key, then the data base is considered to be fully inverted.

A request for information is first processed against the directory to obtain the addresses of the data base records that satisfy the request. Once that has been accomplished, the data are retrieved from the data base to satisfy the inquiry. By maintaining the data addresses in a directory, information requests can be satisfied without having to search through the entire data base. The inverted structure allows for quick retrieval of complex inquiries. All data elements can be accessed with equal ease; therefore, it is better suited for situations where the data retrieval requirements are less predictable than it would be for specific processing functions.

Although the inverted structure provides for easy retrieval, storing and updating can be difficult because of the maintenance of the directory. The directory must be updated whenever a record is added or deleted. Because the fully inverted structure more than doubles the storage requirement and increases maintenance time, it is often used in conjunction with other storage structures. Records can be partially inverted on only a few keys rather than on all the keys. Directories thus become smaller and easier to manage.

DBMS User Environment

We have seen how DBMS can be classified according to the way it supports the logical and physical data structures. Another way to classify DBMS packages is by the language used to initiate data management functions. There are two types of DBMS software: the host language system and the self-contained system. Host language DBMS packages provide extensions to programming languages that aid the application programmer. Such DBMS capabilities are accessible only to programs written in a higher level programming language, such as COBOL. The host language of the DBMS, in effect, enhances the capabilities of the programming language, thus making it easier for the application programmer to access and manipulate the data. Self-contained DBMS packages typically provide all essential capabilities for data creation, update, retrieval, and report formatting. The class of user which directly interacts with the data base can be the determining factor as to which type of DBMS to acquire. Those who interact with the data base can be grouped into two major categories: end users and data processing support personnel. The end uses include those who work with specific predetermined transactions which are repetitive, such as stock control clerks, and those who use the data base in response to unanticipated requests for information.

The self-contained DBMS packages are better suited for users who work in a data processing environment where requests for information are generally ad hoc in nature. These packages minimize the need for application programmers by providing easy-to-use programming capabilities. The user does not need to write a program in a conventional programming language to access the DBMS capabilities. A host language DBMS is usually more flexible in its processing capabilities than a self-contained system and is better suited to uses oriented to support transaction. Some host language DBMS packages also provide easy-to-use data retrieval capabilities.

DBMS Advantages

A DBMS offers several potential advantages to offset its cost. Based on user interviews and industry studies, it has been found that most DBMS packages provide the use with the following advantages:

Ability to respond better to changing information needs

Effective support of on-line access to a data base from remote terminals for data retrieval or processing

Ability to develop programs in response to ad hoc requests for information

Reduction in redundant data

A DBMS can respond to changing information needs more readily than traditional file processing techniques because the data are isolated from the application programs that use them. Thus, changes to the data base can be made with minimal impact on existing programs. This capability is called data independence, and the degree to which the data are independent of the application program varies among the commercial DBMS packages. The higher the degree of data independence provided by the DBMS, the greater the ability to respond to change. However, no commercially available DBMS can now provide complete data independence.

The DBMS advantage most often cited is the effective support of on-line access to a data base from remote terminals for data retrieval or processing. However, the DBMS does not provide the telecommunication functions directly to the user but provides convenient interconnections to other software packages that handle that function. Thus, the DBMS makes application program development in an on-line environment easier.

A DBMS provides an organization with a better environment for developing programs in response to new requests for information. However, the ability of the DBMS to respond to new requests for information depends on how well the data base is designed.

A by-product of an integrated data base and another frequently cited advantage is the reduction of redundant data, which:

Eliminates inconsistencies that can occur when multiple files containing duplicate data are used, thus improving the integrity of the data

Reduces costs associated with maintaining and referencing data stored in separate files

Eliminates duplication of costly data collection and puts responsibility for accuracy at the point of entry

Facilitates management and control of data resources

Conserves costly data storage space

In some cases, not all redundant data should be eliminated. Many organizations have found it necessary to maintain some redundancy and establish interfile links to avoid excessively long processing times. There is a tradeoff between the elimination of redundant data and the efficient use of a computer system.

DBMS Disadvantages

There are several valid reasons for not using a DBMS, depending upon an organization's information processing needs and financial resources. Users have identified several disadvantages of using DBMS technology and instances when DBMS use is not appropriate. Here are some examples:

It affects other computer resources, such as the computer's main memory and direct access storage devices.

It requires an organization either to hire data processing personnel skilled in its use or to provide costly training to its own personnel.

It costs between $34,000 and $120,000, dependiang on which DBMS and what options are purchased.

Users have identified circumstances when traditional file processing techniques may be more appropriate than a DBMS in satisfying an organization's data processing needs. For instance:

An organization does not have a need for or does not want to share data among multiple user groups.

A relatively large portion of the records in a file are accessed each time the file is processed.

An organization does not need an on-line data processing environment.

Differences between Data Base and Non-Data Base Processing

Another method to explain the data base environment is to contrast data base and non-data base processing. The contrast is between the organization of data using data base concepts and traditional file organization. However, it needs to be recognized that the differences are less pronounced as the traditional file organization structure approaches data base characteristics. For example, some sophisticated implementations of an indexed sequential disk file provide many of the characteristics normally associated with data base.

The differences between data base organization and the more traditional file organization are described in Figure 27. This figure lists the more common data base characteristics. These characteristics are frequently referred to as the benefits of data base. For each characteristic, the data base organization supporting that characteristic is described, and then contrasted with the traditional file organization. Note that this figure is a summary of much of the material presented earlier in this book.

Data Base Characteristic	Data Base Organization	Traditional File Organization
Reduces general data redundancy across application files	The DBMS creates and maintains interfile access paths automatically so that the same data may be used by multiple applications.	Each application typically has its own master file, which contains data duplicated in files of related systems.
Reduces the programming effort required for file updating	A program updates data in a single shared data base. The new data are immediately available for all applications.	Each physical file containing the data to be updated must be processed separately. This is usually done at different times, causing discrepancies in various reports.
Reduces the program modification brought about by changes in data definition	Data description is segregated from application programs. Only those programs actually referencing the changed data type need be modified.	Changes in record definition or expansion of record sizes must be reflected in every program accessing the data.
Increases the accessibility of data, by providing multiple access paths and retrieval sequences	DBMS provide automatic generation and maintenance of secondary indexes and logical relationships, which allows tailoring of access to meet the requirements of application systems.	Most traditional file systems support a single access path, so that additional retrieval requirements must be satisfied by search and sort procedures.
Encourages the use of standardized data naming conventions	For many retrieval operations, the applications programmer must use names known to the DBMS. Central data definitions are often maintained in a data dictionary system.	Application programmers often supply their own data names.
Provides data security	Control blocks are generated that specify which data elements an individual application program can access. Control information and undesignated data are not available to the program.	Security systems must be coded as an independent task. Such systems are difficult to write, especially in COBOL.
Provides recoverability	Recoverability is an automatic feature of DBMS. Once processing errors are detected, the system can restore the data base files to the last intact file copy. All transactions against the data base are logged on tape, from which quick file restoration is possible.	No automatic facility is provided; therefore, each application system must program its own recoverability. Standardized recovery procedures are difficult to define and implement.
Reduces operator intervention and associated production errors	Data base files reside on disk.	Tape handling is a major activity in production runs.
Promotes data communication services	Most DBMSs have integrated or interfaced communications monitor programs.	Application systems and data communications are sometimes difficult to integrate within acceptable standards of performance.

Figure 27. Differences between Data Base and Non-Data Base Processing.

Importance of Understanding the Data Base Environment

The need for the auditor to have a thorough understanding of data base concepts and methods cannot be overstated. Data base is a complex technology, and without an understandiang of the nature of data base it will be difficult for an auditor to conduct an effective audit. This does not mean that the auditor need be a technical expert in data base technology, but he or she must understand the terminology concepts, risks, and controls.

It is not the intent of this book to explain data base technology in any depth. Rather, the intent is to provide an overview of the principal concepts. It is strongly recommended that the auditor who will be conducting an audit of data base technology do some individual study or enroll in a formal educational course on data base. The following two references are provided as an aid in determining what is needed and where to find assistance:

Appendix C—Data Base Glossary. This glossary provides the auditor with a listing of common data base terms. If many of these terms are unfamiliar, he or she should acquire more education about data base.

Appendix D—References and Suggested Reading. Appropriate references should be acquired to supplement the auditor's knowledge in data base technology where appropriate.

KEY CONCEPT

Understanding data base concepts is essential for the effective data base audit.

AUDITABLE DATA BASE ACTIVITIES

Problems, concerns, and data base risks cannot be audited directly. Only activities can be audited. The activities described in this book were selected to emphasize audit and control as opposed to representing organizational activities. While some activities may be distinct organizational entities, the auditor's evaluation should concentrate on the controllable and auditable activities as opposed to an organizational unit.

Activities become the vehicle for implementing controls. For example, one cannot just initiate a control to prevent fraud; the control must be implemented within activities. An organization can restrict data access to authorized users which, in turn, should reduce the probability of fraud. In other words, the organization should install specific controls in the security activity, rather than simply creating a general control policy stating that fraud is not permitted.

The data base activities are illustrated in Figure 28. This complex illustration shows the data base environment as well as the activities that occur in this environment. The figure also shows the system of data base controls providing protection against the unauthorized or unintentional access by those interfacing with the DBMS.

Data Base Functions

The major data base functions are illustrated inside the system of data base controls. The center of processing is the DBMS. It is this single piece of software that interacts with the other data base segments.

The main segments of the data base are:

Data base content. The location of physical storage of the data. These are the data that are accessed by users in the fulfillment of their information processing needs.

Security profile. The identification of the data base resources to be protected, and the individuals authorized access to those resources. Traditional file organization only permitted security at the file level, but depending upon the security system used, information in the data base can be protected down to the data element.

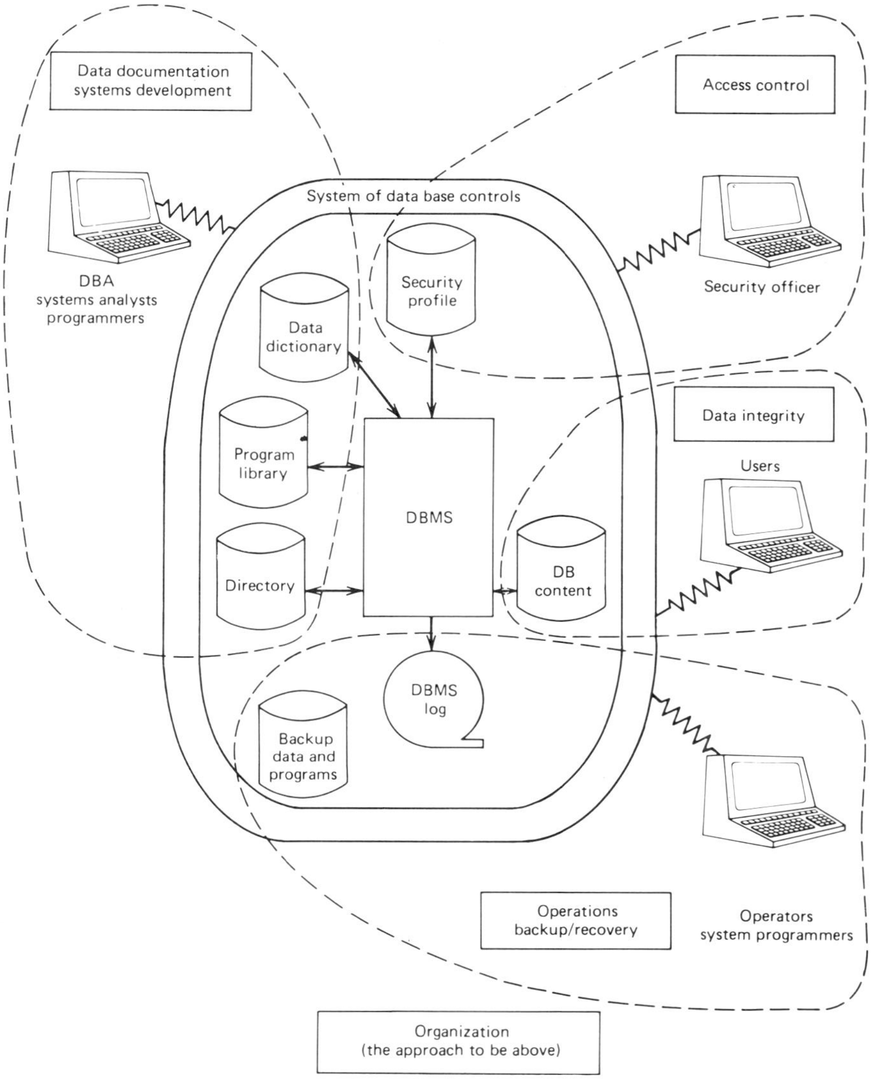

Figure 28. Data Base Activities.

Data dictionary. An automated documentation tool for data. Data elements can be defined, as can the structure in which the data are stored.

Program library. Programs having access to data base resources. Programs are normally stored in a production program library, but the interface to the data base must be either built into the programs or added at execution time.

Directory (sometimes called the data base directory [DBD] or data dictionary/ directory [DD/D]. The directory describes the content of a data base. The data base directory is used by the data base management system in accessing and controlling data. It contains the locations of the data base data.

DBMS log. The data base management system log records data base activity and thus provides an audit trail of data base activity. One of the most common audit trail records is a before and after image, which shows the contents of the data base being addressed both before and after change. In addition, the log normally records usage time, date of activity, special DBMS commands and who used them, as well as operating statistics.

Backup data and programs. Periodically, the information needed to restore operations in the event of a problem must be copied and saved. At a minimum this includes the data base content (which includes the directory) and the programs. All of the material needed to operate the data base should be saved, including the documentation and operating instructions explaining how to execute data base processing.

System of Data Base Controls

The data base area needs a system of controls to assure accurate, complete, authorized, and supportable data. The objective of control remains the same whether the system is manual, computerized using traditional files, or processed using data base technology. However, as the technology gets more complex, so do the controls.

The ring of controls illustrated in Figure 28 is symbolic of the protection provided data base technology. The ring concept is used to illustrate that should an individual break through that ''ring of controls,'' his or her ability to manipulate the system is almost unlimited. The ring also shows that controls are an interrelating group and that penetration can occur at any point within the system. Experience has shown that perpetrators search out the weakest part of the system and penetrate at that point.

The data base technology operation occurs within the system of data base controls. Those using the data base resources should be external to the system of internal controls and interface to the data base through that system of controls. Using this concept, we can view activities by the categories of individuals interfacing with the data base technology. The activities and the individuals involved in those activities are indicated by circles of dotted lines surrounding each of the data base activities.

OVERVIEW OF DATA BASE ACTIVITIES

Understanding the objectives and functioning of the data base activities is an essential part of the data base audit process. Again, the auditor is cautioned that these activities are identified for control and audit purposes, and may not coincide with actual organizational units. However, from a segregation of duties perspective the auditor should assess whether there is an adequate division of responsibilities.

The activities will be explained in more detail in Chapters 6 through 11 (one chapter is devoted to auditing each of the activities), but they are briefly described below.

Organizational Activity

Data base introduces into the organization a new function. With that function comes a shifting of responsibilities. Much of this shifting involves a transfer of responsibilities from the application system development areas and the user areas to a centralized data base administration (DBA) function.

The introduction of data base is normally associated with the organization of a formal data base administration group. This group usually reports within the data processing function, and frequently directly to the data processing manager. The objective of the data base administration function is to oversee and direct the installation and operation of the data base.

The data base administration function normally has line responsibilities for data documentation, system development procedures, and standards for those applications using data base technology. The DBA function also has indirect or dotted line responsibilities to computer operations and users of data base technology through providing advice and direction. In addition, the data base administrator should be alert to potential problems and actively involved in offering solutions.

Studies on the success of data base technology strongly indicate the need for planning. An integral part of this planning is an integration of data base into the organizational structure. This integration requires some reorganization within both the data processing and user areas.

Data Documentation Activity

The transition to data base technology is one involving the switching of EDP emphasis from processing to data. Many existing systems are processing driven, while data base technology involves data-driven systems. This change in emphasis necessitates better data documentation.

If multiple users are using the same data, there is a need for easy-to-use and complete documentation. If there are misunderstandings regarding the data's content, reliability, consistency, and so on, this will lead to problems in the interpretation and use of data. Clear, distinct documentation helps reduce this risk.

Many organizations use standardized methods of data documentation. The simplest method is to use forms and written procedures governing the method of defining data. More sophisticated installations use data dictionaries. The data dictionary can be used as a stand-alone automated documentation tool or can be integrated into the processing environment. It is through this integration that adherence to data definition is assured.

The data base administrator normally oversees the use of the data dictionary. This involves determining what data elements will be documented, the type and extent of documentation requested, and assurance that the documentation is up to date and in compliance with the documentation quality standards.

The documentation requirement for data is a threefold responsibility. First, individuals must be educated into the type of documentation required and provide that documentation. Second, the documentation must be maintained to ensure its accuracy and completeness. Third, the data used in the operating environment must conform to the documentation. If the data in operation are different from the documentation specifications, the entire process will be eroded.

System Development Activity

Data base technology is designed to make system development easier. However, it is only easier when the application system fits into the existing data hierarchy. If the system requirements are outside the data base structure, it may be more difficult and costly to develop that system by using the data base than by using non-data base methods.

The method to ensure that the applications effectively use data base technology is to have data base administration personnel involved in the development process. In other words, more front-end planning and assessment are required to ensure the effective use of data base technology than when data base is not used. This front-end effort also ensures that the application project team understands the resources available through data base technology.

The data base is a continually changing grouping of data. Part of the DBA's involvement in system development is to adjust and modify the structure continually to meet the changing needs of application systems. Thus, the developmental process for data base is twofold: first, to ensure that the applications effectively use the data base; and, second, to establish new data base directions in order to keep the data base in step with application needs.

The system developmental process in data base technology has the following three objectives:

1. To familiarize the system developmental people with the resources and capabilities available for their use
2. To ensure that the proposed application system can be integrated into the existing data base structure, and if not, to modify the application and/or the data base structure
3. To ensure that application processing will preserve the consistency, reliability, and integrity of data in the data base

A problem that often surfaces in the use of data base technology is how to charge for data base usage. Some applications operate more effectively using data base than others. Experience has shown that moving some applications from non-data base to data base technology substantially reduces the cost of processing, while in other instances the cost increases. The reason for this is that the data base must be optimized toward a specific data usage. Obviously, what the data base administrator must attempt to do is to optimize the data base toward the high-usage applications and let the usage be less efficient in the small-volume applications. Data base costs should not be set to discourage the use of data base.

Access Control Activity

One of the major concerns to management about data base is the ready accessibility of information. As more data are placed into a single repository, that repository becomes more valuable to perpetrators. Much of the thrust of the United States Government Privacy Act of 1977 was directed at data base technology.

The access control function has two primary purposes. The first is to identify the resources requiring control and determine who should be authorized access to those resources. The second is to define and enforce the control specifications identified in the previous responsibility in the operating environment.

The access control function can be performed by the data base administration function or an independent security officer. Obviously, an independent function is stronger than the same function that administers the data base. The method selected will be dependent upon the value of the information in the data base and the size of the organization. The more valuable the data, or the larger the organization, the more likely it is that the function will be implemented through an independent security officer.

The enforcement of the security profile for the data base in on-line systems is performed by security software. Some data base management systems have security features incorporated in the DBMS, while others need to be supplemented by security packages. Many of the major hardware vendors, such as IBM, provide security software. However, there are several independent vendors providing general-purpose security software that interfaces with many DBMS systems.

The access control function has the additional responsibility of monitoring the effectiveness of security. Detecting and investigating potential access violations are important aspects of data base access control. First, unless the access control procedures are monitored, violators will not be detected; and second, if violators are not reprimanded or prosecuted, there will be little incentive for other involved parties to comply with access control rules.

Data Integrity Activity

The integrity of the contents of the data base is the joint responsibility of the users and the data base administrator. The data base administrator is concerned more about the integrity of the structure and the physical records, while the users are concerned about the contents or values contained in the data base.

In dedicated files, the integrity of the file is primarily the responsibility of the user. The data processing department has a responsibility to use the correct version of the file and to add those features that protect the physical integrity of the records on the file. However, the ultimate responsibility for the integrity resides with the user, and the application systems need to be constructed to ensure that integrity. This is usually accomplished by accumulating the values in one or more control fields and developing an independent control total which can be checked each time the file is used.

In a data base environment, the traditional integrity responsibilities change. No longer does a single user have control over all the uses of data in a data base. For example, several different application systems may be able to add, delete, or modify any single data element in the data base. In an airline reservation system, any authorized agent can commit or delete a reserved seat for a flight. On the other hand, the data base administrator dosen't have control over the uses of the data in the data base. This means that the data integrity must be assured through new procedures.

The data integrity activity may involve many different groups within an organization. These groups, such as various users and the data base administration function, will share parts of this data integrity responsibility. In fulfilling data integrity responsibility, the following tasks need to be performed:

1. Identify the method of ensuring the completeness of the physical records in the data base.
2. Determine the method of ensuring the completeness of the logical structure of the data base (i.e., schema).
3. Determine which users have responsibility for the integrity of which segments of the data base.
4. Develop methods to enable those users to perform their data integrity responsibilities.
5. Determine at what times the integrity of the data base will be verified, and assure there are adequate backup data between the periods of proven data integrity.

Operations Activity

The normal evolution of data base operations is from the data base administration function to specialized operations personnel and then to normal computer operators. This evolution is necessary so that an organization can develop the appropriate skills and methods needed for training and monitoring regular computer operators. Without taking the appropriate time to develop skills, operators may be placed into a position where their probability of success is minimal.

Operating data base technology is more complex than non-data base technology. Normally data base is coupled with communication technology. This means that two highly technical procedures are coupled, making the resulting technology more complex than either of the contributing technologies.

Most of the day-to-day operations are performed by users. Data base provides the basis for a user-operated technology. One of the advantages of data base is the powerful utilities associated with the technology that are available to the users. One of the more powerful utilities is the query languages, which provide almost unlimited capabilities for users to prepae analyses and reports using the data within the data base.

Operating data base technology poses the following challenges to computer operators:

Monitoring space allocation to ensure minimal disruptions due to space management problems

Understanding and using DBMS operating procedures and messages

Monitoring service levels to ensure adequate resources for users

Maintaining operating statistics so that data base performance can be monitored

Reorganizing the data base as necessary (usually under the direction of the data base administrator) to improve performance and add capabilities where necessary

Backup/Recovery Activity

One of the most technically complex aspects of data processing is recovering a crashed data base. This procedure involves the following four major challenges:

Identifying that the integrity of the data base has been lost

Notifying users that the data base is unoperable and providing them with alternate processing means (Note: These means should be predetermined and may be manual.)

Ensuring and having ready adequate backup data

Performing those procedures necessary to recover the integrity of the data base

Many data bases are operational around the clock during business days, and some seven days a week. It is not uncommon for many thousands of transactions to occur in a single day. Thus, unless recovery operations are well planned, it may take many hours or even days to recover the integrity of the data base. The complexity and planning that must go into data base contingency planning cannot be overemphasized.

The responsibility for data base recovery is normally that of computer operations. However, the users and data base administrators must provide input into the recovery process. The data base administrator usually develops the procedures and acquires the recovery tools and techniques. The user provides the specifications on time span for recovery and determines what alternate procedures are acceptable during this period.

One of the problems encountered is notifying users that the data base is no longer operational. In larger organizations, there may be many users, even hundreds of users, connected to a single data base. It may take longer to notify the users that the data base is not operational than it will take to get the data base back on-line. The group involved in the recovery may not have adequate resources to inform all of the users. Some of the alternate procedures used include:

Messages to terminals if facilities to transmit are available

User call-in to a recorded message indicating the data base is down

Education of users to desired service expectations, and procedures established if those expectations are not met

The backup/recovery activity begins with determining what operations must be recovered and in what time frame. This provides the recovery specifications. From these specifications the procedures are developed and implemented to meet the recovery expectations. Much of the process involves collecting and storing backup data. Backup data are defined as data needed for recovery purposes rather than for day-to-day operational purposes. One of the major files used for recovery purposes is the DBMS log. This provides sequencing and content of data base transactions.

KEY CONCEPT

Auditors are concerned not with risk but audit activities

DATA BASE CONTROLS

The primary objective of data base control is to ensure accurate, complete, authorized, and supportable data. This objective remains the same whether the system is manual, computerized using traditional files, or processed using data base technology. However, while the objective stays the same, the methods of control are frequently new.

The primary objective of control is to reduce risk. Without risk there is no need for control. Risk involves both the frequency of occurrence of an event and the loss per occurrence. Therefore, control can be effective in only the two following ways. (1) Controls can reduce the frequency of occurrence of events, or (2) controls can reduce the average loss per occurence.

Let's look at a risk situation and then observe how controls could work in that situation. As we enter data into a computer system, there is a risk of the entry of erroneous data. If those data are entered erroneously, the risk has been fulfilled and we have a potential loss situation. We can reduce this risk in two ways. First, we can reduce the frequency of occurrence of the entry of erroneous data. Data base technology helps us with that in that we only enter data once and it is used by multiple applications. Therefore, our frequency is reduced and our opportunity for error is reduced. Second, we can instigate controls that will reduce the value of a loss should it occur. We can provide data validation checks that will limit our loss; for example, when a price is entered which varies more than plus or minus 10% from a predetermined price, we can reject that transaction. In other words, we can reduce our average loss per occurrence to within plus or minus 10% of some predetermined amount. Controls that do not fall into one of these two categories are to be considered ineffective controls.

Controls rarely can reduce the loss of risk to zero. In most situations, as the loss approaches zero the cost becomes exorbitant. The cost-effectiveness of data base controls was illustrated in Figure 7. This showed that in an uncontrolled situation, loss, due to risk is high, but, it is reduced as controls are added. Obviously, this assumes that controls are effective. However, as the loss begins to approach zero, the cost of controls begins to accelerate very rapidly.

The figure illustrated the optimal level of control as the point where the cost of controls equals the reduction in risk due to that control. In other words, the optimum control point is the point where it takes $1 worth of controls to reduce the losses by $1. When the cost of control exceeds the loss due to risk, more money is spent on control than is saved. In this situation, we can be considered to be overcontrolled.

Risks \ Activities	Organization	Data Documentation	System Development	Access Control	Data Integrity	Operations	Backup/Recovery
Inadequate assignment of responsibility	✓		✓	✓			
Inaccurate or incomplete data in a data base	✓		✓		✓	✓	✓
Losing an update to a single data item			✓		✓		
Inadequate audit trail		✓	✓		✓		✓
Unauthorized access in a data base				✓		✓	
Inadequate service level			✓			✓	✓
Placing data in the wrong calendar period		✓	✓		✓		
Failure of DBMS to function as specified	✓	✓	✓		✓	✓	✓
Fraud/embezzlement	✓		✓	✓			
Lack of independent data base reviews	✓		✓				
Inadequate documentation	✓	✓	✓		✓	✓	✓
Continuity of processing				✓		✓	✓
Lack of performance criteria	✓		✓			✓	
Lack of management support	✓		✓	✓			

Figure 29. Data Base Risks/Activities Matrix.

When control designers understand the cost-effectiveness of data base controls, they can design controls which provide an economic return. This cost-effectiveness approach to data base controls also eliminates much of the traditional resistance to controls as both the requirement and the economics of control are understood. Controls are viewed by many data processing personnel as a deterrent by management from doing certain acts while, in fact, controls should be designed on a cost-effectiveness basis as are other aspects of automated applications.

The controls included within this book were drawn from discussions with data base administrators, examination of several organizations' control standards and procedures, and search of the data base technology literature. The data base controls included are not exhaustive but, rather, represent the type of controls that are actually implemented in data base organizations.

The list of controls is organized by activity, with many of the controls occurring in more than one activity. However, the controls are classified by the activity in which the control is normally found. The controls are described in the auditing chapters (6 through 12), with a detailed explanation of each control included in Appendix A.

The risks requiring control are listed in the Data Base Risks/Activities Matrix (Figure 29) by a check (√). The controls that are used to reduce these risks are identified in the chapter on auditing that activity.

KEY CONCEPT

New data base risks and activities require new methods of control.

---

part three

CONDUCTING THE AUDIT

New activities, risks, and controls require new methods of audit. The audit process must complement the characteristics of data base technology.

five

CONDUCTING THE DATA BASE AUDIT

Developing the data base risk profile will identify the high-risk data base activities. The identification of the high-risk activities is the prelude to conducting the audit. The risk profile exercise, coupled with the preliminary review, will prepare the auditor to conduct an effective data base audit.

The basic audit approach remains the same whether the audit is of a manual area or a highly technical area like data base. The audit process requires the auditor to set objectives, determine whether or not reliance can be placed on the system of internal controls, and then perform those tests deemed necessary by the auditor. This same basic process will be followed in the data base audit.

The data base audit steps described in this chapter were selected to adapt the standard audit process to data base technology. The process recognizes that there are new activities, new evidence, and new controls, and thus new audit tools and techniques are necessary. The audit steps are designed to lead the auditor through the technological data base maze; however, in following the process the auditor may be required to obtain new skills.

DATA BASE AUDIT PROGRAM

The data base audit program commences at the point where the high-risk data base activities have been identified. The selection of these high-risk activities for audit normally results in an audit assignment defining the scope of the data base audit. For example, the scope may concentrate on data base recovery activities, as opposed to evaluating the completeness of data documentation.

The data base audit program is divided into nine steps. The steps were selected to emphasize the procedures that should be followed in auditing a data base. The same procedures should be followed for each data base activity audited. However, the steps do not need to be performed sequentially; in other words, Step 1 can be conducted for two or more activities concurrently and completed before Step 2 begins for any of those activities.

The recommended data base audit program includes the following steps:

Step 1: Set data base audit objectives.
Step 2: Become data friendly.
Step 3: Identify data base evidence.
Step 4: Identify data base controls.
Step 5: Determine control objectives.
Step 6: Evaluate whether controls accomplish control objectives.

Step Number	Step Tasks	Step Description
1	Set data base audit objectives.	Describe what is to be accomplished as a result of the data base audit.
2	Become data friendly.	Understand both the data base content and the organizational structure of the data base(s).
3	Identify data base evidence.	Document the types of evidence produced by the data base environment that can be used for audit purposes.
4	Identify data base controls.	Document the controls that exist in the data base environment by activity in which they occur.
5	Determine control objectives.	From existing documentation or interview, determine the level of control desired by the organization over the data base environment.
6	Evaluate whether controls accomplish control objectives.	Make a determination as to whether the installed controls meet the data base environment control objectives.
7	Prove data base integrity.	Tests on the data base cannot be used to draw conclusions about the data base until the integrity of the data base has been proved. This step provides reasonable assurance that the data within the data base are accurate and complete.
8	Test data base controls.	Conduct those tests necessary to determine the magnitude of identified control weaknesses.
9	Develop audit opinion.	Develop an audit opinion on both the integrity of the data base and the adequacy of the data base controls.

Figure 30. Data Base Audit Steps.

Step 7: Prove data base integrity.
Step 8: Test data base controls.
Step 9: Develop audit opinion.

The purpose of each step is listed in Figure 30. The remainder of this chapter is devoted to the method of performing each step.

STEP 1: SET DATA BASE AUDIT OBJECTIVES

Experience has shown that data base audits are generally very time-consuming and ineffective. One audit group took over two years to audit a data base, and only stopped at that time because the lead auditor was reassigned. The problem in that instance was that the audit was a probing audit with no set objectives. Because of the size and technical complexity of the data base, as well as the lack of data base skills on the part of the auditor, the auditor was never able to prove the integrity of the data base or the adequacy of controls and thus the audit never ended.

The difficulty in auditing a data base can be attributed to the following three factors:

Data base technology is very complex.

Most auditors lack adequate data base skills.

Most of the auditors' current audit tools and techniques are ineffective in a data base environment.

The solution to the data base audit dilemma is to set achievable and measurable objectives. These provide a high probability of success together with the ability to determine when the audit is complete. Identifying the high-risk activities should be a valuable aid in defining data base audit objectives.

Achievable audit objectives involve the following considerations:

Amount of time available for the audit

Skill of the audit team

Availability of data base audit tools and techniques

Availability and willingness of data base administration personnel to help during the audit

The following are necessary for measurable data base audit objectives:

Objective is defined quantitatively or qualitatively in sufficient detail so that the achievement of the objective is not subject to dispute.

Criteria are included in the objective to measure accomplishment of the objective.

The auditor in charge and audit management agree on the measurement criteria.

It is good practice to limit an audit objective to one activity. For example, the auditor's task is easier when an objective is restricted to the recovery activity than it is when the same objective covers multiple activities. More than one audit objective can exist for any single data base activity.

An example of a good data base audit objective is "to ensure that resources and procedures are adequate to enable data base operations to recover after a problem without loss of data integrity (200-hour assignment)." This is a good data base objective because:

It is something that can be tested—and thus is achievable.

It is measurable in that "no loss of integrity" has been specified.

The criterion for accomplishment (i.e., 200 hours) has been stated as part of the objective.

The objective is restricted to one activity.

The one aspect of the objective that we may still be uncertain about is whether the assigned staff will have the necessary skills. However, we are assuming that they do, and that staff agrees that the number of hours are reasonable.

Data Base Audit Objective Rules

1. Objectives should be achievable.
2. Objectives should be measurable.
3. Objectives should be restricted to a single data base activity.

STEP 2: BECOME DATA FRIENDLY

If a computer language or facility is friendly, it should not be difficult for an individual to use that capability. For the auditor to become data friendly, he or she needs to understand the data in enough detail to be able to use the data easily.

Prior to conducting a physical inventory, it is advantageous for the auditors to become familiar with the area. This helps them know what to look for and where to find particular inventory areas. Becoming familiar with data provides an equivalent capability in a data base audit. Knowing the types of data and how they are stored helps the auditor conduct the data base audit more productively.

If the auditor is data friendly, he or she knows:

1. What data elements are stored in a data base
2. The format by which that data are documented
3. The structure in which the data are stored
4. The method(s) for getting data in and out of the data base

The data base administration function is the key to becoming friendly with the data. This function has the responsibility for administering data, and thus itself must be data friendly.

The auditor should perform the following tasks in order to become data friendly.

Task 1: Obtain inventory of data elements

Experience has shown that it is rare for organizations to have over 1,500 data elements, and most have closer to 1,000. Of these, less than half will have audit significance. Knowing which data elements are available, and then knowing which have audit significance, will be valuable as the audit progresses. If the organization has an inventory of data elements (note that this is the exception rather than the rule), the auditor should obtain a copy of that inventory for his workpapers.

Task 2: Obtain list of what data attributes are documented

The attributes of data are their characteristics. For example, the attributes tell the length, ownership, acceptable values (if appropriate), where generated, where used, data validation rules, and so on. This is the type of information that is available about data elements, which will change from organization to organization. The auditor dosen't need to know the attributes about any specific piece of data at this time, but he or she needs to know what attributes are available for reference at a later time.

Task 3: Identify data base users

The users of the data base tell the auditor the purposes for which the data base is being used. It is necessary to know not specific individuals or programs but, rather, categories of users such as marketing personnel, accountants, bank tellers, and so on.

Task 4: Identify data base structure and data groupings

The auditor should determine whether the data is organized into a hierarchical, network, or relational data base. If there are groupings of data within that structure, those groupings should be identified. In most data base environments these groupings are called subschemas (a subschema is the grouping of data used by a single data base user). The auditor need not know temporary subschemas, but only those used regularly.

Task 5: Identify retrieval tools

DBMS software includes numerous utility programs, many of which are effective in analyzing and retrieving data from the data base. These may prove to be the best audit tools available, making it worthwhile to understand their capabilities.

Task 6: Identify retention and backup procedures

Where, why and how long data retained provide insight into what data are available for analysis by the auditor. Some DBMS log data, for example, may only be retained for a few hours.

Data Friendly Checklist

Figure 31, the data friendly checklist, is designed to assist the auditor in becoming data friendly. It includes the items that need to be performed in order better to understand the data under review. The checklist includes room to indicate the appropriate workpaper reference for information gathered as part of this step.

DATA BASE AUDIT FRIENDLY RULES

1. Inventory the data with financial implications.
2. Identify what data attributes are documented.
3. Learn the tools to analyze and extract data.

STEP 3: IDENTIFY DATA BASE EVIDENCE

The new data base activities and controls produce new evidence. The types of evidence available in non-data base systems may be replaced by new forms of evidence. The auditor must be familiar with this new evidence if it is to be used during the audit process. Many of the controls in a data base environment are prolific, producing large amounts of evidence for audit evaluation.

There are two categories of evidence produced in a data base environment. First is the evidence detailing the activity occurring on the data within the data base. Second is the evidence produced relating to the functioning of data base controls.

The application system only provides audit trail data on application activity. When multiple applications interact with one common piece of data, a means should be established to record this activity in a common location. In normal operation, the evidence that the auditor examines is the DBMS log. It may be necessary to supplement the DBMS log with the application audit trail in order to document data activity fully.

During the conduct of the audit, the auditor will examine evidence in order to develop an audit opinion. Identifying that evidence early in the audit process will assist the auditor in selecting the appropriate audit tests. However, evidence, or aduit evidence, are terms

Number	Item	Response		Workpaper Reference
		Yes	No	
1.	Arrange an appointment with the data base administrator to discuss characteristics and attributes of data base data.			
2.	Ask the data base administrator for an inventory of the data elements on the data base, or, if that list is not available, how to obtain such a list.			
3.	Identify those items within the inventory that have audit significance. Normally these will be financial fields, data identifiers such as employee number or product number, transaction identifiers, and data used in the calculation of financial fields, such as pay rate, product price, etc.			
4.	Determine how data are documented; for example, whether they are documented on a form, a data dictionary, or by other means.			
5.	Obtain a list of what data attributes are documented through the data documentation process.			
6.	Identify the categories of data base users.			
7.	Identify the number of data bases in existence and the purpose for each data base.			
8.	Identify the data base organizational structure for each of the organization's data bases. This also involves knowing which DBMS is used and in which location.			
9.	Identify the major groupings of data for which ready access is available through the data dictionary.			
10.	Obtain a list from the data base administrator of the retrieval tools that may be of value during the audit, and where more information or education can be acquired on the use of those tools.			
11.	Identify the storage locations for backup data.			
12.	Identify the types of data that are retained for backup purposes, such as a DBMS log or duplicate copies of the data base.			
13.	Identify the retention period for the main types of audit evidence, such as the DBMS log.			

Figure 31. Data Friendly Checklist.

that are generally not familiar to data base administration personnel. Therefore, to ask for a list of data base evidence would probably be unproductive. The recommended process for gathering an inventory of data base evidence is to complete the following tasks:

Task 1: Become familiar with common data base evidence

The auditor who knows what to look for will have a much greater opportunity of finding it than the auditor who must rely upon the data base administration personnel for audit guidance. Figure 32 is a list of the most common evidence produced by the data base environment. Note that if you are not familiar with these various types of data base evidence, they are briefly described in Appendix A as part of the control descriptions. The control number(s) is provided in this figure for ease of reference to the discussion of evidence in the appendix.

Evidence	Available		Comments
	Yes	No	
1. Data base management system			
2. Data dictionary system			
3. DBMS logs			
4. Security log			
5. Data base utilities			
6. Data base structure map			
7. Data base verifier reports			
8. DBMS reports			
9. Security profiles			
10. Data base standards			
11. Organizational charts/job descriptions			
12. User complaints/requests			
13. Master terminal operation procedures			
14. Data base operating procedures			
15. Data base recovery procedures			
16. Data base reorganization procedures			
17. Data base integrity procedures			
18. Data base controls			
19. Program change request			
20. Program libraries			
21. Data element inventory			
22. Data base plans/objectives			
23. Data base application data statistics/reports			
24. Review group/control group reports			
25. Data base policies/procedures			
26. DBMS/DB application documentation			

Figure 32. Data Base Evidence Checklist.

Task 2: Conduct data base evidence survey

During the survey segment of the data base audit, the auditor should be inquiring regarding the existence of data base evidence. Much of the investigation will be a natural part of the familiarization process by which the auditor learns the data base operation. Some auditors prefer to provide the data base administrator with an evidence checklist as a basis for the discussion. Figure 32 can be used for this purpose.

Task 3: Document the existence of data base evidence

The auditor should document on the work sheet provided in Figure 33 each piece of evidence identified during the survey. Normally, this type of information is readily available from the data base administrator. Here is the information that should be recorded about each item of data base evidence:

No.	Title	Description	Location	Size	Retention Period	Comments

Figure 33. Inventory of Data Base Evidence.

Number. A unique number assigned by the auditor to each piece of evidence for ease of reference and cross-reference during the audit.

Title. The name by which the evidence is known to the data base administration personnel.

Description. A short unambiguous narrative explanation of the evidence.

Location. The physical storage location of the evidence, and possibly the individual responsible for the evidence, for ease in locating the evidence for audit purposes.

Size. A quantitative measure of the volume of the evidence. This would normally be expressed in terms of records, units of computer storage, or number of pages of documentation.

Retention period. The date on which the evidence will be destroyed.

Comments. Further descriptive explanation about the evidence; for example, suggestions on how to use the evidence during the conduct of the audit.

It is important to identify evidence early in the data base audit in order to ensure that the evidence will be available when it is needed during the conduct of the audit. In many instances, special software will be required to analyze and list the evidence in the format needed for the audit process. Because the preparation of this software may be a time-consuming task, the sooner it is known what evidence is available, and the effort that will be required to obtain that evidence, the greater assurance the auditor has that the evidence will be ready when needed.

IDENTIFY DATA BASE EVIDENCE RULES

1. Identify what evidence is available.
2. Identify where the evidence is located.
3. Identify how long the evidence will be saved.

STEP 4: IDENTIFY DATA BASE CONTROLS

The assessment of the adequacy of controls begins with the identification of data base controls. Experience has shown that this is a very difficult and time-consuming process. However, until the controls have been identified, their adequacy cannot be determined.

Ideally, the data base administration function has already defined the control. Unfortunately, this is rarely the case. A typical comment by data base administration personnel is, "We design data base systems, not systems of controls." This comment expresses the attitude of many data base personnel; they feel control is an integral part of the process and should not be considered to be separate. The concept of a "system of internal controls" is foreign to many data base personnel.

The failure to recognize the need for a system of data base controls causes the following problems in documenting these controls:

Lack of a basis for communication about controls between the auditor and data base personnel

Difficulty in identifying controls from data base processes (note that many data base personnel cannot differentiate between a control and a process)

No single source of control documentation (note that in many instances the auditor is required to document the data base controls)

The normal audit function does not include documenting controls, but it may be necessary if that documentation is not currently available. The auditor should attempt to get the data base administration personnel to document controls. However, if this is not possible, then the task defaults to the audit team.

Methods to Document Controls

Auditors document controls using narrative, checklist, control flowcharting, and matrix methods. While this book recommends the matrix method, the narrative and checklist methods are most common. The major advantage to the matrix method is that it documents controls in a format conducive to assessment.

The narrative method involves describing each control individually. The auditor must identify the control, possibly create a name for the control, describe the functioning of the control, and tell where the control is located. The major disadvantage is the amount of time required to describe the control, and then to assess its adequacy. Poorly written narratives are of little value in the assessment process.

The checklist is by far the most common method for control documentation. A well-constructed checklist provides an extensive list of controls. The auditor can then complete the checklist through interview, or hand the checklist to the data base administration function for completion. The advantage of the checklist is that it provides guidance in the control assessment process. The disadvantages are that the checklist may not be complete, and it is a difficult instrument to use for assessment purposes. The checklist does not show the compensating relationship between controls. The checklist forces a yes or no answer in which a no answer generally means poor controls and a yes answer means good controls. However, in actual practice a no answer to a checklist might be satisfactory if there are other compensating controls.

The control flowchart has received good acceptance in computer auditing, but is frequently difficult to use in a data base audit. The control flowchart in a computer application shows the flow of transactions as they are processed through the application system. The auditor first flows the transactions and then shows the controls on the transaction. (Note: This method is sometimes called transaction flow analysis or transaction flow auditing.) The advantage of control flowcharting is that it shows the location of controls in the system which helps in assessing both over- and undercontrolled situations. The major disadvantage to control flowcharting a data base environment is that data base tends to be a general control and thus does not fit into the application control-oriented flowchart process.

Matrix auditing is a relatively new and powerful concept in auditing. The matrix, when used in auditing, shows two audit variables. The matrix is then used to show the relationship between those variables. The advantage is that the matrix not only shows the relationship between variables, which helps explain the purpose of controls, but also shows compensating controls.

The control matrix includes risks, activities, and controls. The purpose for control is to reduce risk, and controls are located in activities. Therefore, one axis of the control matrix shows the risks and the other axis the activities. The relationship shows which risks occur in which activities. The identified controls are placed in the matrix intersections to show which risks they reduce and the activity in which they are located.

Using a Data Base Control Matrix

A generalized data base control matrix is illustrated in Figure 29 as an activities/risks matrix. The matrix shows the previously described data base risks on one side of the matrix, and the data base activities across the top of the matrix. Within the matrix, the auditor would document the controls being used in the data base environment under audit.

Each intersection of the matrix can indicate that a particular risk is a threat to the indicated activity. The checks in the Figure 29 matrix indicate what data base risks are present in which data base activities. It is in the intersections where a check exists that the auditor should look for controls. Note that this matrix may need to be modified based upon local conditions.

Chapters 6 through 12 in this book are devoted to the audit of each of the seven data base activities. Each chapter will indicate the most common controls for the activity being discussed to reduce the indicated risks. This list of controls (shown in matrix format) should be an aid to the auditor in completing this matrix.

How to Document Controls

Using the matrix approach, the auditor should complete the following tasks in order to identify the data base controls:

Task 1: Determine Activity Risks

Both risks and controls are embedded within activities. Since the basis of control is risk, the justification for having a control is to reduce risk. In order for the auditor to make an assessment of the adequacy of control, the auditor must know the risk which the control is intended to reduce, and because controls are embedded within activities, it is of further value to the auditor to know the specific activity in which the risk is greatest. From this analysis the auditor can determine the risks and the activities in which those risks occur. Note that frequently Figure 13 can be substituted for this task.

Task 2: Identify Activity Controls

The auditor should identify all controls within the auditable activities. The more common controls in each activity are described in the chapter on how to conduct an audit of that activity. Appendix A is also helpful in this process.

Task 3: Match Controls to Risks

The auditor must determine whether or not the identified controls have an impact on the identified risks. If so, the auditor should indicate within the intersection of the matrix which controls are effective in reducing which risks. Again, the chapter devoted to auditing each activity will provide guidance in making this match. The auditor should note that it is not uncommon to have controls for which there is no risk, or a risk for which there are no controls. Very few data base personnel approach the control design process from a risk orientation.

IDENTIFY DATA BASE CONTROLS RULES

1. Identify controls.
2. Determine in which activity the controls are located.
3. Determine which risks the controls are designed to reduce.

STEP 5: DETERMINE CONTROL OBJECTIVES

A control objective is what the user expects from a control. Another method of defining a control objective is as an acceptable level of risk. In other words, it is the degree of risk which the user is willing to accept.

Let's look at an example of establishing a control objective. One of the data base risks is that the level of service will be inadequate. This risk cannot be assessed until we define what is meant by the word "inadequate." Defining the acceptable level of risk or a control objective is the vehicle for defining "adequate." For our example, let us assume that we define adequate in an on-line data base system to mean that a user will receive a response within four seconds 95% of the time. In other words, for every 20 requests, 19 of them will be answered in four seconds or less response time. With this definition of adequate we can now determine whether or not the controls achieve the desired level of risk.

This is a difficult concept for auditors because rarely do users define measurable control objectives. Controls are established to achieve general control objectives, not specific ones. Therefore, the auditor must either make a personal judgment as to what is acceptable, or work with the users in defining the control objectives. Since this is not really an auditor decision, the preferred method is to work with users.

Assuming that a measurable control objective has not been established, the auditor needs to complete the following tasks in order to determine the acceptable level of risk:

Task 1: Identify responsible user

The responsible user is the individual responsible for the risk condition. In our previous example, the risk condition dealt with the adequacy of the service level. This task would require the auditor to identify the individual who is responsible for service level.

Task 2: Explain the acceptable level of risk concept

The concept of defining acceptable level of risk is new to many users. Unless the economics of risk and control are explained to users, the concept of acceptable level of risk is difficult to understand. Users expect that data processing personnel want to take those measures necessary to ensure the most effective processing. Unless they understand the costs associated with zero defects, they are not willing to accept the fact that they will receive anything less than perfection. Once users fully understand that the cost of perfection is unrealistic, and in fact the level of loss is frequently decided by a programmer, the user may be more receptive to this concept. What the acceptable level of risk attempts to define is that point where controls are optimized. If more controls were added, the cost of controls would exceed the savings, and if fewer controls were in existence, the loss associated with the lack of controls would exceed the cost of controls.

KEY CONCEPT

When the user fails to state what loss is acceptable, the auditor must make that judgment in order to develop an opinion of the adequacy of control.

Task 3: Define the optimum control point

The acceptable level of risk is that point where the cost of control is optimized. (See Figure 7 in Chapter 3 for an explanation of the cost-effectiveness of data processing controls.) Once the user has made this decision, the adequacy of control is no longer a matter of dispute, but a matter of fact.

DETERMINE CONTROL OBJECTIVES RULES

1. Identify the magnitude of the data base risks.
2. Determine the acceptance level of loss for those risks.
3. State the achievement of the acceptable level as a control objective.

STEP 6: PROVE DATA BASE INTEGRITY

The auditor cannot develop an opinion about the data base based upon audit testing unless the integrity of the data base has been proved. The conclusions based upon the testing of a sample of the data base cannot be extrapolated to the entire data base unless the auditor is assured of the integrity of the entire data base. This is an extremely important aspect of the data base audit process.

Verifying the integrity of a data base is an extremely difficult process. The data base, unlike traditional computer files, is a composite of data from many areas of the organization. The proof of the integrity of the data base may not be directly confirmable to an external total. The process of proving the integrity may require proof of the individual segments of the data base.

In order to understand the process of proving the integrity of the data base, it is necessary to understand how the data base is structured. The data base is not a single grouping of data held together by a common bond. It is a larger grouping of data which are related in some manner, but normally not in a manner that allows the entire data base to be verified by proving an accumulated total to an external balance.

Organizations rarely have a single data base. It is more common to have multiple data bases which are normally organized by accounting cycles. The more common accounting cycles, which coincide with data base organization, are:

Revenue-related data
Personnel/payroll data
Production data
Expenditures/accounts payable data
Inventory/back order/purchase commitments data

The data base has both physical and logical attributes. However, the programmer is rarely concerned with either of these attributes. The programmer's concern with regard to the data base is only the data needed by that program. In order to understand these concepts, we need to understand how the data base is put together.

Data Base Structure

The data base is a grouping of interrelated data. The data need to be viewed from both a physical and a logical perspective. The physical structure is the place where the data physically reside on a disk storage device, while the logical structure is the way the data are tied together for use.

The physical and logical structures can be illustrated through the analogy of the corporate organizational structure. The physical structure of the data base is analogous to the physical office layout (see Figure 34). If we could view the blueprint of the offices of an

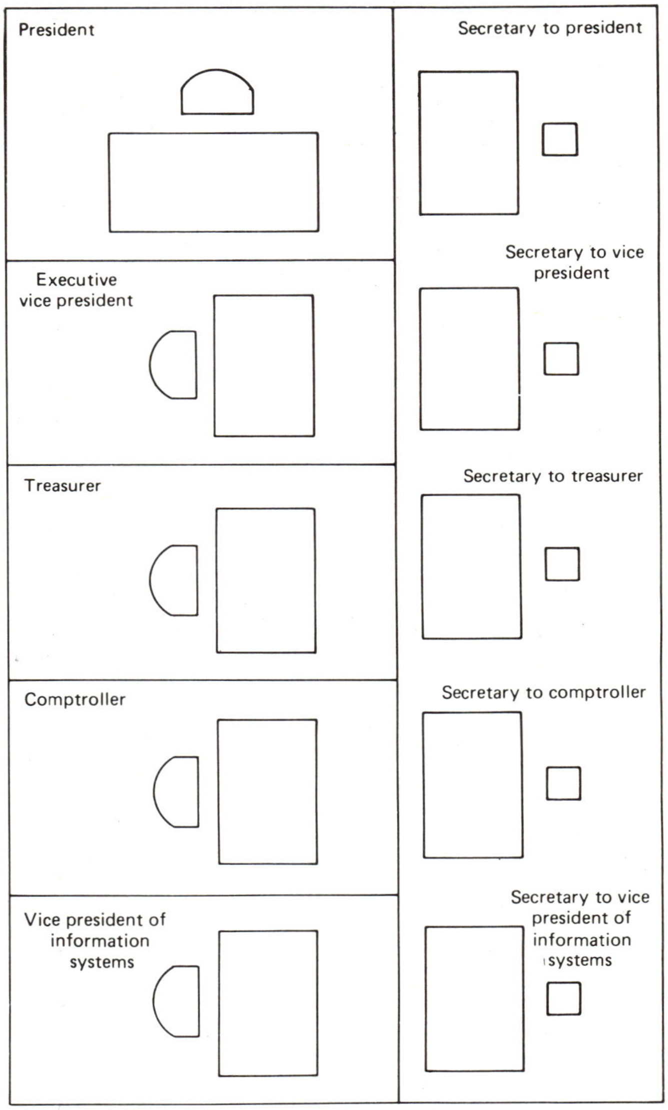

Figure 34. Physical Office Layout (Equivalent to Physical Data Base).

organization, we could see the building and floor and section in which each employee has his or her work station. In Figure 16 we see the physical office layout for the top officers of a corporation. The chart shows where the president and a secretary to the president sit. It shows where the other corporate officers are physically located, so if you wanted to visit them, you would know what building, what floor, and what office to go to. The physical layout of the office is the equivalent of the physical data base. It tells us where a specific piece of information is located.

The individual who works with data is more concerned with how they are logically connected than with their physical location. For example, the fact that the northeast corner on the top floor of corporate headquarters has blue wall-to-wall carpeting might be mildly interesting, but it would be much more valuable to know that the occupant of that office is the corporate president. With regard to the data base, the information about where data are physically located, may be interesting, but it is of little use. The logical structure tells us much more about the data than the physical structure. This is illustrated in Figure 35, which is an organizational chart for the corporation whose physical office layout we observed in Figure 34. Figure 35 shows us who reports to whom so that we can extrapolate the meaning of each position. The physical layout shows that the secretary is physically located next to the president, and we might assume that the two positions have equal importance, but when we observe the logical organizational structure we see that the secretary is in a staff position to the president, but the other officers are in a direct line position. The organizational chart as illustrated in the logical organizational structure (Figure 35) tells us much more about the organization than we learned from the physical layout. In data base terminology, the equivalent of the organizational chart is called the schema. The schema shows the relationship of every piece of data stored in the data base.

Most data base users are not concerned with either the physical data base or the logical data base. They are concerned with those pieces of data which are of value to them in processing. This is a subset of both the physical and logical data base, and is referred to in data base terminology as the subschema. The subschema is the program's or individual's view of the data base.

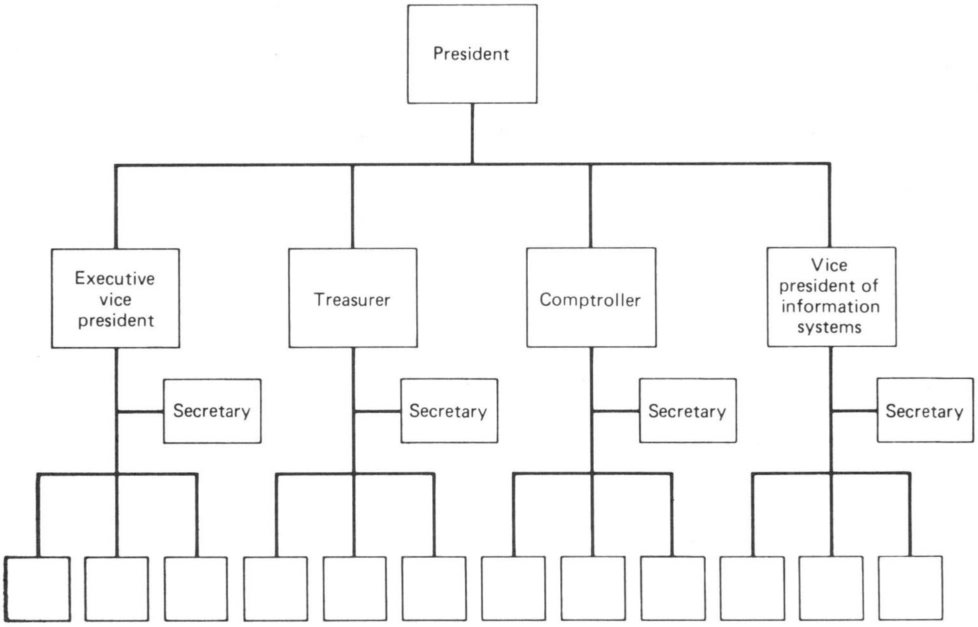

Figure 35. Corporate Organizational Structure (Equivalent to Data Base Schema).

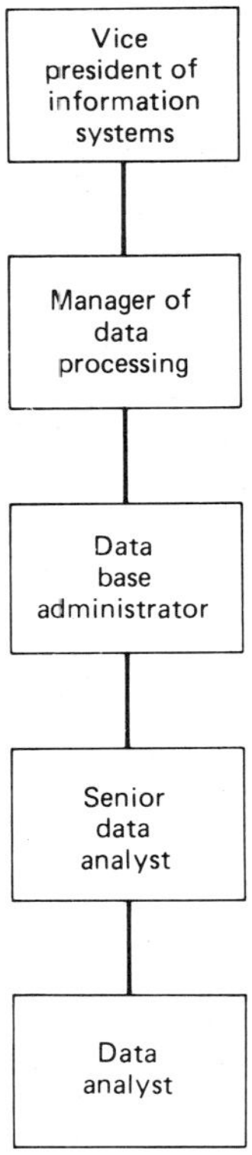

Figure 36. Information Systems Structure (Equivalent to Data Base Subschema).

The equivalent of the data base subschema is illustrated in Figure 36 as the information system structure of the corporate organization we have been studying. The individual viewing this segment of the logical organization (i.e., schema) might be the data analyst. The data analyst would have little concern with the treasurer or comptroller, but would have a lot of interest in the vice president of information systems. The area of interest to the data analyst would be the organizational structure in which the data analyst resides. The data analyst would want to know that within four promotions he could be the vice president of information systems. Likewise, the computer programmer is only concerned with that segment of the logical data base (i.e., schema) which is of interest to that programmer. For example, if the data base contained all of the personnel and payroll information in an organization, but the programmer was only concerned with the data processing department, those pieces of data relating to the data processing personnel would be the programmer's view or subschema of the data base.

Within a data base, there is one physical data base, one logical data base (i.e., schema), but an almost unlimited number of subschemas. In other words, each user of the data base can view the data base differently. It is this concept that causes difficulty in determining that the physical and logical data bases as well as the subschemas are accurate and complete.

Steps to Ensure Data Base Integrity

The verification of the integrity of the data base should concentrate on the accuracy and completeness of the schema. The physical location of data and the number of subschemas need not be of major consideration in verifying the integrity of the data base. If the auditor can ensure that the logical structure is complete, and that the information in that structure is accurate, the auditor will have proved the integrity of the data base.

The tasks that the auditor should follow in ensuring the integrity of the data base are:

Task 1: Understand data base schema

The first part of proving the integrity of the data base is to gain an understanding of the schema. This information is normally obtained from the data base administrator. Many data base administrators can supply the auditor with documentation, or a map describing the logical structure of the data base. This provides the auditor with an overview of both the data contained within the data base and the structure showing the relationship among the data within the data base. This information will establish the basis on which the auditor will verify the integrity of the data base.

Task 2: Determine DBA's integrity methods

The methods used by the data base administrator to ensure the integrity of the data base may be usable by the auditor for the same purpose. These methods may not ensure the accuracy and completeness of each piece of data; rather, they may ensure that the data entered into the data base have been retained in an accurate and complete manner. Most data base administrators have some mechanism to ensure themselves of the integrity of data in the data base. If they do not, the auditor should be doubly concerned about the integrity of the data base.

Task 3: Verify integrity of organizational structure

Most of the data in a data base are held together by pointers. Pointers are a series of direction finders that lead programs through the data base. In other words, record 1 points to record 2, which points to record 3 and so on until the last record in the string or chain has been identified. If there are records for which there is no pointer, or a group of records stops without an indication that it is the end of the chain or group of records, it is considered that there is a broken pointer, and thus the integrity of the structure will not be correct. Data base administrators normally have a utility program that can verify the integrity of the pointers. The auditors should either use this utility program or verify the fact that the data base administrator has recently proved the integrity of the pointers.

Task 4: Verify accuracy of data within the data base

The verification of the accuracy of a data base will be different than that of a computer file in that the data base may, in fact, be many files combined into one grouping of data. With a computer file, the key control fields are totaled and verified to an external source. In a data base, the primary verification will be a proof of existence of the totality of the data base data.

Most data bases are organized into groups of data frequently referred to as "records," "segments," "groups," and so on. The data base should have a control count on these groups of data which can be verified through utility programs. Again, the data base administrator should have the tools for the auditor to use in performing this accuracy verification.

The data base accuracy proof is a two-part process. The first part is the verification of the completeness of "records." This task involves verifying the accuracy of the count of records within the data base. The second part is the verification of the accuracy of data values.

The verification of the individual values in the data base can be accomplished during application audits. The verification of the integrity of the data base records is to ensure that during the audit of an application, all of the needed data are there and can be acquired.

The auditor during the data base audit may wish to verify the accuracy of a test sample of the groupings of data within an individual string of data, or, as commonly known, the subschemas. The auditor should interview some of the users of subschemas to determine whether they maintain an independent count of the groups of data within the subschema and control totals. Note that the data base administrator rarely has this independent total for use in verification. If one or more users maintain such a count and/or control totals (for example, the payroll department might have a count on the number of employees), and if there is one group of data for each employee, that subschema count can be readily verified using the data base verifier utility, together with the values of such data elements as year-to-date gross pay. At the end of this process, the auditor will have reasonable assurance of the integrity of the data base.

If there are no immediate plans to audit applications within the data base, the auditor should verify by test the accuracy of one or more subschema values. The application test is the final proof of the validity of the data within the data base.

PROVE DATA BASE INTEGRITY RULES

1. Learn about the data base structure.
2. Verify that the pointers are complete.
3. Verify that the count of records in the data base is correct.
4. Verify by testing the accuracy of subschema data values.

STEP 7: TEST CONTROLS

Auditors test data base controls for two purposes: first, to determine that controls function; and second, to determine the magnitude of a detected control weakness. The extent of tests conducted is normally based on the adequacy of controls.

Most data base controls are general or environmental controls. For example, the controls govern security, service level, and so on. These controls may be more difficult to test than the application data-oriented controls. For example, it is more difficult to determine that service levels are adequate than it is to verify that a product price has been properly calculated.

Many of the data base risks are not directly related to data. It is for this reason that the testing may be more difficult than application data testing. Not only does it require new tools and techniques, but it also requires new methods to estimate the severity of a detected control weakness.

Selecting Data Base Audit Tools

The data base test tools are described in Appendix B, and the situations in which to use those tools are described in the material covering auditing the individual data base activities. The auditor should be familiar with the data base tools and how to use those tools. In a data base environment, the auditor must understand the data base activities, risks, control, and audit tools.

The selection of the appropriate tool is an important part of the data base process. The primary criteria for determining which tool is appropriate are the evidence being evaluated and the audit objective. To aid in the tool selection process, audit tool recommendations are included in the data base activity auditing chapters for each of the identified data base audit objectives.

Estimating the Magnitude of a Data Base Control Weakness

Once a control weakness has been detected, the magnitude of that weakness should be estimated. Management needs to know both the weakness that exists and its magnitude. Without knowing the magnitude, management does not have the appropriate information to make a control decision. If the severity is low, controls need not be tightened, but if severity is high, then new controls may need to be added.

The four most common methods of estimating the magnitude of a detected control weakness are:

Judgment
History
Cost to fix
Formula

The judgment method is one of the most common ways to determine the magnitude of a control weakness. The auditor, usually in conjunction with the auditee, develops an opinion on what is considered to be the magnitude of the control weakness. This judgment is normally not supported by facts, but in organizations where the auditor is well respected and has a history of good judgment, the estimate is normally accepted by management.

The history method is also a common method used to estimate the magnitude of a control weakness. The auditor or auditee will determine the magnitude of the loss in the past, and then extend that loss into the future to estimate the potential loss if conditions are not changed. In those instances where history is most likely to be repeated, such as with data entry errors, this is a very effective and believable method. However, both history and judgment fall short when the control weakness is in a new area, such as data base. In that instance, the auditor has neither experience or past judgment to rely upon in making future estimates.

The cost-to-correct method identifies both the problem and what it will cost the organization to correct that problem. For example, if an invoice is mispriced, the auditor can determine how much it will cost to correct the invoice, and that then becomes the estimated loss. This is effective in a situation where the intangible loss is very difficult to estimate, and even if it was estimated it would probably not be believable.

The formula method is the newest approach. The method is based on risk analysis which uses the annual loss expectation (ALE) formula (i.e., ALE = frequency of occurrence x loss per occurrence). This formula requires the auditor to estimate the average expected loss for each occurrence attributable to the control weakness and then estimate the frequency of that occurrence on an annual basis. When the two variables of the formula multiply together they produce the annual loss expectation or severity of the loss due to the detected control weakness. This is a more scientific approach to estimating potential loss. It has gained acceptance by many auditors and senior management, but there are many others who believe this is more of a guessing game in scientific garb. The method is more effective when the frequency and average loss can be based upon some testing or historic event.

TEST CONTROLS RULES

1. Understand data base test tools.
2. Test to determine control functions as specified.
3. Test to determine the magnitude of control weakness.

STEP 8: EVALUATE WHETHER CONTROLS ACCOMPLISH CONTROL OBJECTIVE

Well-designed tests provide proof as to whether or not the installed controls accomplish the stated control objectives. This statement is based on two premises: first, that control objectives are stated in quantitative terms; and second, that the auditor estimates the severity of the control weakness. A weakness can be defined as the inability of controls to reduce the loss to zero. In most instances, it is uneconomical to have ''zero'' defects, so there is a control weakness.

In developing an evaluation on the effectiveness of controls, the auditor must:

Consider magnitude of data base risks. The auditor must identify the risks in the data base environment, as these provide the basis for developing the evaluation.

Identify data base control objectives. The control objective defines the acceptable level of loss in a risk situation. Until the auditor understands the control objectives, it is difficult to evaluate the effectiveness of controls. Controls normally will have some degree of effectiveness, and until that effectiveness can be measured against the acceptable level of loss, the auditor is placed in the position of having to establish the loss's standard and then evaluate against the auditor-established standard. The problem is even more difficult in a data base environment, where losses are more difficult for the auditor to estimate.

Identify data base controls and evidence. The auditor must recognize the new data base controls and the new data base evidence. Again, this may be more difficult in a data base environment because precedence has not clearly established good control practices. Also, in many instances data base personnel cannot differentiate controls from data base procedures, leaving it to the auditor to identify controls personally.

Estimate magnitude of control weakness. The final part of the evaluation process comes out of the test process. At the conclusion of the testing, the auditor must make an estimate about the magnitude of the control weakness.

At the conclusion of this process, the auditor will have a series of minor judgments about specific control objectives. The final part of the audit process will be developing an audit opinion based on the totality of information and evaluations made during the audit process.

EVALUATE WHETHER CONTROLS ACCOMPLISH CONTROL OBJECTIVE RULES

1. Identify control objectives.
2. Determine strength of controls.
3. Document control weaknesses.

STEP 9: DEVELOP DATA BASE OPINION

At the conclusion of the audit process, the auditors should develop an opinion on the following two topics:

1. *Integrity of the data base.* The auditor should form an opinion as to whether application auditors can rely on the integrity of the data base when they conduct their audits. If the application auditors can rely on the integrity of the data base, then they can conduct samples and draw conclusions about the data base population from those samples. On the other hand, if the integrity cannot be relied upon, then the application auditors may have to do more substantive testing or conduct procedures to prove the integrity of that segment or subschema of the data base which is used by the application system.
2. *Adequacy of data base controls.* Management needs to know whether the controls over the data base are adequate. This opinion should identify not only whether they are adequate, but how adequate they are. For example, if data base controls are too extensive it might be desirable for management to eliminate some of the controls, while if controls are inadequate management needs to know how much the controls need to be tightened.

Both of the above opinions are important. The opinion about adequacy of controls is needed to adjust the level of controls. The ôpinion about the integrity of the data base is important because it can save the application auditors a significant amount of time during their audits. In actual practice the two opinions are usually closely related. If controls are inadequate, it is normally difficult to substantiate the integrity of the data base, and vice versa.

DEVELOP DATA BASE OPINION RULES

1. Develop an opinion on the adequacy of controls.
2. Develop an opinion on the integrity of the data base.

The remainder of the book is directed at conducting the detailed audit process. One chapter is devoted to each of the previously identified data base activities. These chapters will explain how to conduct audit steps 4 through 8. The last chapter in the book will cover Step 9, developing a data base audit opinion.

KEY CONCEPT

A structure data base audit program provides a higher probability of success for an auditor with minimum data base skills.

six

AUDITING THE DATA BASE ORGANIZATIONAL STRUCTURE

Creating the proper data base organizational structure is one of the keys to success in using data base technology. The impact of data base usage on the organization, coupled with the shifting responsibilities caused by data base, requires changes in the organizational structure. It is important that the changes be made prior to the introduction of data base technology, and that the involved parties understand their specific responsibilites.

Data base, unlike some other data processing technology innovations, must have strong senior management support to succeed. The effective use of data base requires that data be managed as resources of the organization. This only occurs when senior management recognizes the value of information and then takes positive steps to establish the appropriate organizational structure in order to manage information properly.

This chapter defines an ideal data base organizational structure. This structure closely parallels that being used by some recognized leaders in the use of data base technology. The responsibilities for each function are defined in order to show the control responsibilities in data base and how they can best be divided.

The chapter covers the organizational control objectives needed to address data base organizational risks. A detailed audit program for the organizational activity is included. The audit program contains recommended evaluation criteria, together with the controls, audit tests, and audit tools needed to perform an assessment as to whether or not the listed organizational control objectives have been achieved.

ORGANIZATIONAL STRATEGY

Associated with the implementation of data base technology are three distinct responsibilities. They are establishment of data base policy, technical leadership, and administrative responsibilites. The extent of those responsibilities and the organizational implications are dependent upon the use of data base technology.

Organizations develop an organizational strategy based upon who manages data within the organization. Frequently, this strategy is not formal but, rather, a result of management actions or lack of actions. The strategy changes depending upon whether the user manages data or the organization manages data.

The desirable strategies relating to organizational structure are illustrated in Figure 37. The strategy shows that when the users manage data there are few organizational problems, but as the data base become more sophisticated and moves toward management of data as an organizational resource, the problems increase. The strategies listed in Figure

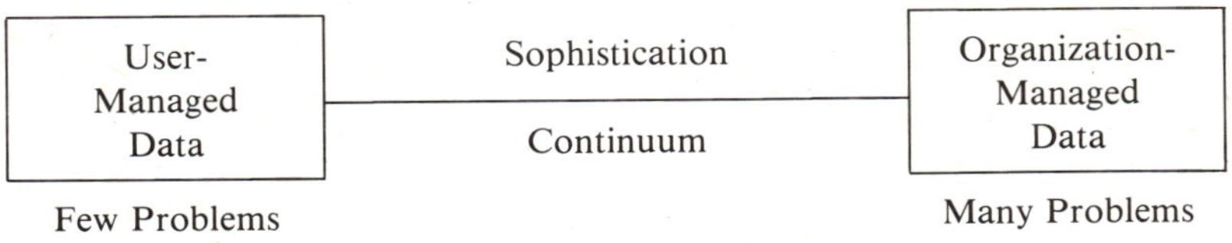

Desirable Strategy	Problem If Strategy Is Not Used
Prime Strategy	
1. To use data base as a management tool	Assignment of responsibilities
2. To initiate a separate group to manage data and data base technology	Assignment of responsibilities
Other Strategy	
1. To segregate duties within the data base administration function	Assignment of responsibilities
2. To establish a data policy.	Assignment of responsibilities

Figure 37. Organizational Strategy.

37 are representative of those that lead toward organization-managed data. When this happens, the problems associated with it are primarily assignment of responsibility problems.

The two prime strategies for managing data as resources of the organization are, first, to consider data base as a management tool, and, second, to initiate a separate group to manage data. This separate group is frequently referred to as the data base administration function. Secondary strategies involve segregating the duties within the data base administration function and establishing a data policy. Both are results of implementing the primary strategies. Again, when these other strategies are used they cause assignment of responsibility problems.

As organizations begin to manage data as organizational resources, it becomes necessary to define the policy, technical, and administrative responsibilities into an organizational structure. The policy level must deal with information strategy and planning, while the technical and administrative levels have responsibility for the implementation of the data policies and plans.

The primary data base concern for the auditor is whether the organizational structure has the proper assignment of responsibility. In those organizations where there is clear segregation among the policy, technical, and administrative responsibilities, there appears to be a much higher degree of success in use and acceptance of data base technology. On the other hand, in those organizations where a single individual or group encompasses the policy, technical, and administrative responsibilities, the probability of problems is significantly increased, and the acceptance and use of data base technology are inhibited due to the lack of appropriate direction.

AUDIT GUIDELINE

Proper definition and assignment of data base responsibilities are essential for an adequately controlled data base environment.

RECOMMENDED ASSIGNMENT OF RESPONSIBILITIES

In establishing an organizational structure for the use of data base technology, both the policy and operational level must be considered. Policy is the senior management responsibility. Operational administrative and technical tasks are a data processing responsibility. It is generally impractical to attempt to have a single individual fulfill both policy and operational responsibilities when data are managed as resources of the organization.

The management structure recommended for a data base environment is illustrated in Figure 38. This structure is designed to identify individual responsibilities as opposed to positions within the data base structure. For example, in a very small organization there may be only a single person serving as data base administrator, in which case that individual may have to perform all of the technical and administrative functions. On the other hand, in some large organizations the data base operational unit may encompass over 100 individuals, and there is a close parallel between the structure shown in Figure 20 and the actual organizational chart of that company.

The policy level should be the responsibility of a member of senior management. This data administrator function need not be a full-time responsibility, but it does need to be

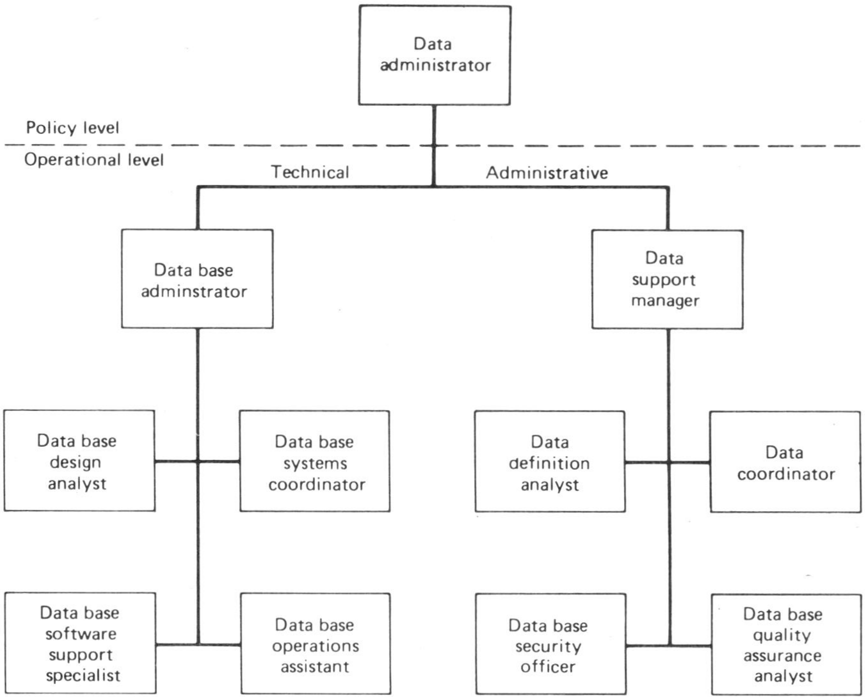

Figure 38. Management Structure Recommended in a Data Base Environment.

assigned to senior management. In some organizations an administrative vice president or vice president in charge of information systems may also perform the data administrator function. However, as the management of data as organizational resources becomes a reality, the data administrator function will consume more and more time of the individual performing that function.

A dilemma faced by many organizations is which background is preferable for the data base administrator—an administrative or technical background. When an organization chooses a data base administrator with a technical background, that individual is normally more concerned with the operation and technical proficiency of the data base than with the use of that data base and interacting with the users. When a data base administrator with a systems or administrative background is chosen, that individual normally acquires technicians to manage the technical part of the data base, and personally concentrates on the administration of data and interface with the users.

The recommended solution is to have two individuals divide the data base administration function. One takes the technical aspects of data base and another the administrative. Again, it is not necessary for either to be a full-time responsibility, although in larger organizations it is more than a full-time responsibility. An approach used by organizations to introduce data base technology is to assign the technical responsibility to systems programmers, and the administrative responsibilities to a member of data processing management.

If an individual is chosen to direct the data base administration function, it is recommended that that individual be an administrator, normally from the systems side of the data processing department. The real problems with data base are administrative and not technical. The technical problems can be resolved with time and effort by data processing personnel. The administrative considerations involve the coordination and support of many parts of the organization and are much more difficult to attain.

Below is a brief overview of each of the identified responsibilities on the recommended data base organizational structure. In addition, there is a list of the typical responsibilities that go with each function. These descriptions and responsibilities can be helpful both in establishment of a data base administration function and in review by the auditor in identifying whether or not the data base responsibilities have been adequately assigned and, if so, whether the assignment of responsibilities is reasonable.

Data administrator. This individual establishes the data policy for the organization. The policy must take into consideration the needs and requirements of the organization as well as those of the user. The data administrator will interpret and define the policy so that the operational units can properly implement that policy. This individual also resolves disputes over jurisdiction, consistency, reliability, and security of information among various users. In some organizations, particularly financial organizations, the data administrator may prepare formal data policy for issuance to users of the information processed by that organization. Detailed responsibilities are listed in Figure 39.

1. Establish data policy for the company.
2. Establish information strategy consistent with information needs of the company.
3. Arbitrate data and information policy disputes among members of senior management.
4. Develop liaisons with other firms' industry vendors and other standards groups to promote advancement of the profession.
5. Work with senior DP management and top corporate management to develop corporate strategies and plans in which information plays a key role.

Figure 39. Data Administrator Job Responsibilities.

Data base administrator. The data base administrator title is given to the individual having technical responsibility for the data base. This individual must study the information needs of the organization and then construct the data base that can satisfy those information needs economically, efficiently, and effectively. This technical individual is not concerned with how the data are used but, rather, that they are entered, stored, and retrievable in a manner that facilitates the use of information within the organization. Primary responsibilities include the selection of data base software and the definition of the physical and logical data structure. Detailed responsibilities are listed in Figure 40.

Data base design analyst. This individual is responsible for designing and implementing the data base structure. Working within the constraints posed by the data base management system and the organizational requirements, the individual attempts to optimize data base productivity and to continue to monitor it so that changes can be made where appropriate. The individual would recommend changes or extensions in the use of data base software and hardware facilities in order to ensure the effective use of data base technology. Detailed responsibilities are listed in Figure 41.

Data base systems coordinator. Application project personnel using data base technology interact with the systems coordinator to understand the data base structure so that they can optimize application systems. This individual is a technical consultant to the application project personnel to ensure that the data needs of the application are being met. This individual is concerned with the structure and retrieval algorithms and not with the meaning or composition of individual elements of data. Detailed responsibilities are listed in Figure 42.

Data base software support specialist. One of the major advantages of data base technology is the series of utilities and capabilities provided with the DBMS. Many organizations, particularly those using data base as an access method, acquire data base technology for the utilities supplied with the DBMS. This individual assists project personnel in using those utilities and capabilities effectively. Many users have direct access to the data base through these utilities. The improper use of the utilities can yield very poor results, so this individual is concerned not only with use but also with productivity in the use of utilities. Detailed responsibilities are listed in Figure 43.

Data base operations assistant. This individual works with computer operations to ensure continuity of processing of the data base technology. When problems occur, this individual helps both diagnose and correct the problem. The individual may train operators in how to use the DBMS and the meaning of and action to be taken on operations messages. Detailed responsibilities are listed in Figure 44.

1. Supervise all technical aspects related to data base activity.
2. Be involved in decisions about acquisition of DBMS and related software and hardware. Manage evaluation and selection process.
3. Maintain liaison with industry, vendors, and standards to ensure a good feel for technical trends, problems, solutions, and alternatives available to company.
4. Answer technical questions for data processing management. Advise data processing management on technical issues.
5. Develop technical plans needed to support long-range data processing activity. Identify technical alternatives available and generate sufficient information for informed decision.
6. Ensure that there are adequate documentation and administrative procedures to control and coordinate the technical activities involved in the data base environment.
7. Make recommendations about prioritization and selection of data base systems development projects.

Figure 40. Data Base Administrator Job Responsibilities.

1. Design the global data base structure for all data base applications and have overall responsibility for all data base related systems development.
2. Assist programmer/analyst in developing logical views of the data base and approve all logical views developed.
3. Select appropriate access method and physical structure of all data.
4. Develop and design backup, audit trail, logging, and other data base support files.
5. Develop and design restart/recovery strategies, procedures, and processes.
6. Develop plans for the orderly growth or migration of data base structures, including global, physical, and logical.
7. Develop and design all data security strategy for data base. Identify security alternatives.
8. Design data base to include requirements for privacy, integrity, and auditability.
9. Develop and select searching algorithms, hash or randomizing routines, secondary indices, data paths used, and other access strategies.
10. Develop strategies to answer the following design tradeoff problems:

    Throughput versus response time (batch or on-line needs)
    Storage efficiency versus retrieval and processing speed
    Flexibility versus efficiency (amount of data independence)
    Complexity versus usage (do you really need to do everything?)

    All of the above must be done in a context of hardware limitations, software limitations, cost constraints, and business needs.
11. Use design tools to model, simulate, or test data base designs, especially when tradeoffs are the ones mentioned above or close to them (i.e., hardware/software limitations, cost, business needs).
12. Recommend techniques or tools to monitor data base activity.
13. Develop and establish criteria which determine when a data base will be reorganized or restart/recovery will be executed. (Note: This is different from No. 5, which relates to an application or system. This item is related to hardware, system software, or recording media problems or user error which requires some action.)
14. Recommend hardware, configuration changes, system software additions, modifications, or deletions.
15. Recommend and work with security officer to develop encryption/compaction strategies, procedures, and algorithms.
16. Assist programmer/analyst in use of data base systems development tools, for example:

    Tools to simplify screen development and formating
    Tools to simplify transaction formating and transmissions
    Tools to diagnose and analyze dumps, traces, and error messages
    Tools for configuration simulation
    Tools for volume testing
    Tools for performance analysis
    Tools for data base fix and interrupt routines
    Tools for interactive data base generation, especially when one uses TSO, data dictionary, library generation utilities, standard subroutines, data base generation utilities, and all associated JCL problems, including mapping routines, statistical summary of calls, hardware or software monitors, billing information
17. Recommend appropriate billing or chargeback algorithms to reflect resources used.
18. Review and suggest refinements based on actual versus predicted performance of data base design. Should be reported at particular point in time such as six months after installation of system.
19. Identify and recommend systems problems which could be addressed by change to system software or addition of replacements for existing systems software. Work with the data base software support specialist to accomplish this task.
20. Define rules or procedures which programmer/analyst must follow in use of DBMS calls or structures. Define rules related to multiple processing, process mode use, concurrency avoidance and interlock (deadly embrace) avoidance, and degree of data independence.
21. Review and approve all application programs for compliance to data base systems development standards.
22. Maintain a complete inventory of data base related software (other than application programs). Inventory show utilities, "fixes" applied, version number, release number, vendors, critical hardware and support system, languages, report writers, query languages, documentation source, individual responsible, local standards manual, and so on as needed to serve as reference and coordinate activity. Note features not to be used, known logic errors, or company restrictions (e.g., warm or cold start).

Figure 41. Data Base Design Analyst Job Responsibilities.

1. Be responsible for the proper installation and implementation of data base systems. Manage and coordinate all maintenance or modification of all installed data base systems. Approve all changes to existing data base systems except when the system is being completely redesigned. Approve all installation plans, procedures, testing, and training.
2. Monitor data base activity from an end user viewpoint to suggest either hardware, software, or user changes. Select terminals, peak activity, user training and skills, business activity, screen formats, downtime to user, slow time (periods of poor response time—often at peak demand periods which is the worst time from a user's viewpoint), number of terminals (cluster) or lines (configuration), use of query or report writers, log-on time, and so on. May all be variables which are monitored and manipulated as needed to provide service level and continuity of processing.
3. Review and approve all new systems for compliance to design and operational standards. Work with data base operations assistant and data base design analyst in the performance of this task.
4. Design, develop, and maintain the billing or chargeback for data base related resources. Develop chargeback strategies that encourage the optimal use of corporate data base resources. Review and control the collection of billing information to ensure accurate chargebacks. Answer chargeback-related questions for management.
5. Manage and coordinate performance tuning activities which relate to data base systems. Set standards related to amount of free space established during reorganization or changes in compaction or encryption algorithms for performance reasons. Set standards for deletion or dumping of old data consistent with processing needs. Develop time tables or schedules for data base migration as processing activity increases.
6. Provide feedback to data base design analyst and programmer/analyst to suggest alternative or better design and programming practices or tools.
7. Use appropriate mathematical modeling techniques to monitor and predict data base system activity. Develop plans of action to provide a smooth transition in an often dynamic data base environment.
8. Use and analyze statistics about information such as disk space use, buffer or queue activity, data base accesses, response time, to plan reorganization or data base structural changes. Prepare reports and charts about this process.
9. Analyze all exceptions in the data base operation to develop strategies to correct this program. Prepare summary reports of these individual exceptions. Analyze and make recommendations about actions that should be taken to eliminate or reduce exceptions.
10. Keep and analyze records of all data base support activity such as logging, backup, audit trails, dumps, and so on to ensure adequate service level and continuity of operations.
11. Review and analyze all systems development activity from an operational perspective to ensure good use of all available resources.
12. Identify long-term training needs.
13. Review overall coordination of security, privacy, and data integrity to ensure consistency and proper consideration for performance needs.
14. Suggest changes to hardware, system software, configuration (change means addition, deletion, or modification) to ensure consistent data base processing capability.
15. Monitor closely some critical data base activity such as use of data dictionary, application of system software fixes, emergency corrections to application programs or data, or use of load modules (libraries).
16. Review all plans for new hardware or software for implication to current or future data base environment.
17. Review and suggest alternatives to operating documents and forms.
18. Work with vendors for planning and coordination of new releases or versions of software and hardware.
19. Prepare and coordinate all long-term data base system schedules and plans.

Figure 42. Data Base Systems Coordinator Job Responsibilities

Data support manager. This individual has administrative responsibilities for use of the data base. The responsibilities focus on the data and the use of those data. This individual need not be a technician or concerned with the physical and logical structure of the data base, although most data support managers understand the logical structure of the data base. This individual has responsibility to ensure that data are properly defined, that people understand that definition, and that the data in the data base will, in fact, be representative of the data definition. Detailed responsibilities are listed in Figure 45.

1. Be responsible for all system software maintenance in the data base environment. Perform installation and periodic generation of the DBMS and DD/D. Adapt software to new configuration and new hardware.
2. Test and certify all new releases, versions, or fixes for various DBMS and related packages.
3. Specifically test and install the following interfaces, especially as installations make changes:
   End user—especially query and report writers
   Application development tools or aids
   Data design modeling, testing, simulating aid
   Operational performance monitors, statistics, and exception reporting packages
   Backup, R/R and reorganization utilities, planning and control software, including logging, audit trail, and dump facilities
   Security, audit and integrity assurance package or features
   Data dictionary and related support facilities
4. Review and suggest changes to operating system or hardware interfaces.
5. Identify, record, explain, suggest impact and possible corrective alternatives for all located security holes such as known "back door," "hooks," "trap doors," unfixed logic errors, and so on. These should be coordinated and controlled with the security officer.
6. Identify all known "bypass" mechanisms which exist on most system software and undertake efforts to control their use. This is done with the data base security officer.
7. Periodically analyze system failure to determine if there is some pattern which appears "causable" (for example, system overload, line dropping). Service disruption or unauthorized activity may be the reason for system fractures. Work with the security officer.
8. Identify controls which depend on specific firmware or microcoding for periodic review (about once every year). Work with the security officer.
9. As new system releases or versions appear, review standards and procedures which relate to the passing of control parameters (e.g., status codes) to ensure consistent and proper treatment. Watch for older applications which may have used even older standards. Changing of parameter handling library routines may adversely affect some application programs.
10. Design, develop, modify, or prepare vendor request for system utilities or software to support data base related activity. This activity will bridge interface problems or entrance processing unique to the company's operations. Work with systems programmers and vendors to provide the system software.
11. Review control and use of data base support output, for example, dumps from buffers, queues, or other intermediate storage (spooled output print files, pools, core storage, registers, screen files, buffered terminals, controllers, or front-end minis). These are often dumped (hex makes it like encryption), but simple scan will reveal little. An innovative programmer could, for example, cause payroll records to be moved into various buffers, then overload or drop lines and cause system failure. Then he would review buffers to find salaries of people he wished.
12. Suggest and recommend additional hardware and system software in support of data base activities.
13. Review vendor documentation, application development standards, and operational standards for impact of system software and software interface coordination. Work with customer and system engineers.
14. Plan, coordinate, direct, and manage the orderly migration and growth of the data base system software.
15. Assist in the preparation of all JCL or parameter control cards for data base system software. Establish standards as needed in this area consistent with security and control needs.
16. Promote a self-tuning, adaptive, self-controlling, and self-regulatory data base environment.
17. Review and evaluate all support packages designed to generate code for use in the data base environment. Implications for data base standards and control are particularly addressed.
18. Work with security officer to maintain program linkage tables and controls. Program linkage tables indicate to which other programs, routines, or commands a program may be linked. A common practice (called "Trojan Horse") used to circumvent security was to imbed one program in another. (Once cleared, the interprogram links up to anything the outerprogram is authorized to do or links up to other facilities if linkage is not controlled (historical problem).) All logs and records reflect processing of outerprogram.

Figure 43. Data Base Software Support Specialist Job Responsibilities.

1. Supervise, monitor, and analyze restart/recovery operations. Analysis should assign probable cause (e.g., program, user, hardware, DBMS, operator, operating system), identify effect on data or transactions, notify effect personnel, suggest corrective course of action, and produce exception report.
2. Supervise and review all master terminal operations. Ensure that operators are properly trained and that documentation and exception procedure provided for applications are correct and adequate. Research and resolve any operational problem with appropriate vendors, analysts, or programmers.
3. Assist in any testing or system development activity to ensure compliance with any or all operations standards.
4. Develop and maintain standards needed to control and manage operational activities related to the data base environment.
5. Ensure that checkpointing procedures are adequate for data base recovery from all possible failures. Typical errors are program failure, system failure, recording media (disk) failure, human error.
6. Develop procedure for timely detection and correction of errors, and prevention of errors (for example, automation of as many human processes as possible).
7. Supervise and review all reorganizations of data base. Ensure that reorganizations are complete, timely, and adequate to maintain required service levels and continuity of operations.
8. Analyze and resolve any data errors or data structure errors detected by reorganization process. Produce exception report and suggest corrective action as well as probable cause of error. Notify appropriate personnel.
9. Identify and coordinate process schedules related to data base activity (e.g., reorganization time, system generation, R/R).
10. Review test and installation of all new system software related to data base operation. This includes all new releases, versions, and fixes. Change standards and procedures as needed to reflect new features, options, or capabilities added as well as hardware and software configuration changes. Ensure that all the above possible changes are documented by vendor, analyst, or programmer. Suggest alternatives which will aid operational efficiency or effectiveness.
11. Schedule and coordinate all on-site and off-site backup of data bases as needed. Ensure that all logs, dumps, audit trails, or other vital record-keeping activities are completely and correctly performed.
12. Supervise all data base conversions (related to data base structure change or change of recording media—new disk drive or computer) to ensure continuity of operations and no data loss or degradation.
13. Perform trouble shooting as needed to maintain service level and continuity of operations. Flag data or transactions affected or in error. Identify probable causes, notify proper personnel, prepare exception report, suggest corrective action, both short term and long term.
14. Use any available redundant data or files to identify or control data discrepancies.
15. Monitor access and use of all libraries or load modules to ensure proper control, maintenance, and generation.
16. Review sufficient usage information to plan and coordinate day-to-day activity.
17. Manage and control the operational use of the data dictionary in support of such functions as system generation, system development, and backup which may be beyond the technical skill of the data definition analyst.

Figure 44. Data Support Manager Job Responsibilities.

Data definition analyst. This individual has prime responsibility for the accuracy and completeness of the definition of data. In organizations using the data dictionary, this individual is normally responsible for that dictionary. The individual may recommend and be heavily involved in the selection and use of data dictionary software, as well as the way in which the data dictionary is integrated into the data base operating environment. This individual normally will establish the standards, forms, and procedures for documenting, modifying, adding, or deleting data from the organization's inventory of data. Detailed responsibilities are listed in Figure 46.

Data coordinator. Users of data work with this individual both to understand and to use data effectively. If auditors want information about the data in the data base, this is

1. Maintain an understanding of information and business needs of the company sufficient to plan and direct the collection and use of data within the company.
2. Develop and coordinate the information available for use in the company. Anticipate or estimate long-term corporate activity which can be aided by availability of particular information or data.
3. Develop plans and procedures that ensure data are accurate, complete, and authorized. User needs related to security, privacy, integrity, and timeliness are identified and coordinated.
4. Make recommendations about prioritization and selection of data base system development projects.
5. Identify data conflicts between users and act to coordinate data usage. For example, assure managers that they are not dependent upon someone whom they can't control for information or data to run their operation. All data needs will be enforced. Also, ensure that no rivalry develops, such as "I won't enter his data until he enters mine" or "Get controllers to collect this information and I will use it." No one wants to do dirty data entry and be subject to criticism.
6. Establish the policy or standards for:
   - Determining information sources to information output
   - Determining information availability
   - Determining information usage
   - Defining data definition policy
   - Determining or establishing data interrelationships
   - Determining use of calculated or derived data
   - Determining redundant or near redundant data (Near redundant data are data related to same-event record keeping, for example, sales transactions: dollar value and number of units sold may not be the same or relatable. Each sales unit sets own price which is not available.)
7. Be responsible for ensuring that users have confidence in the data base systems so that consistent utilization is maintained. This is the major task of the data support manager.

Figure 45. Data Base Operations Assistant Job Responsibilities

the individual they contact. The data coordinator is a consultant to project personnel and other users of data to explain what data are available, and how to acquire those data for use. Detailed responsibilities are listed in Figure 47.

Data base security officer. This individual has responsibility for security of data within the data base. In some organizations, this individual is placed outside the data base processing function. He or she defines the access rules, determines that the rules are being followed, and is normally heavily involved in the methods and procedures for ensuring security over data and the DBMS. In organizations where the security officer reports outside of the data base administration function, he or she normally has a close working relationship with that function. Detailed responsibilities are listed in Figure 48.

Data base quality assurance analyst. This individual is concerned with the quality aspects of the use of data base technology. The individual attempts to define quality from an information perspective and then develop the measures necessary to assess whether or not those quality standards are being achieved. This individual may provide an independent review of the use of data base technology, as well as counseling users on how to obtain the maximum benefits from data base technology. Normally this individual understands both the technical aspects of data base and the user's data needs. Detailed responsibilities are listed in Figure 49.

Use of the Function Responsibility Lists

The responsibilities listed for each of the above data base functions (Figure 39 through 49) are direct control implications. If the auditor determines that a particular responsibility has not been assigned or is included within the responsibilities of another function or of a single individual encompassing multiple functions, the auditor must ask what the control

1. Be fully responsible for all activity related to use of data dictionary. Work with the data base software analyst to ensure DD/D is properly generated and configuration is suitable for company needs.
2. Ensure that all naming conventions are followed. Work closely with data base design analyst and application programmer or analyst during systems development to ensure proper use of naming conventions. The following items should have naming conventions:
   - Data base (schema at all levels)
   - Logical view (subschema)
   - Data items (record, groups of records, and calculated records)
   - Transactions, message formats, and screens
   - Pools, buffers, queues, block, scratch pads (if named)
   - Programs and systems and related JCL
   - Terminals (logical and physical), nodes, and lines (if named)
   - Data sets, partitions, libraries, and routines
   - Access methods (data base and operating system) and randomizer
   - Application program data names
   - User IDs, passwords, user profile
3. Coordinate and control data ownership or data responsibilities with respect to compliance with established policy. Data should be appropriated by cross-referencing to impacted people, programs, or activities if a change is made in data, data structure, or data access.
4. Process any changes to data activity. Coordinate and review:
   - Data (physical or logical)
   - Data relationship
   - Logical views of data
   - Redundant data
   - Secondary indices
   - Data access and processing mode to ensure integrity
   - Data entry
   - Data edit and validation (includes transactions) rules and user needs to ensure validity, consistency, and accuracy
5. Advise users, programmers, and analysts about current and future data use. Ensure well-planned evolution of data base and processing activity given users' changing information needs. Identify current or potential conflicts of data use or definitions between applications or users. Estimate or coordinate estimate of data activity and use.
6. Establish special forms, procedures, or reports to coordinate and manage data development and use in the company.
7. Develop controls to ensure there is complete separation between test and live or production data.
8. Work with security officer and data base operations assistant to identify and control all utilities or techniques which can act outside of the data dictionary (integrated) control. (This does not include application programs which act with integrated DD/D.) Any utility which is specifically designed to or can change data or data structure will be closely monitored.
9. Work with application development analyst/programmers through all phases of project development.
10. Control backup copies of the data dictionary to ensure no security is compromised (e.g., encrypt).
11. Maintain any additionally needed cross-reference glossaries, references, or guide to supplement the DD/D.
12. Review all data entry programs or standards for compliance. Monitor data characteristics, including the following:
    - Range checks
    - Completion/existence check
    - Transaction or sequence of message checks
    - User responsible
    - Physical data characteristics such as format or possible values (A, B, or C) of fields
    - Trend limits
    - Error flag
    - Security
    - Privacy
    - Read, write capability
13. Direct or coordinate the use of such features as data "browsing":
    - Help commands
    - Data research efforts (e.g., keyword in definition search; is there any data related to "customer" and "industry" which marketing or credit department can use)
    - Interactive documentation or direction of low-volume data entry
14. Coordinate all user-prepared report practices to ensure proper use of corporate data.

Figure 46. Data Definition Analyst Job Responsibilities.

1. Serve as a point of contact for data base related information. Particularly, serve end users who do not have an ongoing contact with data base personnel.
2. Coordinate and manage all training services of the company related to the data base environment. This includes end users, programmer/analyst, systems programmers, as well as all members of the data administrator's staff.
3. Keep in touch with vendors, consultants, and industry with respect to services related to training, technology, or management of data base environment. Identify source for contract programming work, contract system software or application software development or data base related research.
4. Be responsible for distribution and publishing of all data base related standards, references, and guides. Identify sources for reference material not available within corporation.
5. Coordinate user manuals and documentation for data base applications.
6. Distribute and file all studies, reports, or white papers on data base related activities.
7. Be available for special studies with users or data processing management. Bring in the appropriate expertise as needed in performing studies. Identify data base opportunities for management. Work with various outside standards and industry groups to share data base experience. Help develop initial project feasibility study for data base systems.
8. Coordinate information which is needed to allow end users and other data processing management to prepare their long-range plans.

Figure 47. Data Coordinator Job Responsibilities.

1. Establish standards, procedures, and controls which are related to security in the data base environment.
2. Identify and investigate any security violations.
3. Develop or monitor user profiles, authorization list, or tables for automated or manual security.
4. Manage and direct activities related to:
   Password distribution, use, and change
   Encryption (and compaction) of data
   Other restrictions to access or process data
5. Resolve any conflicts or disputes related to corporate data security policies at the operational level.
6. Review and make recommendations related to potential security problems or threats. Identify alternative security procedures for management. Assist in security areas related to data security such as terminal, computer room, tape library program or system module libraries, program development or testing security which would ensure more effective security or efficiency in security process.
7. Perform security audits or reviews to determine compliance to security policy and procedures.
8. Personally control access to such things as password tables, authorization list, or encryption devices. Initiate changes in passwords, encryption keys, locks, or card keys at own discretion.
9. Review periodically list of attempted security violations.
10. Review systems at conversion or implementation time to ensure compliance with security policy and procedures.
11. Review software package related to security and features available on software to enhance security. Decide which packages to acquire, and monitor all security package installation, generation, and use. Work closely with data base software specialist in this area.
12. Maintain liaison with security personnel in industry, standards group, regulatory agencies, and vendors to ensure corporate practices are adequate.
13. Review security in areas which do not lend themselves to automated controls and ensure that management is aware of their responsibility in these areas. For example, during R/R, reorganization, or system failures, security facilities may not be in place to control access or provide security. Similarly, some activities tend to compromise security, such as trouble shooting or quick fixes under emergency situations where business needs require that one individual quickly perform several functions which would normally be separated for control purposes.
14. Ensure that controls are in place to coordinate any activity that does not work through the DBMS and the DD/D.
15. Perform configuration reviews to ensure that each component of a typical data base system has consistent security, for example, terminal, lines, nodes, controller, modems, CPU, peripherals, operating system, DBMS, application programs, computer room.
16. For critical data, identify, monitor, and control all possible access paths.
17. Control security over backup or recovery data.
18. Request and foster involvement by internal and external EDP auditors.

Figure 48. Data Base Security Officer Job Responsibilities.

1. Be responsible for consistent quality of activities in a data base environment. Identify and monitor critical activities. Identify and test quality at specific control points.
2. Ensure that there is compliance with authorized activities and that no compromising activities are performed. For example, in production, ensure that:
   - Programmers do not access data descriptions
   - DBA or DSM staff do not routinely operate computer
   - All libraries, data bases, and so on are constantly controlled by someone on DA staff
3. Test on a sample basis such things as:
   - R/R—before versus after
   - Reorganization—before versus after
   - Backup—before versus after
   - New DBMS release
4. Test and monitor activity of user and user management to ensure that they have procedures in place to capture data as needed by the corporation, not only their department. Tests include:
   - Timeliness
   - Accuracy
   - Data entry
   - Data usage
   - Completeness
   - Authorization
   - Error correction
   - Error analysis
5. Receive exception reports (may also be called audit evidence) related to the following:
   - Particular ABEND codes, either program, system, or data base failure
   - Particular status codes if ever returned (for example, security violations by production program—improper read attempted, etc.)
   - Data structure or logical view activity (any changes) for critical data bases
   - Certain periodic cross-reference listing which may highlight potential conflict (especially analysis of the tools—DD/D, DBMS, etc.)
   - Linkage maps of programs to programs for certain critical systems and JCL or JCL libraries
   - Copies of any dumps or traces performed on certain critical systems
   - Generation listings for certain critical software "gens"
   - Data usage statistics for certain critical systems
   - By-product listing and exception report related to use of certain critical utilities (SUPER ZAP) or executed against certain critical systems (reorganization output about critical data base which would reflect any pointer errors)
   - Console logs, system output summaries, schedules, configuration map, SMF data, job accounting data, and so on related to certain critical events; for example, security violations. Also look at system logs, checkpoint logs, message logs, image logs, and other R/R logs.
6. Work through and with the data dictionary to make sure it is the centralized control vehicle.
7. Review master terminal logs or activity reports to ensure compliance to standards related to:
   - Starting, stopping, or modifying all system resources; for example, warm or cold start
   - Execution of purges, flushing, dumps of buffers, registers, data bases, or queues
   - Controlling R/R such as logging interruption, checkpoint scheduling, or log blocking factors
   - Making configuration changes such as reassigning terminals, changing lines, or assigning controller posts
   - Modifying passwords, security, or authorization tables
   - Displaying contents or status of buffers, terminals, control blocks, queues, messages, passwords (security or authorization), tables, addresses, or data bases
   - Changing priority or class codes, job queues, or message queues
   - Using broadcast message facility
   - Inhibiting record-keeping activity, such as statistics, job accounting, SMF, and so on
8. Work with data base design analyst and data base software specialist to develop specific tests for inappropriate use of application development tools on utility-by-utility basis. Tests involve both management of utility and technical use of utility.

Figure 49. Data Base Quality Assurance Analyst Job Responsibilities.

implications of that responsibility assignment are. The audit program that follows for the organizational activity uses many of these responsibilities as evaluation criteria, and presents tests and tools that can be used to determine the impact of the assignment of data base responsibilities.

ORGANIZATIONAL DATA BASE RISKS

The two major organizational risks are:

1. That responsibilities will be inadequately assigned
2. That management will not support data base technology

Secondary risks associated with the data base organizational structure are:

1. That the organization will not detect inaccurate or incomplete data
2. That failure of the DBMS to perform as specified will not be detected
3. That data base fraud/embezzlement will occur
4. That there will be no independent review of data base systems
5. That the data base responsibilities will be inadequately documented
6. That management will fail to define performance criteria

These risks need to be addressed in establishing the organizational structure. An integral part of the audit process is determining that appropriate control is established through the organizational structure to minimize these data base risks. The audit process is facilitated when the risk is known and the acceptable level of risk is defined.

Organizations establish an effective level of risk when they define measurable data base control objectives. This book cannot state an acceptable level of risk for an organization, but does recommend specific control objectives for organizations to use as a model for designing organizational controls and as a base for auditors to use in assessing the adequacy of those controls.

The recommended data base control objectives can be used as audit objectives in assessing the adequacy of control. For example, one of the recommended data base control objectives is that data base responsibilities will be assigned to individuals. This can be turned into an audit objective such as "to determine that there is an individual responsible for each data base responsibility."

Fifteen control objectives are recommended for addressing organizatinal data base risks. The control objectives are listed in Figure 50, together with the data base risk they address (the risk number corresponds to the risk number used in Appendix F) and are described in more detail below.

To assign base responsibilities to individuals. Responsibilities assigned to a group and then not assigned as a specific individual's responsibility may be overlooked. One of the more serious problems in organizations using data base is the recognition by individuals of their specific data base responsibilities. Users frequently believe the data base administration group believes the user has that responsibility.

To see that user retains organizational responsibility for the accuracy, completeness, and security of his or her data. The data base administration function can administer data, but cannot be responsible for its accuracy, completeness, and security. Although the performance of these functions may be delegated to the data base administration group, responsibility cannot.

Number*	Risk	Recommended Control Objective
1.	Inadequate assignment of responsibilities	1. To assign data base responsibilities to individuals 2. To see that user retains organizational responsibility for the accuracy, completeness, and security of data 3. To perform independent reviews to ensure the adequate assignment of responsibilities
2.	Inaccurate or incomplete data in a data base	1. To see that the organizational structure is designed to ensure the adequate assignment of responsibilities
8.	Failure of the DBMS to function as specified	1. To see that the organizational structure is designed to ensure prompt detection and correction of DBMS errors 2. To document data base expectations
9.	Fraud/embezzlement	1. To divide responsibilities so that an individual cannot perform *and* conceal a single event
10.	Lack of independent data base reviews	1. To see that a data base review group is established that is independent of the data base function 2. To define review responsibilities
11.	Inadequate documentation	1. To document department data base organizational responsibilities in the department charter 2. To document individual data base responsibilities in their job description
13.	Lack of performance criteria	1. To define data base expectations in measurable terms
14.	Lack of management support	1. To ensure that senior management defines and enforces data policy 2. To ensure that senior management participates in data base decision making 3. To ensure that senior management supports independent data base review groups

*See Figure 8 for description of risk.

Figure 50. Organizational Control Objectives.

To perform independent reviews to ensure the adequate assignment of responsibilities. An audit function is necessary to ensure the division of responsibilities is adequate and that it works.

To design the organizational structure to ensure prompt detection and correction of data errors. Checks and balances within the organizational structure are important to the identification of errors. Establishing a structure so that one function checks the work of another has proved effective in detecting data base errors and ensuring their prompt correction.

To design the organizational structure to ensure prompt detection and correction of DBMS errors. Ensuring the integrity of data is a joint responsibility of the data base administration function and the user. Many of the controls exist within the DBMS, making it essential that DBMS errors are promptly detected and corrected. Establishing a structure in which one group checks the work of another facilitates this process.

To document data base expectations. Until expectations are defined and monitored the performance of the data base cannot be established. The more measurable these expectations, the greater the probability of satisfied users when they are met.

To divide responsibilities so that one individual cannot perform and conceal a single event. Fraud is more difficult when collusion is required, and unless one individual can both perform and conceal, collusion is necessary to perpetrate a fraud.

To establish a data base review group that is independent of the data base function. Obtaining an independent assessment of the adequacy of performance of the data base functions normally reduces the cost of those functions by early identification of errors and increases management's confidence in the ability of the function to meet its responsibilities.

To define review responsibilities. Resistance to independent reviews is significantly reduced when all parties are aware of those responsibilities and it is known that the review of all functions will be equal.

To document department data base organizational responsibilities in the department charter. The data base responsibilities assigned to each department or group having data base responsibilities should be defined in the charter for that department.

To document individual data base responsibilities in the job descriptions. Each individual having data base responsibilities should have those responsibilities documented and included within his or her job description, so that the individual is aware of those responsibilities and can be evaluated on their performance.

To define base expectations in measurable terms. Performance cannot be measured until criteria are established in measurable terms to evaluate the performance.

To ensure that senior management defines and enforces data policy. The policy on data management should be defined and enforced by senior management. Without this formal policy, there is no basis to develop data procedures, guidelines, and standards.

To ensure that senior management participates in data base decision making. The true expression of interest and support is direct involvement by senior management in the major data base decisions. At a minimum, senior management should be involved in decisions about organizational structure, acquisition of the data base management system and other major software pieces, and data base policy.

To ensure that senior management supports independent data base review groups. Senior management support of independent review groups is expressed through verbal and written testimonials, adequacy of staffing, and an interest in and support of review findings and recommendations.

GOOD ORGANIZATIONAL CONTROL PRACTICES

Data base technology introduces new risks and increases some of the existing risks. Some of the controls used to reduce those new or increased risks are new controls, while others are a reemphasis of existing controls. In order to assess the adequacy of data base controls, the auditor needs to understand both the control and the objective for using that control.

The data base controls described in this book are those used in practice by organizations having data base technology. The controls included are those that organizations state are effective. However, the assessment by the auditor of the effectiveness of a control will depend upon:

The risk being reduced
Magnitude of the risk
Acceptable level of loss

Effectiveness of implementation of the control
Support by management
Compensating effect of other controls

The auditor must take these factors into consideration when evaluating the effectiveness of controls. This is a complex process that is based on auditor judgment. However, the recommended data base audit process is designed to document controls in a manner that facilitates assessment.

The organizational activity risks, together with the controls used by organizations to reduce those risks, are listed in Figure 51. A description of the controls is included in Figure 52, with a detailed explanation of each control in Appendix A. These figures and the control appendix are designed to assist the auditor in evaluating the adequacy of data base controls.

Figure 51 lists the controls that the auditor will most commonly find installed to reduce specific data base risks. For example, the first organizational activity risk is inadequate assignment of responsibilities. The figure states that the control methods to ensure that responsibilities are adequately assigned include the assignment of responsibilities, segregation of duties, rotation of duties, and the use of a risk management team. Thus, if the auditor is concerned over the adequacy of assignment of responsibilities, the auditor might expect to find one or more of the four identified controls to be used by organizations to address the inadequate assignment of responsibilities risk.

The lists of controls in Figures 51 and 52 are not meant to be exhaustive; rather, they are controls used by those organizations with whom the author has had contact. In the opinion of the author, these are the more common controls used in the organizations having data base. However, auditors should expect to find other controls, and should judge those controls on their merits.

DATA BASE ORGANIZATIONAL ACTIVITY AUDIT PROGRAM

The review of the data base organizational activity provides the auditor with:

Evidence on which to base the adequacy of the organizational structure
Familiarity with the organizational structure as a basis for contacts in conducting audits of other data base activities
Identification of the method by which events are approved and occur within the data base organization

The organizational activity data base audit program presented in this chapter is designed to assess audit risk. Figure 50 has identified the control objectives that the auditor should assess for each of the organizational activity risks. To use the audit program, the auditor selects the appropriate control objectives for audit investigation.

The data base audit program in this and other data base activity audit chapters is designed to be used in the following manner:

1. Select risk and control objective

The auditor selects the desired risk and control objective and then refers to the part of the audit program dealing with the specific data base control objective.

Data Base Risks \ Data Base Activity	Controls
1. Inadequate assignment of responsibilities	Assignment of responsibilities Segregation of duties Rotation of duties Risk management team
2. Inaccurate or incomplete data in a data base	System error recovery group
8. Failure of DBMS to function as specified	Output control System error recovery group
9. Fraud/embezzlement	Risk management team Internal audit design review
10. Lack of independent data base reviews	Risk management team Independent review of design changes User signoff Second opinion Data base quality assurance function
11. Inadequate documentation	Operation documentation Data base charters Data base job descriptions
13. Lack of performance criteria	Processing performance standards
14. Lack of management support	Assignment of responsibilities Segregation of duties Processing performance standards Internal audit design review

Figure 51. Data Base Controls for the Organization Activity.

2. Review evaluation criteria

Each control objective has at least one evaluation criterion for the auditor to use in determining whether or not the control objective has been achieved. The most probable controls for each evaluation criterion are listed on the audit program. These are designed to provide the auditor with guidance on identifying the controls in order to develop an assessment about the adequacy of controls.

3. Develop preliminary control assessment

Based upon the controls in place, and the auditor's judgment of the strength of those controls, a preliminary assessment is made regarding the adequacy of controls. Four categories are recommended for the assessment as follows:

Overcontrolled. The auditor believes that the controls are excessive based upon the risk and the control objective.

Adequate. The controls are adequate to reduce the risk to an acceptable level.

Number	Control Name	Control Description
1.	Assignment of responsibilities	Making individuals accountable for their functions
2.	Segregation of duties	Splitting functions so that no one individual has the responsibility for performing a function and at the same time has responsibility for using the results of that function
3.	Operation documentation	Detailing of operating procedures
4.	Output control	Detailing of the procedures for preparing and disseminating output results
5.	Rotation of duties	Limiting the amount of time any one individual has day-to-day responsibility for an operating task
6.	Processing performance standards	The establishment of criteria to measure economy, effectiveness, and efficiency of data base technology
7.	Risk management team	A task force comprising multiple backgrounds identifying the concerns and problems faced when using data base technology
8.	Independent review of design changes	Review of changes to data base applications to ensure compatibility and efficiency by someone outside the application area
9.	User signoff	Concurrence of user that system meets user needs prior to implementation
10.	System error recovery group	Group analyzing and either correcting or assigning correction responsibility for detected data base errors
11.	Second opinion	Review for a second DBA of the work of the originating DBA
12.	Data base quality assurance function	Establishment of a group charged with the responsibility of ensuring a quality data base
13.	Internal audit design review	Review by internal auditors of the adequacy of the design of the data base and using applications
14.	Data base charters	Documentation of the data base responsibilities of departments
15.	Data base job descriptions	Documentation of the data base responsibilities of individuals

Figure 52. Organizational Data Base Controls.

Undercontrolled. The controls are inadequate to reduce the risk to an acceptable level.

Not applicable (N/A). This criterion is not applicable in the organization being reviewed.

4. Conduct audit test

If the auditor suspects that there may be a potential control weakness, or if he or she wants to determine the effectiveness of the identified controls, the adequacy of controls should be tested. The data base audit program provides a recommended audit test to be used in making this evaluation. The program also identifies the evidence needed to conduct that test and suggests audit tools (see Appendix B for an explanation of the audit tools).

Use of Audit Program Example

The data base audit program for the organizational activity is illustrated in Figure 53. Let's review an example of how the audit program can be used.

Let us assume that the inadequate assignment of responsibility is the risk of concern to

Activity Organization **Auditor** ______ **Date** ______

Risk No.	Control Objective and Evaluation Criteria	Probable Control(s)	Control Assessment: Over	Control Assessment: Adequate	Control Assessment: Under	Control Assessment: N/A	Audit Test	Audit Evidence	Audit Tool	Workpaper Reference
1.	*To assign data base responsibilities to individuals*									
	Data base responsibilities assigned to individuals should be documented in their job descriptions.	1 2					Verify that appropriate data base administration job descriptions exist and compare them to recommended job responsibilities to ensure the appropriate division of responsibilities.	11	2	
	Individuals assigned data base responsibility have appropriate skills to perform those responsibilities.	15					Review job descriptions for needed skills and pay grades. Compare employees' personnel folder with job descriptions to ensure individual possesses identified skills.	11	2	
	Responsibility is located in the appropriate organizational unit.	14					Compare location of responsibility to recommended data base organizational structure. Variances should be investigated to be sure that responsibility is appropriate where assigned.	11	1 2	
1.	*To ensure that user retains organizational responsibility for the accuracy, completeness, and security of own data*									
	User and/or data base charter indicates appropriate user responsibilities.	14					Examine charter to ensure that data validity responsibility is assigned to the user accountable for those data.	11	1 2	
	Users maintain independent totals for verifying accuracy and completeness of data base data.	4					Verify that the control totals maintained by the user represent the accumulation of data within the data base.	17 23	16	
	Users authorize access to data for which they are accountable.	7					Verify that the user provides a list of individuals authorized to access data for which the user is responsible.	17 23	16	

1.	*To see to it that independent reviews will be performed to ensure the adequate assignment of responsibilities*									
	An independent group is established to evaluate the data base environment.	10 12 13					Verify that an independent group has been established by management to evaluate the data base environment. (Note: It may be an existing group with a new responsibility.)	11	2	
	The charter of the independent review group should include authority to assess the adequacy of assignment of responsibilities.	10 12 13					Examine the charter of the independent review group to ensure that assignments of responsibility reviews are within the charter.	11	2	
	An independent review group should regularly evaluate the adequacy of the assignment of responsibilities.	10 12 13					Examine a review program and/or review report indicating that the assignment of responsibilities has been reviewed by this group.	24	15	
2.	*To see to it that the organizational structure is designed to ensure prompt detection and correction of data errors*									
	Data base detected errors are controlled by an individual other than the one who created the error.	2 10					Review the error correction procedures to ensure control is vested in a party other than the one who created the error.	17	2	
	Regular reports are prepared for management describing frequency and type of data base errors.	3 10					Examine the report for reasonableness and determine that action is taken where warranted.	24	15	
	Responsibility is assigned to one individual to follow up on errors which are not detected or corrected on a timely basis.	1 5 10					Determine through examination of a department charter or individual job description that responsibility for follow-up on error detection and correction has been assigned.	11	2	
8.	*To see to it that the organizational structure is designed to ensure prompt detection and correction of DBMS errors*									
	Evaluation of the DBMS errors should be assigned to an individual other than the group operating the DBMS.	1 10 11					Determine that assignment for evaluation of DBMS errors has been made and that it is to a group other than the group which operates the DBMS.	11	2	
	A regular report should be issued to management describing the frequency and type of DBMS errors.	3 10					Examine the contents of the report for reasonableness and determine if appropriate action has been taken where necessary.	24	15	
	Responsibility should be assigned to follow up on DBMS errors which are not detected	1 10					Review department charters and individual job descriptions to ensure that the responsi-	11	2	

Figure 53. Data Base Audit Program 1.

Activity Organization Auditor Date

Risk No.	Control Objective and Evaluation Criteria	Probable Control(s)	Control Assessment: Over	Ade-quate	Under	N/A	Audit Test	Audit Evidence	Audit Tool	Workpaper Reference
	or corrected on a timely basis.						bility for follow-up on DBMS errors is assigned.			
8.	*To document data base expectations*									
	Responsibility for defining expectations from the data base environment should be assigned to an individual.	1 9					Review department charters and individual job descriptions to ensure that the responsibility for establishing performance levels for the data base is assigned.	11	1 2	
	Approved data base expectations should be assigned individuals for accomplishment.	1					Determine that the data base expectations are included in individual or group plans and objectives.	8	15	
	Management should be assigned the responsibility for monitoring the achievement of data base expectations.	1 3 11					Determine through examination of individual job descriptions that the responsibility for monitoring data base expectations has been assigned.	11	1 2	
9.	*To divide responsibilities so that an individual cannot perform and conceal a single event*									
	Data base administration personnel should not have any data responsibilities.	2					Determine that all data responsibilities are assigned to the users accountable for those data.	11	1 2	
	The data base control functions should be independent of the groups performing the task being controlled.	2 8					Determine that control functions have been established and that they are independent of the groups performing the data base tasks.	11	2	
	Regular audits should occur in the data base environment to ensure that responsibilities are appropriately segregated.	13					Determine from review of previous audit workpapers that regular data base audits include assessment of the adequacy of the division of responsibilities.	24	2	

10.	*To establish a data base review group that is independent of the data base function*									
	A group independent of the data base administration function should be assigned the responsibility for reviewing the adequacy of data base controls.	2 8 11 12					Determine through organizational charts and group charters that an independent group is assigned responsibility for reviewing the adequacy of data base controls.	11	2	
	The independent review group should be adequately skilled to review data base controls.	12 13 15					Review job descriptions of the review group to ensure they provide for adequate skills.	11	1 2	
	Reviews should be made on a regular basis, and at least once per year.	12 13 14					Determine through review of audit reports and other evidence that the reviews are made on a regular basis and at least once per year.	24	15	
10.	*To define review responsibilities*									
	The review group should have a charter defining the data base review responsibilities.	8 11 14					Examine the review group charter to ensure that it encompasses review of the data base facilities.	11	1 2	
	The responsibilities of the review group should state the scope of data base reviews.	3					Review the independent review group charter to ensure that it defines the scope of data base reviews.	11	2 15	
	The data base administration group should be advised of the review responsibilities of the independent review group.	8 14					Determine through interview with data base administration personnel that they have been apprised of the independent review group and the scope of the review responsibilities.	11	15	
11.	*To see to it that department data base organizational responsibilities are defined in the department charter*									
	Users of data base should have their data base responsibilities documented.	1 14					Examine the charter or other user documents to ensure that the data base responsibilities are documented.	11	2	
	The data base administration responsibilities should be documented.	1 14 15					Examine the charter of the data base administration group to ensure the responsibilities are documented.	11	2	
	The responsibilities of computer operations for operating the data base should be defined.	1 14 15					Examine the charter or other computer operation department documents to ensure the data base operation responsibilities are documented.	11	2	

Figure 53. *(Continued)*

Activity Organization ______ **Auditor** ______ **Date** ______

Risk No.	Control Objective and Evaluation Criteria	Probable Control(s)	Control Assessment				Audit Test	Audit Evidence	Audit Tool	Workpaper Reference
			Over	Ade-quate	Under	N/A				
11.	*To document individual data base responsibilities in their job description*									
	Individual users of data base should include data base responsibilities in their job description.	15					Examine a sample of job descriptions for individuals who use data base to ensure the responsibilities are included in their job description.	11	1 2	
	Data base administration personnel should have job descriptions documenting their responsibilities.	15					Verify that job descriptions exist for data base administration personnel and that they define their job responsibilities.	11	1 2	
	Computer operators who operate the DBMS should have those responsibilities included in their job description.	15					Review computer operator job descriptions to ensure they include operating the DBMS where appropriate.	11	2	
13.	*To define data base expectations in measurable terms*									
	Data base expectations should be defined in measurable terms.	6					Examine the data base expectations or objectives to determine that their completion can be measured.	22	15	
	Data base expectations should be achievable.	6					Through examination and interview, determine that with the existing staff and resources the data base expectations are achievable.	22	15	
	Organizational responsibility should be defined for calculating the degree of accomplishment of data base expectations.	2 12 14					Determine through reports that the degree of achievement of data base expectations has been measured.	22	15	
14.	*To see to it that senior management defines and enforces data policy*									
	Senior management should define the data policy for the organization.	3					Examine the existence and reasonableness of the organization's data policy.	25	15	

	Organizational structure should be established to enforce data policy.	1 2					Evaluate the organizational structure to determine that it is assigned responsibility for enforcement of data policy.	11	2	
	The data policy should be distributed to involved parties.	2					Through interview, determine that parties involved in data base technology are familiar with the organization's data policy.	25	15	
14.	*To see to it that senior management participates in data base decision making*									
	An organization structure should be established that involves senior management in data base decision making.	1					Determine that a steering committee or other structure is established to involve senior management in data base decision making.	11	2	
	Senior management should approve data base decisions.	1					Examine major data base decision documents to ensure that they have been approved or agreed to by senior management.	22	15	
	Senior management should have an organizational responsibility for oversight of data base administration.	1					Determine through evaluation of job descriptions or equivalent documents that one or more members of senior management have specific data base administration responsibilities.	11	2	
14.	*To see to it that senior management supports independent data base review groups*									
	Senior management should get reports of the data base review groups.	10 12 13					Determine through examination of reports that copies have been sent to senior management.	24	1	
	Senior management should be apprised of the failure of the data base administration group to act on the review reports on a timely basis.	10 12 13					Determine that a procedure exists to involve senior management if the data base administration group does not act on review findings and recommendations within a specified time span.	14	2	
	Senior management should approve individual reviews or an annual review plan.	2					Determine that organizational procedures exist for senior management to review and approve review group plans.	22	2	

Figure 53. *(Continued)*

the auditor. The auditor refers to the data base audit program for the control objectives addressing risk 1 (inadequate assignment of responsibilities risk). In our example, let us assume that the only control objective the auditor decides to evaluate is the assignment of data base responsibilities to individuals. Turning to that section of the data base audit program, we note that one of the assessment criteria is that job descriptions exist. The most probable control for this criterion is data base job descriptions (control 15). If these job descriptions exist in the format of other job descriptions in the organization and adequately address data base responsibilities, the auditor would check the adequate column in the control assessment. The audit test is to examine the data base job descriptions to ensure the appropriate division of responsibilities. The audit evidence to do this is the data base job description and the audit tool is the data base function responsibility lists which are included in this chapter. The audit program recommends the audit test, the evidence that the auditor should examine, and the audit tool helpful in examining that evidence. The other two criteria for the identified control objective should be assessed in the same manner. If the test is conducted, the workpaper reference column should indicate where the evidence supporting the auditor's work is located in the workpapers. If no workpapers are prepared, the auditor should initial the workpaper reference column indicating that the audit test has been performed and that no exceptions have been found.

Evaluation of the Adequacy of Organizational Controls

At the conclusion of the audit program (Figure 53), the auditor should have the necessary evidence to develop an opinion regarding the adequacy of the data base organization. This assessment can be made from the evidence gathered in this audit program. However, if the auditor desires to develop an opinion regarding the risk, such as the inadequate assignment of responsibilities risk, then the complete audit must be finished before that opinion can be developed. While it may appear that the organizational structure is inadequate, controls in other activities may compensate for weaknesses within the organizational structure.

The assessment process is described in Chapter 13. This chapter addresses opinions on both data base activities and risks. The recommended audit programs are designed to provide the information used to develop an audit opinion.

seven

AUDITING DATA DOCUMENTATION

The auditor has two interests in data documentation. The first is to assess the adequacy of the documentation to satisfy the needs of the organization. The second is to use the data definition documentation to understand the automated data for potential audit purposes.

In a data base application, data drive processing. Data are the resources, and processing is the means to manipulate those resources. In many a data base environment, maintenance often can be performed by changing data specifications, in lieu of changing programs. These data base concepts increase the need for complete and unambiguous documentation.

This chapter describes good data documentation practices, and the audit procedures necessary to ensure the adequacy of those practices. The types of data base documentation needed are described, supplemented by some examples of data documentation forms. A complete audit program is provided for assessing the adequacy of data documentation controls.

DATA DOCUMENTATION STRATEGY

As with other aspects of data base, the data documentation strategy varies with the sophistication of use of data base technology. As the sophistication increases, organizations normally acquire a data dictionary and then integrate it into the operating environment. At the other end of the sophistication continuum are manually prepared and maintained definitions of data.

Since the inception of data processing, data have been documented. Much of the original documentation was done on manual forms and passed among data processing personnel for use. Most statement-level languages, such as COBOL, provide for a data division which can be used with common definitions of data. In the early days of data processing some of these common definitions were ensured through the use of standardized card decks which programmers would insert in the data division section of their programs.

The acquisition of a data dictionary has been cited by a recent National Bureau of Standards symposium as the most essential element of an effective data base environment. The data dictionary is a centralized and standardized repository of data documentation. Some data dictionaries are used as stand-alone documentation tools, while a more powerful implementation of a data dictionary is to integrate it into the data base environment so that the only means to access the DBMS is through the data dictionary.

The continuum of data documentation strategies as practiced by corporations is illustrated in Figure 54. The illustration shows not only the desirable strategy but also the problem that might occur if the strategy is not used. The auditor should compare this

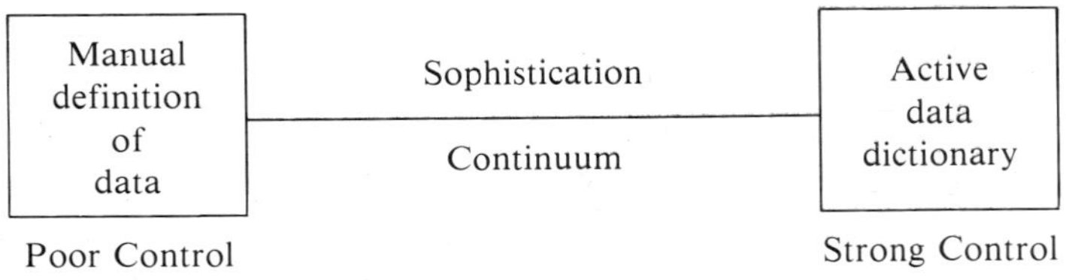

Desirable Strategy	Problem If Strategy Is Not Used
1. To acquire a data dictionary	Inadequate documentation
2. To develop data definition standards	Inadequate documentation
3. To inventory data as an asset	Inadequate documentation
4. To integrate the data dictionary into the operating environment	Operating data may not represent defined data

Figure 54. Data Documentation Strategy.

against the data strategy of the organization under review as a means for the early identification of potential audit problems. Note that many of these strategies may be informal and thus not documented.

The acquisition of a data dictionary is not a widely practiced strategy. Even in which organizations that have data dictionaries, many fail to require their use. Failure to have common data definitions can lead to inconsistent and incomplete processing.

The development of data definition standards is an important part of controlling data. The acquisition of a data dictionary is a convenient method for enforcing standards. Failure to have standards also results in inconsistent and incomplete documentation.

An emerging strategy in organizations that view data as resources is to inventory those data as assets. Few organizations do this, which means they don't know the totality of data used in the organization. Failure to adopt this strategy can result in duplication of data and inconsistency of data usage. Control of data can begin with an inventory of the data.

One of the most powerful strategies an organization can have is to integrate the data dictionary into the operating environment. It is only through this strategy that an organization can be assured that its operating data truly represent the data as defined in the data dictionary. Unfortunately, this concept is used by only a handful of data base organizations.

AUDIT GUIDELINE

The data dictionary is an essential element of control in a data base environment. If it exists, use it; if not, recommend its acquisition.

DATA DOCUMENTATION CONSIDERATIONS

Data documentation falls into two general categories. First is documentation about individual data elements. This documentation describes the attributes and access rules for data elements. Second is documentation describing the data base structure. This explains the data base organization and the results of data base processing.

The methods of recording these two types of documentation vary significantly. It is recommended that the data element documentation and much of the data base structure documentation be recorded on a data dictionary. Experience in the use of data base technology indicates the importance of a data dictionary to the success of data base technology.

Experiences of many organizations have been that as the third user is added to the DBMS, the benefits of a data dictionary become obvious. This is frequently referred to as the "third-person rule." It is at the point where the third user is added that the need for consistent and unambiguous documentation becomes obvious. The problems and questions associated with poor data documentation begin to sap the resources of the data base administration function without a formal data documentation tool.

Data Dictionary

A data dictionary (sometimes called dictionary/directory or catalog) is generally viewed as an inventory of existing types of data in an organization to provide an understanding of their source and use within that organization. A data dictionary can also be viewed as the repository of all descriptive information about the data base such as characteristics, relationships, and access authorities. Such things as origin, primary users (retrieval or update), general comments and descriptions, frequency of use in reports, and interfacing programs may be recorded in this dictionary.

A data dictionary takes many forms in systems today. These user-oriented kinds of information may be retained completely manually or in a fully computerized form. In essence, the data dictionary facility is an adjunct or supplement to the schema definition. A transitional phenomenon is occurring wherein more of the information required in a dictionary is in the schema definition or a combined schema for all data bases within a system. In fact, a strong motivation for the development of a data dictionary sprang from the use of systems with sketchy or incomplete data definitions.

The data dictionary aids the data base administrator with such features as:

- Controlling unique data item names throughout an organization
- Identifying users who may be affected by any changes to data structure or storage structures
- Controlling and policing data conventions and integrity
- Identifying data source and creation responsibility
- Documenting data usage, value, frequency of change, and so on

The above list mentions only a few of the many kinds of information which may be retained in a data dictionary.

Data Element Documentation

The objective of documenting data elements is to have available a common definition for all users. Properly done, this documentation becomes the guideline for the use of an indi-

Data element name
Aliases by which it is known and who uses them
Precise and unambiguous definition
Data element sources
Frequency of change
Person responsible for correctness
Person responsible for data element
Eligibility to read, enter, update, or delete, in detail or in total
Special authority required to read, insert, amend or delete it
Any special restrictions for access
Relationship to other data items
Data validation rules
Programs that can access data elements, and for what purpose
Reports where the data element appears
Data format
Position of data element in the logical data structure in which it appears
Data volumes

Figure 55. Data Element Documentation.

vidual data element. It also shows how and by whom that data element is used within the organization.

A composite of the data documentation requirements as developed by multiple organizations is presented as Figure 55. This shows close to an ideal level of documentation for each individual data element. In practice, an auditor should not expect to find all of this documentation, but should be encouraging the expansion of data element documentation to include these types of documentation.

An explanation of the type of documentation that would be included in each category listed in Figure 55 follows:

Data element name

The data element field name is the unique identifier of the element and the key for addressing the data element. The name may be any or all of the following:

Full name. The name by which the data element is known.

Data element number. A unique numeric or alphanumeric identifier for the data element so that it can be differentiated from all other data elements within the data dictionary.

Mnemonic. The name the data element is called in programming languages, such as COBOL. Some languages limit the data element mnemonic to eight alphanumeric characters, for which the first character usually cannot be numeric.

Aliases by which it is known and who uses them

Data elements may be known by several different names. This may be because a single piece of data represents two pieces of information; for example, when an employee number is also the employee's social security number. In other instances, the same piece of data is called by different names in different parts of the organization, for instance, the number used to represent a customer order may be called order number, purchase order number, invoice number, or requisition number. The system must be able to recognize the same piece of information by whatever name it is called.

Precise and unambiguous definition

The description of the data element should be a complete narrative definition of the element, its purpose, and its use. Since there are normally no physical character limitations on the definition, abbreviations or acronyms should not be used in describing the data element. Long sentences and obscure words tend to cloud the meaning and defeat the purpose of the description. Understanding of one description should not depend upon the understanding of the description of another data element under normal circumstances. The inclusion of examples in the description should be considered if the examples will enchance the clarity of the data element's definition.

Data element sources

The sources are the individuals or programs that originate this particular data element. For example, the addition of an employee number may originate solely from a specific individual in the personnel department, while the customer order number data element may originate from several hundred individuals on the marketing force, and an employee's net pay may originate as a result of a calculation in a specific payroll program.

Frequency of change

A measure of usage of the data element is the frequency with which that data element changes. For example, the employee number would change perhaps each time an employee is transferred, added, or deleted. Other fields like product ordered may have a very high frequency of initiation and change. This type of information is essential to the data base administration group as they attempt to establish a highly efficient data structure. Knowing the number of data elements that might be added, an access affects the organizational structure of the data base.

Person responsible for correctness

This is the individual or department responsible for the accuracy and completeness of the data element. This is the individual who should be held accountable for maintaining controls to ensure the integrity of the specific data element in the data base.

Person responsible for data element

This is the individual who can authorize access to that data element, and who defines the data element.

Eligibility to read, enter, update, or delete, in detail or total

The definition of data should identify who can use that data element for what purposes. The most common usages are read, enter, update, or delete; however, the degree of accessibility can be defined in greater detail. This concept, called granularity, permits data to be accessed by such things as value, date, or relationships.

Special authority to read, insert, amend, or delete data

This refers to the requirement of a special authority to perform what might be considered a special transaction or event, such as changing your own payroll record, or issuing a credit over $999.

Any special restriction for access

If there are restrictions on the authority to access data, they should be specified in the data definition. For example, the plant payroll department may be allowed to access pay rates up to $1,000 a week but not over that amount. Accessibility will be covered in more detail in the chapter on data security.

Relationship to other data items

An important aspect of the data attributes is the relationship of those attributes to the attributes of other data items. For example, there is normally a direct relationship between an employee's pay grade and that employee's pay rate. Understanding and verifying this relationship helps ensure the integrity of data within the data base.

Data validation rules

The tests to be applied to data elements for correctness, the timing of those tests, and whether the item is to be rejected for failing the test are rules that should be included in the documentation. These should be both absolute tests and relationship tests. In some of the more sophisticated data dictionaries, both the data validation programs and the test data to test those data validation programs can be generated automatically from the data validation rules.

Programs that can access data elements, and for what purpose

A record of all the programs that access a particular data element identifies the scope of effort required when the data element changes. The list of programs also determines who should be advised when a data element is changed if the change affects the purpose for which that data element is used. Keeping this list current is essential in assuring the consistent use of data within an organization. If the data dictionary is integrated into the operating environment, this type of information can be generated automatically.

Reports where the data element appears

This is a subset of the information included in the use of data elements, but is oriented specifically toward the people who use the data results in their jobs. In on-line systems, screens where the data element appears should also be listed, as they are, in fact, reports.

Data format

The four most common data formats for the structure of the data element value are:

Alphanumeric
Alphabetic
Sign numeric
Unsigned numeric

Definition of the schema
Definition of the subschema
Data structure
Storage structure
Use of pointers
Use of indexes
Established controls
Data security procedures
Results of control checking
Security problems and failures
Recovery actions taken

Figure 56. Data Base Oriented Documentation.

In scientific applications, the other formats may be used, such as binary.

Position of the data element in the logical data structures in which it appears

Identifying the position of the data structure in which the data element appears is necessary for programs using that particular data element. Frequently, in data bases data elements are grouped into logical units which may be called segments, groups, or records. When data elements are placed in larger groups, the user of the data element is not able to retrieve an element individually, but has to retrieve and process the entire group of data.

Data volumes

This refers to the number of times this specific data element appears within the data base. It is also helpful to indicate original data elements and redundant data elements. In order to improve efficiency of data bases, it may be necessary to repeat the same data element two or more times within a single data base.

Data Base Oriented Documentation

This type of documentation describes the structure and environment in which the data elements reside. Generally, this documentation is more difficult to collect and record. While the data dictionary can be used to store some of the information, much of the information may need to be collected manually and stored by the data base administrator.

The types of information gathered by organizations about the data base environment are listed in Figure 56 and described below.

Definition of the schema

The schema definition, which is the system global view of data, provides a centralized definition of the logical data structue and physical storage structure of a data base. The data and storage structure definitions may be expressed in separate schema languages or portions thereof, or they may be intermixed in a single schema definition language.

The data definition facilities provide both human-oriented and machine-oriented definitions of a data base. The human-oriented communication of data definition can take various forms and be made selectively available to different classes of users. The original written definition of a data base schema, usually the responsibility of a data base administrator, provides the basic form of human-readable information concerning the attributes and structure of the data. Additional forms may exist which provide a graphic data formalism to communicate data structures for human readability. It is also possible to have features which provide for both selective display of schema information to the data base administrator and subschema information for the application programmer or end users. These may take the form of printed or displayed tabular output or graphical representation.

Other considerations involving data base definition and control include:

The degree of explicit control over both data and storage structure as opposed to implicit or fixed methods determined *a priori* by the system. In other words, the user may be allowed a choice of access methods and data structures rather than having them determined solely by the system.

The actual separation of storage structure definition from both data structure and device/medium specifications. The separation of these definitions may provide easier learning by classes of users, increased flexibility, and responsiveness to future changes.

The written data definitions must be processed to produce data directories which are then available to the data base management system or to the programming language compiler for machine processing of requests against a data base.

It may be noted that the structure of the definition is often similar to or more complex than the structure of the stored data themselves and, since the definition is itself a data element, many of the same problems and solutions are involved in both types of storage. It is quite possible, in fact, to store the definition in exactly the same way that user data are stored, and to use the system facilities to access it, implying that there are data structure definitions for the definitions themselves. To avoid an infinite recursion, of course, one initial definition has to be built into the system. (Most of what has been said above could apply equally well to the storage of other types of definitions such as update input definitions or inquiry definitions.)

Storage structure attributes which may be defined include such things as the method of physically recording data structure relationships, actual storage structure, physical techniques, access methods to retrieve data, and physical encoding/decoding.

Definition of the subschema

The subschema definition is an individual or application view of the data base and is intended to provide for separate and multiple views. This facility is the vehicle for multiple languages and user applications to describe only the data and structures with which they are concerned and furthermore to describe them in the form they wish.

A subschema definition provides the following benefits:

A measure of data independence

Integrity and privacy (it limits a user to the subset of data to which he is authorized)

Ability to provide multiple views of the data base

Ease of writing, debugging, and maintenance of programs (it allows programmers to work only with relevant data and not the universe of the data base)

Definition of the mapping between the subschema and the schema

The capability of the subschema to allow differences between the user's view of data and that of the schema may vary greatly. Generally speaking, the schema-to-subschema relationship is a mapping process. The schema-to-subschema mapping produces varying degrees of data independence and access control between programs or users and the centrally controlled data base. The subschema provides for translation of data and storage structure attributes. Some of these variations between schema and subschema views are:

Logical data structure
Value attributes
Order of data items
Schema attributes

A subschema for a given host language such as COBOL may or may not be syntactically the same as that for the host language. For certain language interfaces, the subschema definition language may take the form of the schema definition language. The processing method of interfacing the subschema to the schema can vary from the time of program compilation to the point of execution of each request for data.

A defined subschema may be either written directly as part of the program, or invoked from a library where it was prestored. In either case, the use of a subschema should be subject to the approval of the data base administrator.

When a subschema is defined, a utility could assess the degree of compatibility with the schema in terms of operational feasibility and performance efficiency. Conversely, it would be useful to have a mechanism for defining an ''optimum'' schema given several proposed subschemas. Such a facility could consider input volumes, frequency and response times on requests, and the effect of these on storage structure, access methods, and device medium allocation. Under the present state of the art, multiple users must bargain among themselves or negotiate with the data base administrator in developing a data base structure and subschema acceptable to their application needs yet jointly compatible.

Data structure

The data structure, the user's conceptual view of the data, provides the user with the facility to perceive data as a model of the real world. The data structures are the logical definition of data attributes and relationships among elements of data including data items at the lowest level. The data structure class is the set of data structures provided in a given system.

In discussing data structures, it is essential to differentiate clearly between definition or naming data and the occurrences or actual instances of data. A distinction is made throughout between a data structure schema, which one might say is the variable name, such as ''college,'' and an occurrence of data, such as ''Harvard.'' When an instance or occurence of data is intended, one of these words will be used.

Data structure classes, which indicate the structuring power or capabilities of a system as seen by a user, are composed of elements and the composition of those elements at many levels. The elememts and types of structures which can be composed from other structures build from the following generic structure types, called data elements: item, group, group relation, entry, file, and data base. The lack of power or flexibility of data structuring may impose constraints on the actual data modeling of the ''real world'' situation and on the processing requirements demanded by user applications.

A data structure is constructed by aggregating elements into higher level elements. This process of aggregating data is called data structure composition and is illustrated in Figure 57.

The item is the primitive data element (e.g., ''birthdate'') of which structures of all other types are ultimately composed. A subitem (e.g., ''month'' within ''date'') can best be thought of as having the following characteristics:

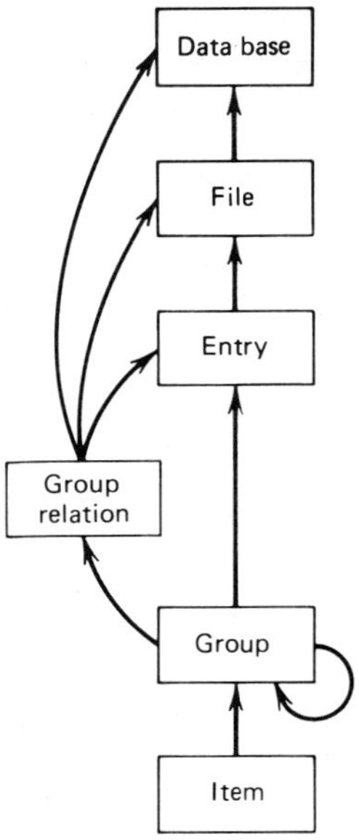

Figure 57. Data Structure Composition.

Its value is a substring of a string-type item value.

It is valued by character position within the item value.

It is considered to be at the same level as the item in the data hierarchy.

A group is a set of items and possibly other groups. A group composed only of items (rather than items and groups) is called a simple group; otherwise it is compound. It may be nonrepeating, in which case it offers a means of giving a name to a collection of elements ("address," "number," "street," "city," and "state"), or it may be repeating, representing a set of elements which can occur more than once within a containing element (e.g., "education" = "college," "degree," and "year," and an employee may have more than one occurrence of "education"). A repeating group always repeats within some higher level element ("employee" above); a set of such occurrences is called an assembly (e.g., all the "education's" for one employee).

There often is a set of one or more items (defined by the user or furnished by the system) which uniquely identify the instances in an assembly. This is called the group identifier. A similar set which determines the order of the instances in an assembly is called a group sequencer. Multiple logical sequences may be allowed for a repeating group.

Groups may be related in several ways. In any relationship, one group has associated with it a set of zero or more (or one or more, in some cases) other groups. This set is a group composition as shown in Figure 58. First, one group may contain another group (e.g., the repeating group "person" might contain the repeating group "skill"). In this case, the name of the parent group includes the value of items in contained groups—if we say PRINT ORGANIZATION UNIT, we get all the "persons," including all the "skills." The set of items and groups immediately below a given group in the structure is called its principal items and groups.

A second kind of relation exists when one group may be superior to another. The relation is similar to "contains," except that the meaning of the name of the superior group does not include values of items in subordinate groups. Referring to Figure 58, a reference to ORGANIZATION UNIT would not encompass any PERSON or PROJECT data. All systems limit the use of this relation to defining a tree structure. Also, almost all systems provide either "contains" or "is superior to," not both.

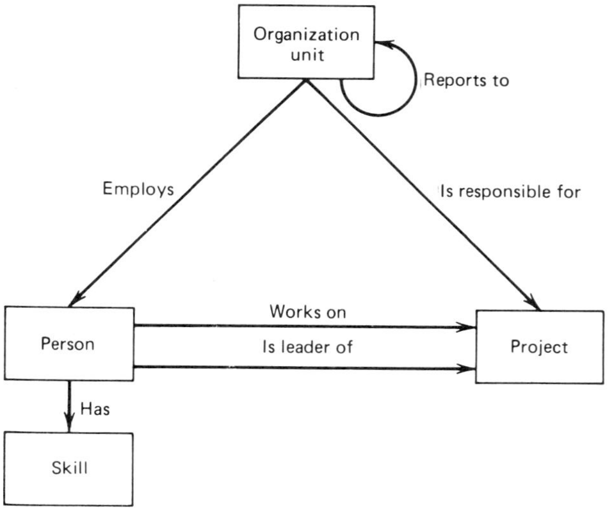

Figure 58. Plex Structure.

The third kind of relation is the group relation which permits multiple interrelationships giving rise to a plex structure. With this type, there may be any number of group relations, each with an individual name (rather than a single "contains" or "is superior to" relationship). An example of a plex structure is shown in Figure 58.

A distinction can be made as to whether a group relation is hierarchical or nonhierarchical. In the former case, a subordinate occurrence is related to specific parents and cannot exist as a free-standing element. The value for "college, degree, year" for a particular employee has no meaning outside his record. In the latter, the subordinate element is a self-contained entity which can exist by itself. An example is a record containing all the data for a given part. This is subordinate to the records for all units using that part, but if no such units happen to exist at a given moment, the part record remains in the system.

An entry is a set of groups and group relations in which one and only one group is the entry-defining group. This entry-defining group is not contained in or subordinate to any other group. Thus, an entry-defining group could be a simple group with no parent, or the "top" group in a hierarchy of compound groups, in the hierarchy of a tree structure, or in a hierarchic group relation. In a nonhierarchic group relation, both the superior and subordinate groups would be entry-defining groups. (If confused, think of the entry as a "record.")

A file is a set of entries. More than one entry type may be defined in any given file. A data base is likewise a collection of entries which are usually related and dispersed physically throughut one or more files defined to the system.

Features may exist which provide for: optional item occurrences, variable length occurrences, a wide range of variety in item types including such special forms as date, geographic coordinate, Boolean, and textual. An additional feature which may be used to control optional item occurrence is a null value (nonexistence) indicator.

Storage structure

The storage structure is the physical representation of a particular data structure on some storage medium. The storage structure is the system's physical view of data, and as such determines the method of placement of and access to data. The storage structure may vary significantly across different systems and can be separated into two generic classes: those permitting sequential access only, and those permitting random access. Within these classes there may be many variants. Sequential access implies data storage where access to the next data element is by association to a previous data element in sequence. The data elements may either be physically contiguous or logically contiguous (that is, linked in some fashion). Random access means that access to a given data element is not related to the access of other data element occurrences. Random access methods may or may not permit sequential access as well; for example, pure hashing does not permit sequential access.

Optimization of storage structure can be facilitated by giving the user or data base administrator some degree of control over its organization and characteristics. Things which might be specified by the user include average and maximum record length; file size; what, if any, indexing or hashing there should be; the nature of the mapping between logical and physical records; which item values are likely to be searched on; whether chaining or a pointer array is to be used; and how records are to be placed ''near'' each other.

Sometimes only a sequential or only a random storage structure is provided. Generally, a combination of both is provided with a selection of specific methods within each generic class. It is possible to have a mixed storage structure within the same data storage space, thus allowing sequential and random access.

The data base administrator may be provided the ability to select the storage structure best suited to the community of users and their modes of use. Any storage structure with multiple users, modes of use, and need for multiple access paths will involve tradeoffs between forms of sequential and random access. If the data base administrator is allowed to declare data items to be indexed or chained and further to declare that only certain values, ranges of values, or partial values are to be included in the index, he has some control over tradeoffs.

Although there may be many methods and broad flexibilities in the choice of storage structures, there is, from the user point of view, a select set of basic tradeoffs. In general, there may be choices available which affect efficiency and capability tradeoffs relative to:

Time versus storage space
Retrieval versus update
Single versus batched access

Data compression is another storage structure feature designed to utilize secondary storage space efficiently. Various techniques are possible, each having different levels of housekeeping to compress and decompress the data on transfer. Compression techniques include encoding standard data values and removing multiple blanks or zeroes. The saving in storage space, transfer time, and number of accesses must be balanced against the cost in additional processing time.

Use of pointers

Pointers are used to connect one data element to another element. ''Address'' and ''pointer'' as used in this discussion are meant in the general sense to refer to any information which can be used to locate an entity. They do not necessarily mean actual memory or file address. The elements are exhaustively retrieved by starting at the first element and following the pointers along the chain until the last element is reached. If a logical ordering is to be represented, the elements can be placed in the pointer sequence in their proper logical order. Pointers are stored with the data elements they connect.

In the chaining pointer technique, each data element contains the address of the next, and may contain pointers to the previous element in the chain, leading back to the beginning of the chain, and to other related elements, such as the "owner" of the chain. The situation in which there are various aggregations and/or sequences among a collection of data elements, with each element possibly belonging to several of them, can be implemented by having one chain for each aggregation or sequence. If an element can appear in a variable number of chains, provisions have to be made to identify the significance of each pointer properly and to handle the variable number of pointers.

A useful technique to specify the end of a collection if it is to be processed sequentially, as in the case of a chain, is to place a distinctive symbol in or after the last element. This technique can be used to mark the end of a variable length value, the end of an assembly, and so on. Similarly, a special symbol can be used as a separator between group occurrences.

Use of indexes

A common way of providing retrieval is through use of indexes. An index is a means of establishing a correspondence between a set of values of an item and a collection of records whose items have those key values and are stored at certain addresses. An index consists of a set of key values and one or more addresses associated with each key value. The index is usually in sequence by key value. If the index is large, it may be broken up into several levels, with the first one, in high-speed memory, giving for each range of key values the address in the file where a finer index to that range is located. That one in turn may lead to another even finer one, and so on.

An index may contain unique key values or ranges of key values. The collection of record addresses associated with an index entry may be represented in any of the ways described previously for data aggregations. For example, if the index contains record addresses only for certain key values occurring at intervals along the sequence, a record with a particular key value may be located by searching the index for the largest key value which is still less than that key value, and then searching for the desired record within the interval.

It is often desirable to set up secondary random access paths so that records can be located by values of any of several different items or sets of items. A file which is indexed by values of every item is sometimes called a totally inverted file. If some but not all items are indexed, the storage structure is called partially inverted. An inverted file can be utilized to find entries which satisfy a combination of conditions. For example, if all "employee" entries with SKILL = 5711 and DEPT = 2013 were needed, the address lists for those two values in the index could be compared. Addresses appearing in both lists are those of entries satisfying the condition.

Indexed storage structures can become very space-consuming and time-consuming to update, depending on how close they come to a totally inverted file. It is here that the tradeoff between retrieval and updating arises most strongly—if the data base is heavily indexed, then retrieval becomes fast. However, when a record is to be added or modified, there is likely to be heavy overhead in making the appropriate changes to the indexes, particularly considering that the indexes are often ordered, and adding a new value may require much data movement.

Established controls

Control documentation should describe the controls in place, and the methods for using those controls. Experience has shown that most data base installations integrate control documentation into general data base documentation. This, coupled with the fact that many data processing professionals are confused as to what are controls and what are procedures, makes it difficult for auditors to go to a single source to gather information on controls.

The chapters covering audits of the data base activities identify the most common controls for those activities. In addition, Appendix A provides information on the description and functioning of data base controls. This insight into how organizations control data base should prove helpful to the auditor in reviewing data base controls.

Data security procedures

Security involves both physical and logical access controls. In addition, the security function has responsibility for monitoring security, taking action where appropriate, and recommending or making adjustments to the security procedures. This process is discussed in Chapter 9.

Results of control checking

An important part of data base documentation is the history of problems. It is only through an analysis of what is going wrong that adjustments can be made to improve controls. The results of control checking may be included in any or all of the following documentation:

Regular control reports. An example is a DBMS log analysis.

Special incidents reports. These may be developed by the data base administration people or by users.

Third-party complaints. Individuals not directly connected to the operation of the data base but users of data base information may note and report problems.

Data base audit reports. Reports by auditors identify control problems.

Independent review group reports. Review groups involved in evaluating data base applications or the DBMS environment may identify and report on control problems.

Experience has shown that many organizations do not formalize the reporting of data base problems. Therefore, for a more extensive list of the type of problems that have been occurring, it is recommended that the auditor interview those people in positions to uncover control problems.

Security problems and failures

Security is normally assumed to work unless there have been detected violations. However, the successful perpetrator may be able to break security and not be detected; in that case security will have failed and that failure will not be known. Therefore, it is doubly important to note and investigate security problems and failures when detected.

Some organizations require formal reports on security problems and failures. Unfortunately, many of these reports only deal with actual losses and do not report suspected problems. The auditor may have to conduct an investigation to obtain a more complete list of potential security problems. Those organizations that have established a security officer function normally have a much better security reporting system than those that do not have a formal security officer function.

Recovery actions taken

Recovery is considered to be one of the most technically complex procedures in the data base environment. The ability to perform a successful recovery operation is essential to the success of data base technology. Information on the actions taken and the degree of success is essential in evaluating and improving the recovery process. These procedures are discussed in Chapter 11.

DATA BASE DOCUMENTATION EXAMPLES

Most data base organizations have forms to document data elements and records. These forms vary significantly among organizations. However, the type of information gathered is relatively consistent from organization to organization.

This section discusses three forms that are typical of those used by many organizations:

Data element description form. This is a method of describing the attributes of a single data element.

Record description form. This is a method for recording both the record characteristics and the data elements contained within that record. (Note: A record in data base may be called a segment or group.)

Data element inventory list. This is an exhaustive list of all the data elements used by the organization.

Data Element Description Form

The data element description form presented in Figure 59 is typical of the forms used by organizations to describe an individual data element. The form can be used for a new data element, to change a data element, or to delete a data element. The form provides space for the following informatin:

Data identification. Space is provided on the form to indicate the data element name, a number which provides a unique identifier for each data element, and a mnemonic used for statement-level languages, together with the detailed description.

Physical characteristics. The physical description should define the length of the data element and identify whether it is alphabetic or numeric. If numeric does it have an algebraic sign where the decimal point is located. If the data value represents a unit of measure such as pounds, that should be indicated. The void state should be indicated if the field is not used. The description should specify what type of information will be contained in the field, for example, blanks or zeros. The field justification indicates whether the value will be right or left justified, and if there is insufficient data to fill the field, the fill indicates what will be placed in the unused positions, for example, blanks or zeros.

Attributes. Information describing the source of the data, the validation checks to be performed on the data element, and the level of desired security should be placed here.

Usage. This refers to the records and files in which the data element is used. The data element description form provides room to indicate the number and name of each file or record where the data element is used together with an indication of that usage. Three usage category columns are provided as follows:

O—This usage originates the data element.
C—This usage changes the data element.
R—This usage only reads the data element.

Record Description Form

This form is completed for each grouping of data or record within the data base. The information contained on this form, in addition to the record name and unique identifier (see Figure 60), includes:

Record attributes. This is an explanation of the purpose of the recora. Additional information indicates the sequence in which the records are accessible, and the retention

☐ New
☐ Change
☐ Delete

Data Desc. Number ______

Page _____ of _____

Data Name: ______________________ Mnemonic ______

Description: ______________________

(Note: Use reverse side for additional detail if necessary.)

Physical Characteristics:

Length ________ Alpha ☐ Numeric ☐ Signed ☐ Decimal location ________

Unit of meas. ________ Void state ________ Justification ________ Fill ________

Data source: (if computed, specify formula) ______________________

Validation checks: ______________________

(Note: Use reverse side for additional detail if necessary.)

Security: ______________________

Input, output and file or record description usage:

Number	Name	O	C	R	Number	Name	O	C	R

Prepared by: ________ Approval: ________ Effective date:

Mo.	Day	Yr.

Figure 59. Data Element Description.

Record Desc. Number

Page ____ of ____

Record name ________________

Function/purpose ________________

Sequence ________________

Retention period ________________

Record volume	Min.	Max.	Average

Source of Record					
Prepared/Used by (Individual or Program)	**Ident.**	**Disposition**	**Type of Activity**	**Unit Volume**	**Freq.**

Data Elements in Record					
Number	**Name**	**Number**	**Name**	**Number**	**Name**

File Usage					
F.D. Number	**File Name**	**O/C/R**	**F.D. Number**	**File Name**	**O/C/R**

Comments ________________

Prepared by: ________ Approval: ________ Effective date:

Mo.	Day	Yr.

Figure 60. Record Description.

period for the record. In addition, detailed information is provided on the volume of records.

Source of records. This section indicates all of the individuals or programs which produce this record. It gives the identification of that individual or program, the disposition of the record, the type of activity such as "enter via terminal" or "create within the program," the unit volume of records produced by this source, and the frequency, such as daily, continuous, or weekly.

Data elements in record. This is a detailed listing of the data element number and name of each data element within the record.

File usage. The file names in which the record is used together with the file description number (F.D.No.) and file usage (O/C/R—see data element form for description of codes) are indicated here.

Data Element Inventory List

During the preliminary review of the data base, it was suggested that the auditor compile a data element inventory list if one did not exist. Some organizations already have compiled this list, and Figure 61 is representative of the type of form used for such a listing. Note that this information can come directly from the data dictionary.

The information contained on the data element inventory list form includes:

No. The unique number identifying the data element

Data element name. The descriptive title given to the data element

Mnemonic. The cryptic data element name used for programming

Owner. The individual responsible for the data element

Bytes. The length of a data element

Type. Indication of whether the data element is numeric, alphabetic, and so on

Description. A cryptic description of the data element

If more information is wanted about any item on the data element inventory list, it should be available on the data element description form. The data element number becomes the method of cross-referencing the two forms.

DATA DOCUMENTATION CONTROL OBJECTIVES

The control objectives given for data base documentation are designed to reduce the risks of an inadequate audit trail, the placing of data in the wrong accounting period, failure of the DBMS to function as specified, and inadequacy of documentation to operate the data base environment effectively. The control objectives are positive statements of control that if accomplished will minimize the data documentation risks. The recommended audit process is to verify whether or not these desirable control objectives have been achieved.

The data documentation control objectives are listed on Figure 62 and described below.

To define data base audit trail requirements

The audit trail in data base is divided between the data base environment and all of the applications that use that environment. Thus, while the audit trail may be relatively simple and straightforward in a dedicated application, it can be extensive and complex in a data base environment. It is important that all of the segments of the audit trail be documented

Page_____of_____

Number	Name	Mnemonic	Owner	Bytes	Type	Description

Prepared by:	Effective date:	Mo.	Day	Yr.

Figure 61. Data Element Inventory List.

Number*	Risk	Recommended Control Objective
4.	Inadequate audit trail	1. To define data base audit trail requirements 2. To divide requirements between the user and the DBA function 3. To document data base deletions
7.	Placing data in the wrong calendar period	1. To define data accounting requirements
8.	Failure of DBMS to function as specified	1. To assign centralized control of external schema 2. To define data independently of the applications that use the data
11.	Inadequate documentation	1. To develop an inventory of data elements 2. To document data in accordance with documentation standards 3. To enforce the use of data as documented

*See Figure 8 for description of risk.

Figure 62. Data Documentation Control Objectives.

so that when reconstruction becomes necessary, the audit trail evidence and its source have been documented.

To divide requirements between the user and the DBA function

The audit trail is partially maintained by the data base environment and partially by the user(s). The responsibility that each has for maintaining the audit trail should be documented so that all parties to the creation of the audit trail are apprised of their audit trail responsibilities.

To document data base deletions

Data base technology provides unique opportunities to delete data from the data base. For example, data can be easily removed during data base reorganizations (the function that reformats the data in the data base). If a record is maintained, through an audit trail history or special deletion forms, the integrity of data on the data base is easier to confirm.

To define data accounting requirements

Recording data in the proper calendar period is a business problem, not a data base problem. However, on-line data bases provide capabilities that make the business problem more complex. For example, banks can receive requests from customers to transfer funds at a future point in time. Having the accounting requirements clearly defined facilitates installing appropriate data base controls to ensure that data are placed in the proper calendar period.

To assign centralized control of external schema

Unless there is independence in establishing the external schema (physical data base), strong users may successfully lobby to structure the data base to optimize their applications. When this happens, some of the data base advantages may be lost.

To define data independently of the applications that use the data

When data are resources of the organization, they must be defined and structured to meet the needs of the organization, not just an individual user. For example, the marketing function may wish to define a sale differently than the accounting function. Without an independent definition of data, data may be defined and stored in a manner that is not useful to the whole organization, but only a single user.

To develop an inventory of data elements

One aspect of the adequacy of documentation is the completeness of the documentation. Completeness cannot be determined until the population being documented is known. An inventory of data elements defines that populatuon.

To document data in accordance with documentation standards

A second aspect of completeness is inclusion of all the needed attributes about the data. Developing good documentation standards, and then documenting in accordance with those standards, ensures completeness of the documentation of the data attributes. Normally this requires monitoring by either a data librarian or a quality assurance group.

To enforce the use of data as documented

If the data base does not represent the data as described in the documentation, people will no longer use the documentation. Once it is known that documentation is out of date, it becomes useless, and it is potentially dangerous in that systems may be designed using the wrong definition of data. As previously stated, the easiest method of enforcement is to document through a data dictionary and then integrate that dictionary into the data base environment.

AUDIT GUIDELINE

Review the adequacy of data base documentation from the perspective of a user and your assessment will usually be correct.

GOOD DATA DOCUMENTATION CONTROL PRACTICES

Control over data documentation doesn't just happen; it must be planned. Control begins by defining the requirements of control and then finding and implementing the methods of accomplishing those requirements. The previously described control objectives can be considered the data documentation control requirements.

Controls are designed to reduce risk and achieve predetermined control objectives. The control objectives become the acceptable level of loss due to the risk. The selection of individual controls will depend upon the magnitude of loss acceptable due to data documentation risks.

The data documentation controls used in data base organizations to reduce data documentation risks are listed in Figure 63 and are referenced to the risk they are designed to reduce in Figure 64. These represent the controls that the auditor may find in the data base environment under review. They are the controls used by organizations having a data base, but are not meant to be an exhaustive list of data documentation controls. In the event that data documentation control weaknesses are identified, this list should prove helpful to the auditor in recommending controls to improve data documentation.

AUDIT GUIDELINE

Good controls result in good documentation. Verify that controls are adequate to produce good data documentation, keep it current, and enforce its use.

DATA BASE DOCUMENTATION ACTIVITY AUDIT PROGRAM

The following audit program (Figure 65) is designed to assist the auditor in assessing the adequacy of data documentation controls. The data base documentation audit program provides the criteria for use by the auditor in evaluating documentation controls. The audit program also provides recommended audit tests and audit tools, together with the most probable evidence to be examined.

The following data base audit program is one designed to evaluate environmental controls. Thus, the emphasis is on control, with the data segment of the audit to be conducted

Number	Control Name	Control Description
16.	Centralized coordination of external schema	Placing the responsibility for coordinating external schema definition in a centralized group
17.	Data element responsibility	Making individuals accountable for each data element in a data base
18.	Conceptual data independence	Establishing the data definition of the organization as opposed to that of individual user groups
19.	Data dictionary system	An automated documentation tool for data
20.	Active data dictionary system	The automatic feeding of the documentation in the data dictionary into the operating environment
21.	Data definition standard	The predefinition by standards of the information to be collected on each data element
22.	Data element inventory	A listing of all the data elements used by the organization
23.	Data element utilization reports	Statistics on the actual use of data elements to supplement the static information on that data element
24.	Data base backout request form	A formal request needed to remove data from the data base

Figure 63. Data Definition Data Base Controls.

Data Base Activity / Data Base Risks	Controls
4. Inadequate audit trail	Data dictionary system Active data dictionary system Data base backout request form
7. Placing data in the wrong calendar period	Conceptual data independence Data dictionary system Active data dictionary system
8. Failure of DBMS to function as specified	Centralized coordination of external schema Conceptual data independence Data dictionary system Active data dictionary system Data base backout request form
11. Inadequate documentation	Data element responsibility Data dictionary system Data definition standard Data element inventory Data element utilization reports

Figure 64. Data Base Controls for the Data Definition Activity.

as individual data base applications are audited. One purpose of auditing the data documentation controls is to assure the data base application auditors of the adequacy of that documentation as they begin to audit base applications.

AUDIT GUIDELINE

Be "data friendly" prior to evaluating data documentation controls.

Activity Data Documentation Auditor ______ Date ______

Risk No.	Control Objective and Evaluation Criteria	Probable Control(s)	Control Assessment: Over	Control Assessment: Adequate	Control Assessment: Under	Control Assessment: N/A	Audit Test	Audit Evidence	Audit Tool	Workpaper Reference
4.	*To define data base audit trail requirements*									
	A standardized method has been established for documenting the data base audit trail.	21					Obtain the procedures and standards for documenting the audit trail and determine their adequacy.	25	15	
	The requirements for the data base segment of the audit trail are documented.	21					Obtain the documentation that defines the data base environment audit trail and determine its adequacy.	26	15	
	Procedures should be defined requiring data base applications to document their audit trail and cross-reference evidence needed in other audit trails.	21					Examine the adequacy of the procedures to instruct application systems to define and document their audit trail.	25	15	
4.	*To divide requirements between the user and the DBA function*									
	Formal procedures should be developed defining how to divide the audit trail between the DBA function and the user(s).	17					Examine the adequacy of the procedure to divide audit trail responsibilities between the user and the DBA function.	25	15	
	Data base audit trail requirements should be defined in a data base procedure.	21					Determine the existence and adequacy of the data base procedures before creating the data base audit trail.	25	15	
	Procedures should be established describing the process data base users should take to develop and coordinate the adequacy of their audit trail with other users of the same data.	17					Examine the procedures and the documentation resulting from those procedures to determine that the user segment of the data base audit trail is documented in accordance with the procedures.	25	15	
4.	*To document data base deletions*									
	Data from the data base should not be deleted other than by the data base applications.	24					Examine the reorganization and recovery procedures as well as the data base maintenance process to ensure that data are not	15 16	15	

							being deleted through those procedures.			
	The history of the data deleted from the data base should be maintained.	24					Examine the methods and completeness of reporting the history of data deleted from the data base. (Note: This may be done through the DBMS log or through an application history log.)	2 3 8	4 7 15	
	An approval process should be used to delete data from the data base.	24					Verify on a test basis that data deleted from a data base has been properly authorized.	2 3 18	4 7	
7.	*To define data accounting requirements*									
	The method of determining into which accounting period financial data will be placed should be determined.	21					Examine the procedures that describe the method for placing data in the appropriate accounting period.	25	15	
	A method should be established to determine the appropriate accounting period for data within the data base.	21					Verify for data that do not belong in the current accounting period that they have been appropriately dated.	23	3 6 16	
	Determine that the documented accounting requirements are in accordance with the organization's accounting policies and procedures.	21					Compare documented data base accounting requirements for data elements with the comptroller's accounting procedures.	23 25	3 6 15	
8.	*To assign centralized control of external schema*									
	The external schema should be developed by the data base administration function.	16					Verify that the external schema developmental process is under the direction of an independent data base administration function.	1 11	15	
	The external schema should only be developed after all of the user requirements have been considered.	16					Verify through workpapers and interview that all of the user's needs have been considered in the development of the external schema.	1 25	15	
	The documentation of the external schema should be maintained by the data base administrator.	16					Ensure that the external schema documentation is prepared and maintained by the data base administrator.	1 11 25	2 15	
8.	*To define data independently of the applications that use the data*									
	A centralized group, preferably the data administration group, should be assigned the responsibility to define data for the organization.	18					Determine that there is an independent group who has the responsibility to define data for the organization.	11	15	

Figure 65. Data Base Audit Program 2.

Activity Data Documentation Auditor ______ Date ______

Risk No.	Control Objective and Evaluation Criteria	Probable Control(s)	Control Assessment: Over	Control Assessment: Adequate	Control Assessment: Under	Control Assessment: N/A	Audit Test	Audit Evidence	Audit Tool	Workpaper Reference
	All known users of information should be contacted regarding their data needs prior to defining a data element.	18					Interview on a test basis users of data to determine that their needs were solicited prior to defining data.	22	16	
	An appeal process should exist for those users who have difficulty using the data as centrally defined.	18					Examine the reasonableness of the appeal process, and determine through testing one or more cases that the process is reasonable.	25	15 16	
11.	*To develop an inventory of data elements*									
	Someone should be appointed accountable for control over the totality of data elements.	16 17 18					Identify the responsible individual and through review of job description or charter determine that the data responsibility has been assigned.	11	1 15	
	An inventory of data elements should be made.	19 22					Examine the inventory of data elements and on a test basis verify its completeness.	21	15	
	The inventory of data elements should be regularly updated.	19 20 22					Examine the procedures for updating the inventory and through test determine that they have been followed.	21 25	2	
11.	*To document data in accordance with documentation standards*									
	Standards should be developed outlining how data are to be documented.	21					Review the data documentation standards and determine their reasonableness.	10	15	
	The data documentation standards should be enforced.	21					Review the documented methods and procedures for ensuring that documented standards are enforced, and on a test basis verify that those procedures function properly.	25	15	
	An appeal process should be formalized for projects which have difficulty complying with the documentation data standards.	21					Examine the appeal procedures and verify through testing that the procedures are reasonable.	25	15	
11.	*To enforce the use of data as documented*									

	Procedures outline the process of enforcing the use of data as documented.	20					Examine the procedures and determine their reasonableness.	2 25	15	
	Procedures or processes exist which detect violations of the proper use of data.	17 23					Select a representative sample of data from the data base to ensure that data and their use are in compliance with the documentation defining those data.	2 23	4 15	
	An appeal process exists for those applications whose needs cannot be met using data as defined.	17 18 23					Examine the appeal process and through testing verify that the process is effective.	23 25	15 16	

Figure 65. *(Continued)*

eight

AUDITING DATA BASE SYSTEMS DEVELOPMENT

A certain level of maturity is necessary before conversion to a data base environment is feasible. In general, data base technology is not appropriate for new data processing departments. It is far better to build data processing skills using simpler technology. When data base technology is introduced into an organization, that organization has two concerns: to convert existing applications to data base technology, and to develop new applications to use that technology. Both concerns necessitate that the systems requirements be evaluated based upon the benefits of data base technology. This evaluation may involve some major modifications to existing applications, or complete rewrites of those applications.

This chapter describes the data base considerations in systems development and provides an approach for evaluating whether or not those considerations have been addressed during the developmental process. A review methodology is provided for each phase of the systems development life cycle. The review methodology emphasizes what is different in a data base application. In addition, some guidelines are provided for the successful development of application systems.

CONVERTING APPLICATIONS TO A DATA BASE ENVIRONMENT

Conversion to a data base environment will generally necessitate a substantial restructuring of the organization's application portfolio to take advantage of the enhanced capabilities of the DBMS. The several possible approaches that permit converting the application portfolio range from an evolutionary approach, in which new or replacement application systems are developed using data base technology, to a revolutionary approach, in which new development is suspended until existing application systems are converted to the new environment. Regardless of the particular approach selected, an ordering of priorities for conversion must be developed for the application portfolio. Within this ordering, the initial applications selected for conversion are of critical importance.

The revolutionary and evolutionary approaches for conversion of the application portfolio to a data base environment actually represent opposite ends of a continuum of approaches. No single approach is universally best. In fact, more than one approach may be operable within a given conversion; that is, certain application systems may be converted on a revolutionary basis while other systems are converted in an evolutionary manner.

In the revolutionary approach to conversion, sometimes called resystemization, one rewrites and restructures existing application systems as necessary to operate under the new DBMS. Generally, one should avoid exclusive use of this approach for the following reasons:

There is the risk of overextension caused by attempting too much, too fast.

Delays in one subproject may impact others.

Insufficient resources may be available for developing new systems during the conversion.

At the opposite extreme of the revolutionary approach is the evolutionary approach in which all new systems are developed under the new environment. Existing systems are not converted but, rather, are replaced at the end of their normal life cycle. This approach reduces the risk of overextension and the impact of delays in subprojects. However, there are disadvantages to an evolutionary approach:

Complex interfaces with existing, conventional systems are generally entailed.

Local inefficiencies and redundancy typically result.

Current organizational deficiencies and constraints may be perpetuated.

Just as the conversion of the entire applications portfolio may be approached in an evolutionary or revolutionary manner, so may the conversion of a single, existing application system. In other words, the entire application system may be converted to the new environment at one time, or the conversion may take place in phases. The latter approach, in which the reporting and update functions are converted gradually, using bridges, has the advantage of early availability of both cross-functional data and the new features of the DBMS. Furthermore, greater flexibility in scheduling the conversion is provided. However, the gradual approach has the disadvantage of redundant development and data storage, and requires increased management to provide and control the conversion bridges.

One temporary measure that may be employed to avoid or postpone conversion is to extract data from existing master files in order to build a transient, integrated data base. This data base is not maintained but instead is recreated on a cyclic basis. The data base is used for cross-functional reporting and analysis. This approach provides early availability of cross-functional data and lends itself to a specialized interrogation language. But there are certain disadvantages to this approach:

Availability of data is achieved at the expense of redundancy and reloading.

Problems of timeliness and consistency may be created.

Basic application limitations are perpetuated.

There are never sufficient resources, nor is it appropriate, to permit continued maintenance and enhancements of application systems during the conversion to the data base environment. Moreover, conversion requires a relatively stationary target. Thus, a moratorium or maintenance (or more accurately on enhancement) may be declared during conversion.

The declaration of a maintenance moratorium must be the result of agreement among user, senior, and data processing management. Senior and user management support is necessary for the conversion. However, if senior management is the primary motivator behind the conversion, there will be some degree of user resistance to a maintenance moratorium. On the other hand, if the conversion is driven by user management, senior management will tolerate a moratorium on maintenance only so long as it does not interfere with normal business functions. In either case, user and data processing management must jointly determine the scope and duration of the moratorium and agree to the circumstances under which it may be modified or cancelled.

A common device for invoking moratoriums is a steering or priorities committee. Composed of data processing and user management, the steering committee is responsible for approving projects and establishing priorities. The steering committee does not manage, nor does it relieve management of its business responsibilities. Rather, it provides a forum for discussion and has power derived from its membership and sponsorship.

Criteria for Selecting Initial Applications

Certain application systems indicate better opportunities for conversion than others. The following types of applications represent good opportunities for conversion:

- An application system using many different master files and/or many internal sorts, indicating the need to represent complex data structures and to support multiple paths between data
- An application with a requirement for on-line inquiry and/or update of interrelated data (A DBMS would still be applicable, although not required, if the data were not interrelated.)
- An application system with chronically heavy maintenance backlogs, suggesting redundant data and/or inflexibility with respect to its data structures
- An application system requiring a broader view of data (either more detail or greater cross-functional breadth)
- An application which crosses functional or organizational boundaries (e.g., project control)
- An application which cannot support basic business needs
- An application which provides data used by other systems

Certain types of applications represent poor opportunities for conversion, for example:

- A purchased application which is maintained by a third-party supplier
- An application which uses historical data and which is processed infrequently
- A recently installed application system which is effective in satisfying user needs

An analysis of the characteristics of the existing applications based on the above considerations will yield a preliminary ordering for conversion of the application portfolio. As the conversion is planned in more depth, the preliminary ordering will be revised and refined to reflect such factors as precedence relationships regarding conversion, level of effort required, and the availability of resources.

In converting to a data base environment, a key decision is selecting the entry-level application. In an ideal world, the initial application would be selected as the vehicle for making mistakes and learning how to convert and how to manage the conversion. It would have a low profile and would not present any risk to the business. However, the realities of the world will force initial conversion which has visibility, contains some element of risk, and must be completed quickly. The factors listed below should be considered in identifying the best opportunity for developing technical competence while simultaneously reducing risk and visibility:

- The application should be representative and nontrivial.
- It should be a good DBMS application (though not necessarily the best).
- It should represent a relatively low risk to the business.
- It should provide sufficient opportunity for learning.
- It should convert either an old system or one that is technically obsolete.
- It should provide eventual visibility as a vehicle for management controls.

It should be "owned" by a vocal, important, but neglected (by data processing) segment of the business.

AUDIT GUIDELINE

Experience shows it rarely pays to convert an existing application to data base technology. View such proposals critically.

DATA BASE SYSTEMS DEVELOPMENT STRATEGY

The data base development strategy can be evolutionary or revolutionary. Experience has shown that to encompass the benefits of data base technology, the revolutionary approach should be taken, recognizing that it may be impractical to do all applications at once. Rarely is data base technology cost effective unless applications are rewritten to optimize the use of that technology.

Four desirable strategies are recommended to help organizations optimize data base technology, as follows (see Figure 66):

1. *To rewrite all existing systems to optimize the use of data base technology.* Unless this strategy is used, the objectives established when acquiring data base technology may not be achieved. The potentially large investment offers few benefits until data are managed as resources of the organization. This normally requires the rewrite of most major applications.

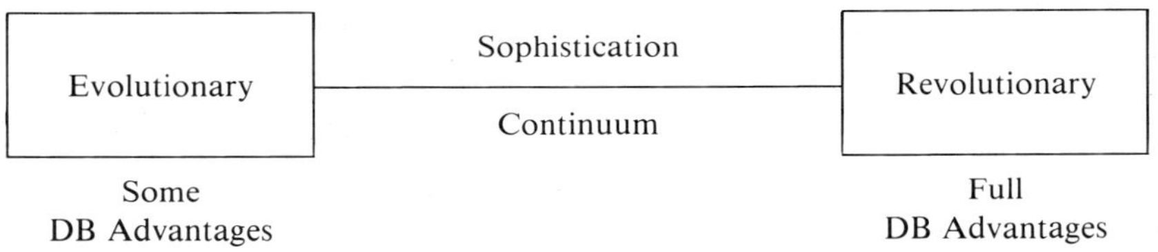

Desirable Strategy	Problem If Strategy Is Not Used
1. To rewrite all existing systems to optimize the use of data base technology	Data base objectives may not be achieved.
2. To establish review points and review groups	System fails to perform as specified.
3. To declare a maintenance moratorium during conversion	Schedule and budget will not be met.
4. To organize a steering committee to establish data base system development plans and priorities	There will be loss of interest in data base technology.

Figure 66. Data Base Systems Development Strategy.

2. *To establish review points and review groups.* The complexity of data base technology makes it advantageous to have applications reviewed by an independent review group during development. If these reviews do not occur, the system may not perform as specified.
3. *To declare a maintenance moratorium during conversion.* Maintaining an existing system while building a new system with rapidly changing specifications requires time and effort. If this maintenance effort is extensive during conversion to data base technology, schedules may be missed and budgets overrun.
4. *To organize a steering committee to establish data base system development plans and priorities.* The process of converting or rewriting large numbers of systems affects the methods of work and responsibilities of many users. Without a steering committee (usually comprising users) to oversee this process, there may be a loss of interest in data base technology and insufficient effort expended on the conversion effort.

The auditor should determine which of these strategies are being used in the organization under review. If the strategies are not used, it may indicate potential problems. This insight will provide guidance to the auditor about areas to be investigated for potential control weaknesses and inefficiencies.

SYSTEM DEVELOPMENT GUIDELINES

The following guidelines for system development were recommended by a panel of data base experts organized by the National Bureau of Standards, and were made based on the experience of the workshop attendees:

Do establish review points. When describing a plan, care must be taken to ensure flexibility in order to support changing/overlooked requirements. Points must be scheduled at which time the plan is reviewed and updated as required. Decisions must also be made as to the appropriateness of proceeding with development.

Do involve end users. The data processing department must be extremely careful not to ignore user input to the development process. No one knows the functional requirements which must be met better than the end user.

Do keep scope reasonable. The scope of the project must be dictated by practicality. Attempt only as much as is attainable within well-defined time frames and technology. Once the scope is defined, stay within its bounds.

Do not stifle prototyping. Modeling is perhaps the best method available for trying out ideas. Encourage validation of concepts through prototyping.

Do shift responsibility to where the expertise exists. Always ensure that responsibility for achieving goals is placed where the ability both to understand and to accomplish them exists.

Do phase the implementation. Within an overall context, ensure that total system conversion is planned and executed in attainable increments.

Be wary of entanglements. System conversion planners must always review commitments with the goal of avoiding crippling dependence upon manufacturers, proprietary packages, and maintenance agreements. Recognize costs/benefits of new technology. Quantify both the advantages and disadvantages of being the first to use new technology.

Do get adequate management commitment. Make sure management knows beforehand what resources and time periods are required, what has been available, and what progress, if any, has been made. Do not let them walk away from it. They are key players.

Do initially select an important but tractable portion of the ultimate and have some results in four to six months. This forces an early and realistic review. One also hopes it demonstrates the new capabilities, emphasizes the ability of the implementors to handle the new technology, and provides better insights into both the technical and operational (people-oriented) problems that the organization will face.

Do introduce your technical staff to the new technology. This is important when you are studying whether to go data base but, also, immediately before and during the initial implementation. Sometimes six months to two years pass from initial study to start of implementation. Further training for the initial decision process is usually ''book learning'' and quite stale by implementation time.

Do orient and educate your users. Next to management, this group is the key to success. They must feel comfortable with what you say. That means they should have a role in deciding what they get and when. In addition, they must prepare themselves for the new modes of operation.

Do keep the user group on your management review team. They can keep you out of trouble. They can change their priorities and needs to fit your capabilities to deliver. They can help you resist pressures for early and extra delivery since they, too, want and need a quality product. By keeping them in the loop, you run less of a risk of surprising them and evoking resistance on delivery.

Do set up a central ''data base control group.'' Useful in any big system or series of related systems, it becomes essential in a data base oriented organization. Such a group may have several levels with differing managers, but these groups must be coordinated. There is a policy level, an implementation level, and an operational level. The implementation group does most of the administrative and design work involved in bringing into being and providing for the efficient structure of the data base(s). The operational level is responsible for the operational integrity of the data base and must take the actions for restart/recovery in addition to any periodic initialization/dumping or consolidation of the actual data base.

Do implement a data dictionary/directory. As a key item common to all systems, it is needed to make the data base a corporate rather than a private entity. Because the data are to be shared across groups who are not responsible for the data, it is essential that the ''meaning'' of each data item be documented. A data item, besides having a name, a form, and values chosen from some well-documented set, has several meanings. One is the English description; another is an operational description of how the value is determined; another is how the data are commonly used and by whom. All of these must be known to avoid confusion and to avoid having data misused.

Do ask for and accept help from the vendor of the data base system. If you are changing hardware at the same time, put pressure and some of the risk on that vendor. Good advice must be available during your learning period. Consultants are useful, not only initially, but also during design and implementation time.

AUDIT GUIDELINE

Data base applications require more time spent on requirements and design than do non-data base applications.

DATA BASE SYSTEM DEVELOPMENT CONSIDERATIONS

Research on testing systems under development shows the following testing accomplishments:

Most errors occur early in the design process. Approximately two-thirds of all errors in the system development process occur during the requirements and design phases.

Testing costs more as the system development life cycle (SDLC) progresses. If the cost to correct a detected error during development took one unit of work during design, it would take 10 units of work to correct during programming and testing, and 100 units of work to correct when the application went operational.

Testing does not detect all defects. At best, testing by the application development team will only detect 80% of the defects.

The above analysis supports the conclusion reached by many data base organizations that there is a very positive return on investment by having an independent review made of an application under development. While some believe that this increases the cost of systems and delays implementation, experience has proven exactly the opposite to be true. An effective review process actually reduces costs and permits systems to be installed quicker. The three most common methods for conducting an independent review are:

1. *Audit participation in system development.* The organization's internal auditors perform a series of mini-audits during the developmental process. These mini-audits are designed to evaluate the adequacy of controls during development.
2. *Quality assurance reviews.* A quality assurance group, normally c omposed of senior data processing personnel, reviews systems at defined checkpoints and normally emphasizes compliance with the system development methodology.
3. *Project review group.* A group comprising users, project personnel, and other interested parties such as computer operations and a data base administrator review the application's ability to satisfy the needs of the user and optimize technology.

The type of review group and the charter given the review group will be dependent upon the concerns of management and the risks inherent in using data base technology. The number of review points and the tasks performed during those reviews should be based upon the charter of the review group. The remainder of the chapter explains a SDLC review methodology that can be used by any of the about three types of review groups.

DATA BASE APPLICATION REVIEW METHODOLOGY

A successful review methodology has the following characteristics:

Formal system development methodology. Unless the review team knows what deliverables will be produced at what phase of the system development life cycle, reviews are impractical. An effective review cannot be made when there are no criteria by which to measure the project team performance.

Formal review methodology. Reviews are only effective when the reviewers know specifically what they are looking for. A bunch of "good ole boys" talking about the system may produce worthwhile results, but is a time-consuming and burdensome method for conducting a review.

Defined checkpoints. The points at which reviews will occur must be known by both parties.

Management support. Data processing management must actively support the review process and let the project team know of that support.

Independent review team. The review team must be independent of the project. This does not mean the project personnel may not be on the review group but, rather, that at a minimum the reviewer does not review his/her own work and that nonproject personnel are on the review team.

The review methodology proposed in this chapter will be based on a five-phase system development life cycle. These phases were selected to emphasize problems encountered in the use of data base technology, and are not necessarily representative of system development life cycles used by any specific organization. The auditor may need to adopt the guidelines presented in this chapter to the system development life cycle methodology in use in the organization being reviewed.

The five phases selected for the data base system development review methodology are:

Requirements phase. The requirements define the goals and objectives to be accomplished from an automated application. Requirements define the product that is to be built. As with any product, the more definitive and measurable the requirements, the higher the probability that the product will satisfy the user.

Design phase. The design develops the blueprint to build the product. During the design phase, a determination is made on how to achieve the system requirements. The design phase translates requirements into specifications from which the executable system can be built.

Program phase. This phase translates the design specifications into machine-executable instructions. Programming translates information that people understand to machine-understandable instructions. The complexity of this phase is dependent upon the completeness and clarity of the specifications provided the programmer.

Test phase. Testing assures that the system is implemented in accordance with the system requirements. During the program phase, data processing people conduct tests to ensure that their product works and performs in accordance with the program specifications. The test phase should be conducted by user personnel to ensure that the system does what the user expected it to do.

Installation phase. A system acceptable to the user must be placed into a production status prior to operating on a day-to-day basis. This conversion from a test status to a production status involves the movement of programs and may also involve changes in data and operating procedures. The conversion phase may be a mini-system in itself, introducing special risks which require special controls.

AUDIT GUIDELINE

Audit participation in the development of data base applications may be the most fruitful use of audit resources.

Data Base Application Risks

The system development process provides an opportunity to implement controls to reduce most of the data base risks. Reviewing the application to assess the adequacy of control

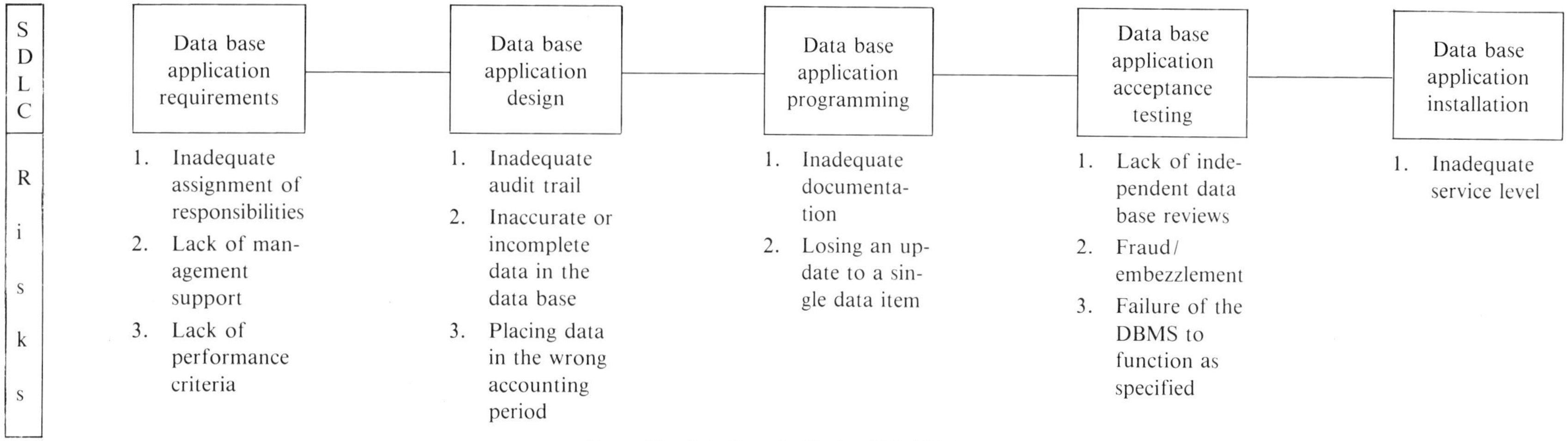

Figure 67. Data Base Application SDLC Risks.

should concentrate on specific risks. The proposed review methodology identifies the SDLC phase risks where it is most effective to address specific risks.

The data base application risks and the phase in which those risks should be addressed are illustrated in Figure 67. These are not the responsibility of the auditor, but are the responsibility of the project team during those phases. At the end of each SDLC phase, there should be a review point at which time the reviewers need to determine whether the project team has adequately addressed the appropriate data base application risks.

System Development Control Objectives

The data base system development control risks are reduced by establishing control objectives and then implementing controls to achieve those objectives. The recommended control objectives for a data base system development project are listed in Figure 68 and described below. (Note: Figure 68 indicates both the risks and the SDLC phase related to the control objectives.)

To divide system development responsibilities adequately among the DBA functions, the application project team, and the user

Each party to the development of an application system should know his or her responsibilities during the developmental process. During the development of dedicated applications, projects can be extensively modified during the developmental process as requirements change. This may not be true in a data base system because of the structure imposed by data base technology. Change may not be economic if the data base structure is affected. Therefore, have each team member know and fulfill his or her design responsibilities to provide greater assurance that the application will be effective.

To ensure that senior management participates in data base application system planning

The importance of involvement of senior management in the use of data base technology cannot be underestimated. Senior management must resolve differences and information users, and they also need to set policy and direction for those users.

To ensure that senior management approves data base application proposals

Involving senior management in the approval process, at least for major data base applications, sends a positive message to the users of management interested in the proper use of data base technology.

To establish performance criteria for all data base applications

The only method to ensure that the objectives for using data base technology are achieved is to establish performance criteria and then measure to determine whether those criteria have been achieved.

To include the audit trail in the design specifications

The audit trail is split among multiple applications in the data base environment. In order to ensure its completeness, the audit trail specifications should be an integral part of the design process.

Number*	Risk	SDLC Phase	Recommended Control Objective
1.	Inadequate assignment of responsibilities	Requirements	1. To divide system development responsibilities among the DBA function, the application project team, and the user
14.	Lack of management support	Requirements	1. To ensure that senior management participates in data base application system planning 2. To ensure that senior management approves data base application proposals
13.	Lack of performance criteria	Requirements	1. To establish performance criteria for all data base applications
4.	Inadequate audit trail	Design	1. To include the audit trail in the design specifications
2.	Inaccurate or incomplete data in the data base	Design	1. To include the methods of ensuring accurate and complete data in the design specifications
7.	Placing data in the wrong calendar period	Design	1. To include the accounting requirements in the design specifications
11.	Inadequate documentation	Program	1. To ensure that documentation conforms to data base documentation standards 2. To ensure that documentation is up to date
3.	Losing an update to a single data item	Program	1. To implement controls to ensure the proper sequencing of updates
10.	Lack of independent data base reviews	Test	1. To establish a test plan 2. To have the test plan implemented or monitored by an independent group
9.	Fraud/embezzlement	Test	1. To test the adequacy of controls
8.	Failure of the DBMS to function as specified	Test	1. To test to ensure that the system achieves specified performance criteria
6.	Inadequate service level	Installation	1. To monitor the installed application to ensure that specified performance criteria are achieved

*See Figure 8 for description of risk.

Figure 68. System Development Control Objectives.

To include the methods of ensuring accurate and complete data in the design specifications

Controls are an integral part of the design process and are needed to ensure accurate and complete data. If the control requirements have not been specified, not only will expected levels of accuracy and completeness be unmeasurable, but the control design process will not be integrated into a system.

To include accounting requirements in the design specifications

When there will be multiple users of the same data, cutoff problems may be introduced in systems design. One user can no longer use the batch control concepts to ensure the placing of data into the appropriate accounting period. These decisions need to be resolved during the design process.

To ensure that documentation conforms to data base documentation standards

Prior to programming, the completeness of the documentation should be verified in order to ensure that programs conform to the design specifications.

To ensure that documentation is up to date

Many organizations require the program design documentation to be complete before they will issue a program number authorizing the compilation of a program. This is but one of many methods organizations use to ensure that the documentation is current.

To implement controls to ensure the proper sequencing of updates

Multiple applications interacting with the same data may need to be performed in a predetermined sequence. If sequencing is important, it must be determined during the developmental process and coordinated with all other applications using the same financial data.

To establish a test plan

Testing is too important to leave to the discretion of the individual programmer. A test plan should be established which identifies the criteria which the data base application must meet to be deemed acceptable, and lays out the ways to evaluate those criteria through testing.

To have the test plan implemented or monitored by an independent group

It is difficult for individuals to test their own work objectively. Having an independent group perform the testing, or the testing performed under the direction of an independent group, significantly increases the number of errors detected during the test process.

To test the adequacy of controls

Perpetrators tend to break control of the weakest point in the system of controls. It is only through testing that the adequacy of controls can be evaluated so that control weaknesses can be identified and corrected.

To test to ensure the system achieves specified performance criteria

The dissatisfaction experienced by many organizations with data base has been attributable to an expectation gap between what users expected and what the data base technology actually delivered. When the expectations are defined and measured, this gap is closed.

To monitor the installed application to ensure that specified performance criteria are achieved

The actual test of the data base application is when it is run in operation. Frequently, there will be differences between the results experienced in testing and the results produced in the production environment. The difference is normally the variable introduced by people. Therefore, it is important to monitor and ensure that the desired level of performance is sustained over a period of time.

DATA BASE CONTROLS

The controls selected for installation during the system development process should be selected to meet predetermined control requirements. In practice, few organizations have a control design methodology. The most common practices are either to leave controls to the discretion of the system designer or to design controls to prevent the recurrence of previously detected data base problems.

The controls listed in Figure 69 are the controls most frequently utilized by data base organizations. No one single organization uses all of these controls. The controls need to be selected based upon the level of risk that is acceptable to the organization. The controls are cross-referenced to the risk that they are designed to reduce in Figure 70. Note that some of these controls are effective against more than one risk. However, they are associated with the risk most closely aligned to the use of the control in practice. A more detailed explanation of these controls can be found in Appendix A.

These data base system development controls are the controls that the auditor should look for and/or recommend during the system development process. The controls and the methodology have proved effective in improving the reliability and integrity of data base applications. Again, it is worthy of note that it is significantly more cost-effective to install controls during the developmental process than to add them through systems maintenance procedures.

AUDIT GUIDELINE

Unless controls are specified that will be implemented, concentrate on control specifications.

SYSTEM DEVELOPMENT ACTIVITY AUDIT PROGRAM

The system development audit program should be conducted as a series of mini-audits. These mini-audits are performed at predetermined points throughout the system development life cycle. As in other audits, objectives are established, an audit program is developed, the audit is conducted, and a report is prepared.

The same audit approach can be used to review purchased applications, enhancements to existing data base applications, and applications to be converted to data base technology. The difference between these reviews and the new developmental project review is the frequency and timing of the checkpoint reviews. Purchased applications should be reviewed during the contractual stages; system maintenance and conversion projects should be reviewed after the design specifications are complete and prior to implementation. The reason for having more review points on a new project is longer duration of the new developmental projects.

The recommended audit process is to conduct a review at the end of each of the five identified system development life cycle phases. An audit program is provided for each of the five review points. A narrative discussion of each review point explains the differences between a data base application and non-data base application at that point in the SDLC.

Number	Control Name	Control Description
25.	Data base administration function	A function that establishes interface standards for systems under development and advises systems analysts and programmers on data base technology capabilities and interface procedures
26.	Application system testing	Methods of assuring that operational systems cannot adversely affect the data base
27.	Formal design process	Using structured methods or automated tools and techniques to aid in the design process
28.	Top management checkpoints	A series of steps throughout the developmental process at which top management will make a decision regarding performance and continuance of the project
29.	System implementation standards	Methods and procedures that must be followed when implementing systems using data base technology
30.	Data base standards	Methods and procedures that must be followed when establishing and operating a data base
31.	Training of personnel	Courses and materials that provide appropriate skills for people using data base technology
32.	System documentation	Sufficient formal written explanation of the data base environment so that its continuity and maintenance can be assured
33.	Review board	A group of managers, users, and data base personnel who oversee priorities and projects using data base technology
34.	Government reporting requirements	A formal method of assuring that the use of data base technology is in compliance with federal regulations
35.	Personal privacy requirements	Methods and procedures of assuring that an individual's privacy has not been compromised through data base technology
36.	Standard progression of new versions	An orderly method of moving from one version of a program or system to a new version
37.	Independent testing	Testing performed by individuals other than those who developed the data base system
38.	Structured programming techniques with walk-through	An organized method of programming with walk-throughs to ensure the process is followed
39.	Design models	Using simulation techniques to test the reasonableness of the proposed design

Figure 69. Data Base System Development Controls.

Reviewing the Requirements Phase

The requirements phase in data base technology emphasizes data instead of processing and system design. User requirements may be satisfied in data base without writing programs through utilization of data base resources. The sophisticated use of data base can provide the following capabilities automatically:

Data validation
Resequencing of data
Limited analysis and calculations
Data formatting and report writing
File maintenance

Data Base Risks \ Data Base Activity	Controls
1. Inadequate assignment of responsibilities	Data base administration function
2. Inaccurate or incomplete data in a data base	Application system testing Formal design process Independent testing Structured programming techniques with walk-through
3. Losing an update to a single data item	Application system testing System implementation standards
4. Inadequate audit trail	System implementation standards Data base standards Training of personnel System documentation Standard progression of new versions
6. Inadequate service level	System implementation standards Data base standards
7. Placing data in the wrong calendar period	Training of personnel
8. Failure of DBMS to function as specified	Application system testing System implementation standards Data base standards Training of personnel Standard progression of new versions Structured programming techniques with walk-through Design models
9. Fraud/embezzlement	Training of personnel Independent testing
10. Lack of independent data base reviews	Review board Government reporting requirements Independent testing
11. Inadequate documentation	Formal design process System implementation standards Data base standards Training of personnel System documentation Standard progression of new versions Structured programming techniques with walk-through
13. Lack of performance criteria	Review board Independent testing
14. Lack of management support	Data base administration function Top management checkpoints

Figure 70. Data Base Controls for the System Development Activity.

Activity Systems Development Requirements Phase Review **Auditor** ______ **Date** ______

Risk No.	Control Objective and Evaluation Criteria	Probable Control(s)	Control Assessment: Over	Control Assessment: Adequate	Control Assessment: Under	Control Assessment: N/A	Audit Test	Audit Evidence	Audit Tool	Workpaper Reference
1.	*To divide system development responsibilities among the DBA functions, the application project team, and the user*									
	The DBA function should be responsible for reviewing application requirements to ensure they are consistent with data base capabilities.	5					Verify that the data base administrator performs a review function of data base application requirements to ensure that the requirements are reasonable based upon existing data base capabilities.	26	1 2	
	The individual responsible for each data element should authorize the use of those data for the application under development.	30					Confirm with the responsible user for key data fields that the application system has been authorized to use those fields.	10 23	2 16	
	Users should conform to existing data documentation in their requirements specification.	30 32					Confirm with the users that the existing definition of data is adequate to meet their requirements, or that they will go through the normal change process for approval prior to finalizing application requirements.	26	16	
14.	*To ensure that senior management participates in data base application system planning*									
	Senior management should ensure that all the involved parties participate in the requirements phase.	28					Ensure that all parties affected by the data base application are involved in the requirements phase.	10 11	16	
	The data base application fits into management's long-range plan.	27					Examine the long-range data processing plan to ensure that the application system is consistent with that plan.	22	16	
	A member of senior management should be a participant in the planning process for the data base application.	28					Confirm that a member of senior management is a participant in the requirements phase of the data base application.	11	16	

14.	*To ensure that senior management approves data base application proposals*									
	Senior management should approve the requirements, budget and schedule for the data base application.	28					Verify that the requirements, schedule, and budget have been documented and that they have been or will be approved by senior management.	22	16	
	Senior management should approve the return on investment for the application system.	28					Verify the return on investment calculation has been made for the data base application and that it has been or will be approved by senior management.	26	2 16	
	Any significant changes to the data base caused by a new application should be approved by senior management.	28					Determine whether significant changes to the data base have been caused by a new application system, and that those changes have been approved by senior management.	3 19 26	7 15	
13.	*To establish performance criteria for all data base applications*									
	User requirements should be stated in measurable terms.	27 32					Examine the reasonableness of the criteria for measuring successful completion of the requirements.	26	16	
	The requirements should be stated in enough detail so that test data specifications could be written from those requirements.	26 27 32					Confirm with the data processing project people that the requirements are stated in enough detail so that they could generate test data to verify compliance.	26	16	
	The measurable objectives should apply to both the manual and automated segments of the application system.	27 32					Examine to verify that the system objectives cover both the manual and automated segments of the application.	26	16	

Figure 71. Data Base Audit Program 3.

The requirements phase for an application system must also be concerned with reliability and consistency of data. The data are no longer used for a single application but, rather, multiple applications. Therefore, a single user cannot control consistency and reliability but, rather, must fit into a structure in which reliability and consistency are defined independently of the applications using those data.

The major difference between requirements in a data base environment and those a non-data base environment is that the data base application must interface into an existing definition of data and data structure. This necessitates allocation of more time and effort to the requirements phase because changes that would have been easy in a non-data base environment may be costly and complex when data base technology is used. This extra effort is associated with changing the data base as opposed to the programs that use those data.

Auditors participating in the requirements phase of a data base application should address the three risks identified with that phase. The requirements phase audit program (Figure 71) provides the criteria and tests that the auditor should follow in assuring the adequacy of the requirements for a data base application.

AUDIT GUIDELINE

The system will never *be any better controlled than it is at the end of requirements* unless *requirements occur during the other phases of the SDLC. Stop poorly controlled systems during the requirements phase.*

Design Phase Audit Program

Designing an application to interface with the data base is different than designing a non-data base application in the following ways:

The reading and writing of data base application require interface commands to the DBMS.

If an integrated data dictionary is used, the data definitions must come from the data dictionary.

Access authority may be needed to access the data in the data base.

The sequencing of processing may need to be coordinated with other application systems.

File maintenance considerations may not be part of the design process.

The design must consider the best method for optimizing the use of data base technology. Some organizations use modeling programs in order to test design principles. Poorly designed data base applications may require extensive processing time.

The data base administrator normally works with the project team during the design of data base applications. The data base administrator can frequently offer suggestions to reduce processing time significantly, or can modify the data base to increase the performance of application systems. The amount of effort expended by the data base administrator is usually related to the volume of expected processing by the data base application.

The audit program for the auditor participating in the design phase of a data base application follows (Figure 72).

Program Phase Audit Program

Programming for a data base application should be simpler than for a non-data base application. The simplicity is attributable to the following:

Programs may not include file maintenance routines.

Data validation programs can be generated automatically if data dictionaries with data validation capabilities are utilized.

Many of the special reports can be written by users.

When system specifications are developed using a structured methodology, fewer changes should occur during programming and testing.

One of the main benefits attributable to data base technology is the powerful utility programs accompanying the DBMS. Programmers and users may be able to achieve many of their objectives using those utilities. Thus, the programming function does not change, but the tools to accomplish the programming tasks change.

The auditor involved in the program phase of a data base application should place primary emphasis on conformance to design specifications and data base programming standards. Deviation from those specifications and standards may cause major problems during operation. Programming of a data base application should be highly structured and if changes occur should be reprocessed through requirements and design.

The special risks that need attention during the programming phase of a data base application are addressed in the following audit program (Figure 73).

Test Phase Audit Program

Testing in a data base environment will not be satisfactory if the only testing is by the application programmer on the application program. The programmer can test the internal program logic, but normally cannot test the interface to the data base. In some instances, this can mean there is no assurance that the application programs work satisfactorily until they are placed into an operational environment.

Some of the newer data base systems provide special testing capabilities. One such example is the IBM System/38. This computer simulates the interface to the data base for testing purposes. In testing, the programmer believes that he is creating, updating, and deleting records from the data base, but in actual practice those processes are simulated and the data base remains unchanged.

Some of the differences that the programmer encounters in testing a data base application versus a non-data base application are listed below:

Except for some of the newer DBMS systems, the programmer cannot simulate the data base for test purposes.

Performance levels are difficult to determine until the program is coupled with the live data base.

The sequencing of events between multiple application systems cannot be tested.

Actual data base conditions may be impractical to simulate for test purposes.

What the above differences show is that unit testing cannot adequately address the data base segment of the application system. This data base testing must either be included in special testing or be left untested until the application goes into an operational status. In mature data base organizations, this ''wait'' concept may be acceptable, as the risk associ-

Activity Systems Development Design Phase Review **Auditor** ______ **Date** ______

Risk No.	Control Objective and Evaluation Criteria	Probable Control(s)	Control Assessment: Over	Control Assessment: Adequate	Control Assessment: Under	Control Assessment: N/A	Audit Test	Audit Evidence	Audit Tool	Workpaper Reference
4.	*To include the audit trail in the design specifications*									
	The detailed specification should be documented for each audit trail objective.	27 32					Review the completeness of the specifications in relationship to the audit trail objective.	26	16	
	The audit trail should include both the manual and automated segments of the system.	27					Review the audit trail specifications to verify that both the manual and automated segments are included.	26	16	
	The audit trail should be stored in a sequence and format that make retrieval and use easy.	27 29					Confirm with audit trail users that the format and sequence are consistent with the use they expect to make of the audit trail.	26	16	
2.	*To include the methods of ensuring accurate and complete data in the design specifications*									
	For key financial fields, such as cash receipts, procedures should be established to maintain independent control totals.	27					Verify for key financial fields that independent control procedures are adequate.	18	11 16	
	The data validation routines should be adequate to reduce data entry errors to an acceptable level.	27 29					Develop or obtain a representative list of data entry errors and verify that the data validation routines would detect those errors.	23	3 6	
	Procedures should be established to verify the integrity of key financial fields on a regular basis.	27 29					Confirm with the user that the file integrity verification frequency is adequate to protect the integrity of the data.	26	16	
7.	*To include the accounting requirements in the design specifications*									
	The fields that have accounting implications should be identified.	27					Verify with the accounting department that all of the key financial fields in the applica-	26	16	

							tion under development have been identified.			
	The accounting cutoff requirement for those key financial fields should be stated.	27					Review the completeness and reasonableness of the documented accounting cutoff requirements.	26	16	
	The data base design specifications should include procedures to ensure that key financial transactions are included in the proper accounting period.	27 29					Verify the reasonableness of the method specified to ensure that transactions are placed in the proper accounting period.	26	16	

Figure 72. Data Base Audit Program 4.

Activity Systems Development Program Phase Review **Auditor** ______ **Date** ______

Risk No.	Control Objective and Evaluation Criteria	Probable Control(s)	Control Assessment: Over	Ade-quate	Under	N/A	Audit Test	Audit Evidence	Audit Tool	Workpaper Reference
11.	*To ensure that documentation conforms to data base documentation standards*									
	Data base program specifications should be completed prior to commencing coding.	27,29 30,32 38					Verify that procedures ensure programs will be specified prior to coding.	10	15	
	The documentation should conform to both the letter and intent of the data base programming documentation standards.	31 32 33					Confirm with data base maintenance programmers that the documentation is adequate for maintenance purposes.	26	15	
	The data base applications should be built to standards that will be in effect when the application goes into operation.	30,32 33,34 35					Confirm with the group setting standards that the standards being used to build the application will be in effect when the system goes operational.	10	15	
11.	*To ensure that documentation is up to date*									
	The documentation should include and be based on the current version of the DBMS.	25 32 33					Identify the DBMS version, and determine that the documentation relating to the DBMS is based on that version.	1	15	
	The documentation should include the recovery procedures for both the automated application and the manual support systems.	25 32					Review the application system recovery documentation for completeness and currentness.	15	2	
	The documentation should be reviewed by an independent party to verify the currentness and completeness of the documentation.	32 33					Review the results of an independent documentation review, and if not performed request a third-party documentation review.	24	16	
3.	*To implement controls to ensure the proper sequencing of updates*									
	Controls should be designed to ensure that a	30					Identify transactions whose processing se-	26	11	

	transaction can't be processed out of sequence.	38					quence is important and verify that controls will ensure the proper sequence of processing.			
	Independent control totals should identify out-of-sequence processing if it has an impact on financial totals.	30 38					Determine if out-of-sequence processing can affect the financial totals, and if so determine if controls are adequate to detect that variance should transactions be processed out of sequence.	26	11	
	Controls should prohibit two users from updating the same data element concurrently.	30					Verify that the DBMS has concurrent update controls.	1	7 15	

Figure 73. Data Base Audit Program 5.

Activity Systems Development Test Phase Review **Auditor** ______ **Date** ______

Risk No.	Control Objective and Evaluation Criteria	Probable Control(s)	Control Assessment: Over	Control Assessment: Adequate	Control Assessment: Under	Control Assessment: N/A	Audit Test	Audit Evidence	Audit Tool	Workpaper Reference
10.	*To establish a test plan*									
	The data base application acceptance test criteria should be defined.	25					Verify that the user and data base project personnel have identified and documented the criteria which should be achieved prior to the system's being placed into production.	26	16	
	A detailed plan should be prepared outlining the type of tests needed to verify whether the data base application achieves the acceptance criteria.	25					Examine the test plan and evaluate the completeness of the plan to measure the acceptance criteria.	17 22	16	
	Responsibilities for execution of each part of the test plan should be assigned.	25					Verify that someone is responsible for executing each part of the test plan.	11	11 16	
10.	*To have the test plan implemented or monitored by an independent group*									
	Someone other than a member of the project team should be assigned responsibility to decide if the data base application is acceptable prior to its being placed into production.	28 33 37					Verify that a non-project person is accountable for the adequacy of the system prior to its being placed into production.	11	16	
	The independent party should be involved in implementing the acceptance test, or monitoring the results uncovered by testing by project team members.	28 33 37					Verify that the individual accountable for the acceptance of the system has gathered sufficient information to make that acceptance judgment.	23 26	3 16	
	The independent testers should certify that the system has or has not met the acceptance test criteria.	33 37					Examine the results of testing to ensure that the individual accountable for acceptance testing has prepared and signed a statement indicating the result of that test.	23 26	3 16	
9.	*To test the adequacy of controls*									

	The threats to the integrity of the data base application should be identified.	25 27					Examine the completeness of the identified data base application risks.	26	16	
	The magnitude of each risk should be determined.	27					Evaluate the reasonableness of the documented magnitude of each data base application risk.	26	16	
	The controls should be designed to reduce those risks to an acceptable magnitude.	30					Verify that the function of controls will reduce the risk from the estimated magnitude to an acceptable level.	23 26	3 16	
8.	*To test to ensure that the system achieves specified performance criteria*									
	The data base application processing should function in accordance with system specifications.	26 37 39					Verify that the processing procedures perform in accordance with systems requirements.	20 22,23 26	3 16	
	Manual system processing should not detract from automated system performance.	26 37 39					Verify that the manual systems can process data at the rates required by the automated application.	22 23 26	3 16	
	The error-handling procedures in the application should prevent the system from malfunctioning when erroneous data are entered into the system.	26 37 39					Verify that the error-handling procedures perform in accordance with system requirements.	22 23 26	3 16	

Figure 74. Data Base Audit Program 6.

Activity: Systems Development Installation Phase Review ______ Auditor ______ Date ______

Risk No.	Control Objective and Evaluation Criteria	Probable Control(s)	Control Assessment: Over	Control Assessment: Adequate	Control Assessment: Under	Control Assessment: N/A	Audit Test	Audit Evidence	Audit Tool	Workpaper Reference
6.	*To monitor the installed application to ensure that specified performance criteria are achieved*									
	Procedures should be established to monitor the performance of application systems for at least a reasonable time span after the application is placed into production.	37					Examine the operational monitoring procedures for data base applications and verify that those procedures are both reasonable and followed.	17	16	
	A group independent of the data base application project should monitor that application in the production environment.	37					Verify that a group independent of the application project team will verify that the expected performance levels are achieved by the data base application after it is placed into operation.	10 11 17	16	
	The results of monitoring the performance criteria should be reported to management on a regular basis.	28 37					Review the frequency and type of reports prepared for management describing the performance of operational applications to determine the reasonableness of the reporting procedures.	10 17	16	

Figure 75. Data Base Audit Program 7.

ated with data base diminishes over time; however, in newer data base installations incomplete testing has caused severe problems.

The following audit program is for use by the auditor when participating in the data base application test phase (see Figure 74).

Installation Phase Audit Program

At the completion of acceptance testing, the application must still be placed into the production status. This normally involves cataloging the programs into a production library, and changing the production control libraries so that the new version of the data base application will be used in production on the proper date and time.

The installation of an application system may or may not affect data base procedures. The simpler applications utilizing existing data and data structure may not have any impact on the use of the data base technology. However, applications that require new data elements or new views of the existing data may require some extensive changes to the data base.

The more common installation requirements for a data base application are:

Reorganizing data base. Changes to the data contained within the data base or the organizational structure of those data may require the data base to be reorganized to accommodate the new application.

Changing security/retention requirements. Adding new data to the data base may change the security classification of the data base and/or the retention procedures for those data.

Acquiring access rights to the data base. Users of existing data within the data base should be required to obtain permission to access those data from the individual or group responsible for the data.

At installation, the user will really know how the data base application performs. Prior to that time, performance could only be evaluated on test conditions, which may not be representative of real world conditions. Therefore, the installation should be monitored closely to determine that the actual performance levels are acceptable, if different than those experienced in testing.

The installation is normally a short phase, but the auditor should remain involved with the data base application because from a user perspective installations have been a particularly troublesome phase of the system development life cycle. The following audit program is for use in reviewing the installation of a data base application (see Figure 75).

AUDIT GUIDELINE

Auditing is not a line function. Therefore, don't be put into a position of certifying data base systems before they go into production. Auditors provide opinions—managers make decisions.

nine

AUDITING DATA BASE ACCESS CONTROLS

Security, unlike many of the other controls, is difficult to evaluate. Even in operation, many organizations are uncertain as to whether or not security controls function. The question that needs to be asked is, "Have the security controls stopped the penetration, or has penetration occurred undetected?" This is not an easy question for the auditor to answer through review and test.

Security over data base takes on greater importance for two reasons. First, more data are contained in a single location than with most non-data base files; and second, more sophisticated software is available to analyze and extract data from the data base. These factors coupled with the newness of the technology make the assessment of security an important part of the data base unit.

This chapter provides the auditor with an audit program for evaluating data base security. The audit program is designed to identify control weaknesses that might be violated by the casual perpetrator. The audit program is not designed to identify weaknesses or methods by which the highly sophisticated perpetrator could break security. If the audit objectives involve the sophisticated perpetrator, it is recommended that security consultants be added to the audit team.

DATA BASE SECURITY STRATEGY

Data processing has been subject to the Bonnie and Clyde security syndrome since its inception. Bonnie and Clyde were bank robbers who robbed banks using the automobile technology while police were still on horseback. In data processing, perpetrators used technology for personal gain before those responsible for security used that same technology as a deterrent to those perpetrators. Data base provides an excellent opportunity for the Bonnie and Clyde type perpetrators.

The security strategy for computers has changed slowly over the years. When business computers first came into use, they were housed in glass-enclosed showrooms, frequently in the front window of an organization, to demonstrate the organization's sophisticated processing method. Regular tours were conducted through the computer room to show off the new facility. As secruity problems surfaced, particularly bombings of computer rooms, the showroom was converted into a fortress. Computers were housed in windowless, impenetrable areas. The emphasis was on physical security.

As technology advanced with the introduction of disk storage, multiprogramming, and telecommunication, new methods of penetration were used. One program could access the instructions and data of another program; one program could explore the entire contents of on-line disk files; access to the system could be achieved through on-line communications; and Trojan horse routines were imbedded in the operating system or an application

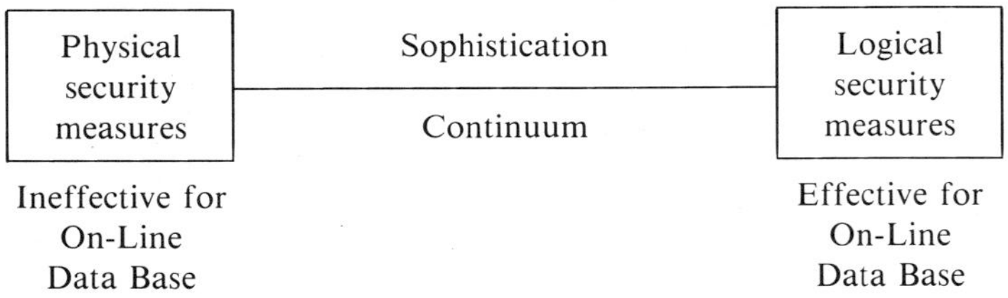

Desirable Strategy	Problem If Strategy Is Not Followed
Primary Strategy	
1. To perform risk analysis	Risks will not be identified.
2. To develop security profile	Security requirements will not be established.
3. To establish a security officer function	There will not be a spokesperson for security.
Secondary Strategy	
1. To implement a security software package	Logical security requirements will be difficult to enforce.

Figure 76. Security/Access Strategy.

program to be activated at some later date. None of these methods required physical access to the computer room. The era of logical security began.

The security strategy of most organizations moves along a continuum of sophistication from physical to logical security (see Figure 76). Physical security remains important but must be supplemented by logical security. Logical security is defined as those security measures operating within the computer's central processing unit.

Logical security can be preventive, detective, or corrective security. Detective security measures do not stop events from occurring, but merely record those events so that the appropriate action can be taken. For example, IBM's SMF records who accessed what resource, and as such can be used as a detective security measure to determine when improper access has occurred. Preventive security measures stop improper access from occurring and normally use passwords for the control method. Corrective security measures take action against improper access, such as shutting down a computer terminal which has failed to enter an authorized password within a reasonable number of attempts.

The computer strategy of an organization can be viewed as moving from physical to logical security. Some desirable security strategies that are indicative of more sophisticated logical security are:

To perform risk analysis. Conducting a risk analysis exercise identifies the threats faced by the data base. Having this extensive list of threats is conducive to adding additional security measures, many of which will need to be logical security measures. If risk analysis is not performed, there may be large risks present for which there are no countermeasures.

To develop security profile. A security profile is a formal definition of who has access to what resources. How to develop this profile is explained later in this chapter. Without such a security profile, it is difficult to develop complete security requirements for the computer.

To establish a security officer function. The establishment of an individual or group having security responsibility for the organization is a formal recognition of the importance of security. It normally takes a catalyst such as a security officer function to focus the necessary attention on security so that the appropriate countermeasures can be installed. Without such a function, the other pressures facing data processing may take precedence over security due to the lack of a spokesperson for security.

To implement a security software package. This secondary strategy normally follows the implementation of the above strategies. Without risk analysis, a security profile, and a spokesperson for security, the acquisition and implementation of a security software package rarely happen. On the other hand, without a security software package the logical security requirements are difficult to enforce.

AUDIT GUIDELINE

In a data base environment, put the audit emphasis on logical security.

SECURITY CONSIDERATIONS

Security in an organization can be viewed as a chain of countermeasures to prevent perpetrators from gaining access to the computer resources. Countermeasures will include such things as a security guard at the entrance to the computer room, the use of passwords, and the shredding of computer reports and carbon paper. Each of these countermeasures is designed to prevent the loss of security over some aspect of data processing.

The links in the chain (i.e., security countermeasures) may be of different strengths. For example, using cryptography to prevent the interception of easy-to-understand information being tranmsitted over communication lines is a very strong countermeasure, while operator security training may be a weak countermeasure. Perpetrators search out and penetrate at the weakest point in the system. One well-known computer abuse expert stated that the cost of tapping transmission lines even without cryptography is significantly higher than a $100 bribe that might be required to acquire that same information from a computer operator. The argument was that if there are relatively weak links in security, it is not economical to strengthen the stronger links through measures such as cryptography until the weaker links have been strengthened.

Security must be continually evaluated in order to identify and improve the weak security links in the system. The objective should be either to create a chain of security around the computer in which the links are of equal strength, or to surround the computer with rings of security so that when one ring is penetrated another ring appears. In the chain concept, the strength comes from links of equal strength, while in the ring concept the strength comes from a series of security measures, all of which must be broken before penetration can occur. Note that the two concepts can be used in conjunction with one another.

Conducting Risk Analysis

The process that is helpful in identifying security risks so that the appropriate countermeasures can be installed is risk analysis. Risk analysis is a science devoted to the identification and determination of the magnitude of security risks. The objective of the process is to utilize the combined talents of the individuals understanding the computer environment in order to identify the risks in that environment. The end result of the risk analysis exercise is a list of threats to the computer area. Management can then determine whether it is worth expending resources to reduce those threats.

Successful risk analysis is usually dependent upon having a trained risk analysis facilitator. This individual organizes, directs, and summarizes the work of the risk analysis participants. Without the facilitator, the process may lack direction and thus fail to produce the proper results.

The security officer normally acts as the risk analysis facilitator. Organizations that do not have a security officer should train one of their senior data processing personnel in risk analysis concepts so he or she can be the facilitator. The risk analysis exercise practiced under the direction of a trained facilitator can be a very productive exercise for the computer function.

Listed below are tasks that are normally followed in conducting a risk analysis exercise.

Task 1: Organize risk analysis team

The selection of the individuals to the risk analysis team is an important part of the exercise. The objective is to bring together people with multiple disciplines and experience on how systems are developed and used within the organization. Without the multidisciplined approach, the risk attention focus might be too narrow.

The good risk analysis team should include following:

Senior management representative
Systems analyst
Application programmer
Systems programmer
Computer operations representative
Auditor
Application system users (normally more than one)
Computer security consultant (if budgets permit)

Task 2: Train risk analysis team

Prior to convening the risk analysis team, some formal training should occur. The training is normally conducted by the risk analysis facilitator or the computer security consultant if used. Training may be formal or informal, but formal classroom training is preferred. The training has three objectives:

1. To explain risk analysis concepts and the individual members' obligations and responsibilities in that process
2. To explain how the team functions, emphasizing the processes that will be used to identify risk
3. To explain the value of determining the magnitude of the risk and describe the process that will be used by the risk analysis team in this magnitude determination

Task 3: Conduct risk analysis exercise

The team is convened for a period ranging from a few hours to a few days depending on the magnitude of the task. The facilitator begins the exercise by explaining the objectives of the exercise, the role and responsibility of each team member, and the method by which the exercise will be conducted. The facilitator does not direct the exercise but, rather, counsels and assists the group in the performance of the exercise.

Risk analysis is an analytical brainstorming session. The analytical aspect requires the team to explain how the risk might occur, while the brainstorming aspect means that no proposed risk can be criticized or rejected without further investigation. While the process can be unstructured, it is normally advisable to focus the attention on specific points of penetration as opposed to rambling. The categories of penetration that might be addressed should include:

Computer terminal facility
Communication lines
Physical access to the computer room
Application programs
Operating software
Vendor and maintenance personnel

At the conclusion of the brainstorming segment of the exercise, the list of potential risks must be consolidated and analyzed, and the magnitude of each risk must be assessed.

The end result of the exercise will be a list of potential risks. Normally there is much overlap so that it becomes necessary to consolidate duplicate and overlapping risks into a single risk category. At the end of this process, a cohesive list of potential risks will have been developed.

At this point, each of these risks must be challenged for validity. The team must agree that each risk is realistic. The objective is to produce a list of risks that pose a real threat to the organization.

The final part of the risk analysis exercise is to determined the magnitude of the risk. The risk analysis team can complete this part of the exercise in any one of the following manners:

Ranking. Rank the risk list from high to low. The first item on the list will be the highest risk to the organization, and the last item, the lowest risk.

Qualitative category. Categorize the risks in the categories such as high, medium, and low. This allows the organization to concentrate first on the higher risks before addressing the medium and low risks.

Judgment. Quantify the risks using judgment. This normally produces a dollar range in which the risk is believed to fall, for example, risk X may result in a loss of between $10,000 and $30,000.

Formula method. Quantify the risk using the annual loss expectation formula. The risk analysis team estimates both the frequency of loss and the average loss per occurrence in order to produce an annual loss expectation.

Task 4: Present results and recommendations to management

The risk analysis facilitator completes this final task. The risk analysis team's role is the identification and quantification of risk. They are not considered security experts and thus are not the proper group to develop conclusions and present recommendations to management, although they normally do provide input into that process.

Normally, the establishment of security controls is recommended to management. A later section in this chapter outlines the more common types of security controls. Since these are representative of security control practices, it is logical to assume that the more effective security control recommendations contain the security controls described in this chapter.

ESTABLISHING THE SECURITY OFFICER FUNCTION

The security officer function has responsibility for computer security in the organization. This function should be differentiated from plant security, which is more of a police-type function, patrolling the perimeters of the organization's property. Obviously, the computer security officer and plant security should work closely together if the latter function exists.

The responsibilities of the data base security officer function have been described in the chapter on data base organization. The actual responsibilities will vary based upon the size of the organization, the types of users, the resources being protected, and the technology in use. To develop the security officer function responsibilities, one need only modify the responsibilities outlined in Figure 48 based on the above criteria.

Two questions need to be addressed in the establishment of the security officer function. These are: (1) How should the security officer function be staffed? and (2) Where should the security officer function report? The answers to these two questions are interrelated.

The following three alternatives have been used in staffing the security officer function:

1. *Security committee.* A group of individuals interested in security is formed to oversee security in the data processing function. This is usually a permanent committee which is assigned specific responsibilities and may have a budget to carry out those responsibilities. In organizations that charge for their services, a budget is usually established for the operation of this committee. Normally the committee is chaired by a member of data processing management and comprises individuals from all of the major data processing sections.
2. *Part-time security officer.* One individual is assigned the security officer responsibilities on a part-time basis. Frequently, this individual is a member of the computer operations department, and the individual's other responsibilities may be related to security. For example, a systems programmer who has responsibility for security software may be made the data base security officer.
3. *Full-time security officer.* One or more individuals are assigned the full-time responsibility of overseeing security in the computer area.

The method selected for staffing the function is normally dependent upon the importance given security by data processing management. The more important security becomes to management, the more resources are allocated to the security of the data processing function. The disadvantage of committees and part-time assignments is the competition for the individual's time by other responsibilities. Unless the part-time individuals are convinced of management's true concern for security, they may not devote the proper attention to it. On the other hand, getting a competent full-time security officer may prove difficult, and without a highly skilled and dedicated individual, the needed protection may not materialize. It is not the type of function in which to place an individual so he or she will not hurt any other segment of the data processing area.

DEVELOPING A SECURITY PROFILE

The security profile is a process of documenting authorized accessibility to data base resources. The profile identifies both the data base resources and the authorized users. The profile documents which user has access to which resource. The security profile is the documentation for the process that (1) identifies the resources in data base technology that require protection; and (2) identifies all of the individuals/terminals/programs that require access to those resources.

The data base security profile can be a data base control mechanism, or it can be part of a larger security system. Some organizations identify all resources subject to control and all individuals requiring access so that they can build the security profile for the organization. The security profile discussed in this book is that for the data base resources. Specifically, it will concentrate on the data resources.

Access can be controlled by individual, by terminal, by program, or by a combination thereof. For example, selected individuals may be restricted to accessing the data base from specific terminals. Even though the individual is authorized to access data, he cannot do it from terminals other than the ones authorized. This may be necessary to increase assurance that the authorized individual is, in fact, requesting access.

The resources listed can be data, groups of data, the entire data base, data base programs, data base utilities, and special data base privileged commands. A security rule of thumb says that all resources should be under the control of the data base security system. It also states that all individuals interacting with the data base should be under the security system. This includes the data base administrator, systems programmers, operators, and even data base administration management.

Accessibility to the data base resources can be defined by type of access. In other words access does not have to mean either complete access or no access. The data processing term for defining the level of access is granularity. This means the fineness of the access control process.

An example of a data base profile is listed in Figure 77. The granularity code for this profile example is as follows:

Data Base Resource / **Program**	**Employee Number**	**Employee Rate**	**Hours Worked**	**Exemptions**	**Weekly Gross Pay**	**Weekly Deduction**	**Weekly Net Pay**	**Year-to-Date Gross Pay**	**Year-to-Date Deductions**	**Year-to-Date Net Pay**
Personnel	F	F								
Payroll	R	R	A	R	C	C	C	U	U	U
Employee benefits	R			F		R		R		
Tax	R				R	R	R	R	R	R
Cost accounting	R				R			R		

Granularity code:
R = read only D = delete
U = update C = calculate
A = add F = full capability
Blank = access not permitted

Figure 77. Data Base Security Profile.

R = read only. The user can only read the data.

U = update. The user can change the value of the data, but cannot add or delete a value.

A = add. This user is authorized to add a new data field to the data base (e.g. adding another employee to the payroll system).

D = delete. The user is authorized to delete one of the data values.

C = calculate. This user can create this field through a mathematical calculation.

F = full capability. This user can perform any of the above activities on the indicated data base resource.

Granularity can be much more specific than the above code indicates. For example, the payroll department may be authorized to read only selected employees' pay rate information, while the ability to change pay rate occurs outside the payroll department. This means that payroll programs can only read pay rates that meet the access criteria. For example, there might be an hourly payroll calculation program, a weekly payroll system, and a monthly payroll system. One program can be restricted then to read the pay rate of an employee only if the pay rate is in the hourly pay range, another payroll program can read pay rates only if the rates are in the weekly pay range, and a third only if in the monthly pay range. Granularity can even go further. It can indicate that pay rates can only be read once per week, and it can also restrict departments for which pay rates can be read or updated. Some DBMS systems have up to 16 levels of granularity fineness in which they can restrict access.

Figure 77 is an example for a personnel data base. The data base resources listed are individual data elements. Five programs are listed in Figure 77. It is these programs that have access to the data elements and thus are the users of that data.

To interpret the data base security profile, it is necessary to understand the granularity codes in the matrix intersection. For example, the personnel program has full capabilities to read, update, add, or delete both the employee number and the pay rate because an ''F'' is indicated at those matrix intersections. However, the personnel program cannot get at any of the other fields in the personnel data base, as those intersections are blank. The payroll programs can read employee number, employee rate, and exemptions, and can add hours worked for the week. The payroll program can also calculate weekly pay and update the year-to-date pay. The access restrictions for the other programs are documented in the data base security profile.

The data base security profile becomes the specifications for enforcement of access control. Enforcement normally occurs through security passwords using a password control system. Obviously, the granularity within the security profile can be no greater than can be enforced by the security system. For example, it would not make sense to differentiate adding and deleting of records if that was not controllable using the granularity code capabilities. The security system dictates the maximum level of security permissible.

Without the enforcement of the access rules documented in the security profile, the exercise of preparing the profile is meaningless. The profile should be prepared by the users having accountability for individual data elements. They should tell the security officer who can access that data element as the basis for completing the security profile.

Once the security profile has been initially prepared and enforced through security software, it must be updated periodically. The updates can be made on a printed version of the security profile when the user indicates changes to the accessibility of data for which the user is responsible. It is generally not necessary to redo the security profile completely after it is first completed. The updates entered into the security system by the application project personnel can serve as the basis for maintaining the currency of reports of data base security.

The tasks involved in creating the security profile are as follows:

Task 1: Identify data base resources

The resources requiring control should be identified. In some organizations, this information can be obtained from the inventory of data elements, specifically those with financial implications. If such an inventory is not available, it would need to be developed in order to create the security profile.

Task 2: Identify security access enforcement mechanism

The preparer of the security profile needs to determine what levels of granularity are included within the security access mechanism. These are the level of granularity that should be used on the data base security profile. As previously stated, it is impractical to document a level of security which is not controllable using the security software.

Task 3: Identify resources requiring access

The preparer of the security profile using SMF or equivalent should identify the most common users of the identified data base resources. In organizations that have a good data dictionary, this information might be included in the data dictionary.

Task 4: Identify individual accountable for each resource

This is the individual who will make the decision on who can access the resource for which that individual is accountable and for what purpose.

Task 5: Document accessibility with the user

The preparer of the profile should interview the accountable user to determine the type of access authorized for the resources under the control of that user.

Task 6: Document and implement security profile

The purpose of the security profile exercise is to enforce accessibility rules in the production environment. The profile becomes the basis for the enforcement. When initially implemented, there may be users who have not been contacted who require access to that information. The enforcement process should provide the capability for making those modifications in a timely fashion.

AUDIT GUIDELINE

Risk analysis is a tool that can help the auditor identify data base access risks.

EVALUATING DATA BASE SECURITY

There are two philosophies of security risks in a data base environment. One philosophy is a people philosophy. That assumes that only people embezzle, not machines, and therefore the security analysis and controls should be placed on people. The other philosophy is that security violations occur through transactions and thus transactions should be the focus of control.

There is merit in both arguments. In actual practice, organizations control both people and transactions. The methods of evaluating the security environment do not vary significantly whether the emphasis is placed on people or transactions.

The security evaluation is one involving assessing the ability of people or transactions to manipulate the data base environment. To circumvent security controls successfully, an individual must be able to perform an event and conceal the performance of that event. In other words, he or she must be able to violate security and then adjust the records so that that violation cannot be detected. For example, assume the security violation involves the changing of an accounts receivable file so that the amount due was lowered. This would be detected through normal controls unless that individual could also change the control total, in which case the security violation and the loss associated with that violation may not be detectable.

One method used to assess the adequacy of the security of the data base environment is to evaluate the segregation of duties within the data base environment. These can be people duties or transactions duties. The process that can be used to determine whether any individual can perform an action and then conceal that action is to identify conflicting functions performed by a single person, in other words, to determine whether an individual is able to perform two events which are conflicting.

The tool that is used to evaluate segregation of function is a conflict matrix. Figure 78 illustrates a conflict matrix for a purchasing data base. The illustration shows an ideal segregation of functions for that system.

The conflict matrix lists on one side the people involved in a function, and on the other side the conflicting tasks that are performed within that function. The checks in the matrix include which individual performs which task.

People / **Conflicting Tasks**	**Request Product**	**Approve Purchase Order**	**Place Order**	**Receive Product**	**Approve Payment**	**Issue Check**
Requester	✓					
Department head		✓				
Purchasing agent			✓			
Receiving clerk				✓		
Payable clerk					✓	
Cashier						✓

Figure 78. Conflict Matrix for a Purchasing System.

The people listed on the left-hand side of the matrix are all of those individuals involved within the particular function. In our conflict matrix example, the evaluated function is purchasing. Note that the Figure 60 matrix uses titles as opposed to names of individuals. Either title or individual name may be used. Note also that the people involved in the purchasing system are from throughout the organization, and not exclusively from the purchasing department.

The conflicting tasks are those tasks that are performed in the fulfillment of purchasing a product, but note that not two tasks should be performed by the same person. Good security procedures indicate that tasks should be divided so that no one individual should be able to perform more than two of the tasks. Identifying the people involved in any given function is not difficult; defining the tasks takes more time and judgment in that that information is normally not readily available.

The people are factual and the tasks are determined by the individual completing the matrix. Both the people and the tasks should be identified before the matrix is completed. The people should be sequenced in the order in which the flow of work will pass, and the tasks should be sequenced in the order in which the tasks occur.

The conflict matrix is completed by indicating in the matrix by a check which individual performs which task. The Figure 78 conflict matrix shows a perfectly segregated environment (indicated by the diagonal line of checks) in that each identified individual only performs a single task. In actual practice, some individuals may perform more than one task. In this case, some of the checks would be on a horizontal line which is indicative of a security problem.

When a security problem is detected, appropriate action should be taken first to determine if any security violations have occurred, and then to close that security loophole. When the data base conflict matrix is used, the solution is normally the reassignment of tasks so that the organization can attempt to achieve an ideal segregation of functions.

DETECTING PENETRATION

One of the dilemmas facing the security reviewer is, "Where is the most logical point at which security penetration would occur?" The answer to this question is sought not only by the auditor, but also by the security officer. The second major question asked about penetration is, "Who is the most logical security penetrator?" This type of information is valuable not only in data base security, but also in detecting and preventing data base fraud.

The tool used to identify penetrators and penetration points is the penetration point matrix. This matrix is a tool devised primarily for fraud auditing, but it has security uses. The matrix can be used to detect the most likely point at which security will be violated, so that security can be strengthened at that point.

The penetration point matrix is a planning tool. It is not a high-precision instrument in that it can pick "the" specific point and individual, but it is a methodical way of analyzing a risk situation to select probable penetrators and penetration points. The technique has been successfully used in many fraud investigations.

The penetration point matrix assigns a score based upon the probability that a specific individual can penetrate a predetermined point in a system. The individual accumulating the most points, and the point accumulating the highest risk score, should be the focuses of strong security measures. The next most critical penetration point can be identified and security measures strengthened at that point if necessary. The process can continue as long as the security personnel believe that the exercise has identified high-risk situations. Let's look at the use of this matrix in order to understand the concept better.

People \ Penetration Points	Request Order	Issue Order	Warehouse	Computer System	Pay Invoice	Approve Invoice	Transportation	Risk Score
Requester	2	1	1					4
Approver		2				1		3
Purchasing agent		(3)	2	2		2	2	(11)
Receiving clerk			1				1	2
Payable clerk			1			1		2
Cashier			1		2	1		4
Data base administrator				3				3
Mail clerk					1			1
Sales person		2				1	1	4
Risk Score	2	(8)	6	5	3	6	4	

Figure 79. Penetration Point Matrix for a Purchasing System.

A penetration point matrix for a purchasing data base system is illustrated in Figure 79. Note that the conflict matrix illustrated in Figure 78 was also for a purchasing data base system in order to contrast the two matrices as evaluating risk in a common application.

The people in the penetration point matrix are all the individuals who have an opportunity to defraud or break security in the purchasing system. Note that in the conflict matrix the people involved were those participating in the system. In the penetration point matrix, those same individuals appear, but we have added individuals such as the data base administrator, mail clerk, and salesperson who do not participate in purchasing but do have an opportunity to defraud the purchasing system. In practice, more people may need to be added, such as a systems programmer, computer operator, and other people believed to have an opportunity to penetrate the system. There is more judgment involved in selecting the people for the penetration point matrix that is required for the conflict matrix.

A penetration point is defined as a point at which security could be violated. Determining these points required judgment on the part of the security individual. The penetration points selected for the purchasing system has some relationship to those in the conflict matrix, but they extend outside of the normal system. For example, the transportation process is cited as a penetration point as is the computer system. A study would have to be made of the system by a knowledgeable security officer in order to determine the complete list of penetration points in the system under analysis.

The matrix must be scored after the people and penetration points are included. The scoring of the matrix again is a matter of judgment, which requires an individual knowledgeable in both the system and the people who have access to that system. The scoring which is used and placed in the intersections of the matrix is interpreted as follows:

3 = individual has a high potential to defraud the system at this point.

2 = individual has an average probability to defraud the system at this point.

1 = individual has a low probability to penetrate security at this point.

Blank = individual has no practical opportunity to violate security at this point.

Each individual's opportunity to break security at each penetration point is assessed and a penetration probability score assigned. In some organizations, two or more people complete these independently and then they use the Delphi technique to agree on a common risk score. The Delphi technique is an iterative approach. It permits each of the participants to see the scores developed by all the other individuals. Each participant is then given an opportunity to change his or her score based on the other participants' scores and arguments. The results are tallied, and the information is sent back to the participants. The process continues until a general consensus is reached.

After the individual intersections have been scored, both the horizontal and vertical axes are totaled. This gives a risk score for each of the people included in the matrix, as well as each of the penetration points. The individual receiving the highest risk score would be the prime candidate for security violations, and the penetration point receiving the highest score would be the most probable point for penetration. In our example, the purchasing agent received 11 points and thus becomes the prime candidate for security violations. The point at which the purchase order is issued received the most risk points of any of the penetration points and thus becomes the most probable point for violating security. The conclusion of this exercise is that the point at which the purchasing agent issues the order is the most likely point for violating security within the purchasing data base system.

It is important to remember that the most probable candidate for fraud may be one of the most respected individuals in the organization. Therefore, this exercise should not negatively affect the standing and prestige that individual has in the organization. What the exercise is showing is that that individual has the greatest opportunity at a particular point. Providing strong security measures at that point not only protects the organization, but it also protects the individual from being accused of a security violations in the event one should occur. Also, good controls keep good people honest.

This exercise should be considered when evaluating security in order to identify the most probable penetration point. The value of the exercise is to concentrate security audits and the development of security measures on the high-risk points. Again, the user is cautioned that this is merely a planning tool for future investigation and is not a highly predictive process. As a rule of thumb, risk scores that are within plus or minus 10% of one another should generally be considered ties.

AUDIT GUIDELINE

The matrix is a control documentation tool that when complete can be used to assess the adequacy of control.

SECURITY CONTROL OBJECTIVES

A large aerospace manufacturer had a sign over the door of the computer room which stated: "All computer operators will be fired on the spot if an unescorted visitor is detected within the computer room." Security was an important part of the aerospace manufacturer's business, and they developed the policy to ensure that operators would challenge an unauthorized individual in the computer room. Let's view two scenarios of the enforcement of that policy.

In Scene 1, an unescorted visitor wanders into the computer room and is detected some time later by a supervisor. The supervisor warns the computer operators that they should have detected and reported the unescorted visitor. The supervisor goes on to state that if there is one more violation the operators will be fired in accordance with the policy.

Now let's look at Scene 2. The same unescorted visitor wanders into the computer room and is detected some time later by a supervisor. The supervisor immediately notifies all the operators that they have been terminated from employment and are to report to the gate of the plant where their paychecks will be delivered. The question posed is, "Under which circumstances will security measures be more stringent?" The answer is obvious.

Data base security risks can be very large. They can mean the loss of financial resources, and they can also mean the loss of business. In our aerospace manufacturing example, if they were unable to protect the secrets provided them under government contracts, they might no longer be eligible for future contracts. Organizations that cannot protect the private information about their employees may lose those employees. Organizations that cannot keep customer and vendor relationships confidential may find they are no longer doing business with those organizations. Security is important.

The recommended control objectives for the security/access activity are listed in Figure 80 and also below.

To assign responsibility for security to a function independent of the one requiring security

Effective security should be directed and monitored by an independent group. When data processing personnel have many on-the-job pressures, security may take a low priority when a job falls behind schedule. It is also difficult for the does to find fault with the security process he/she developed.

To define access to each data base resource

Until the resources and the people authorized to access those resources are defined, security measures cannot be implemented.

To include individuals involved in data base in the access control process

No one having access to the data base should be excluded from the security process. This includes data base administration personnel, operators, data processing management, maintenance, and vendor personnel.

To see that violators are promptly punished

If there is no incentive to comply with security, people will not do so.

Number*	Risk	Recommended Control Objective
1.	Inadequate assignment of responsibilities	1. To assign responsibility for security to a function independent of the one requiring security
5.	Unauthorized access in the data base	1. To define access to each data base resource 2. To include all individuals involved in data base in the access control process 3. To ensure prompt punishment of violators 4. To create logs of security-related activities
9.	Fraud/embezzlement	1. To see that security measures address the common methods of fraud
12.	Continuity of processing	1. To ensure that visitors and service personnel are escorted 2. To assess the risks of security problems on disruptions to processing
14.	Lack of management support	1. To see that management establishes the desired level of security 2. To see that management supports punishment for security violations

*See Figure 8 for description of risk.

Figure 80. Security/Access Control Objectives.

To create logs of security-related activities

In automated environments, the security checking is performed by software packages. Unless logs of potential or actual security violations are created, there may be no basis for taking corrective action.

To see that security measures address the common methods of fraud

Fraud is a potential risk that can only be adequately addressed by study. Knowing how people defraud provides the basis for preventing frauds from occurring.

To see that visitors and service personnel are escorted

Individuals walking escorted in the data base area may be able to perform both disruptive and improper acts without detection.

To assess risk of security problems on disruptions to processing

Sabotage and acts of nature have put many organizations out of business for long periods of time. These security risks need to be assessed and their impact on continuity of processing determined so that appropriate action can be taken to provide for alternate processing facilities.

To ensure that management establishes the desired level of security

Security without management backing is ineffective. Therefore, management should establish the level of security they desire and then support the people and procedures necessary to achieve that level of security.

To ensure that management supports punishment for security violators

One of the major incentives for compliance to security procedures is avoiding punishment. Unless management is actively involved in the punishment process, security measures may go unheeded.

GOOD SECURITY/ACCESS CONTROL PRACTICES

A lot of people talk about the security, but few take action on it. People have great difficulty believing that a problem that has not previously occurred to them will ever occur in the future. It is this type of thinking that leads less than 15% of the drivers to wear seat belts. Most of the drivers not using seat belts have never been in an automobile accident, and they don't believe it can happen to them.

Few organizations have experienced serious security violations. There are normally minor violations, but these can be dealt with and accepted. The major security violations are the ones that prove the greatest risk, and the ones in most need of control.

Few data base organizations have good security procedures. Some banks tape passwords to the teller terminals to make it easy for the tellers to gain access to the computer. In some banks, override passwords are also taped to the terminal in case the regular passwords are unacceptable. Some of these banks have lost large amounts of money due to lax security controls.

Number	Control Name	Control Description
40.	Physical barrier	A physical restraint preventing individuals from accessing data base technology
41.	Surveillance	The use of guards or electronic equipment to detect penetration
42.	Data base malfunction reporting	Reports to management identifying the type and severity of problems occurring with data base technology
43.	Natural disaster and environmental risk	Taking the measures necessary to protect data base technology from acts of God and man, such as fire or earthquake
44.	Maintenance plan	A predetermined schedule for performing maintenance to correct problems before they occur
45.	Security officer function	Appointing one individual accountable for security of data base technology
46.	Security profile	A matching of user needs to data base technology capabilities
47.	Passwords	A secret code or word that individuals or programs must know in order to gain access to data base technology
48.	Password control	Issuance and control over passwords and security keys
49.	Recovery lockout	Locking of files against further updates while recovery is occurring
50.	Access review	A daily review of SMF (IBM's System Management Facility) or equivalent for verifying authorized access to the software partition and data set
51.	Reorganization control	Requiring a data base password to initiate reorganization
52.	DBMS password protection	Locating the DBMS software in a separate password protected storage area
53.	Master terminal control	Restricting system commands to the major terminals
54.	Security reports	Regular reports to senior management describing security violations
55.	Bait records	Dummy records included in the data base to identify when security has been violated
56.	Automatic shutdown	Disengaging of a facility after a predetermined number of invalid access attempts
57.	Conflict matrix	Identification of segregation of responsibilities conflicts
58.	Penetration point matrix	Identification of the point and individual where a security violation is most likely to occur

Figure 81. Data Base Security/Access Controls.

In one large West Coast bank, a consultant sat down at a data base terminal and electronically transferred a million dollars to the consultant's personal bank account in Switzerland. Not only was the consultant not challenged, but the fraud was not uncovered until a few weeks later when that individual attempted to smuggle diamonds which had been purchased in Switzerland back into the United States and was caught by a customs-agent.

Many good controls are being developed to enhance security. The controls used for data base security are listed in Figure 81. This figure provides a brief description of the control, with a more extensive description in Appendix A.

The risks present in the data base access activity, together with the controls to reduce those risks, are listed on Figure 82. This figure is designed to help the security officer and system analyst select controls to address specific risks, and to help the auditor anticipate the type of controls that might be present to reduce identified risks.

DATA BASE ACCESS ACTIVITY AUDIT PROGRAM

The concepts outlined in this chapter have been incorporated into the audit program for the access activity (see Figure 83). The program, as with previous audit programs, provides the criteria for the auditor to use in evaluating access controls. The information gathered from these programs should be used in developing opinions about the adequacy of controls within the data base environment.

AUDIT GUIDELINE

If the auditor does not believe access to the data base is controlled, there is normally no basis for relying on data base controls.

Data Base Risks \ Data Base Activity	Controls
1. Inadequate assignment of responsibilities	Security officer function Conflict matrix
5. Unauthorized access in a data base	Physical barrier Surveillance Data base malfunction reporting Security officer function Security profile Passwords Password control Recovery lockout Access review Reorganization control DBMS password protection Master terminal control Automatic shutdown
9. Fraud/embezzlement	Surveillance Security officer function Password control Access review Security reports Bait records Conflict matrix Penetration point matrix
12. Continuity of processing	Physical barrier Surveillance Data base malfunction reporting Natural disaster and environmental protection Maintenance plan
14. Lack of management support	Security officer function Security reports Conflict matrix Penetration point matrix

Figure 82. Data Base Controls for the Security/Access Activity.

Activity Access Control **Auditor** ______ **Date** ______

Risk No.	Control Objective and Evaluation Criteria	Probable Control(s)	Control Assessment				Audit Test	Audit Evidence	Audit Tool	Workpaper Reference
			Over	Ade-quate	Under	N/A				
1.	*To assign responsibility for security to a function independent of the one requiring security*									
	An independent security function should be established to oversee security of the data base environment.	45					Examine the charter and responsibilities of the security officer function to ensure it has adequate independence.	11	15	
	The individual(s) with security responsibilities should possess adequate skills to fulfill the function.	45					Verify through job descriptions and personnel records that the individual(s) in the security officer function possesses the needed skills to perform the function.	11	15	
	The security officer function should have appropriate reporting lines to members of senior management.	45					Verify that the security officer has regular interaction through reporting or personal discussion with members of senior management about the security of the data base environment.	11 24	15	
5.	*To define access to each data base resource*									
	A list should be maintained of the individuals who are authorized access to the data base.	46 47					Examine the list of individuals authorized for access to the data base and compare that list to the DBMS log to ensure that only those individuals are gaining access to the data base.	3 4 8 9	2 3 9 11	
	A list should be maintained of the data base resources requiring access control.	46					Verify that a list is maintained of data base resources and ensure through analysis of the DBMS log that that list contains all of the resources within the data base environment.	3 4 8 9	2 3 9 11	
	A security profile should be prepared showing which individuals have access to which resources.	46					Examine the existence of the security profile and conduct those tests necessary to ensure that the profile is enforced in the operating environment.	9	11 15	

5.	*To include all individuals involved in the data base in the access control process*									
	Data base administration personnel should be restricted in their access to the data base.	45,47 52 57					Verify through examination of security profiles and security logs that access of data base administration personnel to the data base is controlled.	3 4 9	3 9 11 15	
	Computer operators' and system programmers' access to the data base should be restricted.	45 47 52 57					Verify through examination of security profiles and security logs that access of computer operators and system programmers to the data base is controlled.	3 4 9	3 9 11 15	
	Vendor personnel access to the data base should be restricted.	44,45 47,52 57					Verify through examination of security profiles and security logs that access of vendor personnel to the data base is controlled.	3 4 9	3 9 11 15	
5.	*To see that violators are promptly punished*									
	Security violations should be recorded.	48 54					Examine the procedures for recording security violations and verify that the procedures are being followed.	3 4 24	3 9 15	
	Punishment policy for security violations should be defined.	45					Examine the policy for punishing security violators to determine its reasonableness.	25	15	
	Security violators without due cause should be punished in a timely fashion.	45					Determine that the procedures for punishing security violators are carried out in a timely fashion.	25	15	
5.	*To maintain logs of security-related activities*									
	A data base log (e.g., DBMS log or security log) should record security-related activities whenever the DBMS is in operation.	48 52					Examine the contents of the log recording security activities to verify that those activities are properly recorded.	3 4	3 9	
	Management should determine what security information is recorded on the data base security log.	45 48					Verify that if options are available for recording security information, management (may be security management) selects the options that are recorded on the log.	1 25	15	
	The log of security activity should be evaluated on a regular basis to identify potential security violations.	48 54					Verify through examination of analyses that the data base security log is regularly reviewed and action taken where appropriate.	3 4	3 7	

Figure 83. Data Base Audit Program 8.

Activity Access Control **Auditor** ______ **Date** ______

Risk No.	Control Objective and Evaluation Criteria	Probable Control(s)	Control Assessment				Audit Test	Audit Evidence	Audit Tool	Workpaper Reference
			Over	Ade-quate	Under	N/A				
9.	*To see that security measures address the common methods of fraud*									
	The data base group should acquire information on a regular basis about computer fraud.	45					Verify that the data base function is apprised through publications, consultants, or independent study of the more common types of data base computer fraud.	26	15	
	An analysis should be made on a regular basis to identify the points at which fraud might occur.	50 57 58					Determine that the Penetration Point Matrix or equivalent exercise is performed regularly to identify potential fraud points.	22 26	11	
	Security measures should include the prevention and detection of fraud.	40,41 43,49 50,51 53,55 56					Verify through interview and examination of procedures that the scope of security responsibility includes prevention and detection of fraud.	3,4 9,11 12,13 18,20 24,26	1,2 3,6 7,9 10,11 15,16	
12.	*To ensure that visitors and service personnel are escorted*									
	A procedure should be established to identify visitors when they are in the data base area.	40 41					Determine that procedures are established, such as having visitors wear badges, that enable visitors to be identified quickly.	10 25	2 15	
	Visitors' movements to and from the computer room should be recorded.	40 41					Examine the log of visitors to verify that the presence of visitors in the computer room is appropriately recorded.	4	2 15	
	Procedures should be established to escort and be with visitors and service personnel when they are in the data processing area.	40 41					Verify through observation and examination of procedures that visitors and service personnel are escorted when they are in the data base area.	4	15	
12.	*To assess the risks of security problems on disruptions to processing*									

	The risks due to security problems should be identified.	42,45 50,54 57,58					Verify that risk analysis exercises or equivalent are conducted to identify security risks.	25 26	15	
	The magnitude of the identified security risks should be determined.	45					Verify that annual loss expectation calculations or equivalent have been performed to identify the magnitude of security risks.	25 26	15	
	Management should evaluate the potential impact of those risks on the business and take action accordingly.	54					Verify that the results of the risk assessment have been presented to management and that they have taken action on those analyses.	25 26	15	
14.	*To ensure that management has arranged and/or participated in the desired level of security*									
	Management should participate in the risk analysis exercises.	45					Verify that management has participated in risk analysis exercises.	25 26	15	
	Management should determine the level of security expected based upon the identified risks.	45					Verify that management has provided or agreed to the desired level of security.	25 26	15	
	Management should prepare and issue a security policy for the data base environment. (Note: This may be a broader policy encompassing data base.)	45					Verify the existence and reasonableness of the data base security policy.	25	15	
14.	*To ensure support by management of punishment for security violations*									
	Reports of security violations should be sent to management.	54					Verify that security violation reports are sent to management.	24	15	
	The punishments for security violations should be prepared by or approved by management.	54					Verify that management has developed or approved the punishments for security violations.	24	15	
	Management should represent the point of appeal for security violations, and in that capacity enforce the violation policies thoroughly.	45 54					Review the appeals or changes to security violation punishments issued by lower-level management to determine the reasonableness of support of upper-level management.	24 25	15	

Figure 83. *(Continued)*

ten

AUDITING THE COMPUTER OPERATIONS ACTIVITY

Computer operations in a batch environment place heavy reliance on the computer operators to schedule and process user work. In a data base environment, the initiation for operations switches from the computer operators to the user. Users determine what computer jobs they want run and when they want them, and then, using terminals in their work areas, they initiate those jobs. The responsibility of computer operations shifts from running jobs to providing resources.

The challenge facing computer operations is the integration of data base technology into their current operation. This concept, called "fit," will be a continuing challenge until there is no other technology except data base being utilized. In most organizations, data base and non-data base applications will be run concurrently for the foreseeable future.

This chapter provides an approach for auditing the computer operations activity. The emphasis of the audit approach is on the fit of data base technology into the current operating environment. The controls established to ensure the proper fit not only affect the accuracy and completeness of the data base data, but are instrumental in ensuring an adequate service level and continuity of data base processing.

CONCEPT OF "FIT"

The concept of fit explains how a data base management system should be integrated into the current operating environment. The emphasis in the other chapters has been on how data base management systems interface with the user; this chapter is designed to focus the auditor's attention on how the hardware and system software should be interfaced with the data base management system.

The process of fitting a data base management system easily into the existing or planned environment requires an understanding of that environment. The auditor's contribution to that process is ensuring that the fit is adequately controlled. In this process, it is helpful for the auditor to understand what decisions helped create the current environment, together with the processing objectives that resulted in the implementation of data base technology.

How the end user interfaces with the DBMS is a major consideration in evaluating how the data base management system fits into the operating environment. In this discussion, the current operating environment includes the hardware, the operating system, communications software, and the systems software which comprises application and utility pro-

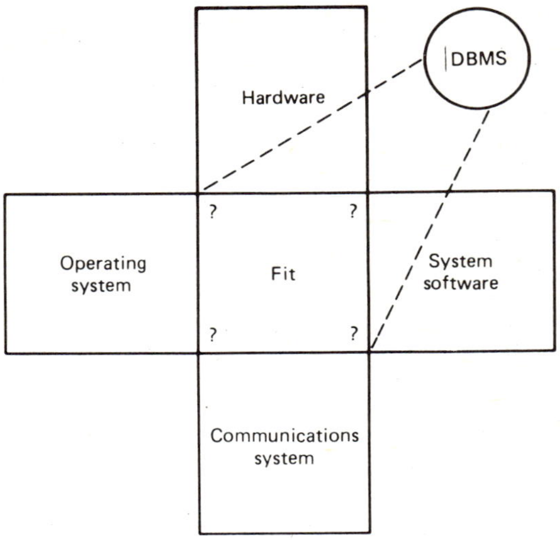

Figure 84. Concept of "Fit."

grams. Interfacing the DBMS usually involves coupling several advanced technologies into one cohesive operating environment.

The operating environment comprises the hardware on which the DBMS will run; the operating system which is the manager of the computer-automated facility; the communication system which may be supplemented by a security system and the transmission of data to and from the DBMS; and the system software which satisfies the user needs in conjunction with the other segments of the operating environment.

The acquired DBMS must fit into that operating environment. Figure 84 shows the DBMS as a round peg attempting to be fit into a square hole. This is the situation many data processing organizations face but fail to recognize.

Squaring off the round edges of the DBMS so that it fits properly into the operating environment involves extensive planning. First, the DBMS selected must be able to satisfy both short-range and long-range needs; second, the tasks must be divided or restructured in the current operating environment (this is the equivalent of restructuring organizational responsibilities among people); and third, procedures must be established to monitor the new environment to ensure that if the data base objectives are not met, adjustments can be made to improve operating performance. The concept of fit involves matching the total operating environment to the needs of the organization. Using this concept, a DBMS would not be acquired until the need could be demonstrated. Fit involves the needs and capabilities of people, economic and performance tradeoffs, the shift of workload from people to equipment, and the integration of the data processing plan into the long-range plan of the organization.

AUDIT GUIDELINE

Review how data base technology "fits" into the other functions performed by computer operations. A good fit normally means a well-run function.

COMPUTER OPERATIONS ACTIVITY STRATEGY

The spectrum of computer operations activity strategy extends from a stand-alone use of data base technology into one in which data base technology fits into the current environment. The stand-alone strategy assumes that data base is just another piece of software and can be dealt with individually. The concept of fit strategy recognizes the difficulty many organizations are having in integrating data base technology into their operating environment.

This operations activity strategy, as with most other aspects of data base technology, cannot be established or implemented by a single group within the organization. The computer operations department may have the responsibility for operating the DBMS, but many of the strategies needed to perform that function effectively must be coordinated with other groups within the organization. For example, the basic strategy involves planning, and it is impractical for computer operations to develop a plan by themselves that involves tasks to be performed by users and other functions within the data processing area.

The desirable strategies for the effective operation of the DBMS (see Figure 85) are:

To develop plan to integrate data base into current environment. The process of integrating data base and non-data base technology must encompass all aspects of the environment if it is to be effective. Not only does it require hardware planning, but applications may need to be modified or rewritten with subsequent changes to the operating system and communication system. If this planning does not occur, the data base benefits may not be realized.

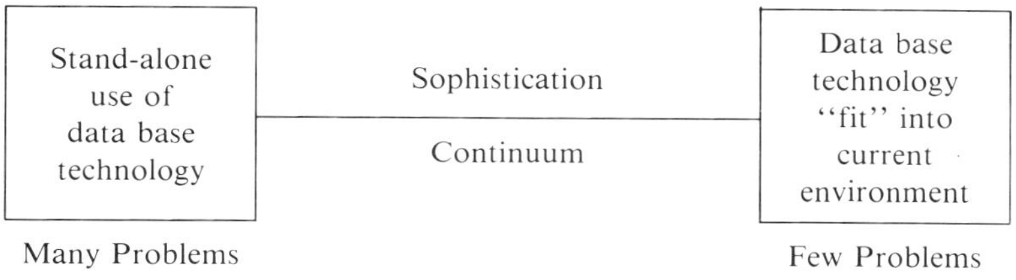

Desirable Strategy	Problem If Strategy Is Not Followed
1. To develop plan to integrate data base into current environment	Data base benefits may not be realized.
2. To define expected service level	Users may disagree on reasonableness of current service level.
3. To monitor operations to ensure expected service levels are achieved	Needed improvements may not be made.

Figure 85. Computer Operations Activity Strategy.

To define expected service level. One of the major dissatifiers of data base technology is the gap between what users expect and what data base administration can possibly deliver. This gap can only be closed by defining the level of service expected in a manner that is agreeable to the users and achievable by the data base administration function. If this does not occur, the users may disagree on the reasonableness of current service level and thus be unhappy with that level.

To monitor operations to ensure that expected service levels are achieved. Computer operations should be able to demonstrate that they have satisfied user service requirements. This will only occur when computer operations monitors and can report on those service levels. If computer operations fails to monitor DBMS operations, they may not make needed improvement to ensure that the users receive the level of service they expect.

The auditor should consider these desirable strategies when evaluating DBMS operations. If computer operations has addressed those strategies and put in place plans and procedures to implement these strategies, the auditor will normally find a well-controlled computer operating environment. On the other hand, if the strategies have not been implemented, the auditor should expect to devote more time and attention to the computer operations activity because the probability that significant control weaknesses exist is high.

AUDIT GUIDELINE

Beware if data base operation expectations are not documented. If people can't document what to expect, how can they hope to be satisfied?

COMPUTER OPERATIONS CONSIDERATIONS

The current or proposed environment for the data base management system exists through the combined interaction of the hardware, system software, and packaged software. This chapter discusses the environment as it exists and areas that can be examined for alteration in order best to fit the data base management system into the environment. The chapter provides the tools to analyze the data base management system characteristics which make it compatible, or incompatible, with the existing hardware and software environment. These factors should be taken into account both during the selection process, when each system should be examined with respect to its hardware and software requirements and features, and after selection, to make sure that the requirements continue to be met.

It is the objective of the designer of a data base management system to furnish as many desirable functions as possible, while at the same time exploiting the hardware and system software resources available. One decision that must be made is which functions will be handled by the data base management system and which will be passed on to the auxiliary software and the hardware. For example, searching a file for a particular record might be done by an intelligent file controller, the file management part of an operating system, or by a routine within the data base management system.

The potential user of a data base management system should take pains to investigate how well the system fits together with the hardware and the other software with which it is to run. If the data base management system has been designed to operate with the user's particular configuration, there must be an assurance that the fit is good. On the other hand, the designer of the data base management system may have tried to mesh with a variety of hardware and/or software, in which case the user must assess the impact of the divergence between the design objective and the system he has in hand. If the design was aimed at a particular level of capability in the environment and the actual hardware or software is more powerful, the extra power may not only be wasted, but it may work in opposition to the data base management system. For example, if the software is constructed using overlays, assuming a nonvirtual machine, and then later installed on a virtual machine, both the operating system and the data base management system would be swapping (paging), and if the physical page does not correspond to the size of the overlay, at least double work will be done. If there actually exists less capacity in the user's system than in the hardware/software system which was assumed in the design, there may be serious degradation in performance of the data base management system. The designer may have tried to produce a tailorable system, more or less independent of the hardware and software. In this case, the evaluation team should make sure that the tailoring process is practical to use, and produces a system that satisfies the user's stated requirements.

User Interface

How the end user interfaces with the system is a major consideration in how the data management system fits into the environment. In this discussion the system includes the hardware, operating system, communications software, system software, and the data base management system.

The user can interface in several ways: on-line, batch, or transaction processing. Each of these ways may require specific hardware and software capabilities. These modes can exist simultaneously and often appear the same to the user and from the user standpoint often overlap. These resource requirements should be understood before processing tradeoff decisions are made.

A major element in the organization of the overall operation is what role, if any, the operating system plays. The data base management system itself often runs under the control of the operating system and usually depends on it for interaction with other programs. In this description it will be assumed that parties of the operating system are responsible for interprogram scheduling and coordination, and for input/output at some level. That assumption is not necessarily always true—the data base management system may perform either or both of these functions.

System Software Environment

A data base management system is seldom written in isolation from other software such as an operating system, utilities, language processors, and application programs. This section discusses the relationships between the data base management system and these kinds of software.

The modularity of the operating system and the data base management system implies a substantial use of resources in housekeeping activities related to systematic servicing of jobs. Each phase of operation of the data base management system starts with input being received from a hardware device whose activity is controlled by a part of the operating system. This input is a request for the data base management system to provide one of its services. The input request is processed by the data base management system so as to produce a number of requests to access the data base. After some initial processing, each such request may be turned over to part of the operating system to complete, resulting eventually in input from, or output to, a storage device. The operating system may transform the data in various ways during this operation before returning control back to the data base management system, which must at some point return some output result to the requestor. In each of these cases the data base management system relies on the operating system to handle the mechanics of data transfer to and from a hardware device. The overall operation of the data base management system itself (its scheduling and its relation to other jobs running on the computer) is usually under the supervision of the operation system, or integrated into it. Many of the operations which have to be carried out for the functioning of a data base management system (scheduling, input and output, data base access) could be done either by the operating system, using its facilities for generalized resource management, or by the data base management system itself.

In considering the division of responsibility, it should be kept in mind that the fact that the operating system could perform a certain function does not mean that it should. It may very well turn out that the operating system does not do all that is required, so that the data base management system still has to carry out additional functions or the operating system has to be modified to include them. These alternatives may be unsatisfactory. It could also be possible that the operating system does all that is required of it by the data base management system but does it so slowly or in such a cumbersome manner that it cannot be used in the environment in which the data base management system must operate. If the data base management system does part of the operation, the interface between the data base management system and the operating system is almost certainly made more complex. If not, then the operating system, which is large, complex, and probably not too well understood, has to be changed. If such a modification is made in-house, the vendor may no longer do maintenance, or maintenance may become impractical. When modifications are made to the operating system, the existing interface between it and the data base management system may no longer work, or, once the changes are made, the user may become locked to the specific release of the operating system and be unable to move to subsequent releases or to new hardware storage devices. Other alternatives are to have the data base management system do everything, effectively combining it with the operating system, or to redesign the operating system completely. Use of operating system functions may also be undesirable if the user has to take a monolithic package which contains unwanted features resulting in a system which is too large or too slow, or both. Thus, the evaluation must balance the increased complexity and lack of flexibility against the advantages to be accrued through the use of operating system facilities. In particular, the evaluation must ensure that the interface between the data base management system and the operating system is as simple and clean as possible.

If an operating system is present and if it carries out all of the functions not directly related to data base management, then at any given time there may be several different kinds of programs running:

- The operating system
  - Scheduling of jobs, processes, and programs
  - Input/output operations
  - Storage device access
- The data base management system
  - Request translation
  - Request processing
  - Data base access
  - Production of output and other results
- Application program
  - Those working with the data base
  - Those unrelated to the data base
  - Those working with the data base as well as unrelated files
- The communication system

Apportionment of Functions

When a data base management system is being fitted into the environment, there are often duplicated functions between it and the operating system. As mentioned before, this normally occurs for one of three basic reasons:

Because the data base management system is written to run with some minimum configuration of the operating system and therefore duplicates more extensively generated versions

Because the operating system does not handle the function as well as the data base management system

Because the impact on the data base management system of possible changes in the operating system will be minimized.

In any examination of a data base management system it is important to understand not only that functions are sometimes duplicated between the operating system and the data base management system, but also where such duplication is done. With a background understanding of this interaction, it is often possible to work out alternative tradeoffs or apportionments so that better use of the system resources can be made.

The apportionment of functions between the data base management system and the operating system is strongly affected by two factors: (1) size of the shared and controlled unit of data, and (2) complexity of processing. The first factor is related to the management and controls of the various levels of shared data. In conventional batch processing where there are a number of separate programs, each using a small subset of the total collection of files, large structures (such as files) can be shared among applications by assigning control of the structures to the applications serially; this is adequate if the applications are willing to wait their turn. If more frequent access to shared data is required, the size of the assignable structure must usually be reduced (e.g., to a record or even to an item) in order to avoid excessive waiting for data by programs. The goal in this case is to arrange for as much concurrency as possible; for example, while one program is processing a record instance, all other instances of that record type are available for use by other programs. Generally, operating systems control data sharing only at a high level, say, on the basis of an entire file. Thus, it is usually necessary for the data base management system to take over the data sharing and arrange for control at the lower levels of record or item instance. The fact that there are very many more elements which must be controlled at this level implies the use of system resources to achieve required concurrency and access control.

The processing required to satisfy a request may vary from very simple, for example, finding a single logical record by a unique key, to complex, like a search through indices and networks of records to find all the records satisfying a certain Boolean condition. The data base management system can generally rely on the data access facilities of the operating system to carry out the simplest functions, but anything further the data base management system usually has to do itself, using the operating system's abilities as building blocks.

Communication Functions

If possible, the communications environment should be selected so that changes which could cascade through to the data base management system are kept to a minimum. If the communications software is included in the data base management system, it should be at least modular to a point that it can be changed independently of the data base management system itself. In a nonstatic environment, as well as with an expanding communications technology, it is clear that there will be changes in network, lines, and terminals during the life of a selected data base management system. Because of this, the communications software is best insulated from the data base management system by having a separate program or procedure to accomplish the interface or by having communications as a procedure within the operating system.

Requests by human users of the data base management system can come from two major sources: batch input devices and terminals. Most operating systems adequately support batch input, but the support of terminal input varies widely. Operating system capabilities of particular importance for terminal requests are communication management, that is, the handling of communication lines, the buffering of messages, and so on; and the ability to schedule application programs on the basis of message content. The presence or absence of these capabilities will have an obvious impact on how the system designer utilizes the operating system. In general, the operating system is much better prepared than the data base management system to handle such problems as changes in the system configuration and modifications to peripheral hardware.

Communication with these devices, especially in the more complex cases, such as on-line systems, is usually done via the operating system. The operating system, for example, may poll terminals until a message is received, check for transmission errors (say, by parity or sum-type checks), and then turn it over to the data base management system for further processing.

An important element to consider in the design of the communications subsystem is the need to check the accuracy of data transmission. This is especially vital in a distributed system in which a data element may arrive at a processing system which has no independent means of checking the reasonableness of the values in that element. Also important are automatic means for requesting the retransmission of data found to be in error.

Hardware Environment

The hardware environment, in most cases, will tend to be the constant element with which all other parts of the system must work. It would be an unusual environment in which a major change in hardware would be made to meet the needs of a data base management system. Some change in hardware can be, and often should be, expected when a data base management system is to be installed. The need for the data base management change which most often occurs is increased use of storage devices and terminals. The data base management system may not itself cause a hardware change but can be part of a general upgrading and expansion of the computing activity.

In considering the hardware environment for the data base management system, there must be close attention paid to the side effects of any change. For example, a change in type of storage device could impact all running programs using the current device type.

In examining the hardware, it is useful first to identify those parts which should be considered static, for example, a CPU on a five-year full payout lease with three years to go. Next to be considered are those parts which can be incrementally increased, for example, spindles of disk storage. Finally those things that can easily be changed should be considered for replacement, for example, native memory by large core storage or double density disks.

On-line data bases and more extensive processing tend to make the hardware configurations for data base management systems larger and more complex than those for conventional processing. Also, the hardware and software that is used may need to have special features because of the presence of multiple users of the data base. To allow them to access the data base without danger to the integrity of its contents, it is vital to provide hardware protection for the system and the data base, and for each program against all the others. For example, memory protection hardware puts each program in a separate partition outside of whose boundaries the program can access only under special precautions, say, by requesting the operating system or data base management system to perform the operation for it, so that access rights can be checked. The data base does not have to be physically located near the users, nor do all the data bases have to be on the same set of hardware. It is now possible to have distributed data bases, distributed computing and computer networks. When the users are not close to the data base, a communication facility must be included unless responses by mail or human (e.g., telephone response) methods are satisfactory.

During the process of considering various data base management systems for acquisition, their hardware requirements must be taken into account. If the data base management system must fit the current environment without change to the hardware or operating system, then the limits of these must be clearly understood before candidate systems are selected. If the hardware and software can be considered for modification to fit the data base management system, then the vendors must be consulted to see if they will make changes. If the changes are made, their effect on vendor support and the cost of modification and future support must be determined.

COMPUTER OPERATIONS ACTIVITY CONTROL OBJECTIVES

Frequently computer operations is not included in the systems planning process. The systems analysts work with users to develop needed solutions and at some time later present the operating requirements to computer operations. Unfortunately, this may be too late to permit computer operations to be an active participant in the planning process.

Control objectives are a desirable by-product of the data base planning process. If computer operations are excluded from any of the planning processes, the objectives for control in computer operations may not be established. From an auditor's perspective, this is a potential void to explore in the audit process.

The data base control objectives in the computer operations activity are designed to prevent problems and disruptions in the operations environment. The control objectives that are desirable in meeting that goal are:

To ensure that data are not lost or changed due to improper operations

The operations activity involves a continuous interface between computer operators and the data base technology. This interaction provides almost unlimited opportunities for error. Control procedures need to be established to minimize the opportunity for error in performing the computer operations tasks.

To protect the data base physically from unauthorized access

Computer operations has little control over access via communication. In many instances, they are not aware that the DBMS is being utilized or who is utilizing that facility. Operations can provide a physically secure plant in which the DBMS operates. This not only involves restricting data base facilities to authorized individuals, but includes those additional steps necessary to ensure that the proper security facilities, both physical and logical, are in operation during all aspects of data base processing, for example, when the facility is being serviced by vendor people, and that there is alertness to unusual situations which might be indicative of a breach of security.

To minimize the frequency of inadequate service levels

There are two aspects of satisfying user service requirements. The first is the achievement of the service specification, and the second is the frequency at which that service is achieved. Both are important. For example, a data base communication system may achieve a four-second average response, but that response is a composite of poor service during the main business shift, and outstanding service on the evening and early morning shifts.

To monitor service level performance

Satisfying user service requirements should not be assumed but, rather, monitored. The fact that users do not complain does not mean they are happy. Taking positive steps to monitor the level of service and then take any corrective action necessary can solve many service problems before they become serious.

To monitor DBMS failures to determine responsibility and implement fixes as appropriate

The DBMS environment is a complex environment comprising people, hardware, software, and operating procedures. Any of these aspects of the environment can and will fail. Monitoring the environment to identify what caused the failure leads to the development of procedures that prevent that type of problem from recurring, or recurring with the same frequency.

To document DBMS operating procedures and controls

Continuity of operations is dependent upon the execution of proper operating procedures regardless of who is performing those tasks. Without adequate operations documentation, the ability of unkilled people to operate the data base effectively is limited.

To plan for expected capacity requirements

The volume of processing on the data base will vary during the course of a day, a week, or over a several-year period. The operations department has the responsibility to provide the operating capacity when needed. This responsibility can be fulfilled by smoothing the workload, adding additional capabilities to handle increased workload, or a combination of these two methods.

To minimize DBMS downtime

Computer operations should initiate those procedures that will reduce both the frequency and the amount of operation downtime after a failure. Part of this planning is to identify the user's requirements for these two variables, and then to initiate the procedures necessary to meet those continuity of processing expectations.

To establish DBMS expectations

The single most important thing a computer operations group can do is to establish user expectation levels that are achievable by computer operations. Most dissatisfiers with operations are a result of undefined factors. If performance criteria are established, the credibility of operations will increase if they can meet those performance criteria. On the other hand, without performance criteria, the user becomes both the judge and the jury on the effectiveness of computer operations, which places computer operations in a position in which they cannot control their own destiny.

The above control objectives should form the basis of the computer operations activity audit program. These control objectives, stated in slightly different terms, are the audit objectives that the auditors should be pursuing. They can also be used by auditors to explain to computer operations personnel good control practices in a data base environment.

GOOD COMPUTER OPERATIONS CONTROL PRACTICES

Traditional computer operation controls are file-oriented controls. The operators in a non-data base environment have the responsibility of mounting the right files at the right time. Although this activity has diminished significantly since the days of heavy reliance on computer tape, the process remains an important part of the operations activity.

The use of data base technology is another step in diminishing the number of mounts and dismounts of computer files. Data base also is an integral part of user-directed data processing which further removes the operation from a minute-by-minute interaction with the hardware. In place of the file-oriented activity, operations is becoming more involved in control tasks.

Many of the controls used by the computer operations activity (see Figure 86) are control-oriented activities. The controls that are evolving out of data base technology are directed toward monitoring the environment and then providing users with the type of information they need to react properly to problems within their operating responsibilities.

The risks inherent in the data base computer operations activity are listed on Figure 87 and cross-referenced to the controls that are being used by data base organizations to reduce those risks. The controls are briefly described on Figure 88 and described in more detail in Appendix A.

Well-controlled data base operation groups use many of these controls. Auditors should use the list of controls to anticipate the type of operation controls they may find during the computer operations activity audit. The presence of these controls, together with well-established control objectives, is indicative of well-controlled operation groups.

DATA BASE COMPUTER OPERATIONS ACTIVITY AUDIT PROGRAM

Computer operations has more tangible facilities than the other activities being reviewed. For this reason, computer operations is frequently viewed as an introductory audit into the computer environment. This remains true in the data base environment if the audit involves the physical facilities. Since these aspects of computer operations auditing do not change from non-data base technology to data base technology, they will not be addressed in this chapter.

The data base operations activity audit program provided is directed toward the risks that are unique or increased in a data base operation. The audit procedures for those risks involve some sophisticated analyses and evaluations. Thus, the auditor for the data base aspects of computer operation should be one of the more skilled members of the audit team.

The following audit program (Figure 89) identifies the criteria whose absence is indicative of a control vulnerability. The auditor should conduct the investigation necessary to determine whether or not the audit criteria have been adequately addressed by computer operations. To assist in this process, the most probable controls are listed, together with the audit test tools used in evaluating the audit criteria.

AUDIT GUIDELINE

Don't use the data base operations activity as a training assignment for new auditors—it's a task for one of your veterans.

Number	Control Name	Control Description
59.	Access authorization control	Means to ensure that only authorized individuals gain access to data base resources
60.	Data error handling	The procedures and timeliness used in examining and correcting detected errors
61.	Remote data transmission control	The terminal controls needed to assure that data are not lost at the terminal site
62.	Central data transmission control	Means to ensure the accuracy and completeness of the communication system for the entire network
63.	Configuration control	Planning and analysis of current and future capacity requirements
64.	Growth analysis	Systematic projection and monitoring of growth statistics
65.	Data base monitor	Use of a monitor (hardware and/or software) to review the efficiency of the data base and the data base application programs
66.	DBMS log analysis	Regular review of the DBMS log to identify abnormal conditions
67.	SWAT team	On-site personnel to analyze and fix problems
68.	Job accounting analysis	Regular review of job accounting information to identify operational inefficiencies
69.	Prerecorded telephone message	Automated techniques for advising users of job status
70.	Operator message procedures	Formal methods for addressing operator messages
71.	Help desk	Single telephone number to call for service

Figure 86. Computer Operations Activity Controls.

Number*	Risk	Recommended Control Objective
2.	Inaccurate or incomplete data in a data base	1. To ensure that data are not lost or changed due to improper operations
5.	Unauthorized access in a data base	1. To protect physically the data base from unauthorized access
6.	Inadequate service level	1. To minimize both the frequency and the impact of inadequate service level 2. To monitor service level performance
8.	Failure of the DBMS to function as specified	1. To monitor DBMS failures to determine responsibility and implement fixes as appropriate
11.	Inadequate documentation	1. To document DBMS operating procedures and controls
12.	Continuity of processing	1. To plan for expected capacity requirements 2. To minimize DBMS downtime
13.	Lack of performance criteria	1. To establish DBMS expectations

*See Figure 8 for description of risk.

Figure 87. Computer Operations Activity Control Objectives.

Data Base Risks \ Data Base Activity	Controls
2. Inaccurate or incomplete data in a data base	Data error handling Remote data transmission control Central data transmission control DBMS log analysis Operator message procedures
5. Unauthorized access in a data base	Access authorization control
6. Inadequate service level	Data error handling Configuration control Growth analysis Data base monitor DBMS log analysis SWAT team Job accounting analysis Prerecorded telephone message Operator message procedures Help desk
8. Failure of DBMS to function as specified	Data error handling Data base monitor DBMS log analysis SWAT team
11. Inadequate documentation	Data error handling Operator message procedures
12. Continuity of processing	Data error handling Configuration control Growth analysis Data base monitor DBMS log analysis SWAT team Job accounting analysis Operator message procedures
13. Lack of performance criteria	Data base monitor Job accounting analysis

Figure 88. Data Base Controls for the Computer Operations Activity.

Activity Computer Operations **Auditor** ____ **Date** ____

Risk No.	Control Objective and Evaluation Criteria	Probable Control(s)	Control Assessment				Audit Test	Audit Evidence	Audit Tool	Workpaper Reference
			Over	Adequate	Under	N/A				
2.	*To ensure that data are not lost or changed due to improper operations*									
	Computer operations should not be authorized to change data values.	59					Review computer operations error correction procedures to verify that they have not changed data values in the conduct of those procedures.	14 17	10 15	
	Communication transmission to and from data base should be adequately controlled.	59 61 62					Evaluate the adequacy of the communication transmission control procedures to ensure the accurate and complete transmission of data.	14 17	10 15	
	Operator activities should be monitored to verify that control procedures are not violated.	59					Review the operations and DBMS logs to identify improper or unauthorized operator activities.	3 14	11 15	
5.	*To protect physically the data base from unauthorized access*									
	Adequate physical measures should be installed to protect unauthorized users from accessing data base facilities.	59					Examine the adequacy of the physical plant to prevent unauthorized access to computer resources.	25 26	15	
	Privileged terminals, such as the master terminal operation, should be both password protected and under the physical observation of a supervisor.	59					Observe the adequacy of protection of privileged data base facilities.	25 26	15	
	Monitor computer operations in order to identify potential control problems.	60					Review the procedures and general control environment to ensure that operations personnel are alert and identifying potential problems before most can become serious.	18 25	15	
6.	*To minimize both the frequency and impact of inadequate service level*									

	Develop procedures to monitor for service level problems.	60 63 64 68					Evaluate the usefulness and effectiveness of service level monitoring procedures as the base for approving service level.	14 25	10 15	
	Predetermine the methods for improving the level of service, should the increased performance be necessary.	63					Evaluate the adequacy of the plans to adjust data base resources to improve service levels if needed.	22	15	
	Establish procedures to advise users of service level problems.	69 70 71					Evaluate the adequacy of the methods used to notify users when service levels drop below predetermined levels of service.	25 26	2 15	
6.	*To monitor service level performance*									
	Data should be gathered that can be used to evaluate performance.	65 66 68					Determine the reasonableness of the performance data collected to measure performance adequately.	26	15	
	The service level performance data collected should be regularly analyzed.	65 66 68					Determine that computer operations regularly analyzes performance data to determine the adequacy of performance.	25 26	2 15	
	Management should take appropriate action where performance levels drop below expectations.	63					Evaluate the analysis of performance information to ascertain that management is taking action where appropriate.	6 8 12 17	2 10 15	
8.	*To monitor DBMS failures to determine responsibility and implement fixes as appropriate*									
	Procedures should be established to record the cause of DBMS failures.	60 66 67					Evaluate the adequacy and implementation of the procedures to record DBMS failures.	3,6 8 25	7 15	
	Analysis should be made of DBMS failures indicating the cause and responsibility for the failures.	60 66 67					Examine the completeness of the reports summarizing and analyzing DBMS failures.	3 6 8	7 15	
	Management should implement fixes on the high-frequency causes of failures.	63					Identify the more common causes of failure and determine if the action taken by management to reduce those causes is reasonable.	3 17 23	3 6	

Figure 89. Data Base Audit Program 9.

Activity Computer Operations **Auditor** ________ **Date** ________

Risk No.	Control Objective and Evaluation Criteria	Probable Control(s)	Control Assessment: Over	Control Assessment: Adequate	Control Assessment: Under	Control Assessment: N/A	Audit Test	Audit Evidence	Audit Tool	Workpaper Reference
11.	*To document DBMS operating procedures and controls*									
	Vendor documentation should be appropriately modified or indicated to document what features are and are not being used by the organization.	63					Examine the DBMS documentation provided by the vendor, and if used determine that it has been appropriately modified based upon the features used by the organization.	1 10	15	
	DBMS controls should be documented.	63					Verify that the operating controls have been documented and are readily accessible by those responsible for execution of the controls.	1	15	
	Computer DBMS operating documentation should be updated as appropriate.	63					Determine that representative samples of new changes to the DBMS environment are reflected in the documentation.	3	7	
12.	*To plan for expected capacity requirements*									
	Users and systems analysts should be surveyed to determine their future requirements.	64					Evaluate the adequacy of the data collection procedures for determining future capacity needs.	3 23 26	3 9 10	
	Capacity requirements should be consolidated and projected.	64					Determine that the capacity statistics collected have been consolidated and a long-term growth projected (i.e., three to five years).	3 23 26	3 6 9 15	
	Resources should be ordered where appropriate to provide for expected capacity requirements.	63					Determine that the needed data base resources can be acquired within the given time frames to meet capacity requirements.	26	15	
12.	*To minimize DBMS downtime*									
	Preventive maintenance should be performed	63					Verify that reasonable maintenance is per-	26	2	

	on hardware and software.						formed on both hardware and software to minimize downtime.		15	
	Anticipation controls should be incorporated into data base technology wherever practical to identify problems before they cause the system to go down.	65					Evaluate the more common causes of system crashes over the past 6 to 24 months and then determine that procedures have been established to anticipate and prevent those crashes from occurring.	23	3 6 10	
	Causes of system abends should be analyzed to identify and act on the more common causes of application system crashes.	67					Quantify the application system abends by cause from the job accounting system log tapes to identify the more common causes of system failures and then determine that appropriate action has been taken to minimize those failures.	23	3 10	
13.	*To establish DBMS expectations*									
	Users should document their data base expectations.	64					Verify that users of data base technology have documented their expectations from that technology.	22	15	
	Computer operations should establish operating performance expectations.	64					Verify that computer operations has predetermined their expectations from data base technology.	22	15	
	The expectations should be incorporated into a plan to achieve these goals.	64					Examine the data base long-range plan to ensure that it is designed to achieve both user and operations expectations.	22	15	

Figure 89. *(Continued)*

eleven

AUDITING THE BACKUP/ RECOVERY ACTIVITY

The establishment of effective backup and recovery procedures is essential to the continuity of data base processing. Backup is the activity that collects the data and procedures needed for recovery. Recovery is the activity that restores the integrity of the data base after it has been lost due to processing problems.

Data base administrators state that recovery is the most technically complex and exacting aspect of operating a data base. The process is too complex to have recovery performed manually, and in addition, without adequate planning, fully recovering the data base may consume hours or even days. An unusual paradox exists in recovery in that the more poorly run data base installations may be the best recovery because they have the most experience.

This chapter describes the process the auditor should use in evaluating the backup and recovery activities. The chapter explains the problems leading to the initiation of a recovery process and the alternatives available to data base organizations for each type of data base failure. A complete backup/recovery audit program is provided, together with recommended audit tests, the controls most commonly found in the backup/recovery activity, and the tools that can be used in the audit process.

DATA BASE BACKUP/RECOVERY ACTIVITY STRATEGY

The common method of approaching recovery in data base technology is to solve the technological problems of recovery. These are very difficult problems and require extensive study and planning. Using this approach, the data base administration function is able to advise users of expected recovery periods. Unfortunately, this approach emphasizes technology and deemphasizes business considerations.

The desirable recovery strategy is to base recovery requirements on business considerations and not technological capabilities. The net result may be the same, but the perspective is at the opposite end of the continuum. Using business considerations as the requirement for recovery, the methods and costs can then be presented and business decisions made regarding the economics of the business recovery requirements.

The recovery continuum illustrated in Figure 90 begins with the strategy based on technical considerations and moves to one based on business considerations. As organizations move along the sophistication continuum toward business-oriented recovery procedures, the following desirable strategies are implemented:

To define recovery requirements. Users of data base technology must define not only the time span in which recovery should occur, but also the percent of cases in which recovery should occur within that time span. This also defines reasonable failure rates.

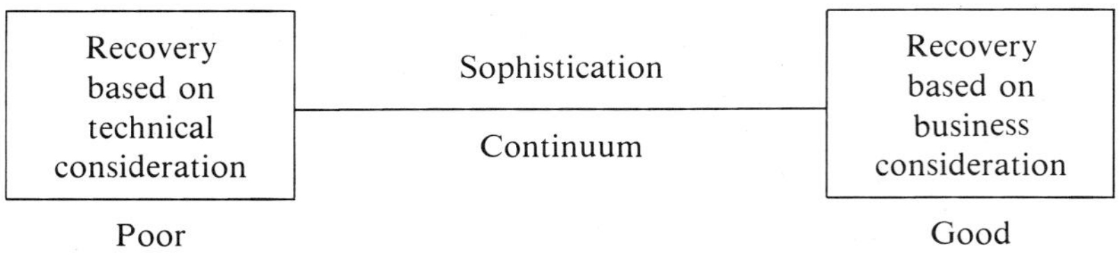

Desirable Strategy	Problem If Strategy Is Not Followed
1. To define recovery requirements	User requirements may not be achieved.
2. To develop a contingency plan	Recovery methods may not be known when problems occur.
3. To establish and monitor failure tolerances	Reasonable levels of performance may not be achieved.
4. To document and test recovery procedures	Recovery procedures may not work.

Figure 90. Data Base Backup/Recovery Activity Strategy.

These user requirements become the input to the development of an effective recovery program. Without stating requirements, the user needs may not be achieved.

To develop a contingency plan. Good recovery procedures don't just happen; they must be planned using the combined knowledge of all involved parties. Contingency plans are documents that have identified the most probable causes of data base failure and present solutions to be followed to recover the integrity of operations after each type of failure occurs. Without a contingency plan, the method of recovering may not be known when failure occurs.

To establish and monitor failure tolerances. It is unfortunate when an organization makes the same mistake multiple times. It is unfortunate when a problem occurs frequently but is not identified as a frequent problem. When organizations both establish failure tolerances and monitor to determine whether or not those tolerances are achieved, they know the type and frequency of data base problems that are occurring. Without reasonable levels of performance established and monitored, the organization cannot develop an effective program to reduce data base failures.

To document and test recovery procedures. Until the recovery procedures are tested, they are speculative procedures. In addition, if they are not documented, the process may not be performed consistently from failure to failure. Unless the recovery procedures are tested, organizations will not know if they work, and if they are not documented they will not know if they work consistently because they probably won't be used consistently.

AUDIT GUIDELINE

Recovery is a business problem first and a technological problem second. Put your audit priorities in this sequence.

DATA BASE BACKUP/RECOVERY ACTIVITY CONSIDERATIONS

The integration of data base technology into the day-to-day operations of an organization increases the need for continuity of computer operations. In many organizations, when the data base goes down, processing ceases. For example, the airline industry is unable to accept airline reservations when the reservation data base is unoperational. Recovery is not only important, it is essential for the survival of the organization.

There are three major functions involved in the backup/recovery activity. First is the retention of data for use in recovering the operation. This includes saving and storing all of the data not needed for production purposes, but needed in the event problems occur. Second is the recovery procedures which enable the data base to be placed into operation. Third is the control procedures designed to ensure the integrity of the data base after it has been lost. These concepts can be easily explained through describing the recovery process.

Data Base Failure Example

The processing flowchart illustrated in Figure 91 represents a payroll application for a construction corporation. The workers are paid on a daily basis for the work performed that day. The payroll system prepares checks for approximately 50 work sites. Each work site is connected on-line to the central data bases.

These are three data bases at the central site. They are separate data bases but all are used in the processing of payroll. Data base A is a work-scheduling cost-accounting system used to record the hours worked on each job. Data base B is a payroll data base that calculates gross and net pay, year-to-date totals for wages, taxes, and benefits, together with the descriptive information on each employee. The transaction data base records and controls the pay information for each work site indicating at which site each worker is to be paid.

The transaction file maintains a list of workers scheduled for each day. This information is provided by data base A and becomes a control on payments for that day. Construction workers' activities are entered into the computer through terminals by expeditors. When the expeditor logs out a worker for the day, that individual's pay is calculated. The individual's time and job(s) worked are recorded on data base A, the data for payroll calculation on data base B, and the payment information on the transaction data base. The disbursing officers located at 4 of the 50 sites can request the paychecks be printed immediately for any worker who wants his or her pay that day. If the worker does not pick up the check, the payroll funds are accumulated.

In the example, a data base failure occurs as data base B is updated. This failure crashes the entire data base system. Let's look at the status of processing at this point in time to determine what must be done to recover operations.

Job status transactions are in the process of being entered when the system crashes. The individuals entering those transactions must be notified as to which have been properly recorded and which must be reentered.

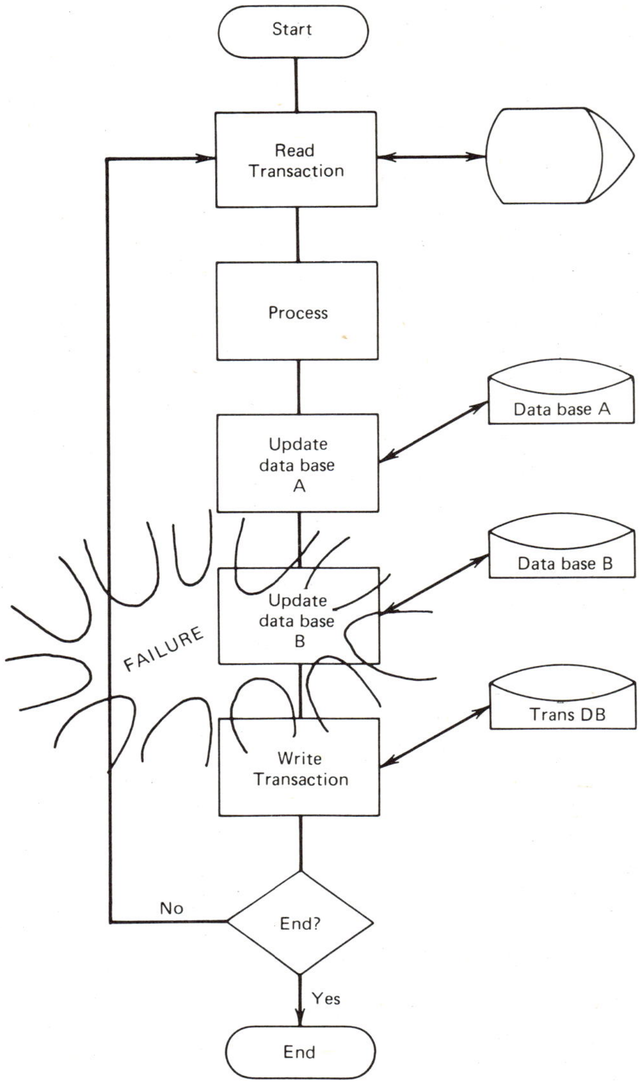

Figure 91. Data Base Failure Example.

Job status transactions have been entered and acknowledged by the system but are being held in a queue awaiting processing. The individuals who entered those transactions must be notified whether or not transactions within the queue can be recovered or whether they must be reentered.

Job status transactions have been updated on data base A, but not on data base B or the transaction data base. The job status transactions on data base A must be retrieved and the appropriate processing performed on data base B and the transaction data base.

The integrity of data base B has been lost. Recovery operations must restore the integrity of data base B to the point where processing stopped and then processing must be picked up from that point.

Payroll information prepared for transmission to the pay sites may not have been received at the time the data base failure occurred. The payroll disbursing officers at each site must be notified of the pay information they should have received to determine whether or not it was lost.

During the time that the operators are scurrying to recover operations, processing must continue at the construction sites. Workers can't stop because the computer is down, so manual means must be invoked to record transactions until they can be entered into the computer. In addition, union contracts may call for the payment of workers on a daily basis, so if the computer is down, alternate means must be performed to pay workers at the construction sites. It is also important to notify the sites as soon as possible that the computer is down, and approximately how long it will be down, so that the sites can begin manual processing procedures.

Couple all the above activities with the need to recover in a short period of time and you begin to see the complexity of the data base recovery process. The process needs to be well planned, for there is little time to react and make decisions during the hectic recovery period. Of course, the degree of risk inherent in the recovery operations will be dependent upon the impact of the break in data base operations on the business system.

DATA BASE RECOVERY RISK

The impact on the organization of a data base failure should be defined by the users of data base. If this impact is defined in quantitative terms, a logical business approach can be made to the recovery process. For example, organizations whose operations are dependent upon the functioning of the data base, such as race tracks who calculate the betting odds based upon bets placed on each race, would not be able to run the race because the payout to winners could not be determined in time. In these instances, recovery is so essential that redundant systems are required to ensure continuity of operation.

Organizations that use the recovery strategy based on technological capabilities rarely identify the impact of data base failure. In those organizations, the auditor must determine the impact of a data base failure and then assess whether the recovery procedures are adequate based upon the business impact. An audit tool is provided to help the auditor in the assessment (see Figure 92).

The data base recovery risk assessment questionnaire (Figure 92) is designed to identify the impact on the organization if a data base failure should occur. Ten criteria are listed which correlate to the magnitude of the impact from a data base failure as follows:

1. *DBMS contains financial data.* The greater the percentage of an organizations's assets/revenue/expenses/budget included within the data base, the higher the magnitude of the impact of a data base failure. (A high risk means a high impact associated with a data base failure.)
2. *Number of diverse users.* The greater number of users, the greater the risk. If these users are diverse, in other words, if they are from different disciplines such as marketing and accounting, the risk becomes very high.
3. *Skill of EDP analyst/programmers in data base skills.* The higher the skill of the project team which develops the application, the higher the probability that they have taken into account the need for recovery. The lower the skills of the project team, the higher the recovery risk.
4. *Number of terminals which can access data base.* The greater the number of terminals, the higher the recovery risk.
5. *Status of data definition.* The more closely the data definition is integrated into the operating environment, the less risk associated with data base failures.
6. *Organizational structure.* The more recognition and authority given to the management of data in an organization, the less the risk, because senior people in positions of data management responsibility normally adequately address the recovery problem.

Number	Risk Criteria	Risk Assessment				
		Very High	High	Average	Low	Very Low
1.	DBMS contains financial data that represents: >30% assets/revenue = VH 30% assets/revenue = H 20% assets/revenue = A 10% assets/revenue = L < 5% assets/revenue = VL					
2.	Number of diverse users: > 2 diverse users = VH 2 diverse users = H > 1 related user = A 1 user = VL					
3.	Skill of EDP analyst/programmers in data base skills: Very high = VL High = L Average = A Low = H Very low = VH					
4.	Number of terminals which can access data base: >100 terminals = VH 75 terminals = H 50 terminals = A < 25 terminals = L 0 terminals = VL					
5.	Status of data definition: Active data dictionary = VL Data dictionary = A No data dictionary = VH					
6.	Organizational structures: DA and DBA = VL DA only = L DBA only = A No DBA = VH					

Figure 92. Data Base Recovery Risk Assessment Questionnaire.

Number	Risk Criteria	Risk Assessment Very High	High	Average	Low	Very Low
7.	Degree of senior management involvement in the data strategy of the organization: Very high = VL High = L Average = A Low = H Very low = VH					
8.	Status of data base recovery program: Documented and tested = VL Documented = A Not documented = VH					
9.	Access to the data base is controlled by: Every user on security profile = VL Most users on security profile = L Non-DP users on security profile = A Only programs on security profile = H No security profiles used = VH					
10.	Audit trails of DBMS processing include: DBMS logs and application trails = VL Application trails only = L DBMS logs only = A No audit trail = VH					
	Total Criteria in Each Assessment Group					
	Risk Assessment Value	+2	+1	0	−1	−2
	Risk Score					

Figure 92. *(Continued)*

7. *Degree of senior management involvement in the data strategy of the organization.* The more senior management becomes involved in data strategy, the less the recovery risk, because those same senior managers are involved when failures occur.
8. *Status of data base recovery program.* The better documented and tested the recovery program is, the lower the risk associated with data base failure.
9. *Tightness of access control to the data base.* Failures can be introduced through unauthorized access, so the tighter the access control, the less the recovery risk.
10. *Extensiveness of the audit trails of DMBS processing.* The more extensive the data base audit trail, the lower the recovery risk.

With each of the recovery risk characteristics are the conditions for use in rating the degree of risk. For example, if less than 5% of the assets of the organization are contained in the data base, the risks should be rated very low. If the assets are between 5% and 10%, the risk is rated low; between 10% and 20%, average; between 20% and 30% percent, high; and over 30%, a very high risk. Using this same methodology, the remaining nine risks should be scored.

The risk assessment is determined by the following four-step process:

Step 1: Total the criteria in each assessment group

The number of risk criteria rated in each of the five risk assessment categories should be totaled. For example, the number of checks in the very high category should be totaled, together with the checks in each of the other risk assessment categories.

Step 2: Multiply by risk assessment value

The risk score for each of the risk assessment categories is obtained by multiplying the total number of criteria in each assessment group by the risk assessment value indicated in the appropriate column on the data base recovery risk assessment questionnaire (Figure 92). For example, if there were three criteria rated very high they would be multiplied by the risk assessment value of "+2" (the score for the very high group) to develop a risk score for that assessment category of +6.

Step 3: Total the individual risk scores

Using algebraic addition, the risk score for the five risk assessment categories should be totaled. This will result in either a plus risk score or a minus risk score. The risk score range will be between +20 and −20.

Step 4: Interpret the risk score

The degree of risk associated with the impact of a data base failure can be interpreted as follows:

Very high risk: +15 to +20
High risk: +5 to +14
Average risk: +4 to −4
Low risk: −5 to −15
Very low risk: −16 to −20

Causes of Data Base Failure

The challenge of data base recovery is the high number of conditions that can cause a failure to the data base operation. Each cause of failure requires different procedures to be used to recover operations, as well as different methods to detect and correct the cause of the failure. The proper identification of these causes and development of recovery procedures addressed to that cause or failure are an integral part of the recovery program.

Listed below are representative samples of the conditions that have caused data bases to fail:

Read/write head scratching the disk surface
Interruption in power supply
Operating system error
Failure of computer operator to follow instructions
Mounting the wrong disk pack
Using the wrong version of the program
Application program abend
Hardware failure
Operating new version of the operating system without making the needed changes to the DBMS
Testing against a live data base with a program containing erroneous logic

Organizations need to categorize potential data base failures into groups and then determine the level of recovery required. The recovery method is then based upon the cause of failure and the level of recovery required. As previously stated, recovery is a business problem the recovery solution for which will be based on the business economics.

The recovery requirements may change depending on the hour of the day that the failure occurs, the day of the week, or the week of the month. For example, a slow recovery might be acceptable to the payroll application on a Monday, but an immediate recovery is needed on a Thursday because payroll must be run on that day. The complexity of the failure itself, together with the options needed in deciding the level of recovery required, can be expressed in a decision table. The data base recovery decision table is illustrated in Figure 93. It gives the categories of failure by type and three levels of recovery, shown below:

Immediate. Recovery should occur within minutes. In some instances, such as the race track example, recovery may be desirable within a few seconds.

Reasonable. At this level, the organization can accept outages for a reasonable period of time, but not extended periods. Note that "reasonable" must be defined. For example, when the banking computers go down they can still process customer business but the service they can provide and the risk associated with that service make it imperative that the computers be operational within a short period to time. Generally, an hour is acceptable.

Slow. The type of processing that can accept a slow recovery is normally a helpful but not essential application involved in the moment-by-moment operation of the organization. For example, a data base that provides for inquiry to products on hand could be down for a day with minimal impact on the organization. Slow recovery is normally considered a recovery process that will have the data base operational the next working day.

Failure Type	Level of Recovery Required: Immediate (within Minutes)	Reasonable (within Hours)	Slow (Overnight)
Hardware failure (CPU)	Hardware redundancy with switching	Hardware redundancy	Emergency hardware maintenance
DBMS or operating system failure	Generally not possible	Restart from check-point	Restart from check-point
Data base unreadable	Dual files	Restart from check-point	Vendor read utility
User-detected errors	Impossible	Analysis and emergency application maintenance	Analysis and correction of application system
Application abend	Impossible	Analysis and emergency application maintenance	Analysis and correction of application system
People failure	Impossible	Analysis and correction	Analysis, correction, and stronger supervision
Terminal or I/O device failure	Hardware redundancy	Use alternate hardware unit or location	Emergency hardware maintenance
Communication line failure	Redundant lines	Rerouting	Messenger
Electrical interruption	Alternative power supply	Restart from check-point	Restart from check-point

Figure 93. Data Base Recovery Decision Table.

Below is a brief discussion of the categories of data base failures and the three recovery methods available (i.e., immediate, reasonable, and slow).

Hardware failure (CPU)

When the central processing unit of the computer fails, the entire processing is lost. With few exceptions, the vendor must be called to service the equipment. When this involves telephoning the vendor and waiting until the vendor finds someone available and sends the personnel to the computer site to provide service, the process is guaranteed to take most of the working day. Even if emergency hardware maintenance is provided, the best recovery that can be normally expected is slow or overnight recovery. If immediate or a reasonable level of recovery is required, then hardware redundancy is necessary. If immediate recovery is required, switching mechanisms are needed to switch processing from one piece of hardware to another, while reasonable recovery permits the movement of files from one piece of hardware to another.

DBMS or operating system failure

When the DBMS or the operating system become unoperational, all application processing ceases. This failure can be caused by a bug in the software, an improper data condition, improper operating instructions, or an application system failure which cascades into an operating system failure. An immediate recovery is generally not possible. A reasonable recovery can be achieved by restarting from a checkpoint, which, depending upon the number of checkpoints and the extent of processing between checkpoints, may take a few minutes or a few hours. Slow recovery would use the same process.

Data base unreadable

If the operating system and DBMS are unable to read information from the data base, processing cannot continue. The cause may be either a disk pack or disk drive problem. If immediate recovery is required, dual files are necessary. Reasonable recovery can be achieved using a checkpoint restart to update an old version of the data base from that point. If it becomes necessary to read a defective disk pack, this frequently can be accomplished using special hardware and/or software in the possession of the vendor. However, this is a slow process which requires integrity checking at the end of the process and normally consumes the working day.

User-detected errors

The application system may execute and produce the application outputs, but the results are unusable. In many instances, these problems will not be detected by operations but, rather, detected by the user. When users notify operations that the results are unusable, an immediate recovery is almost impossible. The application may be recoverable in a reasonable period of time using analysis and emergency application maintenance. In some instances, utilities such as SUPER ZAP are needed to modify the program quickly, or the transaction causing the problem may need to be eliminated from the input stream. Slow recovery can be achieved through analysis and correction of application systems, which may involve a recompilation and test.

Application abend

When an application does not reach a successful completion, processing will be terminated. This abnormal end (i.e., abend) makes immediate recovery impossible. As with user-detected errors, analysis and emergency application maintenance will normally permit recovery within a reasonable period of time, while analysis and the permanent correction of the application system may not be achievable until the next working day.

People failure

Any of the people associated with data base technology can cause it to fail. Computer operators may perform their task improperly. Vendor service personnel may fail to correct an existing condition or even introduce a new condition; security personnel can block out good processing in the guise of protecting the system; users can enter erroneous data; systems programmers can fail to generate the software properly; and application programmers have an almost infinite variety of ways to cause the data base environment to crash. When people are the cause, an immediate recovery is almost impossible. Analysis and correction are required to recover within a reasonable period of time. The proper fix of the problem not only takes analysis and some corrective action, but may require some additional training and stronger supervision.

Terminal or I/O device failure

Any individual component or combination of components may fail. For example, a terminal may become inoperative, an input/output device may fail, or an auxiliary device may malfunction. If an immediate recovery is required, then hardware redundancy is the solution. If the organization can live with a reasonable recovery period, then alternate hardware may be used. Data may be switched from one disk drive to another, or in some instances alternative locations can be sought; for example, a terminal user may perform processing at another terminal location. Slow recovery will occur if the vendor must perform maintenance on the hardware, this will normally prevent processing from restarting until the next work day.

Communication line failure

When communication lines are unable to transmit data or transmit them correctly, operations from outlying areas are terminated. If immediate recovery is required, redundant lines are necessary. Reasonable recovery can normally occur by rerouting information over alternate communication lines. This may involve dial-up service and extra expense, but if included in the contingency plan it becomes a viable backup procedure. If the lines remain down, messenger service can normally carry data from one location to another. This may be a company messenger service or one of the many express services available to organizations.

Electrical interruption

Electrical system failures or extensive fluctuations in voltage can interrupt processing. If immediate recovery is required, an alternative power supply will be required with the ability to switch from one power source to another automatically in the event of a disruption. If reasonable recovery is acceptable, then operations can be recovered from restarting at a point of known integrity. The same process is used for slow recovery, but there are fewer checkpoints.

Making a Recovery Decision

An analysis of the data base recovery decision table shows that immediate data base recovery is normally very costly and in many conditions impossible. Redundancy in hardware and communication lines will provide immediate recovery in many situations, but if the problems are software or people, then excellence of work becomes the best solution as it reduces the occurrence of failure as opposed to correcting the problems due to improper practices. Users demanding immediate recovery should be advised of the costs associated with redundant hardware or extra testing and training to reduce the occurrence of problems.

Organizations can generally provide reasonable recovery with adequate planning. This may involve coordination with vendors and the organization of special teams to assist in recovery once a failure has been detected. Slow recovery is obviously the most economical if users can survive without interacting with the data base for up to a day.

AUDIT GUIDELINE

Prior to auditing recovery, identify the cause of failure that will require the implementation of recovery procedures.

DATA BASE BACKUP/RECOVERY CONTROL OBJECTIVES

The backup/recovery process is usually developed in conjunction with a contingency plan for computer operation. The plan should define the reovery requirements and the means for satisfying those requirements. An integral part of this plan should be the objectives of control in the recovery process.

When establishing control objectives for the recovery process, the following should be considered:

Magnitude of risk inherent in the data base application system

Experience level of computer operations personnel

Sophistication and reliability of recovery tools

DBMS features to record status of processing in the event of a failure

User recovery requirements

Reliability of hardware, power supplies, communication systems, and operating software

The data base backup/recovery control objectives that should be considered as part of recovery planning are (see Figure 94):

To verify controls after recovery to ensure the integrity of the recovered data base

The recovery involves a large number of steps, and itself is subject to error. To ensure accurate and complete processing, the integrity of the data base should be verified after the recovery process is complete and before the data base is used for production purposes.

To maintain records on the recovery process

Maintaining an audit trail of the recovery process provides evidence regarding the correctness and completeness of the steps followed in performing the recovery procedures and improprieties that may have occurred during the process. The records may serve as a basis for evaluating the effectiveness of the recovery process.

To include all segments of the application in the recovery process

Application systems involve both manual and automated segments. Both need to be considered in the development of recovery procedures and in the process to be used for operating the system until the data base can be recovered.

To specify recovery assignments

The recovery period is normally one of great pressure and short duration. It is not the time when people would have to think what to do next, or to develop recovery methods. When individuals know their specific assignments, the probability of a successful recovery increases.

To retain adequate backup data

Recovery cannot occur unless the necessary information is available for that recovery. Backup data includes not only previous copies of the data base, but also copies of pro-

Number*	Risk	Recommended Control Objective
2.	Inaccurate or incomplete data in the data base	1. To verify controls after recovery to ensure the integrity of the recovered data base
4.	Inadequate audit trail	1. To maintain records on the recovery process
6.	Inadequate service level	1. To include segments of the application in the recovery process
		2. To specify assignments
		3. To retain adequate backup data
8.	Failure of the DBMS to function as specified	1. To test the recovery process
11.	Inadequate documentation	1. To document recovery procedures
12.	Continuity of processing	1. To determine expected failure rates
		2. To specify recovery requirements
		3. To define alternate processing procedures
		4. To inform users about service interruptions

*See Figure 8 for description of risk.

Figure 94. Data Base Backup/Recovery Control Objectives.

grams, job control instructions, operating procedure manuals, DBMS logs, and possibly application data. With on-line applications it may be necessary for the terminals to maintain records on the data sent to and received from the DBMS.

To test the recovery process

There is no assurance that the recovery process works until it is tested. Failure should be introduced into data base processing to ensure that both people and the procedures can perform the recovery process correctly.

To estimate expected failure rates

Establishing operational goals is a valuable tool in determining the acceptability of actual failure rates. Having failure tolerances provides goals for operational uptime of the data base environment.

To specify recovery requirements

Users should indicate both the average allowable downtime and the frequency with which that average should be achieved.

To define alternate processing procedures

If the data base operation is an integral part of the business operations, then provisions must be made to continue processing in the event the data base system is unoperational.

To inform user about service interruptions

When the data base is unoperational, users may be unaware of that condition and await service or attempt processing. Where practical, users should be informed that the data base operation is down and that they should use alternate processing means. If downtime estimates can be provided, this should be done, so users can make plans to continue operations manually until the targeted recovery time.

GOOD DATA BASE BACKUP/RECOVERY CONTROL PRACTICES

Recovery is a function that many organizations learn the hard way. Lost transactions, extensive downtime, and excessive user reprocessing are but a few of the results of inadequate recovery procedures. A good recovery process is a well-controlled recovery process.

The backup/recovery activity controls listed in Figure 95 are representative of those used in organizations with good recovery procedures. No one organization uses all of the controls, but many are present in the well-controlled data base organization. These controls are necessary to ensure an accurate, complete, and effective recovery process.

The auditor should assess whether the recovery process under review has both the previously stated backup/recovery control objectives and many of the controls listed in Figure 95. Data base backup/recovery activities that are well controlled normally have few control weaknesses, and thus only require minimal auditing. On the other hand, if the process has not defined its control objectives, and the auditor only finds a few of the common backup/recovery activity controls, the process may have some serious control weaknesses and is a high candidate for audit.

Number	Control Name	Control Description
72.	Before and after images	Data base records before and after processing
73.	Recovery procedures	Automated tools and techniques for recovering integrity of data base
74.	Reorganization utilities	Automated tools and techniques for restructuring and expanding the data base
75.	Data base verifier	An automated tool to assure that all of the data in the data base are properly structured and can be located
76.	Application system failure	Procedures for users to continue operations in the event their applications are not operational
77.	Backup data bases	Copies of data bases made at specific times to use for recovery purposes
78.	Automatic recovery initiation	Automated procedures in place to initiate restart/recovery
79.	Off-site backup	Off-site storage of data base files
80.	System error recovery group	Establishment of a group having responsibility for ensuring continued integrity of the data base
81.	Disaster test	Simulating a disaster to verify recovery procedures function
82.	Contingency plan	Procedures to carry out in the event of a disaster
83.	Recovery audit trail	Record of recovery processing steps
84.	Recovery statistics/reports	Analysis of recovery operations

Figure 95. Backup/Recovery Activity Controls.

Data Base Risks \ Data Base Activity	Controls
2. Inaccurate or incomplete data in a data base	Data base verifier
4. Inadequate audit trail	Before and after images Recovery audit trail Off-site backup
6. Inadequate service level	Recovery procedures Application system failure Backup data bases System error recovery group Disaster test Recovery statistics/reports
8. Failure of DBMS to function as specified	Automatic recovery initiation System error recovery group Disaster test Recovery statistics/reports
11. Inadequate documentation	Recovery procedures System error recovery group Disaster test Contingency plan Recovery audit trail
12. Continuity of processing	Before and after images Recovery procedures Reorganization utilities Application system failure Backup data bases Automatic recovery initiation Off-site backup System error recovery group Disaster test Contingency plan Recovery audit trail

Figure 96. Data Base Controls for the Backup/Recovery Activity.

Activity Backup/Recovery **Auditor** ____ **Date** ____

Risk No.	Control Objective and Evaluation Criteria	Probable Control(s)	Control Assessment: Over	Control Assessment: Adequate	Control Assessment: Under	Control Assessment: N/A	Audit Test	Audit Evidence	Audit Tool	Workpaper Reference
2.	*To verify controls after recovery to ensure the integrity of the recovered data base*									
	Procedures should be established to prove the integrity of the restart point.	75 78 83 84					Ensure that procedures are in effect to prove the integrity of the data base that will be used at a restart point as the basis to recover operations.	14 15 17	2 7	
	Criteria should be established to determine that the recovery process is correctly performed.	75 84					Examine both the documented recovery procedures and the evidence produced during the recovery process to verify that evidence supports the correctness of the actual recovery process.	14 15 17	2 15	
	Procedures should be established to ensure the integrity of the data base after the recovery process has been completed.	75 80 84					Examine the adequacy of the data base tools to prove the integrity of the data base after the recovery process.	14 15	5 7	
4.	*To maintain records on the recovery process*									
	Restart points should be established for the data base recovery.	73					Review the recovery documentation to ensure that it shows what points are available to restart operations after a problem has occurred.	1 15	15	
	Procedures should indicate which recovery software and software tools are used in the recovery process.	73					Examine the results of one or more recovery processes to verify that an adequate audit trail exists indicating which audit software and which recovery tools were used.	15 26	15	
	Provisions should be made to prepare reports describing the failure and the procedures encountered in performing the recovery process.	76					The information generated during the recovery process should be periodically summarized for use by management in analyzing the effectiveness of the recovery program.	26	15	

6.	*To include all segments of the application in the recovery process*									
	Data base recovery procedures should encompass recovering the internal data queues.	73					Determine the adequacy of the method for ensuring that data stored in internal data queues are recovered.	1 15	7	
	Transactions being processed should be identified so that the status of their processing can be determined at the time of data base failure.	73					Examine the adequacy of the method for identifying which transactions have been processed at the point of a failure and which have not.	1 15	7	
	Recovery procedures should be established for each type of data base failure and for each part of the data base environment.	73 80					Verify that the recovery procedures cover both manual and automated processing, and that they provide for the common types of data base failures.	15	15	
6.	*To specify recovery assignments*									
	The data base recovery procedures for operators should be developed and documented.	73					Examine the completeness of the computer operator recovery procedures.	15	15	
	Individuals who will be involved in the data base recovery should be given specific recovery assignments.	73					Examine job descriptions and individual operating procedures to ensure that recovery assignments are given to specific individuals or job functions.	11	15	
	Copies of the data base and related procedures should be referenced to a specific restart point.	77 79					Select a random copy of a data base and verify that it is associated with a specific restart point and the procedures and other data needed to restart operations at that point.	23	6 7 15	
6.	*To retain adequate backup data*									
	The DBMS and other operating logs should be retained until no longer needed for recovery.	72 73 79					Verify that the retention period on the DBMS log equals or exceeds the maximum recovery period for the type of failure that requires the DBMS log.	3	7	
	Backup copies of the data base should be made as often as necessary to satisfy the user recovery requirements.	77					Verify that immediately preceding the point where the data base is copied the recovery could be made in sufficient time to satisfy user requirements.	1 15 22	8	
	Sufficient off-site backup should be available to satisfy user backup requirements.	79					Identify the backup requirements in the contingency plan and verify that backup libraries are in compliance with those plans.	22	15	

Figure 97. Data Base Audit Program 10.

Activity Backup/Recovery **Auditor** ____ **Date** ____

Risk No.	Control Objective and Evaluation Criteria	Probable Control(s)	Control Assessment: Over	Control Assessment: Adequate	Control Assessment: Under	Control Assessment: N/A	Audit Test	Audit Evidence	Audit Tool	Workpaper Reference
8.	*The recovery process should be tested*									
	The individuals involved in recovery should be trained in conducting those procedures.	73					Conduct a simulated disaster to verify that computer operators are adequately trained.	1 15 22	8	
	The recovery procedures should be tested.	73 81					Conduct a mini-disaster test to verify that the recovery procedures work.	1 15 22	8	
	Adequate security should be provided during the recovery process.	73					Evaluate the security procedures to protect the data base environment during the period when the normal operating controls are inactive.	14 15	15	
11.	*To document recovery procedures*									
	User data base recovery procedures should be developed and documented.	73 82					Verify that users have adequate recovery procedures to follow in the event their applitions fail.	12 15 22	8	
	Application project team personnel should have recovery procedures developed and documented for times in which they are involved in the recovery process.	73 82					Verify that the role of the application project team has been included within the recovery procedures.	26	15	
	The procedures to follow in using the recovery tools and recovery software should be documented.	73 82					Identify the recovery software and recovery tools and determine that adequate documentation exists on how to use software and tools in the recovery process.	3 7 15 17	2 15	
12.	*To determine expected failure rates*									
	The expected frequency of data base failure should be determined so that data base reliability can be measured.	73 82					Verify that the actual data base failures are measured against the expected frequency of data base failures.	26	2	

	An acceptable frequency of data base failures should be determined.	73 82					Verify that users and/or data processing personnel have defined acceptable failure rates for data base technology.	12 22	15	
	The acceptable impact on the organization of failures should be determined.	73 82					Verify that the users have determined the dollar impact of failure or equivalent so that logical business decisions can be made on selecting recovery methods.	22	15	
12.	*To specify recovery requirements*									
	The recovery time requirements should be specified.	73 82					Verify that for each data base application an expected recovery time frame has been specified.	26	15	
	Each application should determine whether or not data base recovery procedures are necessary, or whether alternate recovery procedures are satisfactory.	82					Confirm with data base users whether or not it is necessary to recover operations after a data base failure.	12 26	15	
	Resources should be available to meet recovery requirements, or recovery requirements should be changed.	82					Select one of the more critical projects and verify that it can be recovered within the specified time frame.	1 15 22	8	
12.	*To define alternate processing procedures*									
	Alternate processing procedures should be established when it is deemed they are necessary.	76					Confirm with users of the more critical data base applications whether alternate processing procedures are necessary.	12 15	15	
	Alternate processing procedures should be developed and documented.	76					Conduct a mini-disaster in predetermined segments of the system to verify that alternate processing procedures are available and work in disaster situations.	1 15 22	8	
	Controls should be established to ensure the integrity of alternate processing.	73 83					Verify the adequacy of alternate processing controls to ensure accurate, complete, and authorized processing.	15 18	8	
12.	*To inform users about service interruptions*									
	Procedures should be established to notify users when a data base failure occurs.	73					Verify the reasonableness of the procedures to inform users on a timely basis when their data base application is not operational.	12 15	15	
	Priority should be established indicating which applications are to be recovered first.	82					Verify that a priority system has been established for recovery and operations after a failure.	15	15	
	One individual should be appointed to make the decision that a failure has occurred and that alternate and/or recovery procedures should commence.	73 82					Verify that key individuals have been given the responsibility to make a decision on whether or not a failure has occurred, and if so, what procedures should be followed.	11 15	15	

Figure 97. *(Continued)*

The risks common to the backup/recovery activity are listed in Figure 96 along with the controls to reduce those risks. Some of these controls are very effective in reducing many of the risks. This figure is a guide to the auditor in identifying types of controls that are present in the recovery process and where they are most effective. The auditor is cautioned that other controls may have been developed by the organization which address these risks and, if so, may be as effective as the controls listed.

DATA BASE BACKUP/RECOVERY ACTIVITY AUDIT PROGRAM

The best audit of the recovery process is one that introduces an error into the operating environment and then observes the recovery process in action. If computer operations can restore the integrity in a timely fashion, the recovery procedures can be assumed to be effective. Unfortunately, this process would have to be repeated for each type of data base failure in order to ensure that recovery could occur effectively regardless of circumstance.

The backup/recovery audit program proposed evaluates the organization's preparedness to address the recommended backup/recovery control objectives. If these criteria are reviewed and found to be addressed satisfactorily, the auditor may still wish to conduct a simulated disaster in order to ensure that the evaluated procedures do in fact work.

The audit program on pp. 264–267 (Figure 97) identifies the criteria that the auditor should evaluate in order to ensure that the recommended backup/recovery control objectives have been addressed adequately. Each criterion has associated with it the control or controls that the auditor may find implemented to achieve that objective. Audit tests are recommended for the auditor to follow together with recommended audit tools and data base evidence.

AUDIT GUIDELINE

The only sure way to assess the adequacy of backup and recovery procedures is to test them. Consider initiating a disaster test.

twelve

AUDITING THE INTEGRITY OF THE DATA BASE

Verifying the integrity of the data base requires the auditor to take into account the processes which create and operate the data base. Integrity can be verified at a single point in time using audit tests such as segment counts and verification of independently maintained control totals. Unfortunately, there is rarely a single total or test that will provide assurance of the integrity of the entire data base.

Verifying the integrity of a data base for data base application auditors means verifying the process that builds and maintains the data base. This requires the identification and evaluation of those integrity-threatening conditions in order to ensure that the appropriate processes are in place to preserve data base integrity. Verifying the integrity of the data will be a challenge for the auditor.

This chapter identifies the conditions that affect the integrity of the data base and explains how to evaluate the impact of those conditions on the integrity of the data base. The methods used by data base administrators to ensure the integrity of their data base are explained. The data base integrity audit program presented for use in verifying the integrity of the data base utilizes many of the integrity control concepts put into practice by data base administrators.

DATA BASE INTEGRITY STRATEGY

The data base management system and the associated utilities are a very complex and comprehensive package. The data base administrator's function is to integrate this package into the organization and offer it as a resource for the systems people to use in developing and operating computer systems. The concept is basically the same as with other major pieces of software such as the operating systems and the communication systems. These software systems are installed as a resource with the only integrity responsibility assumed by the administrators of those software packages the responsibility that the package is properly generated.

Many data base administrators believe that if the DBMS is properly generated, they have fulfilled their integrity obligations. Other data base administrators have developed elaborate procedures to provide assuance not only that the DBMS works, but also that the integrity of the data within the data base is ensured.

These approaches to data base integrity represent the two ends of the sophistication continuum of data base integrity strategy. The data base integrity strategy illustrated in Figure 98 shows that at the least sophisticated end of the continuum the integrity is assured through reliance on the DBMS, while at the most sophisticated end the data base administrator generates control methods to verify and maintain the integrity of the data base. As the integrity control mechanisms become more sophisticated, the following desirable strategies are implemented:

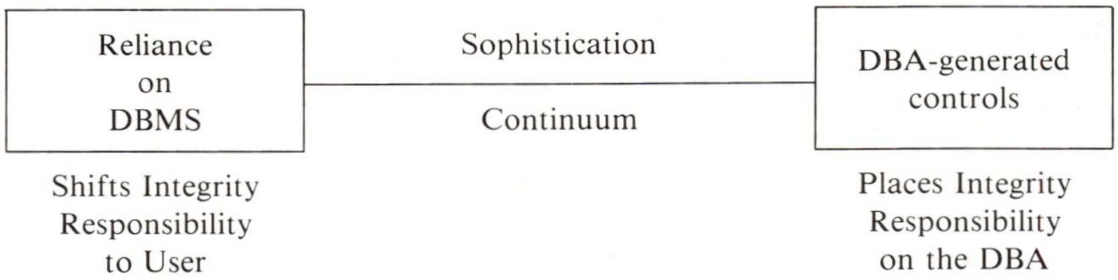

Desirable Strategy	Problem If Strategy Is Not Followed
1. To identify data base risks	Data base risks may not be controlled.
2. To develop data base integrity control standards	The data base integrity may not be adequately controlled.
3. To develop data base application control standards	Data base applications may be inconsistently controlled.
4. To use a standard approach to selecting and implementing DBMS controls	Desirable DBMS controls may not be installed.

Figure 98. Data Base Integrity Strategy.

To identify data base risks. It is difficult to comprehend the need for strong integrity controls until the data base administrator has recognized the integrity risks. The process of identifying those risks is a positive step toward developing the needed controls. Without identification of integrity risks, the risks may not be controlled.

To develop data base integrity control standards. The control standards for data base integrity provide the guidelines for ensuring that integrity. Most organizations have more than one data base, thus justifying the establishment of data base standards. Unless the control standards are established, the data base integrity may not be adequately controlled.

To develop data base application control standards. The applications that use the data base should be provided with the methodology and standards for controlling those applications. The applications are only part of the process in that they must interconnect with the DBMS and other pieces of operating software to fulfill the program's needs. Without a predetermined methodology, the systems analyst and programmers will develop their own control methods which will produce inconsistently controlled applications; in many cases these are poorly controlled applications.

To use a standard approach to selecting and implementing DBMS controls. The vendors of DBMSs develop controls and offer those controls to their customers for use in data base operations. However, the vendors do not require that their customers use those controls, and thus they are discretionary controls. In many organizations, the system programmer or member of the DBA staff who generates the DBMS has authority to select or reject the controls provided by the DBMS vendor. Unless there is a standard approach to selecting and implementing those controls, some desirable DBMS controls may not be installed because the individual generating the DBMS does not understand the implications of omitting them.

The strategy selected by the DBA for ensuring the integrity of the data base will be a major consideration in the amount of audit effort expended to verify the integrity of the data base. In those installations where the DBA has recognized the need for integrity controls and has taken those steps necessary to provide the integrity controls, the audit effort may be minimal. On the other hand, in installations where the DBA only feels obligated to provide a working DBMS, the integrity responsibility resides fully with the user so that most of the integrity evaluation may need to be performed by the auditor.

DATA BASE INTEGRITY CONSIDERATIONS

The data base is the equivalent of a warehouse for data. Problems of verifying the integrity of the products in the warehouse are similar to those of verifying the integrity of the data base. The only sure method of verifying the integrity of the products in the warehouse is to conduct a physical inventory. The same is true of data base technology.

The major difference between the warehouse inventory and the data base inventory is that there is a common denominator for the warehouse products which is dollars. There is no common denominator that can verify the integrity of the data base as easily. Some of the other differences are:

The warehouse has perpetual inventory records, and the data base may not.

Differences between the physical and book inventory in the warehouse can be adjusted with a journal entry. There is no equivalent to adjusting the integrity of the data base.

Misplaced items in the warehouse can be visually located, while in the data base it may be difficult or almost impossible to locate data if a pointer to those data has been broken.

The one similarity is that huge amounts of resources can be consumed inventorying the data base and the warehouse. Therefore, new methods of verifying the integrity of the data base need to be acquired. The approach presented in this book is the equivalent of proving the integrity of the warehouse inventory using random sampling counts. While random sampling won't be used, the sample will be those conditions which if properly addressed provide a high probability that the integrity of the data base has been ensured.

The Data Base Integrity Conditions

The conditions that affect the integrity of a data base are illustrated in Figure 99. Some of these conditions have been discussed in earlier chapters and will be only briefly explained here. The others will be covered in more detail in the following sections.

Accounting controls

Accounting controls govern the calendar period in which the transaction should be recorded. The accounting rules are normally derived from the organization's accounting procedures and/or generally accepted accounting procedures. These accounting regulations need to be converted into processing rules for the data base application.

On-line data base systems do not use the traditional batch control concepts that are designed to place transactions in the appropriate accounting period. With on-line data base applications, transactions can be entered at the convenience of the user. This poses a control dilemma unless controls are established so that the transaction can be identified with the date of the accounting period in which it should be recorded.

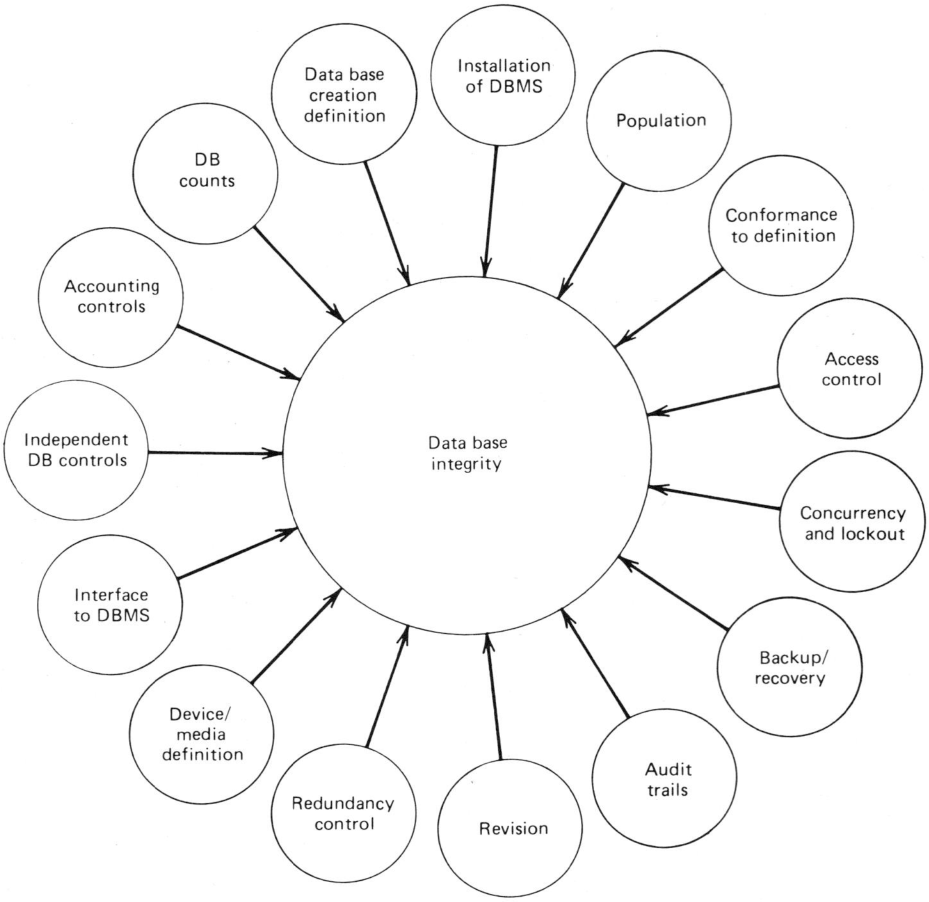

Figure 99. Conditions Affecting Data Base Integrity.

Data redundancy controls

One of the more challenging problems facing a data base administrator is assuring the consistency of redundant data. Early data base concepts pictured one large data base for the organization, but current technology makes this impractical. Most organizations have multiple data bases, with common data elements contained in two or more of these data bases.

Even in a single data base, the same data element may be repeated more than once. This is done primarily because of efficiency of operation. In hierarchical systems, the retrieval method can become very cumbersome and time-consuming unless some data elements are repeated within the data base multiple times.

Data base management system controls do not have the capability to ensure the consistency of data between data bases. In most instances, that control is beyond technological capabilities. For example, if the same element is repeated in multiple data bases and a user updates it in one data base which has no direct communication to another data base, updating the data element in the second data base becomes a user responsibility.

Data base administrators are concerned about the data redundancy problem, but do not have any easy solution. The recommended control solution is the development of specialized routines that monitor the location of these redundant data elements, so that when one of them is updated the automated controls will concurrently update all other locations of the same data element.

Interface to DBMS

Three categories of users have need to interface to the DBMS: (1) the users who need the data within the data base; (2) the operators whose commands and interactions are necesesary to initiate processing, attend to operational problems, and shut down the data base at the end of normal processing; and (3) the technicians who alter the structure and definition of the data base.

All three interfaces need to be controlled to avoid the inadvertent or intentional destruction or modification of data within the data base. Not only should access be controlled for the technicians and operators, but the type of commands available to these individuals should be evaluated. High-risk commands or utilities should be removed from the operating environment in order to provide fewer opportunities for loss of the data base integrity.

Independent data base controls

Users of data base technology have the same options to prepare independent control totals as they did with dedicated files. The method used to develop independent controls must take into account the number of users that can change the data affecting the control total. This is primarily a matter of coordination and method ratehr than a technical problem in creating and checking the control total.

The user can also maintain segment count totals. These accumulate the total number of logical groupings of data within the subschema under the responsibility of the user performing the control check.

Data base counts

Most administrators attempt to maintain a count of the number of groupings of information within the data base. Counts may be by logical groupings such as segments or records, or they may be of physical record. The primary objective of the counts is to ensure that data within the data base have not been lost.

Some data base administrators maintain running counts of information within the data base, while others only use the counts during reorganization. While this control does not address the integrity of the values of data, it does provide that if the hardware and software are functioning correctly, the data values should be correct.

Device media definition

The data base data and indexes must be placed on physical storage devices. This is a responsibility of the data base administrator. The device media control language (DMCL) and storage structure definition facility are tools the DBA uses in the fulfillment of this responsibility. The primary purpose of both the DMCL and the storage structure definition facilities is to provide efficiency and performance tradeoff facilities for the data base administrator. The placement of data on devices based on frequency of use and the placement of data on devices to provide distributed concurrent accesses are two examples of specific features of the DMCL facility. Another data placement feature which may improve performance significantly is one which allows the separation of indexes and data onto separate devices which can be concurrently accessed. In on-line systems the distribution of data occurrences over many separate mass media devices provides a significant performance capability for faster response to multiple concurrent requests.

Data base creation

Creation is the process of accepting new input data and storing it in a previously defined data base. Creation can be achieved in one of three ways:

System-provided creation function

User-supplied host-language program

Updating a null data base with the system update function

Some systems provide no explicit capability other than the update of a null data base, while others provide a full set of support utilities to allow even foreign file input to the creation process. The creation function, given a defined data base, involves two major facilities: definition of the input data and the process of storing the new data according to the stored data base definition. The second step is often called population of a data base.

The creation input definition may take many forms based on the intended or allowed source of input data. The selection of source data input may or may not actually require an explicit creation input definition. Two forms of source data input requiring explicit definition are: (1) foreign files readable by the hardware and operating system, and (2) transactions supplied to the system which are defined by the user.

There are three approaches to handling the format of input to be used in data base creation:

Each data value carries with it the identification of what item it is, and, by implication, where it fits in the data instance hierarchy. Only value creation or replacement is allowed. An example is:

DEPT = RESEARCH
NAME = SMITH, J.
NUMB = 1234
•
•
•
NAME = DEAUX, R.
•
•
•
DEPT = ENGINEERING
•
•
•

This results in an almost trivial implementation, although the item name has to be looked up in the stored data definition each time, which is time-consuming.

The user can define, in some nonprocedural way, the format of incoming data. The format definition languages developed so far are quite elementary—defining fixed positions on a medium, or allowing definitions like "everything up to the next space." In considering more complete input data definition languages, however, the implementor must be sure that the input problems are complex enough to need them, and that they are not too complicated for the user.

The user writes procedures to input all the data. This is the method generally used in connection with host language facilities.

The creation input definition may be explicitly given to the create utility, prestored as a part of the system data definition library, or imbedded in the user's creation program.

Data base population

Data base population places occurrences of data into a defined data base. The establishment of a data base involves a number of steps:

Media selection of input files
Space allocation for the data base
Definition of input data
Provision of input data
The population of the data base

The create function assumes a data base definition exists. Specific features of the population process are exemplified by such things as:

Multiple input and/or multidata base output
Selection of data from input files
Validation of the input data

A primary concern in data base creation is having the system place data into storage in the optimum way, taking advantage of the fact that there is available a large body of data to be analyzed and stored according to a plan. For example, the statistics of keys to be used by a randomizing algorithm can be examined, and the algorithm tailored accordingly. Further, a sequential data collection can be laid out for optimum access, and with the degree of sparseness desired for future insertions. Since the initial body of data is often quite large, special time-saving storage methods can be used during file creation. The data might be sorted into an order which will speed storage. Also, storage operations may be overlapped in a way not possible during normal updating.

Data base revision

Given an established data base, it is usually necessary over time to modify either the physical or logical aspects of those data for such needs as efficiency or new applications. All the user needs and physical performance of a data base cannot usually be predicted and specified at its initial definition.

The revision process normally takes one of two forms: (1) the definition of a new data base with translation of the "old" data base to the "new" data base; or (2) modification or incremental redefinition of an existing data base with either an automatic system restructuring or an off-line utility to adjust the data base to conform to the revised definition. In both of the revision methods a form of redefinition and a possible mapping algorithm between the old (source) data base and new (target) data base are required. These are input to a restructuring function provided as a system utility or a user-written program.

Explicit input of mapping algorithms is needed if the system cannot unambiguously determine them from the given source and target definitions.

The system may very well want to do restructuring on its own initiative, compacting storage space after records have been deleted, and rearranging records, perhaps based on access experience, for greater efficiency. A system may provide for automatic adjustment or restructuring and reorganization within the bounds specified and at the explicit direction of the data base administrator. This capability can give effect to optimization for space or time efficiencies based on system feedback of actual data base usage.

The data base redefinition function allows the data base administrator to redefine a data base selectively. The redefinition may involve both logical data structure changes and physical storage structure changes.

Normally, only two forms of this capability exist, either an actual redefinition facility to modify the present schema, or a complete redefinition based upon a new schema. The actual modification process and form might allow an on-line change to the existing schema or a copy with change to a new schema in order to preserve the original.

Both the schema and the subschema may be modified. Modifications to a subschema data definition in many cases will not require changes to the schema nor data base restructuring. This is dependent upon the degrees to which the subschema is to be modified and its compatibility with or mapping relationships to the schema. For example, an addition of a new data item to the subschema definition would require a schema and data base change only if that item was presently nonexistent in the data base and schema. Likewise, a schema modification ot change privacy locks would not require any actual change to the data base (unless lock values are stored with each entry or record).

Data base redefinition features should include changes to all initially defined data structure and storage structure attributes. Schema definition modifications can include such things as:

Changing validation information
Changing data element synonyms
Modifying privacy locks
Modifying encode/decode specifications

The implementor must be concerned with how to handle programs when a schema or subschema change occurs. It may be that information from the stored definition was used at compilation time to set up absolute values (addresses, lengths, type codes) in the program. When the definition changes, use of this technique requires recompiling the program. In the environment of a large data base, with extensive data definitions and many programs, it would be very awkward to recompile all the programs which use the modified subschema, or even to be sure which programs need to be recompiled. Therefore, it may be desirable to keep data references in the program in symbolic form even after compilation, and resolve them at load time. Some unnecessary work can be avoided if both symbolic and absolute forms are preserved, along with a note of the version of the subschema that was used for compilation. At execution time, if that is still the current version, the absolute values can be used; otherwise the symbolic references have to be reresolved.

A similar situation arises if the schema is modified. In this case it may be necessary to recompile subschemas using it, or the modifications again may be put off to program compilation or execution time.

Upon subschema redefinition or modification it may be necessary to recompile and/or rewrite the application programs utilizing that subschema. Normally, a modification of the program is in order if the changed view of data is to be utilized by the program, although there may be cases in which the program was designed to expect certain evolutionary modifications. The necessity to recompile is a function of system design and binding time of the subschema to both the schema and the compiled program. If the programs or requests which interface the data base are bound to the definitions at compile time, then a recompilation is required.

The act of data instance restructuring may be accomplished via a complete repopulation or an incremental, in-place modification. The method is generally determined by two factors. Repopulation may be the only choice, because that is all the system provides, or because the change to the data structure is so great that it necessitates a full repopulation.

Specific logical restructuring features may include such things as:

Changes to the schema attributes of a data element or structure (for example, changing a data item type)

Addition or deletion of data items

Modification of a data entry structure (for example, create or remove a level in a tree structure; add a new relationship creating a newtwork or plex structure)

Definition of new group or entry types

Conformance to definition

This function applies to all data entering, stored in, or leaving the system. In other words, the validation and conformity of data elements to their definitions cover creation input, update data, stored data in the data base, and data when retrieved by the system.

Both create and update input data may be validated separately prior to being applied to the data base. The method of validation and testing for compliance to definition may vary from complete definition and instance attribute validation to minimize editing checks to no validation at all. The definition against which the instances of data are validated may be imbedded in the process or contained in a separate definition.

It is generally assumed that any create or update functions offered by the data base management system may provide the input validation capability. When the create or update is being accomplished from a user program, it then becomes the user's responsibility to validate the source input data to his program.

Data validation can be accomplished at various levels. Basically, the validation process may cover item type, size and form verification, value validation of many forms (e.g., ranges, sets of values), and relational validation within and between levels of data elements (e.g., different data item value relations, longitudinal checks such as batch totals of specific data item values).

Conformance to data definition applies primarily to the data base. Conformance means that the data as stored and its definition must always correspond. Conformance applies primarily to the structure and schema attributes of the stored data whereas validation pertains to content and value accuracy. For example, utilities could detect broken or erroneous linkages and trigger recovery procedures.

Validation and ensuring conformance to definition of the stored data in a data base may take place at various points in time. Ensuring conformance to definition may occur when data are stored, upon retrieval, or upon initiation by the data base administrator; it may be triggered on time intervals, or system-initiated during slack intervals. The point in time that is most significant to verify conformance is upon initial storage of the data followed by data retrieval. Physical degradation of data or accidental modifications can only be caught via checks upon retrieval.

Some data definition schemes allow for the specification of a value set for each data item, against which incoming or generated values are checked. This can be accomplished easily for input values, but checking generated data requires that a compiler generate appropriate code (presumably a call to a checking subroutine) each time such an item is written. In the case of an interpreter, checking generated data requires that the acceptable values be associated with the item in the stored data description. The same techniques can be used when checking is to be accomplished or procedures are to be invoked upon group instance insertion and deletion. Error checking has to be applied to command inputs as well as data.

The only implementation problem of any consequence in the area of value checking arises when there is along list of individual values in a value set. In this case, it may be possible to use a generalized indexing subsystem. The implementor's real decisions are what to do about an error once it is detected, and how to enable the user to correct it.

One major problem in error handling is the scope of an error. When a bad data item is detected, how much processing should be skipped? Ideally, it should be as little possible consistent with maintaining the correctness of the data base. For example, if one item value in a repeating group occurrence is bad, should only that occurrence be dropped, the whole assembly, or the entire entry? The decision in general should be left to the user. If the input is in the form of separate transactions, then the transaction involved may be discarded, although a problem may arise with totals, checking or otherwise, for the batch of transactions.

The situation is somewhat improved if the system is on-line. In that case, the system can ask the user what to do about an error, or explain how to correct it.

Access control

Access control in a computer system provides protection of the data base from both intentional destruction and improper disclosure. The data base administrator or security officer should be able to assign, control, and modify passwords (access identification and rights). He must also be able to monitor and detect breaches or attempted breaches of access control.

Regulation of access control involved identification, authorization, and monitoring and enforcement with respect to users, data, processes, and even hardware.

Users may be identifiable as individuals or groups via some mechanism such as passwords, tangible objects such as a badge or key, or invariant personal characteristics such as fingerprints or voiceprints. The system may retain a profile of users involving both identification information and their level of authorization to access both the data base and other systems data such as data definitions. Features may exist to establish, display, and modify this user access control profile.

Data access control may take two basic forms: protection of the data from retrieval or update based on schema attributes (e.g., specific named data items), or protection based on value instances of data including data structure relationships. For example, a manager may be authorized to access "salary" only if "department" equals "7916"—his department. The level of data privacy may be applied at all points in a data structure (i.e., data item, group, entry, file, and data base). To provide a reasonably secure access control capability, the value instance form of control is essential.

Program access control may allow the data base administrator to reserve the use of certain more powerful data manipulation commands to selected users. An example is the DELETE command which, if not properly used, may destroy major portions of a data base. Special access control mechanisms may be accommodated by allowing the data base administrator, via data base procedures, to write his own access control routines.

Access control may also exist relative to hardware. The system can retain a profile (similar to the user profile) for terminals or other output devices and control the data that may be allowed to be sent to a given device. Salary information, for example, may be restricted to the printers at the central site and to certain terminals within the organization.

Data encryption is another means of providing data protection. This capability allows physical transformation of data in either their stored or transmitted forms to protect against tapping either the communications lines or direct system input/output to obtain confidential information.

Finally, a level of privacy many times overlooked is the built-in protection within a system which precludes any direct programmer access to the data base. This facility may simply trap all direct input/output calls which do not originate from the data base manager software.

Concurrency control and lockout

In an environment of multiple users sharing data, some forms of concurrent access control and lockout are necessary. Concurrency control and lockout provide protection against undesirable interactions or lost updates in a shared data base environment. The actual responsibility for shared access concurrency control may be and usually is split between the operating system, which is responsible for resource management, and the data base management system.

Concurrency may exist within a single copy of the data base manager or across multiple copies as possibly requried in a multiuser data services environment. In a shared data base environment, the need for concurrency can exist in both batch and on-lines modes.

Following are some examples of concurrency control. If one user is changing values in a collection of records, another user, in general, may not want to output a summary report from them. Also, errors can be introduced into the data base if two users each read the same record, modify it, and, one after the other, write it back—the effect of the first modification and write is lost. The required protection is often implemented by making a user ask for a resource before using it, indicate what is going to be done with it, and, perhaps, specify how other users can access it while he or she has it—in the case of a file, for instance, whether they can read, write, both, or neither. Such a requirement is not limited to file access, but holds true for any shared resource. If the requested resource is not available at that time for the desired use, the requestor is suspended until it is. This, however, raises the possibility of deadlock: A holds resource X and asks for Y, while B holds Y and asks for X. Now neither can continue.

The following conditions must all hold for deadlocks to be possible:

1. Users are concurrently competing for the use of resources.
2. A resource can be under exclusive control of a single user.
3. A user can hold some resources and request additional resources.
4. A resource cannot be forcibly taken away from a user before he has finished with it.
5. A cycle of users exists, with each holding a resource needed by the next.

Deadlocks can be prevented by setting up a restriction to ensure that some one of the above conditions cannot occur. Any of the following is sufficient:

Execute all jobs sequentially, relaxing condition 1.

A user must request all desired resources at one time, relaxing condition 3. This may be undesirable in that a resource may be unnecessarily idle between request and usage.

If a user holding some resources asks for more which are not available, he loses the ones he is holding, relaxing condition 4.

The resources are linearly ordered, and a user may ask only for resources which follow the ones he holds (this avoids cycles), relaxing condition 5.

Backup and recovery

With the emergence of the pooling and sharing of data and the on-line "update in place" environment, data base backup and recovery are essential. Backup is the generation of a copy of a data base at some point in time. This copy may be on either machine-readable or non-machine-processable media. The discussion here is concerned only with machine-readable backup. A backup copy of a data base may be either retained on-line or off-line, and furthermore, it may be segmented to allow selective reloading upon loss of a portion of a data base.

Recovery is a term utilized generically to mean the regaining or the bringing back to an original position or condition. Relative to data, this simply means restoring the data to a previous state. The time of this state may coincide with the time of a backup dump or any point thereafter during which the data have undergone change. The ability to recover a data base to a point in time after which changes have occurred is accomplished by applying a change log to the data.

Audit trails

Audit trails involve the keeping of records on both events and the data activities within a system to allow future examination and verification of what has transpired. In some cases, audit trails provide additional information for recovery of reprocessing of events and the data related to those events. Audit trail information can be recorded on the basis of such things as time, physical location, user, or application. This facility is primarily a function of system software other than the data base manager, but the two work together. The ability of a system to restart from some previous checkpoint requires an audit trail or log of update input transactions with such information as time-stamping, type of update (add, delete, modify), and source of input transaction.

System and data audit trails provide a degree of reliability if they cover error processing facilities as well as recording of input, output, and other data base or system-related events. Error processing facilities related to audit trails may include recording and reporting features. Normally this form of display is handled by a special system utility, yet the interrogation and presentation features could be used.

Installation of the DBMS

The final step in the data base acquisition procedure comes when the vendor presents the data base management system to the user and in return expects a payment. A problem exists at this point for the user in determining whether the DBA is indeed getting an operational system. The complexity of the system often makes it difficult to determine in a short time whether everything is working properly, but there are some basic tests which can provide reasonable assurance.

In determining the reliability of a data base management system, a few facets of the system are often the most critical to a user. These facets include main memory requirements, data base storage requirements, input/output requirements, a multiple user/multiple data base facility, backup and recovery facilities, and possibly a telecommunication capability. When the vendor has shown that the data base management system can accomplish each of these functions within the limits of agreed-upon specifications, the user can feel that the system is basically sound. But while this test may be adequate for justifying payment to a vendor, it does not ensure a viable production system. A new extensive set of tests should be applied prior to embarking on a full-scale production effort.

Main memory is often a scarce resource, and the amount of memory required is a critical factor in the worth of the data base management system. A vendor usually states a minimum size in which his system will operate. This is easily verified when the system is tested; however, this minimum size will normally handle only one user. Production use of the system will involve many users; therefore, a demonstration of incremental main memory increases for each new user, data base, and terminal shold be provided.

Data base storage requirements can also be important, especially if a user has a limited number of peripheral storage devices. Most data base management systems have data storage overhead in the form of control information and data pointers; therefore, there will be some increase in storage requirements beyond raw data requirements. The user should have a data base created using data with known characteristics so that the expansion factor can be appropriately evaluated. This may be easier said than done, since few users know their data this intimately; however, the benefit to be realized is worth the effort.

Input/output measurements are not as easily accomplished as in the measurement of memory and peripheral storage requirements. The most reasonable approach is to have a set of predefined retrieval and modification commands that will be executed against the data base created earlier. With known data and known commands, the vendor should have been able to predict the number of data transfers accurately for each command. The method measuring these data transfers must be agreed on in advance, and will most likely be a utility program provided by the user. These data volumes are likely to be "best case," and the user should assume that average performance will require more capacity.

A production environment use of a data base management system will involve several users and several data bases. Whenever this is the case, the possibility that multiple users will attempt to update a single data base simultaneously is high. If the data base management system provides protection in this area, it should be tested under controlled conditions. A concurrent update capability often involves a program request to "hold" some resource such as a record or block or a data base. An inherent side effect of the holding facility is the possibility for a deadlock situation. If the data base management system purports to protect against this, the user should develop and execute verification tests.

Backup and recovery capabilities must be tested to ensure that, at a minimum, a data base can be restored to a known condition following a data base save and a set of updates. The most obvious way to check this is to save the data base, apply the updates, and save the data base a second time. Then, retaining the second saved data base, reestablish the data base from its original condition with the appropriate data base recovery function and save the data base a third time. A comparison of the second and third saved data bases should result in exact duplication. If this is not the case, then the recovery process does not function correctly. There may be other criteria, such as speed of recovery, which must also meet acceptance standards and should be tested in the process.

DATA BASE INTEGRITY CONTROL OBJECTIVES

Data base organizations approach control from different persepctives. In some organizations, environmental controls are extremely strong, and in others the emphasis is placed on application controls. The control objectives for the data base environment can be oriented toward strong integrity controls at the data base level, or they may be directed toward the applications to ensure the integrity of the data at the application level.

In data base technology the control philosophy is partially dependent upon how the data base technology is used. When data base is used as an access method, there appears to be more emphasis on control in the application, but when data is shared among multiple users, the control emphasis is shifted to the environment. In addition, some organizations put their emphasis on preventive controls, while others make use of detective and corrective controls.

In a well-controlled data processing environment, the auditor could expect to find the following data base environmental integrity control objectives (see Figure 100 for an overview):

To verify the integrity of the initial population of data base

The initial loading of the data base occurs when data base technology is first introduced, and then occurs again during major reorganizations of the data base. This integrity risk must be controlled to ensure that the data are loaded properly.

To validate conformance to data definition

Conformance of the data values to the definition of those data is essential to the effective use of data base technology. Validation routines should verify that compliance. Variance between actual and defined data should not be permitted to exist.

To control access to data modifications

The integrity of the data base cannot be ensured unless access can be controlled. When individuals have unlimited access to the data base, the auditor will not be able to verify the integrity of the data base except at a single point in time using inventory-type methods.

To provide adequate backup and recovery methods

Periodically, the integrity of the data base will be lost through failure of hardware, software, or people. The backup and recovery methods must be sufficient so that the integrity can be restored.

To preserve the integrity of the data base during revision

Periods of revisions to the data base structure are vulnerable periods for integrity. Controls must be provided to ensure that the integrity of the data base remains intact while the data are being reorganized.

To preserve the consistency of data redundancy

The same data elements may be stored more than once in the same data base or in multiple data bases. Controls should ensure that when one of these redundant data values is changed, all other values will also be changed.

To control the placement of data base on media and devices

The data base data are physically stored on computer media and read or written from computer input/output devices. The movement of data to, from, and within those devices must be controlled in order to ensure the integrity.

Number*	Risk	Recommended Control Objective
2.	Inaccurate or incomplete data in a data base	1. To verify the integrity of the initial population of the data base 2. To validate conformance to data definition 3. To control access for data modification 4. To provide adequate backup and recovery methods 5. To preserve the integrity of the data base 6. To preserve the consistency of data redundancy 7. To control the placement of data base data on media and devices 8. To maintain independent data base controls 9. To maintain data base segment counts
3.	Losing an update to a single data item	1. To utilize concurrency and lockout controls
4.	Inadequate audit trail	1. To maintain adequate audit trails to permit reconstruction of processing
7.	Placing data in the wrong calendar period	1. To establish accounting controls to ensure that data is recorded in the proper calendar period
8.	Failure of DBMS to function as specified	1. To verify the proper functioning of the DBMS 2. To verify the correctness of the interface to the DBMS
11.	Inadequate documentation	1. To document the data definitions for creation of the data base

*See Figure 8 for description of risk.

Figure 100. Data Base Integrity Control Objectives.

To maintain independent data base controls

Users are responsible and accountable for data under their control, and should implement those control measures necessary to ensure the integrity of the data for which they are responsible.

To maintain data base segment counts

While it may be difficult for the data base administrator to maintain controls over the value of the data elements, the DBA can maintain counts over the number of groupings of data within the data base. These counts are used to ensure that data are not lost.

To utilize concurrency and lockout controls

When multiple users intereact in the same data base, two or more users may be vying for the same data element concurrently. This can result in lost updates or deadlocked processing unless appropriate controls are included in the DMS.

To maintain adequate audit trails to permit reconstruction of processing

Financial applications are obligated by Internal Revenue Service rulings to maintain audit trails that permit tracing of transactions from inception to control totals, and from control totals back to source documents. Compliance to these requirements necessitates the maintenance of an audit trail. In addition, that information may be used for recovery purposes.

To estalbish accounting controls to ensure that data are recorded in the proper calendar period

On-line data base systems enable users to enter data at their convenience, as opposed to the appropriate processing time. Accounting controls must be implemented to ensure that transactions are processed in the proper accounting period.

To verify the proper functioning of the DBMS

The acquisition of a DMBS and subsequent modifications to that DBMS need to be evaluated to determine that they function properly. While few data base administrators verify the correctness of processing of the DBMS, it is invalid in data processing to assume that software will perform flawlessly.

To verify the correctness of the interface to the DBMS

Interface with the DBMS is the passing of parameters between users and the DBMS. If these parameters are incorrect, improper action will be taken and the integrity of the data base may be destroyed.

To document the data definitions for creation of the data base

The definition of the data used to create the data base should be formally defined, because the form in which data are introduced into the data base at the time of creation may be different than the form in which data are introduced during normal processing. Some of the data definition will be common to both creation and the ongoing use of the data base, and thus can be used for both purposes.

GOOD DATA BASE INTEGRITY CONTROL PRACTICES

The data base integrity controls are some of the more important controls within the data base environment. If these controls are properly implemented they can compensate for control weaknesses in the other data base activities. The stronger the integrity controls, the more the auditor can rely upon the work of the DBA in guaranteeing the integrity of the data base.

The data base integrity controls are closer to pure data base controls than we might observe in other data base activities. Many of the activities such as data base recovery are activities that have also occurred in non-data base technology. However, the controls designed to ensure the integrity of data base technology are mostly unique to data base technology because there is no equivalent to this activity in non-data base systems.

The more common data base integrity controls are listed in Figure 101. Again, though, the auditor is cautioned that most data base administrators have failed to implement these controls. The data base integrity risks cross-referenced to the controls that are used to reduce those risks are listed in Figure 102. In well-managed data base installations the auditor should be able to find many of these integrity controls implemented.

DATA BASE INTEGRITY AUDIT PROGRAM

It is generally good practice for the auditor to review the other data base activities prior to verifying the integrity of the data base. This is normally the most technically complex task that the auditor has in auditing the data base environment. Thus, the more knowledge the auditor has gathered prior to undertaking this audit program, the more effective the auditor will be in verifying the integrity of the data base.

The two options the auditor has in verifying the integrity are (1) to make the exhaustive verification which is the equivalent to a physcial inventory in a warehouse, or (2) to evaluate the conditions which if adequately controlled provide a high probability that the integrity of the data base is adequately protected. It is recommended that the latter method be chosen.

If the auditor desires to verify the full integrity of the data base, it is necessary to verify the completeness of all of the documented subschemas. This requires that the auditor develop the appropriate control totals for each subschema and then trace those control totals to some independent source for verification. However, this method may not cover undefined uses of the data base.

The following audit program describes the criteria that should be evaluated in assessing the integrity of the data base. The audit program lists the most probable controls, together with the evidence produced from those controls and the audit tests that the auditor can conduct to verify the achievement of the specified criteria (see Figure 103).

Number	Control Name	Control Description
85.	Data ownership	Accountability of an individual for each data element
86.	Data discrepancy report	A formal process for the user to report data base problems
87.	QC cards	Quality control cards that are sent between distributed data bases to verify consistency
88.	Redundant data reconciliation	A process that verifies whether or not data redundant in a single or multiple data bases contain the same value
89.	Monitor DBMS log	A review of the control conditions recorded on the log to identify potential problems
90.	Unload statistics	Development of control statistics on a data base prior to use or reorganization
91.	Reload statistics	Development of control statistics after use or reorganization of a data base to ensure all data
92.	Structure verifier	Program developed by the DBA to verify the integrity of that DBA data base
93.	Segment counts	Counts of all the logical groups of data in the data base to ensure that data are not lost or added unintentionally
94.	User control guidelines	Procedures prepared to assist users in controlling data base applications
95.	Data base control standards	Standards describing how to control data base application data
96.	Evaluate DB failures	Reports developed and reviews conducted on data base failures
97.	Subschema controls	Methods for the user to ensure the integrity of the subschema
98.	Program modification and maintenance control	Ensuring of installation of the proper change in the proper version
99.	Adequacy of programmed input validation check	Programmed routines to verify the accuracy, completeness, and authorization of input
100.	Processing intent	Explanation of the objective of management in processing a specific transaction
101.	Concurrent data control	Ensuring that data elements will not be misprocessed due to two or more users processing the same data element concurrently
102.	Deadlock detection and resolution	Breaking of a stalemate in processing between two users

Figure 101. Data Base Controls.

Data Base Risks \ Data Base Activity	Controls
2. Inaccurate or incomplete data in a data base	Data discrepancy report QC cards Redundant data reconciliation Unload statistics Reload statistics Segment counts Subschema controls Program modification and maintenance control Adequacy of programmed input validation check Processing intent
3. Losing an update to a single data item	Data base control standards Concurrent data control Deadlock detection and resolution
4. Inadequate audit trail	Data ownership Redundant data reconciliation Evaluate DB failures Processing intent
7. Placing data in the wrong calendar period	Data base control standards Adequacy of programmed input validation check Processing intent
8. Failure of DBMS to function as specified	Data discrepancy report Monitor DBMS log Unload statistics Reload statistics Structure verifier Segment counts Evaluate DB failures
11. Inadequate documentation	Data ownership User control guidelines Data base control standards

Figure 102. Data Base Controls for the Data Base Integrity Activity.

Activity Data Base Integrity ______ Auditor ______ Date ______

Risk No.	Control Objective and Evaluation Criteria	Probable Control(s)	Control Assessment: Over	Control Assessment: Adequate	Control Assessment: Under	Control Assessment: N/A	Audit Test	Audit Evidence	Audit Tool	Workpaper Reference
2.	*To verify the integrity of the initial population of the data base*									
	Control totals on the initial population should be established.	93 97					Verify the type and extent of controls established over the initial data base population.	1 18 23	15	
	The population after loading should be compared to the preloading control totals.	91 92					Verify that the control totals prior to loading equal the control totals after the population has been loaded onto the data base.	17 18	15 16	
	Initial data base segment counts should be established.	93					Verify that an initial data base segment count has been established and that that count is correct.	17 18	15 16	
2.	*To validate conformance to data definition*									
	The attributes of the data values of each data element should be defined.	95 100					Examine the data definitions and confirm that they include data value attributes.	2	4 15	
	The data validation routines should enforce the data definition data value attributes.	99					Verify that the data validation routines are adequate to ensure that the data in the data base conform to the data definition.	2 26	4 15	
	Data should only be entered into the data base through a process that enforces compliance to data definition.	99					Verify that the only methods by which data can be entered into the data base are methods which enforce the data definition.	2 18	4 15	
2.	*To control access for data modification*									
	Access should be limited to preapproved types of modification.	85 98					Verify that the modifications made to data have been performed under preapproved authorization.	9	15	
	Individuals accountable for data elements should periodically review all accesses to	85 98					Periodically prepare a list of accesses to data elements using SMF log tapes or equivalent,	23	3 6	

	those data elements to verify those accesses are authorized.						and send that information as a confirmation to data base users for them to verify accesses are authorized.		10	
	Before and after images should be maintained on a DBMS log to substantiate changes made to data.	98					Verify that before and after images are maintained on the DBMS log and on a random sample verify that the changes made to data as shown in the before and after image are authorized changes.	3 8	7 9	
2.	*To provide adequate backup and recovery*									
	Copies of the data base should be periodically made for backup purposes.	95					Verify that backup copies of the data base are made at predetermined intervals.	14 15		
	The recovery methods and timing should be consistent with the needs of the application systems.	95					Confirm with a sample of application users that the recovery procedures and timing are adequate for their needs.	1 15 22	8 15	
	Backup procedures should be periodically tested.	95					Perform a disaster test, which involves introducing a flaw into the operational system, so that the recovery of the data base can be tested.	1 15 22	8	
2.	*To preserve the integrity of the data base during revision*									
	Data should not be added or deleted during data base revision.	90,91 92,93 97					Verify that the data base contains the same volume of data before and after the reorganization process.	16 17	5 12	
	Statistics on the content of the data base should be gathered prior to the reorganization process.	90 93					Verify that the DBA develops statistics on the data base prior to revision.	1 16	5	
	Statistics should be developed after revision and compared.	91 92 93					Develop after-reorganization statistics and compare to control totals.	23	5 12	
2.	*To preserve the consistency of data redundancy*									
	The location of all redundant data items should be documented.	88					Examine the documentation of the location of the redundant data elements and confirm through analysis of the subschemas that the list is complete.	6 23	13 15	
	Users of redundant data should be notified of the location of the other versions of those data.	87 88					Confirm with a representative sample of users that they know all the locations of redundant data which they use during processing.	6 23	13 15	

Figure 103. Data Base Audit Program 11.

Activity Data Base Integrity **Auditor** ____________ **Date** ____________

Risk No.	Control Objective and Evaluation Criteria	Probable Control(s)	Control Assessment: Over	Control Assessment: Ade-quate	Control Assessment: Under	Control Assessment: N/A	Audit Test	Audit Evidence	Audit Tool	Workpaper Reference
	Procedures should be established to update all versions of redundant data when one version is updated.	87 88					Confirm through testing that when one version of a redundant data element is updated all other versions are updated concurrently.	6 23	13 15	
2.	*To control the placement of data base data on media and devices*									
	The media used to store the data base, both active and backup copies, should be inventoried.	95					Verify in a data library that all data base copies are inventoried.	23	15	
	The control features contained within the operating system should be utilized wherever possible to control the media and devices.	95					Verify that the operating system control features are used to protect the media wherever practical.	1 14	15	
	Standards should be established regarding the type of medium that is to be used and how the data base is assigned to the specific input/output devices.	95					Evaluate the reasonableness of the data base media placement standards, and confirm compliance to those standards.	1 14	15	
2.	*To maintain independent data base controls*									
	Users of data base applications should maintain control totals on key control fields and regularly verify that the subschema supports those totals.	97					Verify that the detailed records of the subschema support the user-maintained control totals.	23	12	
	Data base application users should maintain segment counts on their subschema and periodically verify those counts.	97					Verify that the detailed segments in the subschema support the segment counts.	23	12	
	All users of a subschema should be involved in developing independent data base totals.	94 95					Confirm with the users of selected data base subschemas that they maintain control totals during processing.	26	15	
2.	*To maintain data base segment counts*									

	Counts of all the segments within the DBMS should be maintained by the DBMS.	93					Verify that the DBMS maintains a segment count total.	1 23	7	
	The segment counts reported by the DBMS should be regularly verified.	93					Verify through tests that the DBMS-maintained segment count is accurate.	1 23	7	
	DBMS segment counts should be verified prior to starting data base operation.	92					Verify through tests of a backup data base that the segment counts are accurate.	1 23	7	
3.	*To utilize concurrency and lockout controls*									
	Controls should be established that prevent concurrent updates.	101					Attempt with two programs to update the same data element concurrently to verify that the controls are functioning.	1	2 7	
	For predetermined conditions, users of the data base application should be prohibited from accessing data (a lockout feature).	101					Identify the lockout conditions and attempt one to verify that the control works.	1	2 7	
	If two application users are deadlocked, DBMS controls should resolve that deadlock condition.	102					Create a deadlock condition to verify that the DBMS can resolve that condition.	1	2 7	
4.	*To maintain adequate audit trails to permit reconstruction of processing*									
	The data base application audit trail should permit tracing transactions to the appropriate control totals.	95					Select a representative number of transactions and verify that they can be traced to the appropriate control total.	23 26	2,3 6,15	
	The audit trail should be able to identify all of the transactions that support financial control totals.	95					Select a sample of control totals and verify that the audit trail can identify all of the supporting transactions that comprise that control total.	23 26	2,3 6,15	
	The audit trail should be retained in accordance with the retention policies of the organization and appropriate regulation.	95					Determine the appropriate audit trail retention period for some key data base transactions and verify that they are retained for the appropriate time period.	23 26	2,3 6,15	
7.	*To establish accounting controls that ensure data are recorded in the proper calendar period*									
	The organization's accounting procedures should be adopted to data base technology.	95					Verify that the accounting procedures are translatable to data base technology, and that the application analyst and data base administrators understand those procedures.	26	15	
	Transactions that have financial significance should be identifiable with the accounting period in which they should be recorded.	95					Verify that the transactions within the data base are identifiable to the accounting period in which they should be recorded.	23	3,6	

Figure 103. *(Continued)*

Activity Data Base Integrity **Auditor** ______ **Date** ______

Risk No.	Control Objective and Evaluation Criteria	Probable Control(s)	Control Assessment: Over	Control Assessment: Adequate	Control Assessment: Under	Control Assessment: N/A	Audit Test	Audit Evidence	Audit Tool	Workpaper Reference
	At the end of each major accounting period, manual reviews should be made to ensure that all major transactions are recorded in the proper accounting period.	95 100					Review the end-of-accounting-period methods used to determine their adequacy to ensure that major transactions are recorded in the appropriate accounting period.	25 26	15	
8.	*To verify the proper functioning of the DBMS*									
	Each new version of the DBMS should be tested to verify that it functions properly.	95					Confirm that the DBMS is tested and review the adequacy of the test procedures.	1	7 15	
	Formalized procedures should be developed to select controls offered by the DBMS vendor for implementation.	95					Evaluate the reasonableness of the control selection procedures and verify compliance to those procedures.	1	15	
	DBMS errors should be recorded and analyzed.	86 96					Examine the results of DBMS failures to verify that they are appropriately recorded, and to evaluate whether DBMS testing has been adequate.	26 12	6 15	
8.	*To verify the correctness of the interface to the DBMS*									
	Standards should be developed describing how to interface with the DBMS.	95 98					Determine the existence of the standards and evaluate their reasonableness.	20 25	15	
	The DBMS interface procedures should be tested to verify they function properly.	95 98					Confirm that the DBMS interface procedures are tested and that the tests confirm that the procedures function properly.	25	14 15	
	DBMS interface failures should be recorded and analyzed.	86 96					Confirm that DBMS interface problems are recorded and analyzed, and whether they attest the adequacy of the interface procedure testing.	23	15	
11.	*To document the data definitions for creation of the data base*									

	The creation data for the original data base or recreation or extension to the data base should be identified.	94 95					Verify that the data used to create the data base have been identified.	23 26	15	
	The data used for creation of the data base should be documented, including both format and attributes.	95 100					Verify the completeness of the documentation of the creation data.	26	15	
	The creation data should be validated as accurate, complete, and authorized.	99					Evaluate the effectiveness of the data validation routines for creation data.	23	3 6	

Figure 103. *(Continued)*

part four

ASSESSING THE DATA BASE

Management wants to know if data base works, is under controls, and is effective. The end product of the audit is a report to management so stating.

thirteen

DEVELOPING A DATA BASE AUDIT OPINION

The end result of a data base audit is an opinion by the auditor on the adequacy of controls and the integrity of the data base. This decision will be used both by management and by auditors reviewing data base applications. Management will make any necessary control adjustments based upon the audit opinion and recommendations; and the application auditors will rely upon the adequacy of the data base controls so that they can select a sample of transactions from the data base and draw conclusions about the entire data base population based upon their samples.

The opinion developed by the auditor on the data base environment is a result of auditor judgment. The auditor is paid for his or her professional advice in interpreting and analyzing the environment. Therefore, while much of the audit process can be automated, and audit tools can be used in organizing and structuring information to make an opinion, the audit opinion must be based upon the auditor's experience and judgment.

This chapter discusses the criteria that should be considered in developing an audit opinion. The skills helpful in developing an opinion are identified. The chapter presents a risks/activities matrix that can be used by the auditor as a tool for assessing the adequacy of controls.

USE OF AUDITOR'S OPINION

The data base environment, like an independent service bureau, performs work for multiple users. Each of these users must rely upon the adequacy of data base controls to protect his or her processing. If these controls are inadequate, they can adversely affect the integrity of user processing.

The audit is a commonly accepted method for verifying the adequacy of controls. However, it would be uneconomical in a data base environment for each user to audit the adequacy of controls, just as it is uneconomical in any service bureau. In service bureaus, the assessment of the adequacy of controls is made by a single audit and then relied upon by auditors reviewing the processing of individual data base applications.

The opinion of the auditor of data base technology is a third-party opinion which should be relied upon in all other audits that require an assessment of the adequacy of the integrity of the data base. The data base auditor should audit the data base prior to the audit of any application that uses that data base. The data base auditor should perform the audit in such a manner that it can be relied upon by other auditors reviewing individual applications.

If control weaknesses are detected during the audit, they should be included in the audit report, together with the action taken by data base administration management to correct those weaknesses. If practical, the auditor should comment on the adequacy of the corrective procedures. This opinion then becomes the foundation for the opinion of auditors reviewing individual data base applications.

CRITERIA FOR CONSIDERATION IN DEVELOPING AN OPINION

The opinion expressed by the base base auditor should be based upon the audit objectives. The audit process describerd in this book divides the data base environment into activities and then provides individual audit programs. For example, the auditor may wish to express an opinion on the adequacy of data base documentation without auditing the other activities.

The audit of any activity results in an assessment of the adequacy of the controls over that activity. In evaluating those controls, there are four criteria that the auditor must consider in developing an opinion, as follows:

Materiality. The magnitude of the assets controlled by the data base

Sensitivity. The importance of the information to the organization, people, or government

Accessibility. The ease with which people can acquire or modify information in the data base

Cost-effectiveness. The economics of controlling the data base

The importance of each of these criteria will vary from audit to audit. For example, the information in some data bases may have little or no sensitivity, while in the other data bases sensitivity may be a major evaluation criterion. In an inventory status system, the disclosure of the information may have little or no sensitivity impact on the organization, while in a personnel system both privacy and competitive considerations make the information very sensitive, requiring strong protection controls.

The four control evaluation criteria, together with the basis of measurement for those criteria, are listed in Figure 104 and described in detail below.

Materiality Control Criterion

Materiality has been the primary audit evaluation criterion since the inception of auditing. Public accountants generally define materiality as a variance greater than plus or minus 5%. Variance is described in terms of individual accounts and/or the totality of all accounts. For example, if the accounts receivable detail record varies by greater than plus or minus 5% from the account balance, that would be considered material, and if the total of all assets varies by greater than plus or minus 5% of the book value of assets, that also would be considered a material weakness.

Internal auditors normally have more stringent definitions of materiality than do independent auditors. Obviously, their objectives are different, and thus the definitions of materiality are different. Alos, internal auditors view materiality over an extended time phase instead of just historically. For example, a control weakness might have resulted in only a few hundred dollars' loss and thus might not be considered material to either the independent or internal auditor until that loss is extended over a reasonable time span, for example, three years. In that case, the potential loss may be many thousands of dollars, and although the loss has not yet occurred, the control weakness would be considered material to the internal auditor.

Materiality can be measured in terms of the magnitude of loss that can occur due to the control weakness, or in terms of actual losses that have occurred. Wherever possible, au-

Criterion	Basis of Measurement
Materiality	Magnitude of control weakness Actual loss
Sensitivity	Compliance to law/policy Visibility Conflict of interest
Accessibility	Segregation of duties Detected penetrations Opportunity
Cost-effectiveness	Return on investment

Figure 104. Control Evaluation Consideration.

ditors should quantify the magnitude of the loss so that a logical business decision can be made by management on the need for strengthening controls. While many auditors are reluctant to measure quantitatively the materiality of a loss, they should be willing to state qualitatively a category of loss such as high, medium, or low.

Sensitivity Evaluation Criterion

Sensitivity of data is a relatively new category of control weakness. It is difficult to express a sensitivity loss in terms of dollars, although this type of weakness does result in a dollar loss.

A sensitivity control weakness is any weakness which will cause the organization to violate a law or policy, or will cause the organization to be sanctioned, investigated, or receive adverse publicity from either the public or private sector. Examples of sensitive areas associated with data base information are listed in Figure 105. Obviously, the type of sensitivity involved will vary according to the categories of information contained within the data base.

The bases for measuring sensitivity weaknesses are failure to comply with laws or policy, the visibility of the sensitive issue, and potential conflict of interest. For example, failure to comply with the privacy laws would be a violation of sensitivity; allegedly improper expenses of corporate officers may place an organization in a highly visible and vulnerable position; and conflicts of interest specifically in the management ranks can cause adverse publicity.

Accessibility Evaluation Criterion

The data base environment comprises electronic evidence as opposed to paper evidence. Thus, the validity of that evidence is dependent upon the adequacy of controls. Unless access to the data base can be controlled, reliance cannot be placed on any of the data base controls.

Illegal transactions	Hiring and promotion (EEOC Affirmative Action)
Bribery (or kickbacks)	Privacy (customer credit records, medical records, etc.)
Political contributions	Confidentiality (employee records, customer lists, etc.)
Offbook accounting (slush funds)	Employee health and safety (OSHA EPA)
Mislabeling transactions (consulting fee, lobbying, liaison)	Product safety (FTC)
Management prerequisites	Pricing practices (inflation antitrust suits, Justice Dept.)
Ethical corporate conduct	Energy practices (energy crisis, DOE)
Socially sensitive inventories	Misleading or false promotional practices (Truth in Lending)
Socially sensitive transactions (any sales to insiders)	
Conflict of interest	

Figure 105. Examples of Sensitive Issues.

Access controls are the most important of all the controls over electronic evidence. The chapter on security of the data base describes the access controls and risks. This chapter provides a good base for developing an opinion on control over access to the data base.

Access controls should be evaluated from two perspectives. First is the adequacy of controls over people as demonstrated through adequate segregation of duties. Second is the access control over transaction processing as expressed through security profiles defining who has access to what resource. People are controlled using environmental controls, while transactions are controlled using application controls.

The evaluation of the adequacy of access controls is measured through the adequacy of segregation of duties, the detected penetrations, and the opportunity for unauthorized access. Both the adequacy of the segregation of duties and opportunities for unauthorized access can be demonstrated through conflict matrices. The analysis of these matrices, coupled with the quantification of the frequency and type of detected penetrations, provides a good basis for developing an opinion on the adequacy of access controls.

Cost-Effectiveness Control Evaluation Criterion

The Foreign Corrupt Practices Act of 1977 stated that events must be controlled unless it was uneconomical to control those events. This required organizations to develop procedures on calculating both the cost and benefits of control. The informal surveys of this researcher indicate that the corporations that can comply with this requirement can be counted on the fingers of one hand.

The two difficulties in developing the cost-effectiveness of control are (1) identifying what is being controlled, and (2) calculating the benefits. The identification of controls and the calculation of costs have not proven difficult for most organizations. In fact, in those organizations that attempt this exercise, the cost calculation is performed with much greater precision than the benefit calculation. Frequently cost is calculated to the nearest $1, and benefits to the nearest $1,000.

The basis for the cost-effectiveness calculation should be reduction of risk. Risk is the sole basis for control; without risk there is no need for control. If there are controls for which no risk can be identified, a control rule of thumb states that the controls are unnecessary. On the other hand, if there is a risk without controls, the organization has a potentially serious control weakness.

The calculation of the control benefit is performed by determining the reduction in risk achieved through the implementation of one or more controls. This requires two calculations. First, the value of the potential loss due to the risk if it is uncontrolled must be calculated; and second, the potential loss after the controls are installed must be calculated. For example, if an uncontrolled situation might result in a $10,000 loss but after controls the potential loss is reduced to $1,000, then the benefit from the control would be $9,000 (i.e., $10,000 minus $1,000 equals $9,000 benefit).

The formula method described in earlier chapters is the recommended method for determining the benefits associated with loss. This formula requires that the expected frequency of occurrence of loss should be multiplied by the expected average loss per occurrence to produce an annual loss expectation value. Risk analysis experts believe that this process performed by knowledgeable individuals is adequate to justify a cost-effectiveness opinion.

The basis for measurement for the cost-effectiveness evaluation is return on investment. The return on investment calculation takes into account the useful life of the control and the value of money. The prime rate banks charge to their best customers can be used for the present value of money. The useful life of the control must be estimated by the individual performing the calculation.

Data Base Skills Needed to Develop an Opinion

The effective assessment of data base controls may require the reviewer to obtain new skills. General skills include a knowledge of management concepts and practices; the theory of computer systems, operations, and software; data processing techniques; management of the data processing function; security of the data processing function; the theory of data base technology; and risk analysis and threat assessment concepts. The specific areas of knowledge helpful in assessing data base technology are listed below:

1. The individual must have sufficient data base technology skills to recognize integrity concerns in the environment and the types and sources of evidence needed to satisfy those concerns.
2. The individual must be familiar with the data base verification methods and techniques that need to be utilized in reviewing data base technology.
3. The individual must have the technical ability to obtain the needed data base evidence.
4. The individual must have the technical ability to evaluate the results of the test.

In order to conduct the test, the individual must know and understand:

1. The data base standards, policies, and procedures (for which compliance is required)
2. The types and location of data base controls used
3. The types and purposes of transactions to be tested
4. The tools and techniques available to assess data base integrity

The individual conducting the review must eventually develop an opinion as to the adequacy of data base control. In order to arrive at this opinion, the reviewer must have a knowledge of the criteria used in developing an opinion regarding the adequacy of controls over data base technology. He or she must also have sufficient knowledge of the data base risks so that an assessment can be made regarding the impact of those risks on the organization. Familiarity with management terminology and reporting practices is another important qualification of the individual conducing the review, so that he or she can properly communicate the implications of control weaknesses to management.

With regard to training, it is assumed that individuals conducting data base control evaluations have had the basic education and experience in a discipline such as accounting, business administration, engineering, or computer science that enables them to perform methodical processes. Experience has dictated that efficient and effective reviews of computer integrity require this basic level of education as a foundation on which to build the additional education and experience needed for this work.

In addition to an individual's basic education experience, he or she will need approximately one academic year or equivalent of education in the subjects considered to be components of the common body of data base technology knowledge needed for this work. To be efficient and effective in conducting more technical reviews, an individual may put in an additional one to five years of on-the-job training or practical experience in performing this work.

CONTROL EVALUATION MATRIX

The adequacy of data base controls can be stated about data base activities or data base risks. These concepts are not mutually exclusive, in that activities contain the controls which reduce the risks. The concept states that the auditor can evaluate the data base environment risk by risk and make an adequacy assessment on each risk or all the risks, or the auditor can evaluate activity by activity and make an assessment on how adequately the activities are controlled.

The audit process described in this book suggests that the auditor evaluate data base activities one at a time. Using this approach, and the risk matrices in each chapter, the auditor can evaluate the adequacy of control in the individual activities. Based on these individual assessments, a total assessment of the data base environment can be developed.

The data base risks described in this book may be present in several activities. Rarely is a single risk isolated to a single activity. Thus, to make an assessment on the adequacy of controls to reduce a specific risk, the auditor may have to review several activities. To assess risk reduction, the auditor must take into account the compensating effects of the controls located in multiple activities all directed toward reducing a single risk.

The data base activities/risks matrix is an evaluation tool for the entire data base environment (see Figure 106). This matrix is a combination of all the risk matrices included in the seven data base activity auditing chapters. The matrix lists the 14 data base risks and the seven data base activities. The control numbers within the matrix represent the controls within each activity that are designed to reduce the indicated risk. (See Appendix A for the explanation of and identification of the controls.)

To use this matrix, the auditor should circle the numbers of the controls present in the activities reviewed. If controls were identified that have not been described in this book, they should be indicated on the matrix. At the conclusion of this exercise, the auditor will have on one sheet of paper all of the risks and all of the controls present in the data base environment. To increase the usefulness, the auditor may want to color-code the circled controls as follows:

Green = strong control
Yellow = average control
Red = weak control

Using this matrix, the auditor can now develop the following conclusions:

Risks for which there are no controls

Activities that have risks which are not controlled in that activity (although there may be controls in other activities)

The adequacy of the total system of controls to reduce each of the identified risks (this incorporates the compensating control concept)

Activities in which there are no controls

The adequacy of the individual activities to reduce the risks present within that activity

The completed data base activities/risks matrix is an effective illustration to add to the data base audit report. The matrix describes in picture form what may be difficult to describe in a narrative report. It also provides evidence to substantiate the auditor's opinion.

THE OPINION

The use of data base technology is controversial even with many data processing professionals. Not only is the technology complex, but it requires a commitment of senior management, user management, and data processing management to utilize the technology effectively. When it is installed, an independent opinion on the adequacy of control and use of data base technology is valuable to all three managements. A positive opinion increases the confidence in the use of technology, and a negative opinion may provide the impetus to change the technology so that it becomes more productive.

This book has emphasized data base controls, but it is to be hoped that it has been broad enough so that the auditor can provide an opinion on any of the following four aspects of data base technology:

Adequacy of controls. This is an opinion valuable to management in adjusting controls, and valuable to other auditors so that they need not duplicate the data base control assessment for each application audit that uses data base technology.

Compliance opinion. This is an opinion regarding whether the implementation of data base technology is in compliance with the organization's policies, procedures, standards, and guidelines and application laws and regulations.

Productivity opinion. This is an opinion on the effectiveness, economy, and efficiency of the use of data base technology in the organization.

Goals and objectives opinion. This is an opinion on whether or not data base technology has achieved the objectives and goals established for the use of that technology.

A good data base opinion should be:

Precise. The wording of the opinion should be such that the reader clearly understands the auditor's assessment of data base technology.

Expressed in quantitative terms. The reader should know the impact of the opinion on the organization. Quantitative terms clearly express the impact of all weaknesses.

Supportable. The auditor must have sufficient evidential matter to support the opinion if it is challenged.

Timely. The audit report should be issued within a reasonable time period after the conclusion of the fieldwork so that it will be of most value to management.

Risks / Activities	Organization	Data Documentation	Systems Development	Access Control	Data Integrity	Operations	Backup/ Recovery
1. Inadequate assignment of responsibility	1,2,5, 7		25	45,57			
2. Inaccurate or incomplete data in a data base	10		26,27,37, 38		86,87,88, 90,91,93, 97,98,99, 100	60,61,62, 66,70	75
3. Losing an update to a single data item			26,29		95,101,102		
4. Inadequate audit trail		19,20, 24	29,30,31, 32,36		85,88,96 100		72,83,79
5. Unauthorized access in a data base				40,41,42, 45,46,47, 48,49,50, 51,52,53,56		59	
6. Inadequate service level			29,30			60,63,64,65, 66,67,68,69, 70,71	73,76,77 80,81,84

7. Placing data in the wrong calendar period		18,19, 20	31		95,99,100		
8. Failure of DBMS to function as specified	4,10	16,18,19, 20,24	26,29,30, 31,36,38, 39		86,89,90, 91,92,93, 96	60,65, 66,67	78,80, 81,84
9. Fraud/embezzlement	7,13		31,37	41,45,48, 50,54,55, 57,58			
10. Lack of independent data base reviews	7,8,9, 11,12		33,34,37				
11. Inadequate documentation	3,14,15	17,19,21, 22,23	27,29,30, 31,32,36, 38		85,94,95	60,70	73,80,81, 82,83
12. Continuity of processing				40,41,42, 43,44		60,63,64, 65,66,67, 68,70	72,73,74,76, 77,78,79,80, 81,82,83
13. Lack of performance criteria	6		33,37			65,68	
14. Lack of management support	1,2,6, 13		25,28	45,54,57, 58			

Figure 106. Data Base Activities/Risks Matrix.

Data base technology is a rapidly changing technology. New features and concepts are being introduced almost daily. These new features may generate new activities or change existing activities, which in turn create risks which require new control. Thus, the auditor's continual evolvement in data base technology is needed in order to apprise management of the magnitude of data base risk and the adequacy of control to reduce those risks while the technological spiral of data base continues.

DATA BASE CONTROLS

Number	Name
1.	Assignment of responsibilities
2.	Segregation of duties
3.	Operation documentation
4.	Output control
5.	Rotation of duties
6.	Processing performance standards
7.	Risk management team
8.	Independent review of design changes
9.	User signoff
10.	System error recovery group
11.	Second opinion
12.	Data base quality assurance function
13.	Internal audit design reviews
14.	Data base charter
15.	Data base job descriptions
16.	Centralized coordination of external schema
17.	Data element responsibility
18.	Conceptual data independence
19.	Data dictionary system
20.	Active data dictionary system
21.	Data definition standard
22.	Data element inventory
23.	Data element utilization reports
24.	Data base backout request form
25.	Data base administration function
26.	Application system testing
27.	Formal design process
28.	Top management checkpoints
29.	System implementation standards

Number	Name
30.	Data base standards
31.	Training of personnel
32.	System documentation
33.	Review board
34.	Government reporting requirements
35.	Personal privacy requirements
36.	Standard progression of new versions
37.	Independent testing
38.	Structured programming techniques
39.	Design models
40.	Physical barrier
41.	Surveillance
42.	Data base malfunction reporting
43.	Natural disaster and environmental risks
44.	Maintenance plan
45.	Security officer function
46.	Security profile
47.	Passwords
48.	Password control
49.	Recovery lockout
50.	Access review
51.	Reorganization control
52.	DBMS password protection
53.	Master terminal control
54.	Security reports
55.	Bait records
56.	Automatic shutdown
57.	Conflict matrix
58.	Penetration point matrix
59.	Access authorization control
60.	Data error handling
61.	Remote data transmission control
62.	Central data transmission control
63.	Computer configuration control
64.	Growth analysis
65.	Data base monitor
66.	DBMS log analysis
67.	SWAT team
68.	Job accounting analysis
69.	Prerecorded telephone message
70.	Operator message procedures
71.	Help desk

Number	Name
72.	Before and after images
73.	Recovery procedures
74.	Reorganizational utilities
75.	Data base verifier
76.	Application system failure
77.	Backup data bases
78.	Automatic recovery initiation
79.	Off-site backup
80.	System error recovery group
81.	Disaster test
82.	Contingency plan
83.	Recovery audit trail
84.	Recovery statistics report
85.	Data ownership
86.	Data discrepancy
87.	QC cards (quality control cards)
88.	Redundant data reconciliation
89.	Monitor DBMS log
90.	Unload statistics
91.	Reload statistics
92.	Structure verifier
93.	Segment counts
94.	User control guidelines
95.	Data base control standards
96.	Evaluate DB failures
97.	Subschema controls
98.	Program modification and maintenance control
99.	Adequacy of programmed input validation checks
100.	Processing intent
101.	Concurrent data control
102.	Deadlock detection and resolution

Data Base Activity *No. 1*
Organizational Structure

Name of Control
Assignment of Responsibilities

Description
A data base environment involves maintaining data independently of the application systems that use those data. This implies that many tasks in the development and operation of application systems would now be performed by new individuals. These individuals must be assigned specific responsibility and be made accountable for their actions. Responsibilities that were formerly performed by the systems analyst and programmer are now divided among them and the data base administration function. Also, some user responsibilities are transferred to the data base administration function.

Evidence
Data base administration charter

Systems analyst/programmer-delegated responsibility

User-delegated responsibility

How to Collect Evidence
Evaluate and assess the charter and responsibilities for the data base administration function, the systems analyst/programmer, and the user.

Evaluate the functions actually performed by the involved individuals versus their assigned responsibilities.

Data Base Activity *No. 2*
Organizational Structure

Name of Control
Segregation of Duties

Description
The operation of a data base involves computer operations, the data base administrator, the systems analyst/programmer, the user, and normally systems programmers specializing in the technical operation of the DBMS. In addition, some organizations have a security officer. In any reorientation of duties, too much responsibility may be given to the data base administrator. Especially in a highly centralized environment, responsibilities should be divided so that no individual can control the results of processing.

Evidence
Data processing organizational chart

Job descriptions in the data base administration function

How to Collect Evidence
Evaluate and assess the adequacy of the segregation of duties based upon the organizational chart and job descriptions.

Review job performances to verify whether or not they comply with the authorized segregation of duties.

Data Base Activity *No. 3*
Organizational Structure

Name of Control
Operation Documentation

Description
The operation of the data base involves several new functions. These include organization of the data base, reorganization of the data base, and generation and maintenance of the DBMS. These are all technical procedures necessitating documentation of the methods of performing the procedures. In many instances, the procedures are performed using software packages which themselves need to be documented. The documentation is needed to assure continuity of processing in case of problems or personnel turnover.

Evidence
Organization and reorganization documentation

DBMS documentation

Computer operation data base operating procedures, including restart/recovery

How to Collect Evidence
Evaluate and assess the adequacy of operation documentation.

Conduct a test in which operators unfamiliar with the operation are asked to operate the data base using only the operation documentation.

Compare the actual operation documentation to the vendor-recommended operation documentation.

Data Base Activity *No. 4*
Organizational Structure

Name of Control
Output Control

Description
Multiple users request common information from data bases. The information might be requested by application programs, utility programs, or query transactions. However, because data base information can be updated by groups independent of those using the data, there can be misinterpretations as to the reliability and timeliness of data. Therefore, output controls must not only restrict access to the authorized individuals, but must also communicate to the users the reliability and timeliness of the data they are obtaining.

Evidence
Output access profiles

Data dictionary output reliability and timeliness descriptions

Descriptive information included in reports

Query language procedures explaining output reliability and timeliness

How to Collect Evidence
Evaluate and review output procedures to assess that they convey the appropriate reliability and timeliness information.

Evaluate and assess the adequacy of the output access procedures.

Initiate one or more queries using a query language to evaluate the completeness of explanatory information regarding the output information used.

Verify the integrity of the output received versus independent control totals maintained by data base users.

Data Base Activity *No. 5*
Organizational Structure

Name of Control
Rotation of Duties

Description
Individuals working with data bases may be in a position to abuse the data. In some environments, this temptation can be reduced by rotating individuals to different functions. For users, this may mean dividing the data base into segments and then rotating clerical people from one segment to another. In the data base administration function, it may mean shifting technical people from one technical aspect of the operation of the data base to another. In computer operations, it may mean shifting operators among various applications so they do not continuously run the same application.

Evidence
Rotation of duty plans and procedures

Notices of transfer of personnel among duties

How to Collect Evidence
Evaluate and assess the rotation of duty plan and procedures.

Verify the movement of people to determine compliance with the rotation of duty plans and procedures.

Data Base Activity *No. 6*
Organizational Structure

Name of Control
Processing Performance Standards

Description
In order for a data base organization to achieve promised performance, specific processing performance standards must be established and plans developed to achieve the standards. This process requires the continual monitoring of actual performance versus standards.

Evidence
Processing performance standards

Procedures for monitoring processing performance standards

Results of monitoring procedures

How to Collect Evidence
Evaluate and assess the reasonableness of the processing performance standards.

Compare the organization's processing performance standards to what vendors state are realistic performance standards.

Compare actual performance to standards, and investigate the causes of differences.

Data Base Activity *No. 7*
Organizational Structure

Name of Control
Risk Management Team

Description
A risk management team identifies and assesses the severity of risk in a data base environment. The risk assessment team normally comprises users, data base analysts, control-oriented personnel such as auditors, and security personnel. This team may be formed for a one-time risk analysis process, or it may convene whenever conditions change, to study a potential new application, for example.

Evidence
Risk analysis team makeup

Risk analysis team policies and procedures

Risk analysis team reports

How to Collect Evidence
Evaluate and assess the adequacy of the makeup of the risk analysis team and their plans and procedures.

Evaluate and assess the completeness and reasonableness of the risk analysis reports.

Conduct an independent audit to identify new risks, or to reassess the severity of identified risks.

Conduct an audit to verify losses associated with the identified risks.

Data Base Activity *No. 8*
Organizational Structure

Name of Control
Independent Review of Design Changes

Description
Review groups, frequently the quality assurance group, review the requested changes to data base applications. The objective of the review is to ensure that the changes are compatible with the data dictionary definition of the data, are consistent with other uses of those same data, and do not adversely affect the efficiency of the data base. This control provides protection for the other users of the data base against the reliability, consistency, and usefulness of data being adversely affected by a change, or performance degraded by the change.

Evidence
Program change request defining the requested change

Charter of the independent review group

Independent review program

Reports or other evidence of the review process

How to Collect Evidence
Examine the charter, procedures, and methods used by the independent review group to ascertain the reasonableness of the review function.

Review a random sample of change requests and the results of the independent review on those requests to verify the reasonableness of the review process.

Data Base Activity *No. 9*
Organizational Structure

Name of Control
User Signoff

Description
Accountability for the accuracy, completeness, consistency, and reliability of data is a user responsibility in the data base environment. Improperly implemented applications can affect the integrity of data. When the user reviews the adequacy of controls in implemented applications, or enhancements to those applications, the probability of adequate data control is increased. User signoff control requires the user to review the adequacy of new systems or enhancements prior to their being placed into production.

Evidence
User signoff procedures

Evidence of user approvals on new systems and enhancements to systems that have gone into production

How to Collect Evidence
Examine the adequacy of the review procedures.

Verify a reasonable sample of new systems or enhancements that have gone into production to determine that they have been approved by the user and contain the user's signature or authorization to be placed into production.

Data Base Activity *No. 10*
Organizational Structure

Name of Control
System Error Recovery Group

Description
Data base errors are normally more significant than non-data base errors because they affect more users. The formation of a system error recovery group is a control designed to provide more effective and timely analysis and correction of errors in the data base environment. The group can be involved with either or both data base applications and the DBMS. The group also maintains statistics on errors and recommends global solutions where appropriate.

Evidence
Charter or job descriptions of system error recovery group

System error recovery group procedures

Reports and statistics produced by the system error recovery group

Evidence produced during the error recovery process

How to Collect Evidence
Survey data base users to ascertain the impact of errors on their operation (a low impact indicates an effective system error recovery group).

Examine the reports and work done by the system error recovery group to verify the effectiveness of their error correction procedures.

Data Base Activity *No. 11*
Organizational Structure

Name of Control
Second Opinion

Description
It is difficult for one individual to gather or interpret specifications, develop and test a data processing product. The work performed by a DBA is new, and may not have the same checks and balances present in more traditional data processing work. The second opinion control requires a second DBA to review the work performed by the first DBA to ensure the accuracy and completeness of the work.

Evidence
Second opinion review procedures

Work reviewed by the second DBA

Error rate in work subject to a second opinion versus error rate in work not subject to a second opinion

How to Collect Evidence
Obtain error frequency from user error reports or job accounting abends statistics.

Examine second opinion procedures.

Examine the work performed by the first DBA to verify the second opinion has been provided.

Data Base Activity *No. 12*
Organizational Structure

Name of Control
Data Base Quality Assurance Function

Description
Data base quality assurance function is established to define and measure the quality in the data base environment. The definition of quality should involve all parties using data base technology, but may vary from application to application. Quality assurance function will work with the data base administration, systems analysts, and users to assist in building in quality and measuring the degree of quality within the data base environment. Quality assurance is charged with improving the process so that quality data base applications can be developed.

Evidence
Quality definition and measurement criteria

Quality assurance review program and procedures

Method of measuring and reporting quality

Quality assurance review reports

How to Collect Evidence
Examine the quality assurance program and procedures.

Examine quality assurance reports and compare them to production results to verify the correlation between the reported quality and the production results.

Review data base projects to ensure that they have been reviewed in accordance with quality assurance procedures.

Data Base Activity *No. 13*
Organizational Structure

Name of Control
Internal Audit Design Reviews

Description
The primary objective of most internal audit design reviews is to verify the adequacy of controls during the design process. The reviews identify the application risks and then make a determination at the point in the design process that the review occurs whether or not the controls are adequate to reduce those risks to an acceptable level. Internal auditors normally use review checklists to conduct the process.

Evidence
Internal audit design review procedures and checklists

Reports produced as a result of the design review

Problems occurring in applications that have had design reviews (to evaluate the effectiveness of design reviews)

How to Collect Evidence
Examine the internal audit procedures and checklists used in conducting the review.

Obtain from user problem reports and job accounting abends on applications reviewed by internal auditors.

Data Base Activity *No. 14*
Organizational Structure

Name of Control
Data Base Charter

Description
The charter of the data base administration function defines the role and responsibility of that group. The formal definition of the group is not only a control for the DBA function, but also describes for other parties involved in data base technology what responsibilities are not part of the DBA function and thus must be assumed by other groups.

Evidence
DBA charter

DBA status reports or time reports indicating work performed by the DBA function

How to Collect Evidence
Obtain from the DBA function their charter.

Compare charter to evidence of work performed, such as the DBA function status reports of time reporting, to verify that the functions performed are in accordance with the charter.

Data Base Activity *No. 15*
Organizational Structure

Name of Control
Data Base Job Descriptions

Description
Job descriptions of the individuals involved in data base technology define their roles, responsibilities, skills, and methods of measuring the effectiveness of those individuals in fulfilling their responsibilities. The job description becomes the basis for hiring someone qualified to perform the function and for measuring performance to verify that it has been adequately performed. The job description also explains to the individual and other parties what is expected from him or her.

Evidence
DBA function job descriptions

Systems analysts/programmer job descriptions with data base responsibilities

User job descriptions with data base responsibilities

How to Collect Evidence
Obtain from the DBA function job descriptions for that function.

Identify systems analysts and programmer positions having data base responsibility and obtain job descriptions for those job functions.

Identify users with specific data base responsibilities and obtain job descriptions for those individuals.

Data Base Activity *No. 16*
Data Documentation

Name of Control
Centralized Coordination of External Schema

Description
The external schema is important in establishing levels of performance, and flexibility to extend applications. The external schema should take into account both present and future information needs of the organization. The organization of that information should then be designed to optimize the use of information in the data base. This design should be centrally coordinated.

Evidence
Policies and procedures for external schema design

Documentation of the external schema

How to Collect Evidence
Evaluate and assess the adequacy of control over the design and implementation of the external schema.

Interview users to determine the adequacy of the information in, and organization of, the external schema.

Data Base Activity *No. 17*
Data Documentation

Name of Control
Data Element Responsibility

Description
Each data element should have one individual or job position accountable for it. The individual has the responsibility for authorizing access to the data element, and assuring the integrity of the data element.

Evidence
Data dictionary

Job accounting system

How to Collect Evidence
Review, or extract from, the data dictionary the responsibility segment of each data element to ascertain that an individual is responsible for that data element.

Prepare confirmations from the data dictionary to send to the responsible individual to verify that he or she accepts that responsibility.

Extract from job accounting systems users of selected data elements. This listing should be sent to the responsible individual to confirm that all users of that data element have authority to access that data element. Differences should be investigated.

Data Base Activity *No. 18*
Data Documentation

Name of Control
Conceptual Data Independence

Description
Conceptual data independence implies that data needs are developed independently of the application systems that use the data. This does not mean that application systems do not feed input to data creation but, rather, that the authority to create and modify data is independent of the applications. In agencies where this is practiced, this normally involves a strong data administration function. A data administrator is frequently a member of senior management.

Evidence
Data administration function responsibility

Data definition procedures

Data dictionary

Application system data definition division

How to Collect Evidence
Examine data administration function to review the data definition policies to determine if they are independent of the application systems personnel.

Examine the information in the data dictionary to determine compliance to the data administration data definition policies.

Examine the data, and data definitions used in application systems, to verify compliance with the data independence policies and procedures.

Data Base Activity *No. 19*
Data Documentation

Name of Control
Data Dictionary System

Description
A data dictionary system is a documentation tool for defining data and their use. Many DDSs are software packages available from vendors. The objective of the DDS is to standardize the definition and use of data. The DDS also can be used to define organization, reorganization, access to data, and other operating information needed to implement a data base environment.

Evidence
Data dictionary policies and procedures
Data dictionary documentation
Data dictionary file

How to Collect Evidence
Evaluate and assess the adequacy of the data dictionary policies and procedures.
Extract information from the data dictionary file and other documentation to verify that the implemented data dictionary is in compliance with the data dictionary policies and procedures.
Test the DDS by entering and/or using data defined in the data dictionary.

Data Base Activity *No. 20*
Data Documentation

Name of Control
Active Data Dictionary System

Description
An active data dictionary system connects the data dictionary to the DBMS in a production environment. A data dictionary can be off-line and used solely as a documentation tool. However, in an active mode application systems cannot access or define data unless those data definitions are processed through the DDS. This is one of the strongest controls in a data base environment since it can enforce access rules in addition to enforcing standardized definitions.

Evidence
Data policies and procedures
Active data dictionary system documentation, policies, and procedures
Job accounting system log

How to Collect Evidence
Assess the data dictionary system to verify compliance to the data policies and procedures.
Extract information from job accounting systems to verify that the active DDS is used in the production environment.
Perform a test which attempts to enter or access data in the data base without going through the active DDS.

Data Base Activity *No. 21*
Data Documentation

Name of Control
Data Definition Standard

Description
The data definition standards describe both the formats to be followed in defining data and the attributes to be included within that definition. In a data dictionary system, these standards may be an integral part of the data dictionary. Standards should also include a method for enforcement, to ensure that all of the defined data are defined in accordance with the data definition standards.

Evidence
Data definition standards

Defined definition of data elements

Enforcement procedures and results of those procedures

How to Collect Evidence
Obtain from the data base administration function the data definition standards.

Examine data definitions from the data dictionary or equivalent and verify that they are in accordance with data definition standards.

Verify that where data definitions are not in conformance with standards, appropriate steps are being taken to bring those definitions into conformance with the standards.

Data Base Activity *No. 22*
Data Documentation

Name of Control
Data Element Inventory

Description
The data element inventory is a listing or accumulation of all the data elements used in the organization. If a single data element is known by multiple names or aliases, they should be cross-referenced in the inventory so that a single data element is not inventoried multiple times, although it may be cross-referenced on the inventory list. At a minimum the inventory should contain the common name or title of the data element, the abbreviated title for use in programming languages, the individual or group responsible for the accuracy and completeness of that data element, and a brief narrative description of the data element.

Evidence
Data element inventory listings

Procedures for gathering and updating the data element inventory list

Data dictionary and program listings

How to Collect Evidence
Obtain the data element inventory list from the data base administrator.

Obtain the data element procedures from the data base administrator and compare the completeness of the inventory to those procedures.

Examine the data dictionary and program listings to determine the completeness of the data element inventory list.

Data Base Activity *No. 23*
Data Documentation

Name of Control
Data Element Utilization Reports

Description
The structure of the data base should be designed so that the most efficient access is to those data elements utilized the most. The data element utilization report is a control that provides statistics on the frequency and type of use of data elements in the data base. The report is normally prepared at periodic intervals as a test to verify the efficiency of the existing data base structure. Variances from projected and actual use may result in a reorganization of the data base.

Evidence
DBMS log

Data element utilization report

Data base structure map

How to Collect Evidence
Obtain from the data base administrator the data element utilization report and data base map.

Compare the relationship between the frequency of use of a particular data element and the ease of access of that data element in the data base structure (use data base map for this determination).

Data Base Activity *No. 24*
Data Documentation

Name of Control
Data Base Backout Request Form

Description
The removal of data elements from the data base can affect multiple parties. For example, if there is a code for which the responsible user indicates there is no more need, that data element will be removed from the data base, yet other users may have a need for it. The data base backout request form is a formal process of documenting the desire to remove data. Also, through either DBA function notices or circulating the form, involved parties have an opportunity to comment on the removal of that data element from the data base.

Evidence
Backout request form procedures

Completed backout request forms

User change requests (to determine if data elements have been deleted and are being rerequested by users)

How to Collect Evidence
Obtain the backout forms and procedures from the data base administration function.

Examine a sample of change request forms and compare with the data elements on the data base backout request forms for duplicates.

Confirm with users that they are being properly advised regarding deletion of data elements from the data base.

Data Base Activity *No. 25*
Systems Development

Name of Control
Data Base Administration Function

Description
The data base administration function has the responsibility for the performance and control of the implemented data base. The DBA function can be a part- or full-time function. The DBA normally has the responsibility for structuring the schema, determining the features in the DBMS that will be utilized, and working with users to optimize applications interfacing with the data base. The data base administrator frequently administers the data dictionary, if one exists.

Evidence
Data base administrator job description

Data base administration procedures

Data base administrator entries into the data dictionary

DBMS documentation and features implemented by the data base administrator

How to Collect Evidence
Examine and assess the adequacy of the data base administrator job description and procedures.

Interview users regarding their assessment of the adequacy of the performance of the data base administration function.

Measure the actual performance of data base utilization against organizational data base objectives.

Examine the completeness and accuracy of data base administrator DBMS documentation. Segments of this documentation should be included in the data dictionary.

Data Base Activity *No. 26*
Systems Development

Name of Control
Application System Testing

Description
Application system testing is the testing of the application system interface with the data base. The testing verifies that the DBMS is providing accurate and complete data to the application system and that the data are being properly returned to the DBMS.

Evidence
Detailed test plan describing the steps to be performed during testing

Test data

Results of testing with corrective action

How to Collect Evidence
Evaluate the adequacy of the test plan.

Evaluate the completeness of the test data, especially in testing program limits and error conditions.

Evaluate the proper functioning of the system based upon the testing results as compared to system specification.

Data Base Activity *No. 27*
Systems Development

Name of Control
Formal Design Process

Description
A formal design process outlines all of the steps and procedures to be followed during the developmental process. Many organizations call this formal design process "structured design" or "system development life cycle." The objective is to utilize procedures that will minimize effort and maximize the probability of building a successful system. A discussion of this process for a data base environment is contained in FIPS PUB 77 [NBS 80a].

Evidence
Formal design procedures

Project plans including the formal design steps in the plan

Completed documents required by the formal design process

How to Collect Evidence
Examine and evaluate the adequacy of the formal design process.

Examine the developmental procedures and products to verify that the process is being followed.

Data Base Activity *No. 28*
Systems Development

Name of Control
Top Management Checkpoints

Description
Top management checkpoints are formal points throughout the developmental process when management will review progress and decide whether or not to continue system implementation. Some organizations only allocate resources from checkpoint to checkpoint. This provides top management with the opportunity to abort or change an unsuccessful project. The number of checkpoints normally varies with the size and importance of the project. Such recommitments of management support are particularly important in a data base environment that requires central coordination of authority.

Evidence
Top management checkpoint procedures

Documentation indicating scheduled checkpoint reviews

Project reports providing the information needed for a checkpoint review

Results of management checkpoint review decisions

How to Collect Evidence
Examine the checkpoint procedures and the adequacy of those procedures.

Review the checkpoint process to determine whether or not checkpoint procedures have been followed.

Examine completed project documentation to verify that all the checkpoint steps were executed prior to the project's going into production.

Data Base Activity *No. 29*
Systems Development

Name of Control
System Implementation Standards

Description
System implementation standards govern the systems analyst and programmer methods for implementing a project. These standards govern the methods for documenting systems, documenting data, developing program specifications, writing programs, testing programs, placing programs into conversion, approval for changes to programs, and the other related methods deemed necessary for the successful implementation of a data base application system.

Evidence
System implementation standards

Procedures governing waivers and deviations from standards

Procedures governing enforcement of standards

Project documentation representing the implementation of standards

How to Collect Evidence
Evaluate and assess the adequacies of the standards and the procedures governing the standards.

Review application systems to determine that standards are followed. This may include (1) review of systems documentation; (2) development of extract programs to review source program libraries and data dictionaries to determine adherence to standards; and (3) analysis of operational data using audit software to validate compliance to standards.

Data Base Activity *No. 30*
Systems Development

Name of Control
Data Base Standards

Description
Data base standards govern the documentation of data, the implementation of DBMSs, and the utilization of the interfaces to the DBMS. The standards include such items as use of passwords, structure of passwords, definition of data, interface of the data dictionary to the DBMS, reorganization, restart and recovery, organization of the schema, and how to deviate from the standards.

Evidence
Data base standards

Procedures governing the use and deviation from data base standards

The data base as the end product of the implementation of the standards

How to Collect Evidence
Examine and assess the adequacy of the data base standards and the procedures governing the use of those standards.

Evaluate the data base to ascertain that the standards have been utilized. Evaluation could include (1) extracting information on the data dictionary regarding DBMS standards; (2) using a data base verifier to examine the integrity of the data base; (3) testing the data base to verify performance standards; and (4) using query languages to investigate the use of standards in the operation of the data base.

Data Base Activity *No. 31*
Systems Development

Name of Control
Training of Personnel

Description
The training of personnel is needed to ensure that individuals controlling or interfacing the DBMS have acquired the appropriate skills. All people involved in data base technology need some training in order to optimize and control the data base properly.

Evidence
Training curricula recommended by data base vendors
Training plans
Training schedules for courses and individuals
Assessment of skills of trainees by course instructors

How to Collect Evidence
Evaluate the amount of training provided versus vendor-recommended training.
Analyze frequency and types of problems occurring that are attributable to individual errors and misjudgments.
Compare actual training to training plans.
Compare actual proficiency of individuals to desired levels of proficiency.

Data Base Activity *No. 32*
Systems Development

Name of Control
System Documentation

Description
System documentation includes all of the documentation needed to operate successfully in a data base environment, and to assure the continuity of processing. Documentation in a data base environment includes data dictionary documentations, schema and subschema documentation, reorganization documentation, data base verifier documentation, and documentation governing the operational performance of the DBMS. In on-line data bases, documentation should also include security, privacy, and access capabilities and restrictions.

Evidence
System documentation standards and procedures
Operating and interface documentation
Actual application system documentation

How to Collect Evidence
Examine and access the adequacy of the documentation standards and procedures.
Evaluate compliance of operating documentation to standards. This normally includes master terminal operation documentation, access and security documentation, DBMS operation and reorganization documentation, and interface documentation.
Assess the adequacy of documentation on the interface between the application system and data base.

Data Base Activity *No. 33*
Systems Development

Name of Control
Review Board

Description
A review board is a group independent of the data base administrator and the application development team. The objective of the review board is to determine that the data base standards and procedures are being followed, and that the implemented systems are meeting the needs of the user. In some organizations, these review boards are called quality assurance, in others, system assurance groups.

Evidence
Review board operating standards

Results of review board reviews

Review board job descriptions and authority

How to Collect Evidence
Examine and evaluate the adequacy of the review board functions and authority.

Evaluate operational systems to verify that the results of the review helped produce an application system that complied with the organization's data base standards and procedures.

Review operational systems to determine that those data base functions and application systems that should have been reviewed were reviewed.

Data Base Activity *No. 34*
Systems Development

Name of Control
Government Reporting Requirements

Description
Development of procedures to assure that the agency complies with federal regulations, such as the Brooks Act, GAO, OMB, GSA, and so on. The data base must be examined to ascertain that it contains the necessary information to fulfill the regulatory agency reporting requirements and that the data are accurate and complete.

Evidence
Regulatory agency reporting requirements

Application system documentation specifying compliance procedures for the reporting requirements.

Regulatory agency reports

How to Collect Evidence
Examine reports to verify compliance with regulatory requirements.

Use the query language to verify that the data base contains the needed information.

Data Base Activity *No. 35*
Systems Development

Name of Control
Personal Privacy Requirements

Description
Federal agencies are required to protect the privacy of individuals. The use of data base increases the privacy threat to individuals. This requires federal agencies to maintain and make available to individuals certain types of data as specified by the Privacy Act of 1974.

Evidence
Personal privacy requirements and procedures

Data base procedures regarding protection of individual information

Privacy information destruction periods and procedures

Security measures designed to ensure privacy

How to Collect Evidence
Evaluate and assess the security procedures and measures.

Evaluate the destruction procedures for compliance with privacy regulations.

Attempt access to private information without proper authorization to test the adequacy of the privacy procedures.

Attempt to extract private information after the date on which it should be destroyed.

Data Base Activity *No. 36*
System Development

Name of Control
Standard Progression of New Versions

Description
Control of changes to data base applications is an important aspect of controlling the data base itself. Improper changes can affect the integrity of the data base. The standard progression of new versions control is a method of controlling version numbers so that the changes to programs are processed in an orderly and controlled manner. Before a new version number is issued, the program changes going into that version must be properly approved by management.

Evidence
Version control number procedures

Approved change request forms

Version number issuance control documentation

Program library reports

How to Collect Evidence
Compare the new versions of programs going onto the program libraries with the version control number program.

Select a sample number of new versions and verify that all changes to those versions have been properly authorized (source code compare can be used to identify differences between two program versions).

Data Base Activity *No. 37*
System Development

Name of Control
Independent Testing

Description
Testing by the individual who develops the process has been shown to be no more than 80% effective. Developing new versions of the data base becomes a difficult testing challenge. Independent testing involves verification by a third party that the data base performs as specified. Many organizations require that the independent tester sign off on the tests prior to the new DBMS version's going into production.

Evidence
Independent test procedures

Results of independent testing

User-detected problems relating to DBMS problems

How to Collect Evidence
Obtain from an independent test group the test procedures and results of those tests.

Examine user-reported problems and determine that they are associated with inadequate testing of the DBMS and supporting systems.

Data Base Activity *No. 38*
System Development

Name of Control
Structured Programming Techniques

Description
Defective systems and difficult-to-maintain systems pose threats to the integrity of the data base. Structured programming techniques are designed to develop sound and easy-to-maintain logic for data base applications. Many structured techniques not only demonstrate the completeness of logic but also provide for walk-throughs by peer groups to ensure further that the structured procedures are followed and have resulted in sound logic.

Evidence
Structured programming methods and procedures

Documentation for systems and programs developed using structured programming techniques

Walk-through analysis reports

Program change requests for structured programs

How to Collect Evidence
Examine the structured walk-through procedures to ensure an understanding of the method.

Examine the system and program documentation for data base applications to verify compliance with the structured methodologies.

Examine the program change requests and results of structured walk-throughs to determine that the process is being followed and produces programs with minimal problems.

Data Base Activity *No. 39*
System Development

Name of Control
Design Models

Description
Many users and project teams are uncertain of the effectiveness of data base applications until those systems are coded and run in a test environment. Design models permit the simulation of design specifications so that the project and users can test the reasonableness of the proposed design before the programs are specified and coded. This is both a productivity tool and a control to ensure that the project will be done in accordance with the needs of the user as opposed to implementing the specifications.

Evidence
Design modeling procedures

Project results produced through design model simulation tests

User change requests after implementation

How to Collect Evidence
Examine the design model methodology and confirm that the process is being properly utilized.

Review user-initiated change requests for applications that have used design model simulation to determine whether the process is effective in eliminating design problems at the point in time that tests were conducted.

Data Base Activity *No. 40*
Data Base Access

Name of Control
Physical Barrier

Description
A physical barrier is a structure that prevents unauthorized individuals from accessing the data base and/or accessing terminals that can access the data base. Examples of physical barriers are locked rooms, guards at entrances to data base resources, or key locks activated by magnetically encoded cards.

Evidence
The physical site

Physical barrier security procedures

How to Collect Evidence
Examine the adequacy of the physical barrier.

Test the functioning of the physical barrier by attempting to enter a secure area undetected.

Data Base Activity *No. 41*
Data Base Access

Name of Control
Surveillance

Description
Surveillance is the observation of the functioning of the area in which the data base and/or terminals having access to the data base reside. Surveillance is normally performed by supervisors or trained security personnel. Surveillance can be continuous or periodic.

Evidence
Job descriptions indicating surveillance responsibility

Location of responsible individuals in a suitable location for surveillance

Surveillance procedures

How to Collect Evidence
Observe the individuals performing the surveillance function.

Examine job descriptions to verify that surveillance is a part of the job, and evaluate the adequacy of surveillance procedures.

Test the adequacy of surveillance by attempting to gain undetected access to the data base resources.

Data Base Activity *No. 42*
Data Base Access

Name of Control
Data Base Malfunction Reporting

Description
Malfunction reporting is the formalization of the data base error reporting process. Malfunction reporting normally involves a form that identifies problems or malfunctions, identifies the cause of the malfunction, and makes recommendations as to the course of action. In some organizations, this function is performed by a group of specialists who do the error analysis, but not the correction.

Evidence
Data base malfunction reporting reports

Data base malfunction reporting procedures

Results of data base malfunction reporting

How to Collect Evidence
Examine malfunction reporting reports and procedures to determine the adequacy of the procedures.

Examine the results of malfunction reporting to determine that the procedures have been followed.

Review the malfunction reports to determine that problems are being corrected in a timely fashion.

Examine machine logs to identify problem conditions to verify that there is a malfunction report for the conditions tested.

Data Base Activity *No. 43*
Data Base Access

Name of Control
Natural Disaster and Environmental Risks

Description
Studies by computer vendors have shown that many computer center problems are associated with natural disaster and environmental risks. These involve such conditions as water overflow problems on floors above the computer room, floods of computer centers in flood-prone areas, and small fires. Investigation should be undertaken to identify the natural disaster and environmental risks, and then to develop appropriate procedures and measures to reduce the probable loss should those disasters occur.

Evidence
Identification of emergency situation

Natural disaster and environmental risk analysis procedures

Insurance coverage and other countermeasures

How to Collect Evidence
Examine natural disaster and environmental risk analysis, the results of the risk analysis procedure, and the protective procedures.

Examine insurance and other measures adopted to reduce the probable loss.

Data Base Activity *No. 44*
Data Base Access

Name of Control
Maintenance Plan

Description
Maintenance occurs on both the data base hardware and the data base software. During these maintenance procedures, the data in the data base may be accessible to the maintenance personnel. Maintenance procedures should be designed to minimize the risk of maintenance personnel's either intentionally or unintentionally accessing or modifying the data base.

Evidence
Maintenance agreement with vendors or other contractors

Maintenance operating procedures

Procedures governing contractor on-line interface to an organization's hardware

How to Collect Evidence
Examine and assess the adequacy of the contractual and operating maintenance procedures.

Observe contractor maintenance to verify that it is performed in accordance with contract agreements.

Examine hardware and the associated controls governing contractor on-line capabilities to access an organization's hardware.

Data Base Activity *No. 45*
Data Base Access

Name of Control
Security Officer Function

Description
The security officer is an individual or group having the responsibility for security in a data base environment. This may be a full- or part-time function. The function is responsible for the documentation of security over the data base, and the monitoring of the security procedures that enforce access specifications. The security officer normally is external to the data processing function. The function is described in Office of Management and Budget Circular A-71 [OMB 78].

Evidence
Security officer job descriptions

Security officer procedures

Results of security officer investigations

How to Collect Evidence
Examine and assess the adequacy of the security officer job description and procedures.

Review the findings and recommendations of the security officer to determine their reasonableness, acceptance by concerned groups, and the support provided the function by senior management.

Independently assess the adequacy of security.

Data Base Activity *No. 46*
Data Base Access

Name of Control
Security Profile

Description
The security profile matches user need with data base resources. The profile can be by both user and data base resource. A used profile indicates all of the resources accessible to that user. A data base resource profile indicates all of the users that can have access to a designated resource. The objective of the security profile is to implement management's security policy through data base technology.

Evidence
Security profile documentation

Security profile as included in the DBMS, the data dictionary, or security software system

Security log

How to Collect Evidence
Compare the implemented security profile to the authorized profile to determine compliance between management intent and practice. Examine the security log first to verify that security procedures are being followed, and second to identify potential security violators. The examiner can attempt to obtain unauthorized data.

Data Base Activity *No. 47*
Data Base Access

Name of Control
Passwords

Description
Passwords are identifiers used by people to gain access to data base resources. Passwords can be any combination of characters, or may be special words known only to the individual in the system, such as the maiden name of an individual's mother. Passwords are normally changed periodically. The individual to whom the password is assigned is the only individual who should know that password. The password file should be well protected.

Evidence
Password procedures
Computer password file
Security log

How to Collect Evidence
Test the password procedures. The use of passwords and protection given them in practice should be assessed to determine if they are adequate. In addition, attempts should be made to violate the password procedures. The security profile can be reviewed to identify potential password violators.

Data Base Activity *No. 48*
Data Base Access

Name of Control
Password Control

Description
The password control governs the issuance, changing, and deletion of passwords from the system. It is also applicable to other forms of security such as the use of keys in terminals and point-of-sale equipment used for security purposes. The password control function maintains either manual or automated logs on who has passwords, and frequently contains statistics on password abuse such as attempts to access unauthorized resources and invalid password attempts.

Evidence
Security logs
Password protection procedures and logs
Security officer violation reports
Employee terminations and transfers

How to Collect Evidence
Analyze logs containing security information, such as job accounting logs, DBMS logs, or other security logs for potential security violations.

Review implementation of password control to ensure that terminated employees are promptly deleted from the security file and that passwords are changed at reasonable intervals.

Obtain from the security officer password violations as a means of determining the effectiveness of password control processes.

Data Base Activity *No. 49*
Data Base Access

Name of Control
Recovery Lockout

Description
The recovery process for data base can occur many different ways. It is possible that users can access all or part of the data base during the recovery process. The recovery lockout control prevents files from being updated while the recovery is occurring, but may allow inquiry during that same period.

Evidence
Recovery lockout procedures and processes

Method of notifying users that files are in a recovery lockout mode

How to Collect Evidence
Examine the completeness of the recovery lockout procedures and user notification processes.

Attempt to update the data base files at a time when the recovery lockout procedures are in force.

Data Base Activity *No. 50*
Data Base Access

Name of Control
Access Review

Description
According to the "Bonnie and Clyde syndrome," perpetrators will learn how to circumvent new technology before the adequate controls can be developed and enforced. A continual review of the access process to the data base is one of the best ways to prevent and detect access problems. The most common method is a daily review of the logs containing access information, such as SMF (IBM's System Management Facility) or equivalent to list potential security violations for analysis purposes. Where problems occur such as a large number of unauthorized accesses at a specific terminal, action can be taken to reduce those threats.

Evidence
Security logs

Access review reports

Access profiles

How to Collect Evidence
Analyze the access review reports or conduct an analysis of the security logs to identify potential security threats.

Obtain security officer reports on access violations to verify that the review procedures are effective in detecting the identified access problems.

Survey users for their input on access violations as a cross-check against the effectiveness of the access review procedures.

Data Base Activity *No. 51*
Data Base Access

Name of Control
Reorganization Control

Description
The reorganization process in a data base is a highly vulnerable process in that data can be modified, deleted, or lost through ineffective reorganization procedures. Reorganization control requires authorization by management to perform the reorganization and a password system to make certain that the reorganization process cannot occur until management has given the appropriate password authorization to permit it.

Evidence
Reorganization control procedures

Reorganization statistics and reports produced by the reorganization utilities

Job accounting log

How to Collect Evidence
Acquire the reorganization control procedures from management and the reorganization reports and statistics from the individual conducting the reorganization process.

List from the job accounting tape when and by whom the reorganization process was performed and compare to the reorganization control procedures to ensure that each of those instances was authorized.

Data Base Activity *No. 52*
Data Base Access

Name of Control
DBMS Password Protection

Description
The utilities and commands provided in a DBMS package provide the capabilities to modify data within the data base, as well as to modify improperly the operations of the DBMS. Password-protecting these commands and facilities provides assurance that they will only be used for the proper purposes. The DBMS resources should be identified and then included in the security profile indicating who has access to which DBMS resources. The profile should be under the control of management.

Evidence
Data base security profile

DBMS password protection procedures

Job accounting log (indicates use of facilities)

How to Collect Evidence
Obtain from management the DBMS protection procedures and logs indicating enforcement of those procedures.

Obtain a listing of DBMS features used from the job accounting system and compare to the security profile to verify that they were used by the authorized individuals.

Data Base Activity *No. 53*
Data Base Access

Name of Control
Master Terminal Control

Description
The master terminal is used to execute privileged DBMS commands. Master terminal is any terminal that is so designated by the system, and thus is then authorized as the only terminal from which those commands can be issued. The master terminal control involves the process of designating which terminal or terminals will be considered the master terminal and then assuring that the system commands are restricted to that terminal.

Evidence
DBMS list of system commands

Master terminal procedure manual

Job accounting system log

How to Collect Evidence
Review the available system commands to ensure that those having a control implication are restricted to the master terminal.

Identify which terminals are designated as master terminals and assure they are properly protected.

List from the job accounting system users of the master terminal and functions performed on the terminal to verify they are properly authorized.

Data Base Activity *No. 54*
Data Base Access

Name of Control
Security Reports

Description
Security reports are reports issued to senior management describing individually or in summary the type and frequency of security violations occurring in a data base environment. These should be regular reports issued either on a predetermined frequency or after each security violation. The reports usually indicate the type of violation, the perpetrator (if known), the impact of the security violation expressed in dollars or other appropriate quantitative measures, and the recommended or implemented changes to security to prevent the violations from recurring.

Evidence
Security violation reports

Security violation reporting procedures

How to Collect Evidence
Survey users to identify security violations.

Obtain security violation reports and compare to user-detected security violations to determine the completeness of the security reports.

Confirm with senior management that action has been or is being taken on identified security violations.

Data Base Activity *No. 55*
Data Base Access

Name of Control
Bait Records

Description
Bait records are records placed on data bases which contain predetermined information. For example, on a vendor name and address subschema, the security officer may place as a bait record the security officer's name, using a unique middle initial and home address. If those individuals are contacted, the security officer or other individual entering the bait record will know immediately that the file has been compromised and can take appropriate action.

Evidence
List of files having security implications

Bait record procedures and inventory of bait records

Data base which includes bait records

How to Collect Evidence
Survey the individuals placing the bait records to verify security violations.

Examine files to verify that the indicated bait records are, in fact, on the file.

Data Base Activity *No. 56*
Data Base Access

Name of Control
Automatic Shutdown

Description
An automatic shutdown control disengages a terminal from data base operations after a predetermined number of invalid access attempts or an invalid process has occurred. For the control to be effective, a supervisor should be required to reopen the terminal and refuse to let the individual causing the shutdown to reopen the terminal. Frequent practice is to shut down a terminal after three invalid access attempts in a row, or an attempt by an authorized user to perform an action for which he or she is not authorized.

Evidence
Automatic shutdown procedures

Job accounting system log

Log of terminal shutdowns listing cause of shutdown

How to Collect Evidence
Attempt to perform an unauthorized event from a terminal and determine that the terminal does, in fact, shut down.

Obtain from the security log indications of the number of invalid accesses by terminal and compare that to the shutdown log to verify that the process is working.

Obtain and examine the record of the adequacy of the shutdown procedures.

Data Base Activity *No. 57*
Data Base Access

Name of Control
Conflict Matrix

Description
The conflict matrix shows the relationship between tasks that should be segregated and the people who perform those tasks. In an ideally controlled environment only one individual will perform one of the tasks. The objective of the matrix is to identify inadequate segregation of duties, and identify the individual having too much responsibility (note that the use of the conflict matrix and an example are given in Chapter 9).

Evidence
Completed conflict matrix for the data base environment

How to Collect Evidence
Evaluate the data base environment conflict matrix and the action taken where segregation of responsibilities conflicts occur.

Data Base Activity *No. 58*
Data Base Access

Name of Control
Penetration Point Matrix

Description
A penetration point matrix identifies potential penetrations of data base systems and the point at which those penetrations can occur. The matrix shows the probability that a perpetrator can enter the system at the identified penetration points. The probabilities for each potential perpetrator are totaled, as are the probabilities for improper entry to the system at the penetration point. The matrix then shows which of the potential perpetrators has the greatest probability to break security and at which point (note that the penetration point matrix is described in Chapter 9).

Evidence
Completed penetration point matrix

How to Collect Evidence
Analyze the penetration point matrix and determine that appropriate action is taken to increase security at the high-risk points.

Data Base Activity *No. 59*
Data Base Access

Name of Control
Access Authorization Control

Description
Access authorization control ensures that only authorized individuals gain access to data base resources. Access control in a data base environment is normally automated through the implementation of user profiles. These profiles provide an index showing what resources an individual is authorized to access. These user profiles can be as specific as the situation warrants. Advanced DBMSs can restrict individuals to specific functions such as "read only" and can further restrict to the value of the field accessed. For example, a given user might have read and update access for pay rate fields of $300 per week or less, read only access for fields of between $300 and $1,000 per week, and no access for fields of more than $1,000 per week.

Evidence
User profiles cross-referencing individuals to resources

Access authorization sheets signed by a security officer or equivalent

DBMS documentation outlining security implementation procedures

Security violation listings

How to Collect Evidence
Extract and examine security violations from security logs.

Examine security profiles and documentation authorizing those profiles.

Test the security of the system by attempting to access data elements for which the individual accessing is not authorized.

Data Base Activity *No. 60*
Computer Operations

Name of Control
Data Error Handling

Description
Data error handling is the procedures and timeliness of examining and correcting detected errors. This process can be partly manual and partly automated. The automated segment uses default attributes, which make corrections automatically and then produce messages asking people to verify the correctness of the automated correction procedures.

Evidence
Error correction procedures

Error correction logs indicating when corrections were made and who authorized the corrections

Listings of errors

Error suspense files, such as a file of error messages awaiting correction

How to Collect Evidence
Examine error correction logs to validate the fact that corrections were made and timeliness.

Examine completeness of error detection and correction procedures.

Extract from error suspense files and examine the types of errors and the length of time the errors have existed.

Data Base Activity *No. 61*
Computer Operations

Name of Control
Remote Data Transmission Control

Description
The terminal, or remote site, needs to establish control over data transmitted to the central site. This control normally involves a count of messages, as well as a control over the value, such as dollars, transmitted. In addition, the control also provides assurance that the message is transmitted accurately.

Evidence
Documentation of local data transmission control procedures
Documentation of remote terminal operating and correction procedures
End of transmission period reconciliation documentation

How to Collect Evidence
Examine remote terminal operating, error detection, and other control procedures.
Prepare and transmit test transactions to verify the proper functioning of the terminal control procedures.
Interview terminal operators regarding the adequacy of the control procedures and the type of control problems encountered.

Data Base Activity *No. 62*
Computer Operations

Name of Control
Central Data Transmission Control

Description
Central data transmission control ensures the accuracy and completeness of the communication system for the entire network. The central function has responsibility for polling the terminals and for maintaining control by terminal so that the users can receive control information at the end of a transmission period. The central data transmission control normally is implemented using vendor-purchased software.

Evidence
Documentation of the central communication system implemented features
Central communication control logs
Terminal signon, signoff procedures
Communication log

How to Collect Evidence
Examine and verify the adequacy of the control procedures in a central communication system.
Extract and examine the control information in the communication logs.
Examine and investigate the types of errors occurring in the central communication processing.

Data Base Activity *No. 63*
Computer Operations

Name of Control
Computer Configuration Control

Description
Providing adequate capacity for the data base environment requires long-range planning and ordering and preparing for upgrades of hardware and software. Some equipment has a 24-month or longer lead time so that without adequate planning capacity may not be available when needed. Computer configuration control requires current and future projects to indicate capacity requirements so that they can be accumulated and integrated into a plan to assure that appropriate data base capacity is available when needed.

Evidence
Short- and long-term capacity needs by current and future projects

Consolidated capacity plan

Orders, letters of intent, or other steps taken to ensure the availability of future capacity when needed

Vendor order backlog for critical components

How to Collect Evidence
Examine capacity plans to identify critical hardware components.

Confirm with vendors delivery schedules for critical equipment and verify that hardware letters of intent or orders have been placed where appropriate to get the equipment within the needed time frame.

Confirm with the DBA function that software performance can satisfy the required data base capacity.

Data Base Activity *No. 64*
Computer Operations

Name of Control
Growth Analysis

Description
Growth analysis is a systematic process of projecting and monitoring the growth of the data base environment. The control provides input to space management both for determining when reorganization should occur and for determining when additional storage capacity is required. The input to growth analysis can come from the DBMS operating statistics and from users of the data base. Without this type of control, the performance of the data base can degrade significantly.

Evidence
DBMS operating statistics

User transaction volume projections

Data base mapping statistics

Job accounting system space management problems

How to Collect Evidence
Compare the growth projections to available data base space to ensure adequate space for processing.

List from the job accounting system log space management problems to verify the adequacy of the analysis of data base space.

Data Base Activity *No. 65*
Computer Operations

Name of Control
Data Base Monitor

Description
The more efficiently the data base operates, the more tasks can be shifted from people to the automated segments of data base technology. If the expected performance levels drop, the benefit of using data base technology may be negated. Hardware and software monitors are used to measure continually the performance of the data base so that adjustments can be made where appropriate. The control requires the predefinition of expected levels of performance, and then the use of monitors to verify the achievement of those expected levels of performance.

Evidence
Reports produced by hardware and software monitors

Performance objectives and goals

Procedures and manuals on the use of hardware and software monitors

How to Collect Evidence
Obtain the results from using the hardware and software monitors and compare them against the expected levels of performance.

Learn how to use the hardware and software monitors and then measure data base performance using those monitors.

Data Base Activity *No. 66*
Computer Operations

Name of Control
DBMS Log Analysis

Description
The DBMS log contains data on the use of the data base resources, operating statistics, and the evidence supporting transaction processing. Because of the large volume of data recorded on the DBMS log, most of the information is coded. To analyze this information, it is necessary to understand the codes to determine the types of analyses that can be performed on this information. Some DBMS logs have analysis utilities, and as data base technology matures these analysis utilities should become more sophisticated.

Evidence
DBMS log

Other evidence as needed to support individual DBMS log analysis

How to Collect Evidence
Prepare analysis using DBMS log analysis utilities or other equivalent utilities to extract the needed information from the DBMS log.

Compare the extracted information against standards of performance or other evidence needed to evaluate the data base performance.

Data Base Activity *No. 67*
Computer Operations

Name of Control
SWAT Team

Description
A SWAT team comprises senior data processing technicians given the responsibility for diagnosing and correcting problems at the time of occurrence. SWAT teams are normally provided authority to make emergency program fixes, and to eliminate troublesome transactions in order to complete processing in a timely fashion. Application and user personnel should verify and confirm the SWAT team fixes and make the permanent changes necessary. In many organizations, the SWAT team is either present during all operating shifts or on call.

Evidence
SWAT team charter and job descriptions

SWAT team procedures

Error reports and analyses prepared by the SWAT team

Data base rerun statistics

How to Collect Evidence
Obtain from the SWAT team their charter, job description, and a sampling of error reports and analyses.

Compare SWAT team corrections to rerun and other error statistics to determine the effectiveness of the action taken by the SWAT team.

Data Base Activity *No. 68*
Computer Operations

Name of Control
Job Accounting Analysis

Description
Job accounting systems run in conjunction with operating systems to record operating statistics. The more common statistics include job starts, job stops, resources utilized, and abends. Analysis utilities are particularly powerful with IBM's SMF. Analyses indicate who uses operating resources, for what purposes, and the volume of resources consumed.

Evidence
Job accounting system logs

Job accounting log utility analyses

How to Collect Evidence
Use analysis utilities to analyze and list data on the DBMS log tape.

Compare the data produced by the analysis to standards or other measures of performance to evaluate the performance of the DBMS environment.

Data Base Activity *No. 69*
Computer Operations

Name of Control
Prerecorded Telephone Message

Description
A major dissatisfier in a data base environment is uncertainty over when jobs will be executed. Telephoning for this information is often frustrating. If a prerecorded message is available at a readily accessible phone number, users can call that number and unless their job is listed as being late, with a new expected time, they can expect their job to be delivered on time.

Evidence
Special telephone number with prerecorded message

Job status file

How to Collect Evidence
Dial status telephone number and listen to recorded message.

Extract behind-schedule jobs from job status file, and determine that they are included on the recorded message in a timely fashion.

Data Base Activity *No. 70*
Computer Operations

Name of Control
Operator Message Procedures

Description
The types of requests made of computer operations normally fall into categories. Developing standard replies to messages normally results in more satisfied users. It also simplifies the work of computer operations personnel in that they have been trained in the appropriate way to address user telephone requests. These procedures indicate the type of information that should be given out, or to whom the message should be addressed.

Evidence
Telephone request procedures

Training sessions given operations personnel in the use of those procedures

How to Collect Evidence
Evaluate completeness of procedures and observe operations personnel answering telephone requests.

Make telephone requests to determine that appropriate answers are being provided.

Data Base Activity *No. 71*
Computer Operations

Name of Control
Help Desk

Description
The help desk is a single telephone number for users to call. Two approaches are used in staffing the telephone. First is to select the secretary of the operations manager and the second is to use the more technical operations personnel. Help desks ensure that user responses are handled in a timely fashion and that type and frequency of messages are logged, and they also ensure that special users get the appropriate attention. For example, a request from a senior officer may be directed to the manager of computer operations.

Evidence
Help desk telephone number listing

Help desk procedures

How to Collect Evidence
Examine the completeness of the help desk procedures and observe the handling of requests to the help desk.

Ask users whether they are aware of the facility and find it valuable.

Make a request to the help desk and evaluate the correctness of the information.

Data Base Activity *No. 72*
Backup/Recovery

Name of Control
Before and After Images

Description
Before and after images show segments of the data base both immediately before and immediately after processing. The images can be used to review the results of processing and for recovering the data base after a problem caused the loss of integrity. The images are normally recorded on the DBMS log.

Evidence
DBMS log

How to Collect Evidence
List or display the desired images by printing the transaction data from the DBMS log.

Data Base Activity *No. 73*
Backup/Recovery

Name of Control
Recovery Procedures

Description
In a data base environment, the integrity of the data base can be lost independently of application system failures. The data base loss can be due to hardware problems, data base management system operating problems, or reorganization problems, or as a result of users interacting with the data base or its operating mechanism.

Recovery procedures provide both the documentation and the step-by-step tasks that must be performed to recover after a data base failure. Recovery procedures are invoked when the integrity of the data base has been lost. The recovery procedures normally begin at a point of known integrity, and then, using the before and after transaction images from the DBMS log, processing is reconstructed from the point of known integrity to the point of known failure.

Backup data are those data not needed for production purposes, which may be needed in the event of a data base failure. Backup data include the DBMS log, copies of the data base at a fixed point in time, recovery procedures documentation, application system logs, and so on.

Evidence
Operator's recovery manual
User's recovery manual
Recovery audit trail
Data base recovery procedures
Data base operating and security procedures
DBMS data integrity control procedures
DBMS log
Backup copies of data base
Application program library
Recovery operating procedures

How to Collect Evidence
The recovery documentation should be reviewed to determine if it is sufficient to conduct the recovery process.

The adequacy of the backup data can be verified during the recovery process. The adequacy of the backup data to recover the data base can be verified at the completion of a recovery process.

Examine and assess the adequacy of the data base loss recovery procedures.

Simulate a disaster to test the adequacy of the recovery procedures.

Examine and assess the adequacy of the data base data integrity procedures.

Data Base Activity *No. 74*
Backup/Recovery

Name of Control
Reorganizational Utilities

Description
The reorganizational utilities are the documentation of the step-by-step tasks needed to be performed to restructure the data base. The physical and logical data bases periodically need to be restructured to meet the changing needs of the users. In addition, the space allocation formula may have to be changed to free up additional space for changing user requirements. Periodically, all the needed changes are put together and a data base is reorganized in accordance with those desired changes. Due to the complexity of the process, reorganizational utility programs are needed to help the data base administrator perform the process.

Evidence
Reorganization procedures
Reorganizational utility documentation
Reorganizational audit trail

How to Collect Evidence
The proper functioning of the reorganizational utility is normally verified using a data base verifier. The verifier can determine that all the pointers are complete and that the data base structure changes have been accomplished. In addition, normal DBMS statistics provide assurance that data were not lost during the reorganization processes.

Data Base Activity *No. 75*
Backup/Recovery

Name of Control
Data Base Verifier

Description
A data base verifier is a software package that reviews the integrity of the data base to ascertain that all designated paths through the data base are complete. These paths are normally marked with pointers, and if a pointer contains a wrong address the data following that broken pointer are lost. Data base verifiers are normally used after a data base is reorganized or recovered.

Evidence
Documentation of the functioning of the data base verifier

Output listing of results from operating the data base verifier

Operating log indicating the data base verifier has been executed

How to Collect Evidence
Examine the results of executing a data base verifier.

Test the operation of the data base verifier by "breaking a pointer" and then running the verifier to determine that it identifies the broken pointer.

Examine the documentation of the functioning of the data base verifier.

Data Base Activity *No. 76*
Backup/Recovery

Name of Control
Application System Failure

Description
Failures in a data base environment can be attributable to both the DBMS and the application system. In the event of failures in the application system, data base processing may be only partially complete. The procedures include those steps to reinitiate processing, determine the integrity of the application data queues, and back out or complete partially completed processing.

Evidence
Application system failure documentation

Application system failure audit trail

How to Collect Evidence
The application system failure procedures should be periodically tested. If an application system failure has not occurred recently, it may be valuable to simulate a failure midway through system processing.

Data Base Activity *No. 77*
Backup/Recovery

Name of Control
Backup Data Bases

Description
Backup data bases are copies of data bases at restart points—points where the integrity of the data base is assured and from where recovery can commence. The backup data base is normally made with a dump utility which copies the image of the data base onto a new file dump.

Evidence
Documentation of the procedures for creating backup data bases

Documentation to substantiate the structure of the data on the data base

Backup data base retention procedures

How to Collect Evidence
Examine the backup data base procedures and retention period documentation for adequacy

Perform a physical examination to verify the existence of the backup data base

Create a disaster testing situation to verify that the operations personnel can recover processing using the backup data base.

Data Base Activity *No. 78*
Backup/Recovery

Name of Control
Automatic Recovery Initiation

Description
Many operating systems can recognize DBMS and data base application problems. Where these problems can be categorized and common recovery solutions provided, those recovery solutions can be automatically initiated. Routines and utilities can be catalogued to be invoked at the time predetermined data base problems occur. This facilitates the restart and recovery processes in order to minimize downtime.

Evidence
List of common data base problems together with predetermined solutions

Automatic recovery initiation procedures

Recovery analysis reports

How to Collect Evidence
Examine the recovery report to verify that the automatic recovery initiation procedures are invoked in a timely fashion and provided the appropriate recovery solutions.

Survey users whose applications have been recovered using the automatic recovery initiation routines to confirm that the application was properly recovered.

Data Base Activity *No. 79*
Backup/Recovery

Name of Control
Off-Site Backup

Description
The data base in many organizations contains the official records of that organization. If the data base is lost so are the official records of the organization. A disaster in the main site or sabotage by operators can result in the loss of all on-site copies of the data base. Storing copies of the data base off-site can either minimize the loss or provide available backup copies depending on the frequency at which copies are made and stored off-site.

Evidence
Rental or other agreement providing off-site storage facilities

Inventory of the backup copies stored off-site

How to Collect Evidence
Visit off-site storage facility and confirm that the appropriate data base backup exists.

Simulate a disaster requiring operations to reinitiate data base operations using backup copies of the data base.

Data Base Activity *No. 80*
Backup/Recovery

Name of Control
System Error Recovery Group

Description
The system error recovery group is a committee of key users and technical people organized for the purpose of recovering the data base. The technical people perform the technical aspects of the recovery, while the users establish recovery priorities and coordinate the manual processing that must occur until the data base is recovered. These are normally part-time assignments. The recovery team is quickly assembled whenever the data base crashes.

Evidence
System error recovery group charter and responsibilities

Reports and results from implementation of system error recovery group concept

How to Collect Evidence
Observe the group in action during the recovery process.

Simulate a disaster to verify that the group can be assembled quickly and is adequately skilled.

Confirm with users the effectiveness and correctness of the recovery process when directed by the system error recovery group.

Data Base Activity *No. 81*
Backup/Recovery

Name of Control
Disaster Test

Description
Organizations frequently spend large amounts of labor and resources developing disaster plans for execution in the event of a data base disaster. If it becomes necessary to utilize these procedures, the organization is normally in a precarious position; if the disaster procedures don't work, the potential loss is high. A disaster test simulates a disaster so that the procedures can be tested at a noncritical time.

Evidence
Simulation of the disaster

Results of conducting the disaster test

How to Collect Evidence
Conduct or observe the disaster test as it occurs.

Data Base Activity *No. 82*
Backup/Recovery

Name of Control
Contingency Plan

Description
A contingency plan is the methods and procedures to be followed by the data base organization in the event of a serious problem or disaster. The plan normally identifies alternate facilities and sites, the individuals and data included within the recovery process. Contingency plans attempt to identify all possible causes of problems and then develop solutions for those problems in the event they should occur.

Evidence
Documentation of a contingency plan

Training sessions and procedures for individuals who will participate in the plan

How to Collect Evidence
Evaluate the completeness of the contingency plan.

Conduct a simulated disaster and observe the effectiveness of the contingency plan in action.

Data Base Activity *No. 83*
Backup/Recovery

Name of Control
Recovery Audit Trail

Description
The recovery process is a complex process involving a large number of individual steps. The recovery audit trail records the steps that are performed, the sequence of those steps, who is accountable for those steps, and any special actions taken during the recovery process. This audit trail is valuable in pinpointing accountability for improper acts as well as discovering potential weaknesses and offering solutions to those problems.

Evidence
Recovery audit trail procedures

Documented recovery audit trail from a representative number of recovery procedures

How to Collect Evidence
Obtain the recovery audit trail procedures and the audit trail documentation from computer operations.

Review the audit trail documentation for potential violations of audit trail procedures and other improprieties.

Data Base Activity *No. 84*
Backup/Recovery

Name of Control
Recovery Statistics/Report

Description
Recovery statistics are provided by the recovery team, recovery utilities, the DBMS, and many of the logs in operation during the process. These statistics need to be accumulated in order to evaluate the effectiveness and correctness of the recovery process. The statistics can be used to compare the effectiveness of the recovery process over a period of time, or to compare different methods or teams in their ability to perform the process in a timely fashion.

Evidence
Manual recovery reports

Operating logs

Statistics produced by recovery utilities or other DBMS facilities about the recovery process

How to Collect Evidence
Analyze the operating logs for recovery information.

Analyze recovery summary reports and/or gather the recovery information available from the utilities and facilities that provide recovery information.

Data Base Activity *No. 85*
Data Base Integrity

Name of Control
Data Ownership

Description
Data ownership signifies that one individual is responsible for each data element. Responsibility involves approving access to use the data element and implementing the procedures necessary to ensure the integrity of the data. Many users may have the authority to read, enter, delete, or update a data element, but only one user should be charged with accountability for the integrity of data.

Evidence
Inclusion of individual responsible for data elements in the documentation for data elements.

How to Collect Evidence
Review data dictionaries to verify that accountability attribute is complete.

Review manually prepared data definition documentation to verify that accountability attribute is included.

Data Base Activity *No. 86*
Data Base Integrity

Name of Control
Data Discrepancy

Description
Users of data base applications should be provided a tool for formal reporting of data base problems. A data discrepancy report is such a tool. The data discrepancy report is normally a preprinted form distributed in advance to users of the data base for completion when they perceive processing to be improper. The report is completed and forwarded to the data base administration group for investigation and action if appropriate.

Evidence
The data discrepancy report form

Procedures for completing the data discrepancy report form

Forms completed by users noting data base administration action

How to Collect Evidence
Check with users that they have a supply of the forms on hand and understand how to use the forms.

Examine completed forms and verify that reasonable action is taken in a timely fashion on the reported discrepancies.

Data Base Activity *No. 87*
Data Base Integrity

Name of Control
QC Cards (Quality Control Cards)

Description
A major problem in a distributed data base environment is ensuring the consistency of data values that are resident in more than one data base. The QC cards include the appropriate data value at a given point in time. The cards are distributed to all individuals responsible for a data base (usually data base administrators) to verify that the data elements in question contain the proper value at the proper point in time.

Evidence
QC cards
QC procedures
Data bases
DBMS logs

How to Collect Evidence
Obtain from the data base administration personnel a representative sample of QC cards.

Verify at the appropriate point in time in one of more data bases that the values in the QC cards represent the actual data base, or evaluate DBMS logs for the appropriate point in time for the last use of that value to determine that it was consistent with the value of the QC cards.

Data Base Activity *No. 88*
Data Base Integrity

Name of Control
Redundant Data Reconciliation

Description
Redundant data pose a problem in ensuring consistency of those data within a single data base or among multiple data bases. If all of the locations of a specific data value are known, reconciliations that verify that the same value is in all data locations can be used to prove the accuracy of the data base. Normally the organization must develop its own reconciliation utility and maintain a library of locations of redundant data elements in order to perform the reconciliation.

Evidence
Library listing locations of data elements which are redundant in one or more data bases
Data reconciliation procedures
Data reconciliation reports

How to Collect Evidence
Search the data base mapping procedures for locations where the same data element is used more than once.

Use reconciliation utilities or if not available trace and dump utilities to verify consistency of redundant data.

Survey users to determine data redundancy consistency problems.

Data Base Activity *No. 89*
Data Base Integrity

Name of Control
Monitor DBMS Log

Description
The DBMS log provides operating statistics on the data base environment. These statistics should be monitored by the data base administrator to verify the proper functioning of the environment and to make operational adjustments where necessary. The monitoring process is not a searching process but, rather, one directed toward gathering specific statistics so that degradations and performance or effectiveness can be detected early and adjustments made before they become serious.

Evidence
DBMS logs

DBMS monitoring reports

How to Collect Evidence
Use DBMS utilities to prepare special reports, or other utilities to provide the needed data from the DBMS log.

Data Base Activity *No. 90*
Data Base Integrity

Name of Control
Unload Statistics

Description
The reorganization process restructures the data within the data base and may at the same time add new capabilities, subschemas, and so on. In this process, new pointers and indices are created. It is a point of great risk in that data may be lost in the process or be unacceptable after the reorganization. Unload statistics provide sufficient information to permit the integrity of the data base to be verified after reorganization.

Evidence
Unload statistics

How to Collect Evidence
The necessary data base statistics can usually be accumulated using the data base verifier or equivalent utility which analyzes and lists the statistics on the content of the data base.

Data Base Activity *No. 91*
Data Base Integrity

Name of Control
Reload Statistics

Description
After the data base is reorganized, statistics necessary to verify the integrity of the data base are accumulated. This can be accomplished with a data base verifier or equivalent utility that will analyze the contents of the data base to provide the necessary verification statistics. These reload statistics are then compared to the unload statistics to prove the integrity of the reorganized data base.

Evidence
Statistics provided on the content of the data base at the conclusion of reorganization

How to Collect Evidence
Analyze the reorganized data base using a data base verifier or equivalent to accumulate the appropriate statistics.

Compare the unload and reload statistics to confirm or disprove the integrity of the reorganized data base.

Data Base Activity *No. 92*
Data Base Integrity

Name of Control
Structure Verifier

Description
The integrity of the data base is difficult to prove because each implementation of data base is different. The structure verifier is a unique program normally developed by the data base administrator to verify the integrity of the data base. The structure verifier is normally coupled with routines which accumulate totals during data base processing for later verification by the structure verifier.

Evidence
Statistics produced by the structure verifier

Internally developed control totals by the DBMS

Externally developed control totals by data base applications or users

How to Collect Evidence
Develop and operate a statistics verifier program.

Utilize DBMS features (normally through user exits) to accumulate totals during processing for later verification.

Data Base Activity *No. 93*
Data Base Integrity

Name of Control
Segment Counts

Description
For efficiency purposes, data elements within the data base are normally grouped into segments, groups, or records. These logical groupings of data can be counted to develop segment counts. At periodic times these counts can be verified against the control total to ensure that all segments are accessible. Segments can be lost due to broken pointers or improper processing.

Evidence
Reports on segment counts

Internally produced segment counts

Reports showing confirmation or variance between counts and actual segments in the data base.

How to Collect Evidence
Develop and operate a DBA-developed utility to count and verify the segments within the data base.

Evaluate reports produced by segment count utility programs showing the correctness or incorrectness of the segments within the data base.

Data Base Activity *No. 94*
Data Base Integrity

Name of Control
User Control Guidelines

Description
User control guidelines are guidelines provided to users explaining how to control data base applications. The controls take into account that multiple users access the same data values concurrently, and thus control in a data base environment involves multiple users rather than single users. The procedures assist users in developing the appropriate control mechanisms to address the data base risks.

Evidence
Documented user control guidelines

System development and maintenance documentation indicating that the guidelines have been utilized

How to Collect Evidence
Examine project documentation to verify conformance or nonconformance to the control guidelines provided users by the data base administration group.

Data Base Activity *No. 95*
Data Base Integrity

Name of Control
Data Base Control Standards

Description
Data base control standards provide the methods that users must follow in the entry, validation, use, and deletion of data from the data base. The standards should govern both manual and automated procedures. The standards should also provide a mechanism for enforcement.

Evidence
Documented data base control standards

Supporting documentation indicating that the standards are followed by data base users

Reviews indicating that standards compliance has met the intent of the standards

How to Collect Evidence
Obtain from review groups statements that indicate that data base applications have complied with the data base standards.

Obtain copies of the data base control standards from the data base administration group.

Data Base Activity *No. 96*
Data Base Integrity

Name of Control
Evaluate DB Failures

Description
An environment as complicated as data base will periodically fail. Information on each failure should be collected, consolidated, and analyzed to install measures to reduce future failures. The evaluate DB failures control is a formal process for documenting each failure and then consolidating the individual reports into periodic data base failure analyses. These summary reports should be evaluated individually and then failure trends should be plotted to show whether performance is increasing or decreasing.

Evidence
Data base failure reports

Data base failure analysis reports

DBMS logs

Operating system logs

Job accounting system logs

How to Collect Evidence
Analyze the information contained on the various data base environment logs to identify failures of the data base and causes of failures indicated on the logs. Compare these to the failure reports to determine completeness of those reports.

Evaluate the individual failures and summarize failure reports to assess the types and frequency of data base failures.

Data Base Activity *No. 97*
Data Base Integrity

Name of Control
Subschema Controls

Description
The subschema is the user's view of the data base. It is the subschema that contains the information which the user is accountable for and should control. Subschema controls are those application controls implemented by the user over the integrity of the subschema. These can include segment counts, control totals on specific data elements, or other types of controls applicable to the user application.

Evidence
Subschema control procedures

Subschema control totals

Subschema utilities and/or application control routines

How to Collect Evidence
Confirm with user the existence and type of subschema controls.

Acquire subschema control reports.

Use subschema control utilities and/or application programs containing control-proving routines to verify the functioning and correctness of subschema controls.

Data Base Activity *No. 98*
Data Base Integrity

Name of Control
Program Modification and Maintenance Control

Description
Program modification and maintenance control ensures that the proper change is installed in the proper version. The control also ensures that the proper program version is placed into operation at the correct time. This control normally involves establishing program version number control. Several versions of the same program can exist on both the source program library and the object program library. Changes to the program, and versions of the program being placed into production, are all controlled on version number.

Evidence
Version number standards defining the allocation and use of version numbers

Source program library version number control listings

Object program library version number listings

Program change requests cross-referenced to source program version number

Object program production cross-referenced to version number by date

How to Collect Evidence
Examine program change requests to determine whether they are referenced to version number.

Examine control listings produced by object program library and source program library software package control listings.

Examine console typewriter log indicating the production version number of the object program in operation, and then compare that to the version that is scheduled to be in production.

Data Base Activity *No. 99*
Data Base Integrity

Name of Control
Adequacy of Programmed Input Validation Checks

Description
Input validation checks take on greater significance in a data base environment. This is because many programs use the same data for processing, thus, the need for increased reliability. Input validation checks include reasonableness checks,, limit checks, range checks, comparison to acceptable values in a table, cross-reference checks between fields, and anticipation checks. In a data base environment, the checks should be documented in the data dictionary.

Evidence
Input validation check descriptions included in the data dictionary

Audit program input validation specification

Results of input validation testing

Application systems that automatically generate audit programs from data dictionary specifications

How to Collect Evidence
Examine data dictionary documentation.

Examine input validation programs and supporting validation specifications.

Test input validation programs by preparing a representative sample of test transactions to verify that the programs function according to specifications.

Interview data control clerks to determine the types of problems occurring due to inadequate input validation.

Data Base Activity *No. 100*
Data Base Integrity

Name of Control
Processing Intent

Description
The intent of processing should be clearly defined. This is normally defined at the transaction level and should explain the purpose of each transaction and the type of processing that occurs on that transaction. This documentation should be located so that all of the processing intent for a single transaction is easy to obtain.

Evidence
Transaction flow analysis flowcharts and documentation

System documentation

System flowcharts

How to Collect Evidence
Examine system flowcharts and documentation.

Develop transactions flow analysis flowcharts.

Develop matrices that follow the flow of the transaction through programs and indicate in the boxes of the matrices the type of processing occurring in each program.

Data Base Activity *No. 101*
Data Base Integrity

Name of Control
Concurrent Data Control

Description
Concurrent data control ensures that data elements will not be misprocessed if two or more users process the same data element concurrently. Most data base management systems provide a control that limits change to one program at a time. If a second user wishes to change a data element that is in the process of being changed, that second user is temporarily denied access to the data element.

Evidence
DBMS concurrent update control procedures

Application program control procedures that validate the propriety of the DBMS controls

How to Collect Evidence
Examine and assess the adequacy of the DBMS concurrent update control procedures.

Examine and review the application control procedures.

Conduct a test that attempts to update a data element while that data element is in the process of being updated by another user.

Data Base Activity *No. 102*
Data Base Integrity

Name of Control
Deadlock Detection and Resolution

Description
Deadlock occurs when two users engage in a processing situation in which each is holding a data element wanted by the other and will not release that data element until it receives the data element the other user is holding. For example, user A has data element one and wants data element two, while user B has data element two and is holding that until user A frees data element one. Most commercially produced DBMSs have routines to detect and resolve deadlocks.

Evidence
Documentation of DBMS deadlock detection and resolution procedures

Listing of detected unresolved deadlock conditions

How to Collect Evidence
Examine and verify the adequacy of DBMS deadlock detection and resolution procedures.

Create a deadlock condition as a test, to determine if the detection and resolution features function properly.

DATA BASE AUDIT TOOLS

Auditors have not developed special tools for auditing in a data base environment. In fact, many of the current audit software languages do not provide capabilities to analyze and develop reports on information contained in a data base. Many auditors have utilized the concept called "conversion to a flat file" which means that the DBA is asked to create a sequential file from a data base subschema (i.e., flat file) so that the auditor can analyze that file using auditor software capabilities.

Auditors in a data base environment are following the practices used by auditors twenty years ago when they adopted the tools of the data processing professional for audit purposes. Most of the audit tools used by auditors in a data base environment are data base tools which are proving effective for audit purposes. Unfortunately, these do not use auditor language and do not include some of the features auditors would like, such as sampling, but are effective in getting the job done.

Listed below are the more common data base audit tools, followed by a more detailed explanation of each tool:

Data base Tool Number	Data Base Tool Name
1.	Data base responsibility list
2.	Data base compliance test
3.	Auditor software
4.	Data dictionary utilities
5.	Data base verifier
6.	Query language
7.	DBMS utilities
8.	Disaster test
9.	DBMS log utilities
10.	Job accounting log utilities
11.	Data base matrices
12.	Subschema creation
13.	Data base structure map
14.	Data base simulation/modeling
15.	Data base environment verification
16.	Data base application verification

1. Data base responsibility list

One of the major data base controls is segregation of duties with the appropriate assignment of responsibilities. The data base responsibility list divides the organization and associated responsibilities by function. To use this tool, the auditor should become familiar with these lists (Figures 39 through 49) and then compare the actual organizational structure and assignment of responsibilities to these data base responsibility lists.

The responsibilities contained in the data base responsibility lists represent the ideal. In larger data base organizations, the auditor should expect the actual organizational structure to resemble closely the ideal structure. On the other hand, in smaller data base organizations the auditor should be more concerned over the division between policy and technical administrative responsibilities than over the individual job function breakdowns.

2. Data base compliance test (to data base policies, procedures, and standards)

Compliance testing in a data base environment is similar to compliance testing in any other audit environment. In a data base environment the auditor must understand the data base policies, procedures, and standards in order to perform compliance tests to those policies, procedures, and standards.

The data base environment is a general control, and thus much of the control is defined in the policies, procedures, and standards. If the intent and letter of the policies, procedures, and standards are not followed, the strength of the data base environmental controls may suffer. This process involves (1) identifying the data base policy, procedure, or standard; (2) determining whether it is applicable to the specific situation under review; and (3) determining whether the area under review complies with those policies, procedures, and standards.

3. Auditor software

Auditor software provides an automated analysis tool designed for auditor need. The audit software is usually developed in a language familiar to the auditor and provides the type of capabilities the auditor needs. Specifically these are analysis commands, statistical sampling, and ease of report writing, including several levels of totals.

Auditor software for use in a data base language must be able to address the data base directly, as do data base applications. The language specifications indicate which DBMSs they can interface. If the audit software language cannot interface with the DBMS, then the ''conversion to a flat file'' concept must be involved in which the auditor receives from the data base administrator a sequential tape or disk file for analysis using the audit software package. However, the auditor should be cautioned that the file received from the data base administrator must be verified before conclusions can be drawn about samples from that population.

4. Data dictionary utilities

The data dictionary contains the data elements used in a data base environment, together with multiple attributes about those data. Earlier chapters in this book have explained the types of attributes that are common on a data dictionary. The auditor has two interests in a data dictionary: first, as a source of information about the data and the attributes within the data base; and second, as a source of audit evidence that can be analyzed for such information as whether an individual is named responsible for each data element.

The auditor can use the data dictionary by reviewing printouts of the individual data element. These are normally available from the data base administrator. However, the auditor can also use the data dictionary utilities to perform analyses and develop special listings for audit purposes.

5. Data base verifier

The data base verifier is a generic name of a utility that can be used to prove part of the integrity of the data base. At a minimum, data base verifiers prove the completeness of pointers, and develop counts on the number of segments and/or physical records within the data base. These analyses provide assurance that there are no broken pointers and give counts that are valuable in proving the integrity of the data base.

The auditor can use the data base verifier to check the completeness of pointers, to do some integrity checking before and after a reorganization, to develop counts of data base segments or records at a given point in time, or comparison to statistics manually maintained by the data base administrator. Note that this is a very technical package and requires advanced skills for use.

6. Query language

One of the most powerful tools available for the auditor in a data base environment is the query language. In fact, many organizations acquire a DBMS specifically to gain the capabilities of the query language. In those circumstances, the data processing function may use the data base as a sophisticated access method, as opposed to taking advantage of the data base technology.

Auditors will generally find that query languages are more powerful and faster than audit software languages. Normally the only facility missing in the query language is statistical sampling, and that can be added by cataloging a statistical analysis program in the application library. Using query languages, auditors can do on-line analysis at a terminal as well as developing files for later analysis, or have audit reports printed for later analysis by the audit staff.

7. DBMS utilities

The acquisition of a DBMS includes a series of analytical utilities. These utilities serve two purposes. First, they are for the use of the data base administration group in creating and maintaining the DBMS. Second, the utilities provide the ability to acquire and analyze data within the data base. It is the second set of utilities that is of most value to the auditor.

The auditor should obtain a list of available data base utilities that have value in the audit process. Examples would be utilities that can do such things as "trace and dump." That utility, for example, would enable the auditor to trace through the data base for certain types of information and then dump or list it on a report. Many of the utilities are designed for special analyses, but if it is the type of analysis the auditor desires, these utilities are generally easy to use and efficient.

8. Disaster test

A disaster test is a disaster condition simulated by the auditor. In many instances, the auditor will select a segment of the DBMS or an application as a test to determine whether the operations group can recover that DBMS segment or application system without the resources available in the computer room.

The auditor simulates the disaster by entering the computer room unannounced and informing the shift supervisor that a disaster test is being conducted. Obviously, the test has been cleared with senior data processing management first. The auditor then obtains the information that is needed for recovery purposes and removes that from the operations area. The information removed would be the disk packs on which the data base is contained, the program libraries, any other files required, as well as job control statements and operator instructions. The operations group is then asked to recovery the operation using backup facilities and recovery procedures. It is strongly recommended that this test only be conducted during a time when processing volume is low. Sometimes the auditors tape and seal the information on a Friday afternoon and then the operators come in Saturday, assuming the computer is not normally run on Saturday, to conduct the disaster test.

9. DBMS log utilities

The DBMS log is a running history of data base operations. The log normally contains before and after images which show the processing before and after it occurs, operating statistics, use of data base resources, and so on. The utility programs can analyze and list information contained on the DBMS logs. Note, however, that the DBMS logs are normally only retained for a short period of time.

The DBMS log contains many thousands of records, all of which are highly coded. Many of the utilities are technical to use, meaning that the auditor must have good sound knowledge of the DBMS in order to use the DBMS log and utilities effectively. On the other hand, it is a very extensive audit trail of data base operations and can provide some powerful analysis of operations.

10. Job accounting log utilities

The DBMS is another operating program to the operating system. As such, the functions performed by the DMBS, as well as data base applications, are recorded on the job accounting log. While this log is used in both data base and non-data base environments, it contains statistics on job starts, stops, abends, use of data base resources, and so on. The job accounting system utilities are well developed and provide easy analysis of the log information and produce some potentially very valuable and easy-to-interpret audit reports. The best utilities are available for IBM's Systems Management Facility (SMF).

11. Data base matrices

Data base matrices show the relationship between two data base variables. The matrix can be used for documenting the environment as well as for analyzing the results of documentation. The matrix also provides the advantage of putting large amounts of information in a small space for analysis purposes.

This book has presented three different uses of the data base matrix. First is the conflict matrix (see Chapter 9) showing the relationship between people and tasks to analyze segregation of functions. Second is the penetration point matrix showing the relationship between potential perpetrators and system penetration points (see Chapter 9) to identify vulnerabilities for fraud. Third is the risks/activities matrix showing the controls installed in the activities to reduce specific risks (see Chapter 13). Other matrices can be developed to meet specific audit situations.

12. Subschema creation

A subschema is a user's view of the data base. The auditor is a user and can create a subschema to meet specific audit needs. The data base offers potentially significant audit analysis capabilities for the auditor as auditors begin to create their subschemas as needed.

The subschema can be created through the normal data processing system development process or created dynamically. The system development method for creating subschemas is normally more efficient, but may cause the auditor to lose some independence as opposed to the dynamic creation of a subschema. On the other hand, the systems route to creating subschema is a more permanent creation and this is available over a longer period of time. Auditor-created subschemas can be used with auditor software that can interface with the DBMS. Dynamically created subschemas are a features of most query languages.

13. Data base structure map

Mapping routines provide the equivalent of a picture of the data base. The mapping routines are used primarily by the data base administrator for analysis of the content of the data base. They can be used for analysis to increase the performance of the data base operation, or to verify the presence or structure of data within the data base.

Data base structure mapping routines are complex to use, and complex to interpret. For the auditor to use the routine he or she would need highly sophisticated data base skills. However, the auditor may be able to obtain potentially valuable audit information by discussing the process with the data base administrator, and learning how the data base administrator uses the analysis and the type of information available through an existing data base map.

14. Data base simulation/modeling

Simulation/modeling packages enable the data base administrator to determine how the data base will function using a specific organizational structure. The efficiency of a data base varies significantly depending upon the organizational structure. The simulation/modeling routines permit the data base administrator to try different variations of a data base structure without incurring the expense of actually creating a data base.

Auditors would use the simulation/modeling routine if they had a concern over the efficiency of the data base. The tool might be used to demonstrate to management that additional controls would not significantly impact performance, or that acceptance of a systems recommendation would increase data base performance. The use of the simulation/modeling routine requires the auditor to have a good understanding of data base structure and operations.

15. Data base environmental verification

During the course of the data base audit, the auditor will collect extensive documentation produced by the DBMS and/or the applications that use the data base. This documentation can be used by the auditor to verify that an event has occurred and/or occurred properly. The auditor will also use procedures, job descriptions, and so forth as a base to verify whether the actual data base environment is as stated in the evidence collected by the auditor.

16. Data base application verification

During the course of the audit, the auditor will produce or receive reports, files, application documentation, and other evidence relating to the data base applications. The auditor will use these as the basis of verifying that some application event has occurred and/or has occurred properly. The verification process is used as an audit procedure to assess the correctness of the application processing and procedures.

GLOSSARY OF DATA BASE TERMS[1]

Alias. An alternate name. Each data unit may have one or more aliases. Aliases can be assigned to accommodate different languages, software systems, and/or user conventions.

Attribute. A characteristic of a data unit or a data relationship; e.g., name, type, function, source, length, base, units, scale, precision, representation, owner, user, relationship, structure, order, etc.

Business entity. A logical or conceptual entity, which is of interest to an enterprise.

DA. Data administration.

Data administration (DA). A function responsible for developing and administering the policies, procedures, practices, and plans for the definition, organization, protection, and efficient utilization of data within a corporate enterprise. This function is chartered to manage data as valuable corporate resources.

Data availability. The state in which data are physically present in the data base in an acceptable, processable form to all authorized data users.

Data base. A named group of interrelated entity record sets sharing a common data base directory. A conceptualization of all the data available to one or more (or partial) application systems. Generically, the term data base can also be used to describe all of the data (both manual and automated) which are of interest to the user organization(s).

Data base administration (DBA). A function responsible for developing and controlling the definition, organization, protection, and documentation of the data base(s) in accordance with data administration plans, policies, procedures, and standards. This function provides technical DBMS liaison support to applications development and systems personnel.

Data base management system (DBMS). The data processing system consisting of tripartite interaction among the requester, data base administration (DBA), and the data base manager (DBM).

Data base manager (DBM). The combination of hardware and software which controls and processes all requests for data base services in accordance with rules defined by DBA.

Data base descriptive language (DBDL). A language for DBA which provides a format and precise vehicle for describing data, how they are stored and retrieved, and how they are related.

Data base directory (DBD). That part of the data dictionary/directory which is used by the DBM in accessing and controlling data. It contains the data descriptions which are derived from DBDL statements.

Data dictionary (DD). That part of the data dictionary/directory which describes, for human interpretation, the characteristics of data. Data described need not be under the control of the DBM.

Data dictionary/directory (DD/D). A term used to describe the contents of both the data base directory (DBD) and the data dictionary (DD). Since there seems to be some overlap between the contents of the DBD and the DD, it is convenient (and perhaps necessary) to consider the DD/D as the data base used by both applications.

Data element. The smallest unit of physical data about which attributes are defined.

Data entity. A logical or conceptual grouping of data relating to a person, place, thing, or event.

Data maintainability. The state in which the information systems and the data base have been designed to ensure an acceptable level of change flexibility and prevent the occurrence of an unacceptable level of performance degradation.

[1]From *Establishing the Data Administration Function*, (Chicago: GUIDE International Corporation, 1977). Reprinted with permission.

Data management (DM). (DA function) A function responsible for data administration planning and policy development; research, communications, and training; data resource control, data resource accountability, and for providing data management policy liaison support to data processing, user, and corporate management.

Data management. (generic function) The function of organizing, cataloging, locating, storing, retrieving, and maintaining data.

Data management standards. A term identifying those standards and controls required to ensure that distributed data-related tasks, executed in organizations through the corporation, are executed in accordance with DA data management policy.

Data quality. The state in which the validity and timeliness of data have been assured to a degree of acceptability by the enterprise.

Data redundancy. The state in which data are contained more than once in a data base. The redundant copies of the data may be in the same or different forms. Redundant data may or may not be derived. Data redundancy may be planned (for performance considerations) or unplanned.

Data security and privacy. The concept that units of data can be altered, viewed, or processed only by users who have the proper authority and the "need to know."

Data standardization. The concept that the characteristics of each shared data element (i.e., name, definition, responsibility, usage, format, etc.) are defined and accepted by all data users throughout the corporation.

Data timeliness. The state in which the currentness of data in the data base is compatible with the enterprise's currentness requirements for those data.

Data validity. The state in which the content accuracy of data has been assured by the application of user defined tests of acceptability.

DBA. Data base administration.

DBD. Data base directory.

DBDL. Data base descriptive language.

DBM. Data base manager.

DBMS. Data base management system.

DD. Data dictionary.

DD/D. Data dictionary/directory.

Distributed Computing. The concept of being able to distribute the power of a large, central computer among many remote users, wherever they are located.

DM. Data management.

Entity. A person, place, thing, or event about which data may be recorded.

Information Processing System. The computer system hardware and software components of an information system. Its general functions are the collecting, storing, and referencing of information.

Information System. An organized approach on the part of an enterprise to manage its information resource. It consists of people, information, functional business systems, and an information processing system.

Password. A unique string of characters that a program, computer operator, or user must supply to meet security requirements before gaining access to data.

Producer of Data. An organizational unit that collects and/or generates data, and inputs that data into the corporate data base. A producer of data may also be a user not only of its own data but of data collected and entered into the data base by others.

Teleprocessing. The processing of data that are received from or sent to remote locations by way of telecommunication lines.

User. An organizational unit that accesses and uses data residing in the data base.

BIBLIOGRAPHY

Adams, Donald L., "System to Audit Aspects of the Data Dictionary," *EDPACS*, May 1976, pp. 1–4.

A very good analysis of what a DD is and how it functions.

American Institute of Certified Public Accountants, *The Auditor's Study and Evaluation of Internal Control in EDP Systems* (New York, 1977). 67 pages.

A framework for analyzing the control in an EDP environment is proposed.

Auerbach, *The Auditor and Data Base Management* (2-06-11), *Data Processing Management*, 1977. 12 pages.

Good review of audit concerns and difficulties in auditing DBMS.

Bjork, L. A., Jr., "Generalized Audit Trail Requirements and Concepts for Data Base Applications," *IBM Systems Journal*, No. 3, 1975, pp. 229–245.

The use of audit trails for recovery and review is discussed.

Brebach, Gresham T., "Data Base Administration," *Price Waterhouse Review*, No. 2, 1975, pp. 18–27.

The duties and responsibilities of a typical DBA are defined.

Burns, Kevin J., "Keys to DBMS Security," *Computer Decisions*, January 1976, pp. 56–62 (5).

Security considerations in a data base environment are outlined.

Curtice, Robert, M., "Integrity in Data Base Systems," *Datamation*, May 1977, pp. 64–68.

Various recovery and fallback techniques are reviewed.

EDP Analyzer, "Installing A Data Dictionary," January 1978, pp. 1–13.

Practical problems of using and operating data dictionaries are discussed.

EDP Analyzer, "Integrity and Security of Personal Data," April 1976, pp. 1–14.

The Privacy Act and its implication for data base management are investigated.

EDP Auditors Foundation for Education and Research, *Control Objectives* (Hanover Park, Ill., 1980). 208 pages.

A good framework for audit and analysis of all aspects of a data processing operation is presented.

Grimes, J. R., and Gentile, E. A., "Maintaining Internal Integrity of On-Line Data Bases," *EDPACS*, February 1977, pp. 1–14.

An explanation of data base audit programs used by Bell Telephone is presented in detail.

Government Accounting Office, *Data Base Management Systems—Without Careful Planning There Can Be Problems*, June 29, 1979.

GUIDE International Corporation, *Distributed Computing in the Early 1980s—The Environment and the Requirements*, (Chicago, 1977).

Project data processing needs in the 1980s and associated hardware and software.

Lefkovits, Henry C., *Data Dictionary Systems*, Q.E.D. Information Sciences, Inc. (Wellesley, Mass., 1977), p. 358.

Features and use of data dictionaries are discussed as well as specific data dictionaries (LEXICON, CINCOM DD, DB/DC DD, DATA MANAGER, DATA CATALOGUE, UCC TEN).

Leong-Hong, Belkis, and Marron, Beatrice, *National Bureau of Standards Publication 500-3 Computer Science & Technology: Technical Profile of Seven Data Element Dictionary/Directory Systems*, (Washington, D.C.: National Bureau of Standards, 1977) 38 pages.

Characteristics, features, and uses of the DD are discussed.

Lyon, John K., *The Database Administrator* (New York: John Wiley & Sons, 1976). 170 pages.

Varies from light reading to deep jargon, but covers the subject.

Martin, James, *Computer Data Base Organization—Second Edition* (Englewood Cliffs, N.J.: Prentice-Hall, 1977). 713 pages.

McFadden, Fred R., ''Costs and Benefits of A Data Base System,'' *Harvard Business Review,* Vol. 56, Jan.–Feb. 1978, pp. 131–139.

Minami, Dr. Warren N., ''Data Administration: Key to Better Management,'' *Journal of Systems Management,* May 1976, pp. 40–44.

The position and function of the data administrator are outlined.

National Bureau of Standards, *Data Base Directions—The Next Step,* National Bureau of Standards Special Publication 451, 1976. 158 pages.

Proceedings from NBS and ACM workshop in October 1975. One session was entitled ''Auditing and the Data Base'' and a very concise statement of audit difficulties was developed.

National Bureau of Standards, *Guideline for Planning and Management of Database Applications,* Federal Information Processing Standards Publication 77, 1980.

National Bureau of Standards, *Guideline for Planning and Using a Data Dictionary System,* Federal Information Processing Standards Publication 76, 1980.

Patrick, Robert L., *NBS Special Publication 500–24—Performance Assurance and Data Integrity Practices,* National Bureau of Standards (Washington, D. C., January 1978), 53 pages.

This report identifies 67 practices currently in use to control a sophisticated computer environment.

Reneau, J. Hal, ''Auditing in a Data Base Environment,'' *The Journal of Accountancy,* December 1977, pp. 59–65.

Access controls in a data base environment are suggested.

Ross, Ronald G., ''Placing the DBA,'' *Journal of Systems Management,* May 1976, pp. 25–33.

A detailed analysis is made of a DBA's need to do both high-level and detail design work.

Statland, Norman, and Winski, Ronald T., ''Distributed Information Systems, Their Effect on Your Company,'' *Price Waterhouse Review,* No. 1, 1978, pp 54–63.

Smaller distributed computers are discussed as they affect a typical firm.

Wiorkowski, Gabrielle, K., and Wiorkowski, John J., ''Does a Data Base Management System Pay Off?,'' *Datamation,* April 1978, pp. 109–114 (4).

Summarizes a user survey of the impact of generalized DBMS on DP operations.

Yosaki, Edward K., Sr., ''The Many Faces of the DBA,'' *Datamation,* May 1977, pp. 75–79.

The problems of placing the DBA in an organization are explored.

DATA BASE EVIDENCE

1. *Data base management system.* The software package that manages the data base.
2. *Data dictionary system.* An automated documentation tool for data.
3. *DBMS logs.* A history of all the transactions occurring during data base operations.
4. *Security log.* A listing of accesses and potential security violations.
5. *Data base utilities.* A variety of utilities, normally included with the DBMS, that perform much of the day-to-day maintenance on the DBMS.
6. *Data base structure map.* A pictorial representation of the data base structure. This can be produced by a utility program.
7. *Data base verifier reports.* A listing of integrity problems in the data base structure. Produced each time the data base verifier utility is executed.
8. *DBMS reports.* Periodic status reports produced by the DBMS providing statistics about the content and operation of the DBMS.
9. *Security profiles.* A listing of the resources accessible to individual users.
10. *Data base standards.* The required procedures and methods for operating and interfacing with the data base.
11. *Organizational charts/job descriptions/charters.* The assignment of responsibility, segregation of duties, and creating accountability for actions.
12. *User complaints/requests.* Documentation of the problems and needs of users.
13. *Master terminal operation procedures.* The process for performing privileged maintenance on the DBMS.
14. *Data base operating procedures.* The instructions provided operations for the day-to-day operation.
15. *Data base recovery procedures.* The instructions provided operations on how to prepare for and conduct recovery after a data base failure.
16. *Data base reorganization procedures.* The instructions provided on when and how to reorganize the data base.
17. *Data base integrity procedures.* The manual or automated methods used by data base administration, operations, and user personnel to verify the proper functioning and content of the data base.
18. *Data base controls.* The guidelines provided users of data base to help ensure the integrity of the application data.
19. *Program change requests.* Requirements submitted by the user to change data or processing.

20. *Program libraries.* Facility to store and control data base application source and object code.
21. *Data element inventory.* A list of all the data elements used by the organization.
22. *Data base plans/objectives.* Short- and long-term plans, goals, budgets, and objectives for the use of data base technology.
23. *Data base application data statistics/reports.* Control-oriented information produced or available from data base applications.
24. *Review group/control group reports.* Control-oriented data base information produced by or available from control functions.
25. *Data base policies/procedures.* The direction established by management for data base technology and the methods established to achieve those policies.
26. *DBMS/DB application documentation.* The instructions on how to use, maintain, and operate the DBMS and the applications using the data base.

DATA BASE RISKS

Number	Risk
1.	Inadequate assignment of responsibilities
2.	Inaccurate or incomplete data in a data base
3.	Losing an update to a single data item
4.	Inadequate audit trail
5.	Unauthorized access in a data base
6.	Inadequate service level
7.	Placing data in the wrong calendar period
8.	Failure of DBMS to function as specified
9.	Fraud/embezzlement
10.	Lack of independent data base reviews
11.	Inadequate documentation
12.	Continuity of processing
13.	Lack of performance criteria
14.	Lack of management support

INDEX